Praise f
Extraordinary

D0825236

"*Extraordinary Rendition* reminds us of the power of art and the necessity of literature. In stories, essays, and poems that are as varied and diverse, contradictory and complicated as we are, the writers in this deeply humane anthology shed light and bear witness to one of the complex conflicts of our time. Ru Freeman has made a book unlike anything I've ever read. It's a great contribution not only to the conversation about Palestine, but to the larger one about peace and justice."

—Cheryl Strayed, author of *Wild*

"This is a book that Americans who believe they're interested in a 'just peace' between Palestinians and Israelis should read. It's a wide and diverse and eloquent book of witness. And it's a revelation, and it's shocking. And it's tragic."

—Richard Ford

"These varied writings—passionate, anguished, wry, intelligent—combine to produce a uniquely complex and powerful testimony. This is an extraordinary political-literary intervention."

—Joseph O'Neill, author of *Netherland*

"The question of Palestine can sometimes feel like a long night of despair. But not with this new collection in sight! Here are witnesses, shining like stars."

—Amitava Kumar

"*Extraordinary Rendition* stands in the tradition of engaged artists, speaking in defense of liberty and justice—values that ought to be universal but just as often are used as fig leaves by history's victors. Here, renowned writers turn their words to battered, defiant, and beautiful Palestine (a place whose oppressors receive the backing of America, a country whose passport many of these writers hold). Its a risky stance, but the best art takes risks. Inside find nuance, challenge, empathy deep into the bone."

—Molly Crabapple

"In *Extraordinary Rendition*, an eclectic range of American writers break through the stereotypes and distortions of our media and provide a far more nuanced, penetrating, and three-dimensional portrait of Palestinians, their history, and the political realities they face daily. The range of genres and approaches make this a necessary and timely anthology, and it should be read by as large and wide-ranging an audience as possible."

—David Mura

Extraordinary Rendition

AMERICAN WRITERS
ON PALESTINE

EDITED BY
RU FREEMAN

OLIVE
BRANCH
PRESS

An imprint of Interlink Publishing Group, Inc.
www.interlinkbooks.com

First published in 2016 by

OLIVE BRANCH PRESS
An imprint of Interlink Publishing Group, Inc.
46 Crosby Street, Northampton, Massachusetts 01060
www.interlinkbooks.com

Anthology selection © 2015 Ru Freeman
All essays © 2015 the various authors

Published by arrangement with OR Books, LLC, New York

All rights reserved. No part of this book may be reproduced or transmitted in any form or
by any means, electronic or mechanical, including photocopy, recording, or any information
storage retrieval system, without permission in writing from the publisher, except brief
passages for review purposes.

Cataloging-in-Publication data is available from the Library of Congress.

ISBN 978-1-56656-060-3 paperback
ISBN 978-1-56656-070-2 hardback

This book is set in the fonts Pobla and Colaborate.

Cover illustration: Marlene Dumas "Wall Weeping," 2009, oil on linen, courtesy of the artist
and David Zwirner, New York/London

Printed and bound in the United States of America

10 9 8 7 6 5 4 3 2 1

To request our complete 48-page, full-color catalog, please call us toll free at 1-800-238-
LINK, visit our website at www.interlinkbooks.com, or send us an e-mail: info@interlink-
books.com

Anywhere You Look

in the corner of a high rain gutter
under the roof tiles
new grasses' delicate seed heads
what war, they say

Jane Hirshfield

For my father, GAMINI SENEVIRATNE,
who believed that this work was necessary
&
for RICK SIMONSON, who helped it unfold.

Contents

Making Sense

RU FREEMAN

"How does one write about this place? Every sentence is open to dispute. Every place name objected to by someone. Every barely stated fact seems familiar already, at once tiresome and necessary. Whatever is written is examined not only for what it includes but for what it leaves out: have we acknowledged the horror of the Holocaust? The perfidy of the Palestinian Authority? The callousness of Hamas? Under these conditions, the dispossessed—I will leave aside all caveats and plainly state that the Palestinians are the dispossessed—have to spend their entire lives negotiating what should not be matters for negotiation at all: freedom of movement, the right to self-determination, equal protection under the law."
—TEJU COLE

Over Christmas and New Year of 2008, Israeli bombs fell on Gaza, killing 1,417 people, 313 of them children. On a long-distance phone call, after he had read a piece I had written on the Huffington Post about having decided not to attend the inauguration of a president I had spent more than two years campaigning for, my father asked me this question: What are American writers saying about this? A lifelong advocate for global social justice, who had never needed a reminder that we are always either participant or perpetrator, my father spoke on into my silence. There were American writers, he said, who had written about the Vietnam War. Then, he added, "It was your publisher who brought out that book. Can't you get them to do the same for a volume of writing about Palestine?"

What can and cannot be done in America is a question that carries enormous hope on the part of people who do not live here, and a corresponding despondency on the part of those who do. I could have gone into an explanation of it but I, raised by such a father in a family where what needed to be done was what we focused on, never the obstacles to that work, knew better than to make excuses. I hung up the phone, marveling at the fact that my father would not only know about such a collection of writing, but that he would possess a copy of it, now long out of print in its nation of origin, stored in his tropical home where there were routine massacres of white-ants who marched forth to devour his books, and I set about seeing what was possible.

The publication he was referring to had august origins. In 1937, writer and activist Nancy Cunard and W. H. Auden had posed a singular question to 200 authors: "Are you for, or against, the legal government and people of Republican Spain? Are you for, or against, Franco and Fascism? For it is impossible any longer to take no side." 147 authors responded, including Samuel Beckett, Evelyn Waugh, H. G. Wells, Ezra Pound, and T. S. Elliott. The writing that resulted was published as *Authors Take Sides on the Spanish War* (Left Review, 1937).

Thirty years later, in 1967, building on that tradition, as they put it in their opening remarks, editors at Simon & Schuster undertook a similar exercise regarding Vietnam, and asked a different question: "Are you for, or against, U.S. intervention in Vietnam? How, in your opinion, should the conflict be resolved?" The responses resulted in the collection, *Authors Take Sides on Vietnam* (Peter Owen, 1967). The 160 writers in the collection included James Baldwin, Nelson Algren, Simone de Beauvoir, Allen Ginsberg, Doris Lessing, William Burroughs, Graham Greene, Italo Calvino, Robert Graves, Harold Pinter, John Updike, James Michener, Marianne Moore, and Arthur Miller.

Forty-three years later I believed like my father did that surely we might ask ourselves a similar question about Palestine. Along with poet Matthew Siegel, with whom I had disagreed bitterly and publicly, I began a Facebook page urging other writers to join us in speaking about Palestine and Israel. It seemed long overdue that our generation of writers, people who understood the power of the written word, face our responsibility to add our voices to a vital conversation. Yet despite much wringing of hands, and the horrific news out of Gaza that ticked across the TV screens, nobody joined. I wrote to publishers asking if they might be willing to carry out such a project. There was no response. For four years the project stalled, the Facebook page remained silent.

In 2014, I asked again for a simple show of hands. Who might speak for Palestine?

The impetus to ask a group of writers to reflect on the ongoing assault on the thin and shifting borders of Palestine, and the people who are confined to that tenuous landscape, became impossible to set aside in the face of the 2014 assault on Gaza, an assault in which Israel claimed it hit 5,226 targets within the 139 square miles that constitute Gaza, and one which left 2,104 Palestinians killed, including 495 children, and 10,626 injured, many critically. Parallel to the bombing of Gaza was the simultaneous incursion into Palestinian neighborhoods in the West Bank which went unmentioned in the American press. It resulted in the largest land-grab by Israel since 1948, with the seizure of $3.5 million worth of Palestinian property within and surrounding Jerusalem. In the face of such numbers, and the fact that we as Americans, willingly or not, fund the perpetration of such violence through our taxes, but more so by our silence, I felt that we needed to confront the reality that Cunard articulated in 1937: it is impossible any longer to take no side.

Against the backdrop of what had transpired, it would have been easy enough to gather a group of people who could give us facts and figures, history and conjecture, attack and defense. Yet the 2,402 square miles of Palestine, and the 3.9 million people who live within its fragmented territories occupy a larger moral and ethical space, particularly for American writers, one which is critical to the way we look at the world into which we release all our artistic endeavors. We need, as artists, to be able to hear the beat of that larger world, to provide in its hour of need, some perspective that can move toward a recognition of the fact that our hands too are stained—if we remain silent—with the blood of others.

We are fond of identifying ourselves with victims during certain historical moments: We were all Americans (during 9/11), we were all from Newtown (in the aftermath of that shooting), we were all Trayvon Martin/Michael Brown/Eric Garner, we all rose and fell with the Berlin wall and with Nelson Mandela. Yet we are rarely inclined to commit our art to documenting how, exactly, this comes to be. How do, in this case, the injustices experienced by Palestinians belong to us all? What makes us identify with people and a cause that is geographically remote but pulses with an intimacy that belies that distance? How does the giving and receiving of help sharpen our resolve on other fronts, and strengthen our bonds, and what forms can that solidarity and empathy take? Is it direct and literal, or oblique and fragmentary?

In an article titled "Poetry & Inhumanity: Anti-War Art: Nearly Impossible?" written for *The Best American Poetry* (August, 2014), Sara Eliza Johnson takes issue with Noah Berlatsky's article in *The Atlantic* ("Anti-War Art: Nearly Impossible"), which was written in the context of the July attack on Gaza by the Israeli Defense Forces. Belatsky concludes that such art is almost impossible, that the prettifying (through narrative, aesthetic inference, etc.) drive of the artist distances the consumer, and renders the art itself irrelevant in terms of it having any impact on the machinery of war. Johnson, on the other hand, argues for writers, poets in particular, to consider their response to state-sanctioned violence, which extends from police brutality (Ferguson) to the subsidizing of terror in other nations (Iraq, Iran, and Palestine). To support her argument for art that removes the space we often leave between ourselves and the misery and horror experienced by "others," she points to Thomas Hirschchom's *The Incommensurable Banner* (2008), a visual art installation that depicts photographs of dead victims of the "War on Terror," a piece that serves to create discomfort, to nag at our conscience, to observe that this dead body is, in fact, not us, but that we are deeply culpable in its existence. That discomfort is a useful way to describe the space that the writers in this collection were asked to occupy.

◆ ◆ ◆

The spirit behind this anthology is that it would first compel us to set our names down beside each other as writers willing to remove the barrier between the story we hear and/or are told, and ourselves. Secondly, that it would permit the creation of a new way of thinking about how we, as writers and readers, might raise our voices against the seeming inevitability of war and a culture of dispossession and invasion that has been allowed to remain unquestioned for too long. As Mourid Barghouti writes in his memoir, *I Was Born There, I Was Born Here* (2012), "The weaker party in any conflict is never allowed to tell his own story," for the enemy will not allow a competing narrative. The story that *is* told, that the Palestinians are "wrong, defective, and deserving of the pain that they have brought upon themselves," is given life through the deliberate muting of the Palestinian voice. It is into that ruinous silence that the writers gathered here pitch their voices and, together, construct sure footing. How they chose to engage with Palestine—which today is both the heart and conscience of the world—varied with each writer. Many provided a preface to their work, and those introductions appear either before or after their pieces according to what made the most sense in the flow of the entire anthology.

In compiling their work, I have delineated sections which serve to frame a series of pieces that move around or within a common theme. I did this out of consideration for readers who might wish to read this anthology in sections rather than as it ought to be read, in order of appearance, for they proceed from opening to close as a single narrative of exploration that, like our imagination, moves both forward and back, linking what is observed to what is remembered, and what is hoped for. The writers are in unintentional but direct conversation, and the issues which one writes about bleed organically into those raised by others.

A poet and a novelist, Roger Reeves and Colum McCann, open this collection. Both writers use the concept of flight to release sorrow like kites into the air, setting it free from the mundanity and ultimate uselessness of known facts. Reeves uses the brilliant conceit of a lynched Black man disintegrating and floating over the world, hovering over Gaza and onward, to look at what links a thirty-year-old African American man to the massacres taking place in Palestine. McCann responds with a story written when he was just twenty-five years old. It is a tale that uses a Hebrew myth heard in a Baptist Church in Texas to speak about the violence in Ireland—with its divergent loyalties of the past, one side with Palestine, the other with Israel—but whose narrator's burden could be held equally by a young man in Derry or an old man in Gaza. Both the poem and the story reveal the place where our skill at harnessing our words to our imagination gives us writers the ability to hold multiple realities, central to all of which is grief, in our hands.

Chana Bloch's Israeli pilot, who not merely dismisses but refuses to acknowledge the destruction he has caused, is made human again at the end of Ramola D's story about the death of five daughters, even as Ravokovich's dead Arab is brought to life in those same girls in the seconds before they are incinerated. Dwayne Betts grapples with the vacuum that takes the place of news about Palestine, and sets the stage for Ed Pavlic's unfolding of the layers of journalistic subterfuge that surround our understanding of what occurs in a country we are responsible for crucifying, but rarely name. The extent to which mostly Western journalists themselves participate in a pro-Israeli narrative was revealed to me in stark terms when I was told by a seasoned war correspondent in Ramallah that there is no place safer for a reporter than in Gaza. "The chips that Israeli authorities place in a press-pass allow them to track your every movement," I'm told, "and we get telephone calls on the hour from the authorities to both inform us of where they might bomb, and to make sure our safety is not compromised." No journalist will ever admit to this practice, and yet not doing so stains the bravery to which they lay claim, and tarnishes the stories they file. Such realities underscore the importance of the testimony of these writers and poets.

Writers as varied in their aesthetic as Rickey Laurentiis, Lawrence Joseph, Kiese Laymon, Farid Matuk, and Naomi Shihab Nye take up the call to Americans to understand that our national myopia regarding a history of violence against our own, from Ferguson to New York City, is bound tightly to our dismissal of the violence that unfolds in the streets of Gaza. It is a connection that Palestinians understand only too well, as is evidenced by their words of solidarity to the protestors in Ferguson, as well as the poignant graffiti that is scrawled over Israel's 26.24-foot high, 430-mile long wall of apartheid, that denote Ferguson as a neighborhood of Palestine. Indeed, the broken, shuttered, litter-strewn streets of Aida refugee camp are chillingly reminiscent of America's inner cities. What funds are available for the beautification of any Arab neighborhoods are withheld by Israel, its garbage-collectors threatened, and its building permits revoked; there is, in such places, overwhelming evidence of the effort by Israel to force a sense of despair upon the populace, a scent that is found in equal measure down the streets of Jackson, Mississippi, or New Orleans, Louisiana. There is, equally, a similarly institutionalized system of racism even more blatantly revealed with signposts that warn Israelis (read White in America), from going into those neighborhoods and further, as of 2010, stating that it is against Israeli law to do so; it is, quite simply, a policy constructed to prevent the cross-pollination of experience, ideas, cultures, and the knowledge that might permit the co-resistance that must precede co-existence.

Without seeing such streets for oneself, it is easy to understand the impotence felt by Peter Mountford as he confronts what he describes as righteous rage, the "circle dancing" of an "us" which can safely leave a "them" outside. The call and response to his dilemma harkens back to Roger Reeves' opening statement as well as forward to Leslie Jamison, who uses the deadly intertwinings of the drug war in Mexico, which provides the backdrop to a literary conference, to embrace both ignorance and speech, as well as to Duranya Freeman's nineteen year old bravery, and her resolution that the only political stupidity is to remain silent in the face of injustice.

The question of the right to speak is also taken up by Tomas Morin, as he reflects on how we engage with electoral politics, and then move on from the policies which are formulated without our consent and lead to perpetrations we do not condone and cannot abide, but do. Morin's supermarket in suburban America takes shape again in a tunnel in Gaza described by Matt Bell who spends endless hours on YouTube, watching the construction of these defiances. They are, in fact, filaments that connect refugees in Lebanon with those clinging to life in Gaza, and they act both as a means of survival and a capitulation to Jordan which, Israeli politicians hope, will eventually absorb the population of Gaza into its fold. There is, in fact, no daily act undertaken by the people of Palestine whose consequences do not reverberate throughout their country and beyond into the lives of every exiled Palestinian.

Tess Gallagher picks up several threads, her ladybugs saving children from a burning house echo Ramola D, and foreshadow Nathalie Handal, and her assertion that all soldiers should mind doll buggies pulses at the heart of what is advocated by all these writers. The Trojan Horse of Gallagher's imagination pushes against the walls snaking through Arizona and Gaza, scattering populations from Tijuana to Tel Aviv, a purer innocence setting us all free.

Children abound in this collection. Cristina Garcia's longing for the name of each broken child is answered by Kafah Bachari's story of Lala, a girl in a red-riding-hood coat wandering through the rubble of Gaza. Unwittingly, the self-immolation of an Orthodox boy in David Gorin's poem evokes four children on a beach, Mohammad, Ismail, Zakariya, and Ahed Bakr, children who are mourned in many of these pieces, and held up as a call to see more closely, as Kim Jensen urges, and to reject the glib rhetoric of false parity as Susan Muaddi Daraj decides to do. America's own fallen angel, the one unmourned by her nation, Rachel Corrie, returns to life and to death in the words of those like Schumacher who served as she did, and in those who remember her in their poetry, as Philip Terman does, as a daughter.

Indeed, Corrie is a figure held up as the face of America's conscience not only by these writers, but by the people of Palestine. She is mentioned repeatedly by Gazans, and in the beleaguered West Bank city of al-Khalil (Hebron) stands a cafe named for her. A young man in Nablus tells me when I ask about the undeservedly warm welcome we get as Americans, that social media changed the way Palestinians look at Americans. "Finally," he says, "during Gaza last year, we got to see that Americans cared about us." Without a trace of irony he muses what the response in America might have been had Rachel Corrie been bulldozed by the IDF in this time of Instagram, Snapchat, and split-second sharing of news, if video of her death had been captured and broadcast around the world via cell-phones. "Perhaps we will be free now," he says.

Central to this anthology is, of course, the question of whether the language of poets and writers can transform what seems intractable, and it is articulated by Askold Melnyczuk and Jane Hirshfield, and answered repeatedly by the voices of what I prefer to call sight rather than witness (for witness presumes an equal partnership in what has been suffered whereas sight acknowledges the luxury of distance and safe passage). That sight, whether imagined or real, is heard in Fanny Howe's scant few lines which mirror the little that is left and the magnitude of the loss, and Claire Messud's narrative which moves through impotent dreams and wakeful nightmares. Imprisonment for the crime of creating art itself is revealed in the farcical trial observed by Ammiel Alcalay, and picked up and arrayed in the poetry of Phillip Metres and Steve Willey. It is answered also in how language delineates the negotiation of space, a theme that runs through several pieces. Alan Shapiro's reflection on the re-construction of physical history and the memorializing of violence moves into Ahdaf Soueif's description of the erasure of a culture in Silwan, homes and personal stories dismantled through artifice and cunning.

There is no attempt on the part of Israel to conceal the methods by which it seeks to obliterate a people. The political savagery that underlies the destruction of places like Silwan, is physically evident in the hills of Galilee where Israel's "South African Forest" of invasive pine has buried the Palestinian village of Lubya with its orchards of almond and olive trees. That forest is only one of eighty-six public parks that sit on ethnically cleansed Palestinian villages, and it bears the distinction of being the only one ever visited by its foreign Jewish benefactors who apologized in person, this year, for unknowingly donating the money that went toward its planting.

The concrete version of this travesty is iterated everywhere. In the Anastas home trapped on three sides by a soaring 30 foot wall that prevents the Christian inhabitants from operating the businesses they ran on the main thoroughfare between Bethlehem and Jerusalem; in the network of tunnels being dug by Israeli authorities beneath the Haram al-Sharif, in a series of defilements and excavations that threaten the structural integrity of the al-Aqsa Mosque, the third holiest shrine for Muslims; in the IDF-supported settlements which are now built a fair distance from each other, which "necessitates" the construction of wide roads to connect them for reasons of "security," alongside other infrastructure, thereby confiscating more land belonging to the Palestinians; in the water that is pumped out from beneath the West Bank and sold back to the Palestinians at four times the price, with delivery never certain. It is an Israeli organization, Zochrot, that points out that the gleaming city of Tel Aviv is built on the Palestinian villages of Al-Sumayil, Salame, Abu Kabir, and Al-Manshiyeh among others. It is hard not to question the integrity of academics who meet in Tel Aviv University's faculty lounge which was the former home of the sheikh of Sheikh Munis, even as they insist that Tel Aviv rose out of a barren desert.

Sadness is too small a word to encompass what has taken place in Palestine, and yet use it we must. Tom Sleigh's critical insistence on the necessity of acknowledging not merely grievance but grief is illustrated in his poem, "A Wedding in Cana, Lebanon 2007," and in the words of several writers speaking as both observers and victims. If there is mourning for what ails us, what has befallen people who are not us, but are us, it is voiced also in the numbered notes of the artist and writer Robert Shetterly, who has been commissioned to draw art on the wall that imprisons Palestinians, in the poetry of lament and ardor of Nathalie Handal, writing from Bethlehem as the bombs dropped around her in July, 2014, as it did in Gaza, and the body of Dina Omar's brother, buried in foreign soil, and the bit of earth her Israeli friend brings back from the home to which she herself cannot return, the pink-brown dust of Palestine that she presses onto her brother's grave in West Covina, California.

This is not an anthology of agreement but rather of resolve. An effort by writers to utilize the tool which we have been gifted, that of the imagination, to embrace ambiguity and uncertainty, to see color in a place where color has itself been outlawed in favor of the stark dichotomies that dissolve empathy, the blacks and the whites of intractability. Aquifers water the trees of settlers in Kazim Ali's diary, but the meaning of those trees, in planting, in uprooting, and in movement, is voiced as sorrow by Alice Rothchild. Caryl Churchill's play, "Seven Jewish Children: A Play About Gaza," evokes the opposite response in the minds of two Jewish writers, a poet and a novelist, Jason Schneiderman and William Sutcliffe, and yet both arrive at a similar conclusion which acknowledges helplessness and the quest to understand. In the Israeli town of Sderot, Kazim Ali writes of a sculptor welding together a menorah created from the fallen rockets from Gaza, while inside Gaza, he and Robert Shetterly observe children collecting spent gas canisters to use as toys, or to line their meager gardens.

This is, above all, a conversation, for we are bound by our words, which inform the way we move through the news of our world, and what we choose to do with that information. We tunnel, collectively, diligently, holding ourselves accountable for what we do and do not know, searching in Matt Bell's words for "the marker that may push through to another side." A side no less safe, or fraught, but new nonetheless. A place where the "informed compassion" called for in Susan Muaddi Darraj's essay is given body in Sarah Schulman's call to action, and her insistence that the point of solidarity is to be effective.

◆　◆　◆

It made sense to append to this collection a summary of findings by the Russell Tribunal, a convening of an international people's tribunal on Palestine. It is included here as a way of supporting other efforts such as ours, those made by ordinary citizens, predominantly writers, who refuse to absolve themselves of the duty to take action on matters that are pertinent to the humanity with which we are concerned in our art.

Included also as an appendix is Marlene Dumas' note for her exhibit *Against the Wall*, from which the cover for this collection is taken. Dumas broke from her usual style to paint the series to visualize the significance and dissonance of the wall that hems in the people of Palestine, and she details the reason for this shift in her note. Interestingly, both the title of Robert Shetterly's work and hers juxtapose the wall of faith and goodwill with the wall of ideology and hatred, and both invoke the Palestinian poet Mahmoud Darwish. The photograph that she gifted to us, *Wall Weeping*, was chosen for the way it reflects the sinew and muscle of this collection of writing, where we acknowledge the existence of a wall, the realities that it attempts to conceal, the people pressed up against it with nowhere to go, and those who also raise their hands, not in surrender but with deliberate intent, to disintegrate its false boundaries.

This anthology includes three writers who have no affiliations of residency or citizenship with the United States, though their work is well known in this country, and they have each traveled within the United States and are familiar with an American audience. They are Ahdaf Soueif, William Sutcliffe, and Steve Willey. I solicited their prose and poetry because they provided a perspective that enhanced the anthology as a whole, while not altering the parameters that I had set since, like the anthologies that preceded this one, my task was to ask a group of writers whose country was involved in the violence being perpetrated but who may not naturally be inclined to write about that to do so. There is ample work to fill many volumes with the poetry and prose of other contemporary writers beyond the borders of America, particularly Palestinian writers such as Mourid Barghouti, Adania Shibli, Sahar Khalifa, Najwan Darwish, Suad Amiry, Raja Shehadeh, and Mahmoud Shukair, to name a few, who write movingly and with passion about Palestine. Anthologizing those voices in a single volume that is also translated into the English is a vital undertaking and one that I hope will be taken on by someone with a far more intimate and deeper knowledge of that work than that which I possess.

In choosing which pieces should be included, I erred on the side of engagement rather than dictate. There are only two exceptions to this, Janne Teller's submission which reminds us of the importance of history, "I Wish I Had Words," and the closing poem in the anthology, Steve Willey's "Postscript," which urges and challenges us this way:

> Say Free Palestine
> It starts in your mouth
> It ends in the streets
> Say Free Free Palestine
> Say its been good writing to you
> Say it clear as hell
> And then say it again
> Free Free Palestine
> Go on I know these words are in you.

I chose these two pieces because, in a milieu where violence is perpetrated through the affirmation of theories of creation and promise written or divined from our personal sacred texts, we must surely make room for the known and empirical truths of war and occupation. Further, this writing that we have collectively committed to print and the public eye constitutes the freeing of our own voices, our own new visibility, as well as an invitation to our fellow writers who, too, hold these words within their conscience.

While some writers, usually the most secure in their careers, expressed fear of backlash from an un-named and un-seen "them," many more were open to persuasion, to be nudged away from safe places or a sense of helplessness. Tomas Q. Morin was one such writer, who went back and forth through stages of attempting, giving up, and rallying again, and whose poem, "Extraordinary Rendition," has given the collection its name. It is a choice that insists on reclaiming the truer, higher meaning of words that have come to imply the removal of human beings from their own environment, to be held without charge or access to legal or emotional recourse in a foreign country, a routine practice of the American government. By using these terms instead to describe the courage of the writers in this book who, in their turn, pay homage to the greater courage of the Palestinian people rendered helpless by the systematic destruction of their lives, I hope to dismantle our national tendency to acquiesce to the manipulation of the language to which we must preserve our access. That, too, is part of the battle we fight. It is a title that honors the worth and work of each of these writers who chose to come forward to offer up work that they themselves frequently felt was flawed, or insufficient, or did not "fit." I look at this work now, set one beside the other, and note only this: that each writer's work speaks both fearlessly and flawlessly of a specific moment or revelation, but that taken together, they speak with equal power of a larger whole, one which demonstrates that our writerly preoccupations arc inevitably toward justice.

Ru Freeman
Jerusalem, Palestine
May, 2015

PERSPECTIVE

ROGER REEVES

During the summer of 2014, most mornings I woke, ran, and on the way back from my run listened to NPR broadcasts because I found the news chattering over the airways to be a welcome immersion into the world after running through the farm and cattle lands in Marfa, Texas. Often, a wild turkey, which I affectionately named Turkey Tom, greeted me when I pulled up to the house which caused me to linger in the car because I had been warned about this particular turkey's penchant for sadistic irascibility. While waiting for the turkey to become disinterested in my presence, NPR often chronicled the ongoing siege in Palestine: the death count, the children playing soccer on the beach killed in an airstrike in front of journalists, the bombs that "knocked" on the roof as warnings for larger, more ballistic-laden bombs, more death counts. The dead seemed to be lining up outside the car. Eventually I would make my way inside and continue to listen to the report. The death counts, the communities razed, the news of more destruction became overwhelming, as these events should be. And I struggled with what to do with that sense of feeling overwhelmed. Naturally, I turned toward writing, but I was stuck on the question of appropriation. The Palestinians killed were not my people. They were not my kin. These deaths were not the lynchings and police killings of black bodies in America of which I am permitted to speak about because those are my people. But were these my people? Was I allowing a false sense of political correctness to hush and silence my protest, my pen? Was I being too cautious? Rather than obfuscate the thorniness of an African-American man in his mid-thirties writing about the political situation in Palestine, I built that contested territory into the poem, which happens to be a long poem from the perspective of a lynched man whose body disintegrates. As his body disintegrates, it travels on the wind, in the mouths and on the hides of animals to other parts of the world. What would a lynched man see or think about Gaza? The answer is this poem. What follows are several sections from that very long poem.

From "On Paradise"

IF THE ANGELS BEGIN TO EAT MEAT, DO NOT BLAME
THE CHILDREN FOR LIGHTING EACH OTHER ON FIRE.
HALOES ARE BORN OF SUCH DISASTERS.

◆ ◆ ◆

In Gaza, leaflets announce the beginning of exile.
No time to take the dead down from the eaves
Or pull of the ass
Out of the ditch. The shadows fed with candles,
The linens, the dates, the riverbank
Famous for holding exile, bruised, everything bruised,
The water binding one name
To another—Darwish, Zaqtan, Joudah, Osman, Khdeir, Reeves—one exile
Pushed like a horse over the side
Of a canyon into another.
Already, the children's lips swell from the night-
Stick beating them into famine. In a house, a woman
Watches her dead children disobey
Her calling for them to rise.
What will revive our dead?
And then the shelling began,
And the dead rushed toward the walls,
Pressed their open mouths against the stone
As if to eat the whole house before it came down.

The dead, if allowed, will eat the whole house.
The House of Lords and the house held up by rope
And wet corpses. The empty house
And the horse house. When Moses struck water
From a stone, a house,
But not a house
For him, but a wandering for questioning. But once again,

28

A house even if a God keeps a body
Wandering outside of its gates.
And what have you forgotten this morning?
Who will teach the trees to walk out of this country
Toward exile? It is July, or it could be March, the radio returns
As the golden abacus: *more than eighty dead,*
More than one hundred dead . . . more . . .
Everyone turns toward the house
Of numbers in war. What should be done with language in war?
Will language be house enough in war?
What have I forgotten this morning in war?
When the days have been taken down
And washed from beneath the fingernails of the dead
And the children bear the bones
Of the living on their backs like a beggar bears a sack of pots and silver
Pans to a closed door and famine,
Who will guide the blind sky toward the city in need of sight?
What will happen to the visions of the old men?
It is July, the liquor of dust fumbles us into cows
Groping a desert for home . . .
Then I looked down and saw the world I was entering . . .
The wild turkeys, those dinosaurs in the trees,
The apricots, and ditches of water,
And I asked my companion where are we.
And he said *Paradise, but over there.*

◆　◆　◆

How shall we account for all the foreign metal in our bodies in Paradise?
Must we relinquish it once we enter?
Who will gather it in gold boxes
Embossed with a stag hanging from a tree?
Is the gathering a type of forgetting or merely a letting go?
We give up our metal
Because no one wants to upset Paradise:
The fish, the bees churning honey,
The hunters throwing hound after hound
At an antelope that has succumbed to the hunt, to Paradise,
Succumbed to knowing that its running is not rescue but pleasure,
A pleasure in being taken over and over again.
In Paradise, all pleasure is of being taken.

You know this already.
Even the hunter who stands above his dead
Antelope whispers a prayer into the mouth and nose of the animal
Because he, too, remembers
When he once allowed a blind piece of metal to break him
Across a roof in a foreign country.

◆　◆　◆

Death invented us—every morning
With the swallowtails in the wild grapes,
The bottles of wine humming
In their gasps and broken lips,
In the hardened red light of a dog licking
At the vulture dead
On the side of the road.
Accidental or merely a gun
Slipping into the wet of our mouths,
Our alien heat
Erases itself quickly.
Once, my mother dreamt openly
Of a deer falling from her womb, the legs broken,
The grass below her red, steaming, bucking.
Nothing kept the fence
Between her dreaming and my punctured body
Whole. The swallowtails lick at the broken glass;
Some call it the surface of a lake.
To black—my hands for this work.
The swallowtails remove the eyes from the skull
Of a deer. Or is it a man?
What is it like to break the blue sky with another's eyes,
To rip the world into landscape
And witness it only as that what cannot blink?
The dead refuse to blink.
It is why we burn them
Or throw them
Hand over hand beneath the ocean
In the shadow of an island shaped like a coffin.
Dawn has moved past safety.
Everything rising from a bed or hole of steam
Will fail. My father's heart, his penis.

The dog circling his mother's teat.
About suffering, the swallowtails
Taught the living very little, though the children reached inside
The mud nests and threw the eggs on the ground.
They wondered why their parents ran
Toward nothing,
What clearly would dry, what felt wet in their hands.
Every morning, invention forgives
Our weakness for our belief in it.

COLUM McCANN

I wrote this story, "Cathal's Lake," twenty-five years ago. It's a young man's story and there is a lot that I would change about it now, but I am not here to tear myself asunder, or to edit my own imagination.

The story was written, first off, as a magic realist story, in other words a distinctly and overtly political one. All my South American heroes (Marquez, Galleano) were immediately political in their intent, but they were never overtly political. They preserved the mystery. They did not dictate meaning.

I knew I wanted to write about Northern Ireland, where my mother comes from, and where I had spent several of my summers. I had a gut instinct about what I wanted to say, though no idea how I would say it, and the idea for digging swans out of the soil possibly resulted from a mixture of Irish mythology (The Children of Lir) and contemporary poetry (Seamus Heaney's "Digging"). I wanted to write about sadness and futility and the availability of a narrow bridge of hope through the overwhelming despair of the North.

I also wanted to write about the Lamed Vavniks, or the Tzadikim Nistarim, a story that I was immediately struck by when I heard it (in a Baptist church in Texas of all places). The Lamed Vavniks were the 36 "righteous ones" or "hidden saints," who carried the sorrows of the world on their shoulders. There is one saint, however, who has lost his line of communication with God and so is cursed to bear his sorrows in silence. That's what attracted me—the silence, the curse, the loneliness.

It was, of course, a Hebrew myth, but it struck that it was also, in essence, an Irish story. And as we know there are at least two sides to every story. So, from the very outset I felt as if I were writing a story that—because of the link with the Lamed Vavniks—would also be a Palestinian story. This might sound odd, but there is as much Gaza as Derry in this story. It struck me that Cathal might very well be digging in the olive groves of another disputed territory.

But hopefully the point of the story is that Cathal does not, in the end, fly a flag. He is cursed to dig. He must bear the sorrows and give them flight.

I recognize now that a writer's politics can be as dangerous to him as his own greed. The idea of writing an immediately political story can be very limiting. We can become so overly conscious of our message that we can lose the mystery, or the human element. It is far too easy to bring the disease of politics to our stories.

Writers are not politicians and they should not try to be. This is not to deny the ability to make political statements, but the best statements come from within language and within rhythm and within mystery.

I think most of us are tired of other people (i.e., politicians) telling us what to think. What we love is being allowed to think. The best writing allows. It never proclaims. We make a mistake if we condescend to bare, absolute meaning. What we need is heart too.

One of the reasons why the peace process (now seventeen years old) worked in Northern Ireland is that our writers did not, in general, take distinct sides. Writers of every stripe and background called for a cessation of violence. That's what mattered. They called for the sadness to be opened up and dissected, which eventually filtered into the political sphere. They recognized that the cessation of violence was an opportunity to open a space not just in the political arena but in the level of each individual's consciousness.

This is where our stories matter. This is where we recognize that our fences must be fixed.

Cathal's Lake

It's a sad Sunday when a man has to dig another swan from the soil. The radio crackles and brings Cathal news of the death as he lies in bed and pulls deep on a cigarette, then sighs.

Fourteen years to heaven, and the boy probably not even old enough to shave. Maybe a head of hair on him like a wheat field. Or eyes as blue as thrush eggs. Young, awkward, and gangly, with perhaps a Liverpool scarf tied around his mouth and his tongue flickering into the wool with a vast obscenity carved from the bottom of his stomach. A bottle of petrol in his hands and a rag from his mother's kitchen lit in the top. His arms in the beginnings of a windmill hurl. Then a plastic bullet slamming his chest, all six inches of it hurtling against his lung at one hundred miles an hour. The bottle somersaulting from the boy's fingers. Smashing on the street beneath his back. Thrush eggs broken and rows of wheat going up in flames. The street suddenly quiet and gray as other boys, too late, roll him around in puddles to put out the fire. A bus burning. A pigeon flapping over the rooftops of Derry with a crust of white bread in its mouth. A dirge of smoke breaking into song over the sounds of dustbin lids and keening sirens. And, later, a dozen other bouquets flung relentlessly down the street in memorial milk bottles.

Cathal coughs up a tribute of phlegm to the vision. Ah, but it's a sad Sunday when a man has to go digging again and the lake almost full this year.

He reaches across his bedside table and flips off the radio, lurches out of the bed, a big farmer with a thick chest. The cigarette dangles from his lips. As he walks, naked, toward the window he rubs his balding scalp and imagines the gray street with the rain drifting down on roofs of corrugated iron. A crowd gathering together, faces twitching, angry. The boy still alive in his house of burnt skin. Maybe his lung collapsed and a nurse bent over him. A young mother, her face hysterical with mascara stains, flailing at the air with soapy fists, remembering a page of unfinished homework left on the kitchen table beside a vase of wilting marigolds. Or nasturtiums. Or daisies. Upstairs in his bedroom, a sewing needle with ink on the very tip, where the boy had been tattooing a four-letter word on his knuckles. Love or hate or fuck or hope. The sirens ripping along through the rain. The wheels crunching through glass.

Cathal shivers, pulls aside the tattered curtains and watches a drizzle of rain slant lazily through the morning air, onto the lake, where his swans drift. So many of them out there this year that if they lifted their wings in unison they would all collide together in the air, a barrage of white.

From the farmhouse window Cathal can usually see for miles—beyond the plowed black soil, the jade green fields, the rivulets of hills, the roll of forest, to the distant dun mountains. Today, because of the rain, he can just about make out the lake, which in itself is a miniature countryside—ringed with chestnut trees and brambles, banked ten feet high on the northern side, with another mound of dirt on the eastern side, where frogsong can often be heard. The lake is deep and clear, despite the seepage of manured water from the fields where his cattle graze. On the surface, the swans, with their heads looped low, negotiate the reeds and the water lilies. The lake can't be seen from the road, half a mile away, where traffic occasionally rumbles.

Cathal opens the window, sticks his head out, lets the cigarette drop, and watches it spiral and fizzle in the wet grass. He looks toward the lake once more.

"Good morning," he shouts. "Have ye room for another?"

The swans drift on, like paper, while the shout comes back to him in a distant echo. He coughs again, spits out the window, closes it, walks to his rumpled bed, pulls on his underwear, a white open-necked shirt, a large pair of dirty overalls, and some wool socks. He trundles slowly along the landing, down the stairs to make his breakfast. All these young men and women dying, he thinks, as his socks slide on the wooden floor. Well, damn it all anyway.

◆　◆　◆

And maybe the soldier who fired the riot gun was just a boy himself. Cathal's bacon fizzles and pops and the kettle lets out a low whistle. Maybe all he wanted, as he saw the boy come forward with the Liverpool scarf wrapped around his mouth, was to be home. Then, as a firebomb whirled through the air, perhaps all the soldier thought of was a simple pint of Watney's. Or a row of Tyneside tenements with a football to bang against the wall. Or to be fastened together with his girlfriend in some little Newcastle alleyway. Perhaps he was wishing that his hair could touch his shoulders, like it used to do. Or that, with the next month's paycheck, he could buy some Afghan hash and sit in the barracks with his friends, blowing rings of Saturn smoke to the ceiling. Maybe his eyes were as deep and green as bottles in a cellar. Perhaps a Wilfred Owen book was tucked under his pillow to make meaning of the whistles on the barbed wire. But there he was, all quivery and trembling, in Londonderry, his shoulder throbbing with the kickback of the gun, looking up to the sky, watching a plume of smoke rise.

Cathal picks the bacon out of the sizzling grease with his fingers and cracks two eggs. He pours himself a cup of tea, coughs, and leaves another gob of phlegm in the sink. The weather has been ferocious this Christmas. Winds that sheer through a body, like a scythe through a scarecrow, have left him with a terrible cold. Not even the Bushmills that he drank last night could put a dent in his chest. What a terrible thought that. He rubs his chest. Bushmills and bullets.

Perhaps, he thinks, a picture of the soldier's girlfriend hangs on the wall above the bunk bed in the barracks. Dogeared and a little yellow. Her hair all teased and a sultry smile on her face. Enough to make the soldier melt at the knees. Him having to call her, heartbroken, saying: "I didn't mean it, luv. We were just trying to scatter the crowd." Or maybe not. Maybe him with a face like a rat, eyes dark as bog holes, sitting in a pub, glorious in his black boots, being slapped and praised, him raising his glass for a toast, to say: "Did ya see that, lads? What a fucking shot, eh? Newcastle United 1, Liverpool 0."

All this miraculous hatred. Christ, a man can't eat his breakfast for filling his belly full of it. Cathal dips a small piece of bread into the runny yolk of an egg and wipes his chin. In the courtyard some chickens quarrel over scraps of feed. A raven lands on a fence post down by the red barn. Beyond that a dozen cows huddle in the corner of a field, under a tree, sheltering from the rain, which is coming down in steady sheets now. Abandoned in the middle of the field is Cathal's tractor. It gave up the ghost yesterday while he was taking a couple of sacks of oats, grass clippings and cracked corn out to the swans.

Shoveling the last of his breakfast into his mouth, Cathal watches the swans glide lazily across the water, close and tight. Sweet Jesus, but there's not a lot of room left out there these days.

◆　◆　◆

He leaves the breakfast dishes in the sink, unlatches the front door, sits on a wooden stool under the porch roof, and pulls on his green Wellingtons, wheezing. Occasional drops of rain are blown in under the porch and he tightens the drawstrings on his anorak hood. Wingnut, a three-legged collie who lost her front limb when the tractor ran over it, comes up and nestles her head in the crook of Cathal's knee. From his anorak pocket he pulls out a box of cigarettes, cups his hands, and lights up. Time to give these damn things up, he thinks, as he walks across the courtyard, the cigarette crisping and flaring. Wingnut chases the chickens in circles around some puddles, loping around on her three legs.

"Wingnut!"

The dog tucks her head and follows Cathal down toward the red barn. Hay is piled up high in small bales and bags of feed clutter the shelves. Tractor parts are heaped in the corner. A chaotic mess of tools slouches against the wall. Cathal puts his toe under the handle of a pitchfork and, with a flick of the foot, sends it sailing across the barn. Then he lifts a tamping bar, leans it in the corner, and grabs his favorite blue-handled shovel.

Christ, the things a man could be doing now if he wasn't cursed to dig. Could be fixing the distributor cap on the tractor. Or binding up the northern fence. Putting some paraffin down that foxhole to make sure that little red-tailed bastard doesn't come hunting chickens any more. Or down there in the southernmost field, making sure the cattle have enough cubes to last them through the cold. Or simply just sitting by the fire having a smoke and watching television, like any decent man fifty-six years old would want to do.

All these years of digging. A man could reach his brother in Australia, or his sister in America, or even his parents in heaven or hell if he put all that digging together into one single hole.

"Isn't that right, Wingnut?" Cathal reaches down and takes Wingnut's front leg and walks her out of the barn, laughing as the collie barks, the shovel tucked under his shoulder.

He moves back through the courtyard again, the dog at his heels. As he walks he whisks the blade of the shovel into the puddles and hums a tune. Wonder if they're singing right now, over the poor boy's body? The burns lightened by cosmetics perhaps, the autumn-colored hair combed back, the eyelids fixed in a way of peace, the mouth bitter and mysterious, the tattooed hand discreetly covered. A priest bickering because he doesn't want a flag draped on the coffin. A sly undertaker saying that the boy deserves the very best. Silk and golden braids. Teenage friends writing poems for him in symbolic candlelight. The wilting marigolds jettisoned for roses—fabulous roses with perfect petals. Kitchen rags used, this time to wipe whiskey from the counter. Butt ends choking up the ashtray. Milk bottles very popular among the ladies for cups of tea.

He reaches the laneway, the wind sending stinging raindrops into the side of his face. Cathal can feel the cold seep into his bones as he negotiates the ruts and potholes, using the shovel as a walking stick. In the distance the swans drift on, oblivious to the weather. The strangest thing about it all is that they never seem to quarrel. Yet, then again, they never sing either. Even when they leave, the whole flock, every New Year's Eve, he never hears that swansong. On a television program one night a scientist said that the swan's song was a mythological invention, maybe it had happened once or twice, when a bird was shot in the air, and the escaping breath from the windpipe sounded to some poor foolish poet like a song. But, if it is true, if there is really such a thing as a swansong, wouldn't it be lovely to hear? Cathal whistles through his teeth, then smiles. That way, at least, there'd be no more damn digging and a man could rest.

He unlatches the gate hinge and sidesteps the ooze of mud behind the cattle guard, and tramps on into the field. Water squelches up around his Wellingtons with each step. The birds on the water have not seen him yet. A couple of them follow one another in a line through the water, churning ripples. A large cob, four feet tall, twines his neck with a female, their bills of bright yellow smudged with touches of black. Slowly they reach around and preen each other's feathers. Cathal smiles. There goes Anna Pavlova, his nickname for his favorite swan, a cygnet that, in the early days of the year before the lake became so choc-a-bloc, would dance across the water, sending flumes of spray in the air. Others gather together in the reeds. A group of nine huddle near the bank, their necks stretched out toward the sky.

Bedamned if there's a whole lot of room for another one—especially a boy who's likely to be a bit feisty. Cathal shakes his head and flings the shovel forward to the edge of the lake. It lands blade first and then slides in the mud, almost going into the water. The birds look up and cackle. Some of them start to flap their wings. Wingnut barks.

"Shut up, all of ya," he shouts. "Give a man a break. A bit of peace and quiet."

He retrieves the shovel and wipes the blade on the thigh pocket of his overalls, lights another cigarette, and holds it between his yellowing teeth. Most of the swans settle down, glancing at him. But the older ones who have been there since January turn away and let themselves drift. Wingnut settles on the ground, her head on her front paw. Cathal drives the shovel down hard into the wet soil at the edge of the lake, hoping that he has struck the right spot.

All of them generally shaped, sized, and white-feathered the same. The girl from the blown-up bar looking like a twin of the soldier found slumped in the front seat of a Saracen, a hole in his head the size of a fist, the size of a heart. And him the twin of the boy from Garvagh found drowned in a ditch with an ArmaLite in his fingers and a reed in his teeth. And him the twin of the mother shot accidentally while out walking her baby in a pram. Her the twin of the father found hanging from an oak tree after seeing his daughter in a dress of tar and chicken feathers. Him the twin of the three soldiers and two gunmen who murdered each other last March—Christ, that was some amount of hissing while he dug. And last week, just before Christmas, the old man found on the roadside with his kneecaps missing, beside his blue bicycle, that was a fierce difficult job too.

Now the blade sinks easily. He slams his foot down on the shovel. With a flick of the shoulder and pressure from his feet he lifts the first clod—heavy with water and clumps of grass—flings it to his left, then looks up to the sky, wondering.

Christmas decorations in the barracks perhaps. Tinsel, postcards, bells, and many bright colors. Pine needles sprayed so they don't fall. A soldier with no stomach for turkey. A soldier ripping into the pudding. Someone chuckling about the mother of all bottles. A boy on a street corner, seeing a patch of deeper black on the tar macadam, making a New Year's resolution. A teacher going through old essays. A girlfriend on an English promenade, smoking. A great-aunt with huge amounts of leftovers. Paragraphs in the bottom left hand corner of newspapers.

Another clodful and the mound rises higher. The rain blows hard into Cathal's back. Clouds scuttle across the morning sky. Cigarette smoke rushes from his nose and mouth. He begins to sweat under all the heavy clothing. After a few minutes he stubs the butt end into the soil, takes out a red handkerchief and wipes his forehead, then pummels at the ground again. Go carefully now, or you'll cut the poor little bastard's delicate neck.

◆　◆　◆

With the mound piled high and the hole three feet deep, Cathal sees the top of a white feather. A tremble of wet soil. "Easy now," he says. "Easy. Don't be thrashing around down there on me." He digs again, a deep wide arc around the swan, then lays the shovel on the ground and spread-eagles himself at the side of the hole. Across the hole he winks at Wingnut, who has seen this happen enough times that she has learned not to bark. On the lake, behind his back, he can hear some of the swans braying. He reaches down into the hole and begins to scrabble at the soil with his fingernails. Why all this sweating in the rain, in a clean white shirt, when there's a million and one other things to be done? The clay builds up deep in his fingernails. The bird is sideways in the soil.

He reaches down and around the body and loosens the dirt some more, but not enough for the wings to start flapping. One strong blow of those things could break a man's arm. He lays his hands on the stomach and feels the heart flutter. Then he scrabbles some more dirt from around the webbed feet. With great delicacy Cathal makes a tunnel out of which to pull the neck and head. With the soil loose enough he gently eases the long twisted neck out and grabs it with one hand. "Don't be hissing there now." He slips his other hand in around the body. Deftly he lifts the swan out of the soil, folding back one of the feet against the wing, keeping the other wing close to his chest. He lifts the swan into the air, then throws it away from him.

"Go on now, you little upstart."

Cathal sits on the edge of the hole with his Wellington boots dangling down and watches the wondrous way that the swan bursts over the lake, soil sifting off its wings, curious and lovely, looking for a place to land. He watches as the other swans make room by sliding in, crunching against one another's wings. The newborn settles down on a small patch of water on the eastern side of the lake.

Somewhere in the bowels of a housing complex, a mother is packing away clothes in black plastic bags. Her lip quivers. There's new graffiti on the stairwell wall down from her flat. Pictures of footballers are coming down off a bedroom wall. A sewing needle is flung into an empty dustbin where it rattles. Outside, newspapermen use shorthand in little spiral books. Cameras run on battery packs. Someone thinks of putting some sugar in the water so that the flowers will last longer. Another man, in a flat cap, digs. A soldier is dialing his girlfriend. Or carving a notch. Swans don't sing unless they're shot way up high, up there, in the air. Their windpipes whistle. That's a known fact.

Cathal lights his last cigarette and thinks about how, in two days, the whole flock will leave and the digging may well have to begin all over again. Well, fuck it all anyway. Every man has his own peculiar curse. Cathal motions to his dog, lifts his shovel, then leans home toward the farmhouse in his green boots. As he walks, splatters of mud leap up on the back of his anorak. The smoke blows away in spirals from his mouth. He notices how the fencepost in the far corner of the field is leaning a little drunkenly. That will have to be fixed, he thinks, as the rain spits down in flurries.

ERASURE

I Wish I Had Words
Ode to a Land

JANNE TELLER

I wish I had words
There is the land, there the disappearing words
Buried are the people, dust and alphabetic rubble. Correct
spells celebrating the sins of another. Oh, vowel waltz,
History, that fairy story, everyone's beloved bride. And one and two and
three and four
Reconstruct,
your chosen word
Justice my amnesic cat, sleeps in prayer for her quarter life left, nine's done down
alleys, gunned down, at dizzying speed. And
one and two and three and four, around and nothing, ever more. No
rousing Tom
So what can I add to this pantomime of injustice in slow motion?
At dizzying speed?

◆　◆　◆

Here are the numbers—help dig up the Alphabet of Palestine:

I:　Once there was a land and there were people on this land. Once there was a people in a land that set out to eliminate another people. They almost succeeded. Once there was a people that had been almost eliminated which were given a land. (For future safety, it was said. To get out of the way, was not said.) The land, the people that had almost been eliminated were given, was not the land belonging to those who had done the eliminating. It was the land of a people who had done nothing but be governed by one empire for centuries, then be occupied for decades by another, which we here will call the fourth people. Strangely, it can be said that it was the fourth people (and friends of theirs) who gave the land of the First people to the third people, due to the crimes of the second people. This was an injustice called justice.

43

2:   The first people are named the Palestinians. The second people the Germans. The third people the Jews. The fourth people the English.

3:   Strangely, no one said give the third people Nordrhein-Westfalen. Or Saxony. Or Bayern. Or Baden-Württemberg. Even writing it here, feels a sacrilege. But why? Wouldn't that have been a justice called justice?

4.1:   It's terrifying and true: Six million Jews were killed in Holocaust. 6,000,000! By the Nazi regime. Yes, helped by some neighboring countries. Yes we speak about unspeakable horrors. Yes we speak about Europe. By 1948, less than 1,000 Jews had been killed in conflicts with the Palestinians and Arabs (in the same conflicts 5,200 Palestinian & Arabs had been killed by Jews).

4.2:   Altogether, in all confrontations and wars with the Arabs and Palestinians ever since 1920 until today—i.e., in almost one hundred years—a total of 25,000 Jews have been killed; not even 0.5 percent of the number of Jews killed by the Nazis in one decade. (In the same one hundred-year period, 91,105 Arabs & Palestinians have been killed by the Israelis).

4.3:   In the bombings of Gaza in the summer 2014 alone, 2,300 Palestinians were killed, including 513 children. In the same conflict, seventy-one Israeli were killed, of which sixty-six were soldiers, and one was a child. The number of Israeli Jews killed by Palestinian terrorism in all of the history of Israel from 1948–2014 is 3,791 persons.

4.4:   Since the year 2000, a Palestinian is fifteen times as likely as an Israeli to be killed by reasons of the conflict. Nothing said yet about how the living live.

5:   On June 26, 1945, the Charter of the United Nations was signed, creating the United Nations with the purpose, *"To develop friendly relations among nations based on respect for the principle of equal rights and self-determination of peoples . . ."*

6:   Two years later, on November 29, 1947, the UN General Assembly adopted Resolution 181, recommending the creation of independent Arab and Jewish States on hitherto British-occupied Mandatory Palestine.

7:   The second people accepted the plan. Nations friendly to the first people, the Arab nations, rejected the plan: what had happened to the UN Charter principle of national self-determination, which grants populations the right to determine their own destiny?, they asked. The first people stood to lose half the land.

8: 1948. War was. War was over. The first people lost much more than half the land. And more than 700,000 of their people were now refugees, displaced and dispossessed. The remainder lived in Gaza and the West Bank, at this stage controlled by two of their maybe overly friendly neighbor lands. We call those Egypt and Jordan.

9.1: Census, consensus—and Britain's own census of 1922: says that in 1914, 689,272 people lived in the land. Of these, less than 10 percent (less than 60,000) belonged to the Jewish faith. Eight years later, in 1922, 11 percent were Jews, 78 percent of the population is counted to be Muslim, 9.6 percent Christians. By 1947, the population had swelled to around two million people, of whom 32 percent (630,000 persons) were Jews, 60 percent (1.2 million) were Muslims, and 8 percent were Christians.

9.2: Historically, only before the sixth century AD did Palestine have a non-Muslim majority, namely Christians. Only before the first century—long before Islam's existence, and before the spreading of Christianity—was there ever a Jewish majority living in the land.

9.3: In 2013, 4.4 million Palestinians lived in the occupied territories, and 1.7 million Palestinians lived within Israel; totaling roughly the same number of Jews living in Israel.

10.1: The Balfour Declaration of 1917 (a public letter from the then United Kingdom's Foreign Secretary to Baron Walter Rothschild, a leader of the British Jewish community, for transmission to the Zionist Federation of Great Britain and Ireland), stated that: "... *his Majesty's government view with favour the establishment in Palestine of a national home for the Jewish people, and will use their best endeavours to facilitate the achievement of this object ...*"

10.2: Was it forgotten that the Balfour Declaration continued: "... *it being clearly understood that nothing shall be done which may prejudice the civil and religious rights of existing non-Jewish communities in Palestine ...*"? Or was it never meant?

11.1: The Universal Declaration of Human Rights was adopted by the United Nations General Assembly on December 10, 1948.

11.2: It didn't say: *The sins of one people against another can be washed clean by committing a sin against a third people.*

11.3: It said: "*All human beings are born free and equal in dignity and rights. They are endowed with reason and conscience and should act toward one another* in a spirit of brotherhood"; "Everyone is entitled to all the rights and freedoms set forth in this Declaration, without distinction of any kind, such as race, color, sex, language, religion, political or other opinion, national or social origin, property, birth or other status. Furthermore, no distinction shall be made on the basis of the political, jurisdictional or international status of the country or territory to which a person belongs, whether it be independent, trust, non-self-governing or under any other limitation of sovereignty"; "No one shall be subject to arbitrary arrest, detention or exile."

12.1: Descendants of the original 700,000 Palestinian refugees number today 4.9 million. Within Palestine alone, there are eight refugee camps in the Gaza Strip, housing altogether 1.2 million refugees, and nineteen refugee camps in the West Bank, housing a total of 741,000 refugees. The remainder live abroad, in camps, as asylum seekers or as stateless non-entities. The few lucky ones are residents in one incidental land or another.

12.2: Internationally, for Palestinian refugees, twelve camps are in Lebanon, ten in Jordan, thirteen in Syria (where, by now the refugees must have fled to yet new camps). Burj el-Shemali, Shatila, Qabr Essit, Homs, Marka, have you heard their names? Generation after generation are born, grow up, die in the camps. Many camps date back to 1948, others have come to later.

13.1: All Jews, everywhere in the world, of all nationalities—also safe American Jews, safe Canadian Jews, safe Scandinavian Jews—have an automatic right to settle in Israel and become full Israeli nationals & citizens any time they wish.

13.2: No Palestinian refugee, no matter how precarious his living conditions, no matter if he were born on Palestinian land to Palestinian parents, and has lived in refugee camps ever since, is ever allowed to return to his land. Palestinian refugees living abroad have no right of return. Even if they are stateless. Even if their lives are in danger. Even if they live in squalid refugee camps that their families fled to—due to the establishment of the Israeli State, on their land.

14: The Bible is not a history book. Nor is it a deed.

15: History be told, what came before: the land was tilled. The olives grew, the lemons. People called it home: trees, lakes, stony mountains, fertile valleys and the sea. Children were born. Old people died. Butterflies and scorpions. A place like many others, people working the auburn hills, people resting under white and pink almond trees. A place like none other: in towns, people searching their Gods. For thousands of years.

16.1: In 1967, six days. June 5–10. Blitz-war and the Palestinian territories were no longer governed by its Arab neighbors, but by Israel. Of the territories taken in the war, only Egypt's Sinai was later freed. To this day, the West Bank and Gaza is occupied by Israel for forty-eight years.

16.2: The Palestinian people have lived forty-eight years under Israeli occupation.

17.1: History be told, what came after was the daily humiliations, the land of honey and milk turned into the land of no opportunity—for the first people. The land of squalid buildings, because the occupying rulers will give no permits to restore, the land of no movement, check-point after check-point run fastidiously by the rulers, the land of transport separation, special roads where no Palestinian must go (even though the roads are built on land owned by same Palestinians), special Jews-only public transport, and a wall. All cutting off Palestinian people from their own land.

17.2: How can the Palestinian people till the fields to which they no longer have access? Yet, seven years of no tilling, and the land falls to the State, i.e., the Israeli State, Not the Palestinian authorities. Explain Justitia who can?

17.3: Yes, intifada after intifada. Actions of terror against Jewish-Israeli civilians. I don't believe in violence. But what are people to do, when their land is occupied? When they face daily violence and torture at the hand of the occupiers? When their children are arrested, or shot for throwing stones at their tormenters? For just being there? When their daily life is at stake? Their access to their fields, and thus their livelihood, is cut off, access to water is cut off, to electricity, health care, schools, jobs? And the entire world looks on and does nothing? Why is it that what elsewhere is called freedom fights, resistance, war—why in these lands is it called terror? I am not a believer in violence. I'm against violence in all forms, particularly against unarmed civilians—no matter their denomination. But can anyone in all honesty tell me that their own people would never pick up arms, if they were crushed and choked by an occupation power with a thousand times their military might, and the world stood by doing nothing? Why is it that in this one place on earth, the violence committed by the occupying ruler is so much more palatable than the one carried out by the people suffering the occupation?

18.1: It's not easy to make literature out of law. Not even when there are many of them. For one and not for another people. Today there are more than fifty such laws—adopted by the Israeli Government. Elsewhere, such has been named apartheid.

18.2:   It's easy to make injustice out of law. Laws are made by people. It's as easy to make unjust laws as it is to make just laws.

19.1:   There can be many reasons—it all depends on the perspective and who's in power—to choose one word rather than another. *Settlement* is a word of many meanings, only one of which carries an image of one group of people violently throwing off the land another group of people, who hitherto lived on, owned and tilled this land. *Land grab* would be the other word.

19.2:   In 2014, almost 700,000 Israeli settlers lived on land internationally recognized—by all governments in the world—to belong to Palestine. Three hundred eighty-two thousand settlers lived in 121 settlements in the West Bank, and 300,000 in settlements in East Jerusalem. All these settlements are officially established and supported by the Israeli government.

19.3:   Begun upon the 1967 war, the settlements annex to the territory of Israel a continuously growing amount of Palestinian land. The fourth Geneva Convention says, *"The Occupying Power shall not depot or transfer parts of its own civilian population into the territory it occupies."* The International Court of Justice has declared the settlements illegal, as has many other organs of the international community. Still Israel continues to support and expand them. Latest, in June 2014, the Israeli Government announced a plan for 3,300 new settler homes in the West Bank and East Jerusalem. In another move shortly after, at Gvaot near Bethlehem, an additional 400 hectares (1,000 acres) were expropriated for settlements.

19.4:   The West Bank looks like a leopard skin with the spots growing larger and more numerous, as more and more settlements are established. The roads to the settlements cut off the Palestinians from their neighbors, their nearby towns, the water supplies—and their own land. For each new spot, more Palestinian people are thrown out of their houses, thrown off their land, denied access, while the country is turning unlivable, ungovernable. It happens every day? Does anyone think this is not intentional? Have you looked at the maps?

20:   Blood isn't pretty. Ethnic Cleansing isn't pretty. Occupation isn't pretty. Could that be the reason that the land that does the occupying doesn't allow its own people to visit the land it occupies? Be why the occupying powers get very angry, to the point of considering it treason, if any of their own terms the occupied territories, occupied?

21:   There are walls, and borders, and check points, and citizens divided into class A, B and C, and no more days at the sea, of course, and lots of family that you don't see, of course, and A cannot easily go to B who cannot easily go to C, and vice versa, and even if you can see from Jerusalem to Bethlehem, if you're a Bethlehemite, you cannot marry a Jerusalemite, or rather you can, but you cannot get a permit to change towns, and if you still do, your children can register nowhere, they are no ones. There is an estimated 10,000 such children—what do you call them: non-children?—born within a marriage, yet who cannot get social security, cannot go to school, are alive yet do not exist.

22:   I know, I know, I know: an enormous injustice, an unspeakable horror, was done to the second people who were almost eliminated in the land of the third people—who however still have their land. I know, I know, I know, this injustice was begun at smaller scales throughout history by many a land, many a people. But I also know, I know that no injustice justifies another injustice.

23.1:   Also Jews say stop. Many. All around the world. The Jewish Voice for Peace in the US in August 2014 called for an end to the assault on Gaza and an end to the occupation of Palestine. This was echoed in statements by many other Jewish organizations and individuals. The International Jewish Anti-Zionist Network of Jewish survivors and descendants of survivors of the Nazi genocide have stated, *"We unequivocally condemn the massacre of Palestinians in Gaza and the ongoing occupation and colonization of historic Palestine. We further condemn the United States for providing Israel with the funding to carry out the attack, and Western states more generally for using their diplomatic muscle to protect Israel from condemnation. Genocide begins with the silence of the world. We are alarmed by the extreme, racist dehumanization of Palestinians in Israeli society, which has reached a fever-pitch. In Israel, politicians and pundits in The Times of Israel and The Jerusalem Post have called openly for genocide of Palestinians and right-wing Israelis are adopting Neo-Nazi insignia."* In Tel Aviv, thousands of Jewish-Israeli citizens demonstrated against the 2014 bombings in Gaza. Prominent Jews, like Naomi Klein, said not just, no more, not in my name—but also that it's time to boycott Israel to force it to relinquish the occupation. The Argentinian-Jewish-Israeli pianist, Daniel Barenboim, went so far as to take on Palestinian nationality.

23.2:   Also soldiers have eyes, ears. Voices. Some break the silence, and courageously tell: *"Our mission is to disrupt"*—these were the exact words—*"to disrupt and harass people's lives,"* said one. Another said: *"We went into Ramallah with no reason, security-wise. We turned Ramallah upside down, real hatred, we arrested eighty people that night. We went crazy. What do you mean? We broke the lightbulbs of every house we went into with the butts of our weapons—as an operational pretext, we claimed that the light bothered us. We used the butts of our weapons, the barrel—physical violence on an indescribable level."* A third: *"There are people who . . .*

Okay, I killed a kid, okay. They laugh. Yes, now I can draw a balloon on my weapon. A balloon instead of an X. Or a smiley (soldiers draw marks on their weapons to signify people they killed)." I could go on and on. The testimonies do—and these are from the Israeli soldiers themselves. How much is it necessary for the world to hear before it hears?

24:   Also the leaders of the people who are descendants of the people who were almost eliminated, who got the land of another people that they themselves are now trying to eliminate (at least from the land), have ears. Yet, all the international calls keep demanding the same. Like the first one, adopted unanimously by the UN Security Council on November 22, 1967, Resolution 242: referring to *"inadmissibility of the acquisition of territory by war and the need to work for a just and lasting peace in the Middle East in which every State in the area can live in security."* . . . Demanded ia, : (i) *"Withdrawal of Israeli armed forces from territories occupied in the recent conflict;. . ."* as well as all the following Resolutions 338 (1973), 446 (1979), 1322 (2000), 1397 (2002), 1402 (2002), 1403 (2002), 1405 (2002), 1435 (2002) and 1515 (2003), on the basis of which United Nations Security Council on May 13, 2004, adopted Resolution 1544, calling *"on Israel to respect its obligations under international humanitarian law, and insists, in particular, on its obligation not to undertake demolition of homes contrary to that of the law."* But all have fallen on deaf ears. Of the Israeli government.

25.1:   Where are all the words spoken, written? What happened to them? I have no other words than those already used by others. If I had a stone, would I throw it? No, it's not for me. Violence is a way backwards, not forwards. Instead, I prefer to cast my pen. This is not a text, this is a mirror. A mirror of omission anno 1948–2015. A mirror of horrific injustice, disparity and desperation. A mirror of perpetuation. A perpetuation of the crime that started with the Holocaust, and now is continued endlessly by the victims of that very holocaust onto a people who weren't the perpetrators. A mirror of a people who for decades are being ethnically cleansed from their own land, while the world looks on. A mirror onto which we must cast our pens, and shatter it . . .

25.2:   One state on all the land for all the people, no division of the land, perhaps two provinces (as was once foreseen by some international powers), would be the most beautiful, most long term sustainable, solution, honoring the land itself. But this may not be realistically achievable—at present. Then, since everyone has known for long that a reasonably fair—or perhaps rather one should say the presently realistically do-able—solution would be a clear division along the 1967 borders with minor adjustments for later developments, Jerusalem as a shared protectorate, and abolishment of all Israeli settlements on Palestinian lands. Give equal rights to Palestinians, also right of return. And economic compensation for property lost or destroyed. World guarantee of just and peaceful societies, of safety and law and order—paid by Germany and Europe—of course to the Jews, yes—but so very much finally, finally: *also* to the Palestinians!

26:   The power of the alphabet lies in the hands of those in power.

◆　◆　◆

New York, February 2, 2015

NOTES

Source for D 1 & 2: Jewish virtual Library
Source for E: United National Charter, Article 1.2
Source for K 3: Articles 1,2 and 9 of the Universal Declaration of Human Rights.
Source for L: UNRWA
Source for W 2: www.breakingthesilence.org.il

SINAN ANTOON

Very few works can capture the magnitude of a catastrophe and of its effects and afterlives. Ibtisam Azem's *The Book of Disappearance* confronts the memory of loss and the loss of memory. It goes to, and comes from, the heart of Palestine: a site of ongoing violent material and discursive erasure. In her novel, the ghosts of history and of its victims still roam the streets of Palestine (even though the names have been changed) and haunt the colonizers and their descendants. They restate the question(s) once again and demand justice and recognition. Literature achieves one of its most powerful effects; preserving memory and defending life with beauty.

From *The Book of Disappearance*

by *Ibtisam Azem*

(Translated from Arabic by Sinan Antoon)

Nothing but the sea. I always come back to this spot. Here, Jaffa is on my left and the sea spread out before me. I leave Tel Aviv behind. I don't see it and it doesn't see me. I leave its buildings and noise. The sound of the sea overpowers the sounds of the city. I know it is behind me, but I couldn't care less about its existence.

Although we didn't spend much time together, I feel your presence everywhere in this country. What is "much" anyway? I had wanted to bring you to this spot in particular. Hoping you would try to remember if you, too, loved it in the past before my grandfather whom I never knew left. Perhaps you two walked here once? This spot is not far from your house in Manshiyye.

I'm mad at you. Your memory, which is engraved in my mind, has all these holes in it. Am I not remembering all that you told me? Or was what you told me incomprehensible? I was very young when I started to listen to your stories. Later, when I turned to them for help, I discovered the holes in them. I started to ask you about them. But the more I asked the more you got mixed up, or maybe I did. How can things not get mixed up? I was certain that there was another city on top of the one we live in, donning it. I was certain that your city, the one you kept talking about, which has the same name, has nothing to do with my city. It resembles it a great deal; the names, orange groves, scents, al-Hamra Cinema, Apollo, weddings, Prophet Rubin's feast, Iskandar Awad St., al-Nuzha St., the Sa`a square . . . etc. Where are all these names from? We walk together and you mention other names too. Names not written on signs. I had to learn to see what you were seeing. Ugh and all those people! I got to know all their problems and how they were forced to leave Jaffa. I know all the boring details about their lives and some interesting ones too. I know all the jokes they used to tell. All this without having met a single one of them. And I probably never will.

Your Jaffa resembles mine, but it is not the same. Two cities impersonating each another. You carved your names in my city and so I feel like I am a returnee from history. Always tired, roaming my own life like a ghost. Yes, I am a ghost who lives in your city. You, too, are a ghost, living in my city. We call both cities "Jaffa."

You were the exact opposite of the others. They couldn't talk about their catastrophes as they took place. Even when they would dare open the door of memory, they would only open it just a bit and only many years later. You did the opposite. The last time I asked you about how they kicked you out of Manshiyye and forced you to go to Ajami . . . and how you lived with the Hungarian family they brought to share your house with you. You said, "My tongue is worn away from words. Don't ask me anymore. They didn't stay long in the house we were forced to go to. We were lucky. It's enough, Grandson. What good will it do to talk about it. Even words are tired."

You used to say that you would walk in the morning but could not recognize the city. Nor could you recognize the streets. As if they, too, were displaced with those who were forced to leave. My child eyes back then tried to imagine the scene the way you described it. "As if the darkness swallowed them. As if the sea took them hostage." That is how you described your days and those who were forced to leave and go beyond the sea. But you didn't say that the population of the city went from 100,000 to 4,000. No, you didn't say that. But you said that you couldn't recognize your city after they had left. What sense of bereavement! I cannot comprehend these figures. Nor can I understand what it means for a city to be emptied like that. I, who was born and raised in Jaffa after Jaffa had left itself!

You used to eat oranges voraciously. I thought you loved them, but I was surprised when you said that you didn't. You said you only started eating oranges after they forced you out of Manshiyye to Ajami. They fenced Ajami with barbed wire and declared it a closed military zone. Why did you eat oranges then if you didn't like them? Were you exacting revenge against those who were on the other side of the sea yearning for Jaffa's oranges? You always complained that the cypresses on the sides of the streets lost their meaning after *that year*. They stood there doing nothing except dusting the sky. You used to say that and laugh as if knowing that it was meaningless. But you insisted that those trees were meaninglessly big. You didn't like oranges when you were growing up, you said. You only loved their scent and blossoms. But "after they left, everything took on another meaning or no meaning at all . . . I began to love seeing people eat oranges, but I, myself, never liked them . . . I ate them, but never liked them. Oh, enough already! I'm tired of blathering. Let's talk about something else. You ask too many questions."

You said you used to walk down the streets laughing out loud with your father. Barbed wire surrounding you for more than ten years. No one could leave Ajami except with an official permit. They even stole Jaffa's name when they placed it under Tel Aviv's administrative custody. Is this why I dislike Tel Aviv? Did I inherit this lump in my throat from you? Why do I still live in it then? "Why shouldn't you? This is Palestine . . . these are Jaffa's villages and it'll always be ours," you said to me. But then you fell silent as if speech was painful.

You said you went out with your father in what can only be described as a fit of madness. You walked with him and greeted strangers to fool him into believing that what he himself had said was true. That everyone had returned to Jaffa. You said he was demented and saw everyone there. Ten years passed and he couldn't get used to his new Jaffa. Can one get used to his *nakba*? They changed street names into numbers to remind you that you were in a prison called Jaffa. As if you needed anyone to remind you of that. You said that your father saw Bus no. 6 coming on time and saw his partner, Zico, giving him back the keys to the "mobilia" warehouse they co-owned. You always said "mobilia" instead of "furniture" because you loved the sound of it. Had I not seen this Zico in a photograph with my grandfather I would've thought he was a figment of your imagination. Zico. What kind of name is that anyway? Was that his nickname? I asked you. You said you didn't know. He was your father's partner and owned furniture stores in Jaffa. "They looted the country and the people, so you think they wouldn't loot furniture? Of course! And how many times have I said I don't want to talk about this. My father became demented and died of his heartache after that year. Why do you keep asking? How many times do I have to give the same answers? Please, sweetheart, for God's sake."

Then you went back to your silence.

You realized that your father was demented when he knocked on your door one cold morning. He said that Zico had visited him during the night and said they could go back to bring the furniture from the warehouse and open the stores. You didn't say anything when you heard him say that. You stopped arguing with him when he yelled and said that he wanted to go back to his home. When you told him he was at home he accused you of lying. At first you didn't understand what was taking place. Then you realized that he was demented, all of a sudden. And you realized that he was going to die all at once as well. You took him by the hand and walked with him on his last morning. "I walked and felt I was going to the gallows. The Israelis could have killed us. We weren't allowed to just go out whenever we pleased. There was barbed wire everywhere. We were in prison and he was determined to leave Ajami. God saved us. I don't know how. I was reciting the Kursi chapter from the Qur'an all the way. I was terrified." You took a deep breath after that last sentence. As if all the air in the world wasn't enough to fill your lungs. Sixty years later and you would still feel a tightness of breath when you talked about the *nakba*, your *nakba* and Jaffa's. Your Palestine. You took him by the hand and greeted the strangers as if they were the city's people. You said that God must've heard your prayers because no one stopped you to ask for permits. Pedestrians nodded as they responded to your greetings in a language they didn't know. As if everyone had agreed to let him bid his hometown farewell. When you returned home he said he was going to bathe and sleep a little. But you knew that this was it. Did he take a bath because he knew he was about to die? Did you do the same? Is that why you took a bath before leaving and refused to let anyone come with you? You hadn't left the house for six months. Did you want to die alone by the sea? Survivors are lonely.

This Is Just a Place

NATE BROWN

I.

I was sixteen when my brothers moved out of the cramped bedroom we shared. Matt left first. Having finished a year of community college, he stuffed his Chevy Sprint with his clothes, his Ibanez guitar and gear, and an enormous collection of CDs, and drove his hatchback less than a mile down the road to his newly rented apartment. Six months later, Aaron followed. He'd stopped attending high school halfway through his senior year, which broke the tacit understanding with our parents that we could live at home so long as we were in school. If Aaron insisted on dropping out, then my parents were done housing him. That's how he found himself packing his own car with his things—more clothes and CDs, a fat stack of fantasy novels—and driving that same mile down the road to live with Matt.

For a long time, Matt worked at the HomeTown Buffet where he served roast beef and turkey at the carving station. Aaron worked at the mini mart near our house where, as kids, our father had occasionally sent one of us with a handwritten note and a ten-dollar bill to buy him a pack of Marlboro Lights and a York Peppermint Patty. We could use the change to buy a Twix or a Clearly Canadian for ourselves. It didn't seem strange to me then that a father might do this, or that a gas station attendant would sell cigarettes to a child provided he had a note from his father. Nor did it seem strange that my brothers would move out only to end up a mile from home. We lived in California's San Joaquin Valley, where small things—that Twix bar, a balsa wood plane, the short mile between my parents' house and my brothers' apartment—satisfied us.

Growing up, my brothers and I knew that our family didn't have much money, but no one ever uttered the word poor. It had too much power, and we'd have been ashamed to use it. It was better to say blue collar or, better, working class, which emphasized work and connoted a kind of respectability. By affirming that we worked for what we had, we kept shame at bay. Money or no money, we seemed to be telling ourselves, we were a family that wasn't too stupid, stubborn, or lazy to work. In retrospect, our avoidance of the word poor was a defensive posture that smacks of a libertarianism that makes me uncomfortable today. It's not lost on me that in central California, when we thought of truly poor families, it wasn't households like mine that came to mind. Migrant workers—men, women, and children from all parts of Mexico, Central America, and Southeast Asia—struck us as poor. We were something else. We were not them.

Looking back, I understand that part of the shameful discrepancy in our language had come from some actual, extant differences between white families like mine and my classmates from Hmong and Mexican families. While my brothers and I knew that our shared bedroom and our second-hand clothing set us apart from peers who had more, we also knew that in a place like the San Joaquin Valley, three white boys who had enough to eat, who had security, who lived in a safe part of town, and who didn't have to skip school to work in an orange grove would seem ridiculous had they described themselves as poor. Growing up and going to school in the valley provided us with early lessons both in the power of language and in the unique and ugly human capacity to set oneself apart. Even at the lower end of the economic spectrum, we recognized that there was a long way to fall. And like the small, bullied kid who turns and punches the smaller kid next to him, we felt better than the even poorer kids in our classes. We felt apart.

I mention all of this because I want to make it clear that in spite of the basic facts of my family's own poverty, we were raised by parents who recognized our relatively better circumstances. My brothers and I had jobs. We were paid a minimum wage for those jobs and had pay stubs to prove that we'd paid our taxes, luxuries compared to the off-the-book migrants who were overworked and underpaid and, ironically, constantly accused of laziness. My parents, both native speakers of English and both raised in Visalia, have never been written off or doubted or suspected of criminal activity merely because of their accents, their clothing, the color of their skin. Lean though our childhood was, our parents often packed us into the car and drove us to the wild and rolling foothill town with the giant candy store we adored. Or they'd load up the car with snacks and drive west to the pebbly beach at Morro Bay where we'd fly cheap, plastic kites, and collect sand dollars and stones from the shore, returning home long after midnight, sand in our pockets and between our toes.

II.

The spring after my brothers moved out, my mother was offered a job with a technology company in San Francisco. It marked a colossal change of fortune. She saw her income double and, quite suddenly, my family no longer seemed that poor. My parents paid down debt. They bought a new car. A different future started to come into focus, and as a result, I studied harder. I participated in clubs and school plays. I attended football games, soccer matches, and school dances. In 1999, my brothers joined the Marine Corps and went to boot camp as I was applying to universities that, just eighteen months earlier, I hadn't known existed. I remember thinking at the time that had my mother's new job come earlier, Matt and Aaron might not have joined the Marines at all.

But by August of 2000, both of my brothers were at duty stations as I boarded a plane with my bags packed for my first year at Cornell. I'd scarcely been out of California, and I'd never been on a plane before. I hadn't visited any colleges, hadn't interviewed with any admissions officers, hadn't met any alumni. I'd seen snow—on the ground, up in the Sierras—but I'd never seen it actually fall from the sky. And then, very quickly, I found myself moving 2,700 miles away from home. Somehow that seemed less odd to me than the idea of both Matt and Aaron as Marines. In just under three years, we'd gone from sleeping within five feet of one another to living thousands of miles apart.

Those first months in Ithaca, I felt as if I'd stumbled into the place. I was under-prepared, intellectually and climatologically. I'd not studied enough in high school to do well in my college math and science courses, nor had I understood precisely how cold it would be. It's one thing to read about the average winter temperatures in New York's Southern Tier and another to experience them. By October, I had to call my mother and ask her to order me a new coat. I got the worst GPA of my life that first semester, and I'd learned lessons in drinking too much and staying out too late. That year, the one bright spot had been the recruitment meeting for the *Cornell Daily Sun*.

I began by writing reviews, then moved on to arts features and copyediting. As a junior, I ran the arts supplement that was published each Thursday. Later, I ran for editor-in-chief, and when I got the job, I was surprised and scared. It was more than a full-time job's worth of hours and effort on top of coursework, but I took the position, and that first fall, I wrote dozens of editorials, edited numerous others, ran meetings, oversaw the newsroom, and reported to our board of directors. It felt good, and it felt important, and even if the *Sun* was subject to the blunders and fumbles that all student papers are subject to, the position gave me a new feeling of seriousness. For the first time in my adult life, I read, watched, and listened to the news obsessively—I'm still a news junkie.

The early 2000s were a strange, difficult period for newspapers, including college dailies. Having refined their websites, many newspaper's digital products had become their physical paper's biggest competition. Why buy the paper when you could read the same stories online and for free? At least part of that answer to that nagging question came from the web's double promise of an expanded readership and of greater interactivity between readers of the paper and the reporters and editors who created it.

Today, we're all familiar with (and perhaps tired of) simple, immediate online interactivity. Comment sections, long threads of argument on Facebook, and rapid-fire Twitter reply chains have become an intellectual bargain basement fully stocked with tiresome, frightening, racist, misogynistic, and classist commentary. In 2003, it was not yet so obvious that ubiquitous online interaction and reaction would help disseminate terrible ideologies alongside—or, rather, just underneath—any number of news stories, editorials, and blog posts.

The relatively novel ability to drop the editors of a publication an email reduced the time between a reporter printing the news and a reader reacting to it, which came with an attendant problem: knee-jerk emails to the editor often set off long chains of letters to the editor in which readers would reply to one another rather than to the story that'd started the conversation. Subsequently, most online news venues have instituted policies that require that letters to the editor address only content originally published by that publication, and not to subsequent reader commentary.

But if you were in Ithaca in 2003 and picked up an edition of the *Sun*, it was as likely as not that you could flip to the letters page and see second- and third-tier responses to the thoughts and ideas expressed in other people's letters to the editor. This was how Jim came into my life.

I should say here that the most interesting and contentious section of any college paper is the op-ed page. It is where excited, opinionated, and occasionally obnoxious students take their best stabs at reflecting on the big stories. In the fall of 2003, those included the wars in Iraq and Afghanistan, the increasingly contentious relationship between politicians on the right and left, and the Second Intifada that raged on half a world away. There were constant columns about what Israel should or should not do about what it saw as Palestinian aggression, and there were rejoinders and rebuttals that cited Israel's massively superior firepower and its tendency to employ disproportionately hostile military tactics.

At twenty-one, I felt less than capable of making judgments about the ongoing violence between Israelis and Palestinians because, as a white man who was raised a Lutheran in California's hot middle, I'd known exactly one Muslim, Mr. Al-Askari, a friend of our family who taught at my high school for years, and one Jew, Shoshanna, whose family had to drive to the nearest temple, forty-five minutes north in Fresno, in order to attend Shabbat services. Put more bluntly: I was sheltered from the violence and strife between Israelis and Palestinians because it seemed remote, foreign, and of little consequence to my life.

I'm ashamed now of my ignorance, but I'm more ashamed that it took me nearly my entire college career and the Second Intifada for me to ask why the ongoing bloodshed seemed so inevitable to everyone. The answer came one very cold October night in the form of a letter to the editor from an attorney in another state. Jim's position was clear and his sentences were cogent. These were things we looked for in letters, as so many of them were purely stupid, poorly written, or irrelevant. I was selecting letters for the next day's edition, and as with any letter (or article, for that matter), I wrote the short headlines that introduced them. For

Jim's, I appended the headline "War will cease only when Palestine is willing to compromise." While neither the headline nor Jim's letter aligned with my own then-nebulous views on Israeli-Palestinian conflict and violence, it seemed to encapsulate Jim's argument. I saved the file, printed the proof for review, sent it to paste-up, and put the paper to bed. Our deadline met, the staff and I went home.

When I arrived the next afternoon to get started on the following day's paper, I had a message from Jim waiting in my inbox. He was displeased. He asked that I call him to discuss the manner in which we'd published his letter, so I called. He explained that in using the word Palestine in the headline I'd written, I'd implied that such a place actually existed which, as far as Jim knew, it did not. I argued the point that to use the Palestine was to describe not merely the place but also the political body of people (though, of course, there was cause to describe the region as Palestine, too). He was having none of it. The conversation remained cordial enough, if flatly curt, and over the course of the forty or so minutes that we spoke, he asked if I was Jewish. I told him I didn't see what my religious affiliation had to do with anything. After explaining that I might understand better if I were Jewish, he demanded, for the sixth or seventh time, that we run correction, which I was unwilling to allow.

Without intending to do so, I'd stumbled into a longstanding debate about nomenclature, about appropriate signifiers and semantics, as if that debate was the one we should have been having, rather than a debate about adherence to treaties, rules of warfare, and civilian casualties. As if the true ugliness of the then-ongoing Second Intifada was held within the words we used to describe the conflict and not in the ugly details of the conflict itself. Ultimately, my associate editor stepped in and acted as ombudsman. She refused to run Jim's correction, but offered to run a clarification stating that the author of the letter preferred the wording "War will cease only when Palestinians are willing to compromise." Just like that, an argument with an upset reader had wiped the word Palestine from our pages, as if there weren't millions of people in the world who referred to Palestine as their home.

By that time, I'd long understood the importance of nomenclature and of self-description. I'd avoided describing my childhood as one of poverty because I felt the word didn't appropriately describe my family's work ethic. Especially since I was at a wealthy school, I'd stuck to describing my family as working class in an effort to communicate my respect for my background. It was my history, after all, and my family. It seemed to me that describing us as poor would have been to strip us of our hard-earned dignity. It wasn't until my fight with Jim that I was fully aware of how dedicated some people are to stripping others of theirs, and of our own complicity in permitting it.

III.

I hadn't thought about Jim, his letter, or our semantic pissing match in a long time, and it was only when watching the gruesome images from Gaza this summer that I thought of the episode once more.

In July of 2014, an Israeli naval vessel shelled a beach in Gaza, killing four young cousins who were playing there. It was a horrifying moment during a war that consisted of little else but horrifying moments. The images in the *New York Times* reminded me of some of southern California's industrial coastline, a hybrid of warehouses, blocky apartment buildings, and sand peppered with bits of wood and shell. I remembered our parents in the days before their new car and the San Francisco job, how long those drives over to Morro Bay seemed at the time. I know now that those jaunts must've been an incredible stretch for my parents—the tank of gas, the kites, knickknacks from the shell shop, hamburgers at the beachside restaurant. It must have strained their pocketbooks. Still, playing on that beach, my brothers and I got to be exactly what we were: kids, happy to be out of the house, playing in the sun, running from the chilly foam of the broken waves that chased us up the beach.

The deaths of the children killed on the beach in Gaza last July were no less horrifying or less tragic because they were Gazans, yet, as the *Times* reported, upon acknowledging that they'd launched the attack, the Israeli Defense Forces called the deaths "a tragic outcome." The semantic sleight of hand minimized the death of those children in a way that I've rarely seen. In the IDF's sidestepping acknowledgement of responsibility, those cousins were not little boys. They were not children. They were not even Palestinians. They weren't even collateral damage or casualties, words that might too closely identify their deaths with military intention. No, those boys had become a single, tragic outcome.

The same year that I served as editor-in-chief of the *Sun*, I took a seminar on the poetry of A. R. Ammons, who had recently passed away after having taught at Cornell for decades. In his poem "In Memoriam Mae Noblitt," Ammons employs a refrain that stabbed me in the gut the first time I read it. "This is just a place" appears throughout the poem and acts as a linguistic ballast in a poem that's otherwise filled with celestial motion and sorrow. It's a phrase that had long held meaning for me, so much so that one day, when I was in graduate school in Madison, Wisconsin, I got drunk at a bar and walked across to the street to a tattoo parlor where I had those words needled into my chest. Aaron had long since been injured in Iraq and had come home to recover. Matt was serving his second tour. Partially, I'd gone to get the tattoo in solidarity with my brothers, who had both gotten ink while in the Marines. But the phrase was also a reminder that while it was all right to feel nostalgic about that little shared bedroom, my parents' shoestring-budget trips to the beach, and about the children my brothers and I had once been, it was also okay to stop mourning the loss of that time, that home.

In ten years, my wife and I have had addresses in seven different cities. Yet, I've never stopped picturing my parents' house when the word "home" is uttered. And when I think of the phrase tattooed on my chest, I recognize that it's an odd luxury to change one's notion of home. I may feel nostalgic for moments from my childhood, and I may regret the loss of intimacy with my brothers, but my parents still live in that bungalow. The big lemon tree is still just outside of my childhood bedroom window. The gargantuan split-leaf still sits squarely in the middle of the front yard. Their home has never been denied me, has never been taken away, and it occurs to me while thinking of notions of home, that the phrase *this is just a place* might smack of a glib privilege that refuses to acknowledge the circumstances of others—leveled homes near Israeli settlements, bombed apartment buildings in Gaza that are now little more than busted concrete and rebar. I can imagine that few things would fix your notion of home more permanently than its forcible seizure or destruction, than being told that what you've long called home belongs, in fact, to someone else.

This is a world in which words and names have power, so much so that four dead children can be called an outcome and an entire people can be denuded of their connection to their homes merely by describing them as Palestinians while steadfastly refusing to recognize the word or the concept of Palestine.

If there is a path to lasting peace, I wonder if it resides not merely in deeds—restraint, compromise, mercy, treaties, the laying down of arms—but also within language itself. Perhaps peace will come when we can watch a Palestinian woman press a finger to an atlas and say, This is the place. This is home. And we admit that each of us knows what she feels.

DWAYNE BETTS

For a long time I've been fixated on a few images. While Palestine isn't on the news, there are often these photos. This one photo struck me, as I tried to work out how to speak to this trauma that seems so distant. I don't know. The pictures help—they help frame things for me, because in this one, the little girl just knows something we don't. The value of pink in a war zone, of flowers in the hair. In a lot of ways the photo is more important than the poem—the one gets me to the other, but I'm not sure if it's any way words can get to the understanding that little girl has.

Nothing About Palestine
Is On The News Tonight

the living, too, like the dead, receive no airtime,
not here in America, where the days news
is deflated footballs and a running back who
shouts out his real Africans as an act of revolutions.
nothing about Palestine will be on the news tonight,
our eyes fixated on would be snow storms & scandals,
we too fixated on the lives of broken celebrities
to contemplate a world where the dead only have cache
with their mourners. a kid I once knew wore a black
& white keffiyeh over his face, each day he mourned
some loss. add all his losses up & you get all those
small circles around his head pulling his eyes
toward the ground, as if he feared stepping in a grave.
the solemn look in his eyes: all I knew of him & all I know
of Palestine. eyes turn too quickly toward hurt
& you imagine only hurt is there, only the broken,
battered bodies you imagine gives you a way to pretend
to understand the world. I know so little of Palestine.
the entire history of my knowledge captured by a photo,
a little girl my oldest son's age. she carries a pink umbrella
that catches the light from the sun, it's upraised,
as if to shield her from the aftermath of shellings
all around her; she has flowers in her hair & looks
toward whoever holds the camera, that hand is
obviously a stranger, her look quizzical, as if she doesn't
understand why he documents her on this sunny day,
umbrella upraised to protect her from the shards of war
that have turned her path to school into ruins.

The Goal Is Clarity

ED PAVLIC

In the weeks since returning from the West Bank I've been tuned into the news, the news that stays news, and the news that isn't news at all. The top story in the *New York Times* on Wednesday, July 9, 2014 begins "Israel and Hamas escalated their military confrontation on Tuesday. . ."[2] Inches away, the World Cup story allows, "The final score was Germany 7, Brazil 1. It felt like Germany 70, Brazil 1."[3] The juxtaposition of balance on one hand and the exaggeration of how unbalanced the World Cup rout felt on the other is too close to ignore. I dare say, with warfare again in the open in the region, it's worth tracing its contours in our media, in our minds, and in our lives.

I know. It's the oldest of old hats to note the distended shapes American journalism creates to preserve the Israel-first, false impression of some symmetry or parity between interests and powers in the contested territory split, shared, and struggled over by people known as Palestinians and Israelis. Even the names are disputed. Many Palestinians would refute the idea of "Israelis" and simply say Jews. Many Israelis have contended that, in fact, there are no "Palestinian" people. It's territory—rhetorical, ethical, religious, ethnic, and geographic—so complexly, at times, hideously, contested that many people in the West, certainly in the US, simply look away. As a person who, since childhood, has lived a life athwart American racial codes and territories, I've always kept an eye on Israel/Palestine for the focused, if challenging, clarity it can offer one's perspective on American experience. That might sound strange. But, it's true. In a recent tour of the West Bank with the Palestinian Festival of Literature, in fact, I found much clarified.

This clarity is not complete, of course. It's based on my own observations as well as conversations with people such as Ray Dolphin from the United Nations Office for the Coordination of Humanitarian Affairs in occupied Palestinian

---

[2] Steven Erlanger and Isabel Kershner, "Israel and Hamas Trade Attacks as Tension Rises," *New York Times*, July 8, 2014, http://www.nytimes.com/2014/07/09/world/middleeast/israel-steps-up-offensive-against-hamas-in-gaza.html

[3] Sam Borden, "Goal, Goal, Goal, Goal, Goal, Goal, Goal, and Brazil's Day Goes Dark," *New York Times*, July 8, 2014, http://www.nytimes.com/2014/07/09/sports/worldcup/world-cup-2014-host-brazil-stunned-7-1-by-germany-in-semifinal.html

territories (UN OCHA), Dr. Tawfiq Nasser, Director of the Augusta Victoria Hospital in East Jerusalem and Omar Barghouti, founding member of the Palestinian Campaign for the Academic and Cultural Boycott of Israel (PACBI). While touring the region, I was also reading, widely and variously and, at times, all night long (jet lag): James Baldwin's letters (one from Israel) published in *Harper's* in 1963; Etel Adnan's incomparable two-volume, *To look at the sea is to find what one is* (2014); Sarah Schulman's great memoir of (Jewish American) political re-awakening, *Israel/Palestine and the Queer International* (2012); the report, "East Jerusalem: Key Humanitarian Concerns" (2011), and the "Humanitarian Atlas" (2012) put out by the UN OCHA; and the Legal Unit Annual Report (2013) from the Czech-run Hebron Rehabilitation Committee. The Hebron Rehabilitation Committee recorded over six hundred violations of Palestinian human rights during the calendar year, 2013. The report contains month-by-month charts in which each violation has its entry. Incidents are tabulated by category: against people; against property; by settlers; by Israeli soldiers. This daily array of violence presents, for one, a background I've yet to see appear in American media reporting the abduction and murder near Hebron (in Arabic, Al-Khalil) of three Jewish teenagers in June.

There's active and latent anger and violence everywhere in the region. But, according to these sources, even in so-called "Palestinian" territory (occupied by and often under the control of Israeli military personnel), there's absolutely no parity in the legal, military, and social contests between Israeli power and Palestinian struggle. One is a contemporary bureaucratic state whose legal

system vigorously operates to sustain and increase its hold on geographic territory and is possessed of a cornucopia of surveillance and weapon systems to back it up. The other is a disparate array of factionalized, anti-colonial resistance that uses smuggled and home-built weapons when not employing such high-tech systems as slingshots and cutlasses or simply throwing stones. Simply put there's no contest here.

Looking around, say, at the closed-off, shut down and vacant business district in Hebron, Shudada Street, or at the scorched guard tower and murals of martyred and imprisoned Palestinian leaders at the Qalandia checkpoint in East Jerusalem, Baby Suggs' comment from Toni Morrison's *Beloved* rang in my ears, "Lay down your sword. This ain't a battle; it's a rout." Staring at children at play in the Hebron streets under the shadow of iron bars and barbed wire and under the watch of Israeli guards with machine guns, or, just down the street from there, staring at armed soldiers, near-children themselves, deep in so-called Palestinian territory at yet another checkpoint, this one stenciled with a mural: "Free Israel," I heard June Jordan's visions, in "Requiem for the Champ," of Brownsville, Brooklyn in the 1980s: "This is what it means to fight and really win or really lose. War means you hurt somebody, or something, until there's nothing soft or sensible left."

Let's stipulate that the Palestinian Authority does its best. But, the reality is that the PA is, at best, superintendent to Israel's occupation. The people know it; many resent it. At bottom, they work for the landlord. They're in dialogue with Baby Suggs. Hamas, meanwhile, newly beset, again, now by el-Sisi's rule in Egypt, and contested within Gaza by even more militant factions, seems to be playing out the gambit June Jordan observed in the blasted out Brooklyn blocks of the 1980s. At the core of the Palestinian struggle, however, is the fundamental—not to say universal—urge that the Israeli/Jewish people—from their point of view, the oppressor—will not lead normal lives while Palestinians live in cages of restrictions made of law, concrete, and razor wire and very often watched over by men with machine guns. That Palestinian aim, in fact, isn't foreign to an American sensibility, not at all; it's incoherently twisted deep in the core of what America

is supposed to afford people ("freedom") while at the same time it's there at the crux of what the United States has inflicted on subordinate, mostly non-white, populations of people, within and beyond its borders, since before it existed and until today.

This is the basis of the disturbing power of clarity the situation in Palestine/Israel affords an American viewer. When and if, that is, one is allowed a glimpse. This is why the American media operate in the way they do and it's at the heart of why most Americans look away. In order to admit the most basic, blatant facts in the one situation—and exactly to the degree one finds a home in the American "mainstream" (itself an incoherently contested mythology), or "dream"—people would need to radically adjust primary illusions about the country in which they live: "individual achievement," "equality of opportunity," "an open society," etc. In short, clarity about Palestine destroys the mainframe illusions of American whiteness, no matter the color of the person who aspires to it. No wonder Palestinians identify to the extent that they do, and they do, with the African American freedom struggle, and with the history of American Indian quarantine and displacement, in the US.

Recently returned from Palestine, this week, I found myself re-engaged with the psychological gymnastics of contemporary life wherein media images of LeBron James' free agency and Neymar's fractured vertebra butt up against gruesome political and social intensities—massacres in Coastal Kenya, 82 shootings and 14 dead in Chicago over the Fourth of July, and, of course, renewed warfare in the West Bank and Gaza—as well as duties such as teaching my five-year-old to ride a bike in the parking lot across the street. The struggle is to keep some semblance of perspective and proportion.

So it was on Wednesday morning that I found myself reading aloud to my wife, Stacey, from front-page stories in the New York Times as she got ready for work. One story frankly depicts Germany's rout of Brazil, 7–1, from Tuesday, July 8 plain enough. Another, though, just inches apart on the page, frames conflict between forces in Gaza and Israel as a "military" contest of some plausible parity. "Israel and Hamas Trade Attacks as Tension Rises" reads the headline over a photo of a sizable explosion in an urban era. The silent suggestion in the headline being that the photo could be from either an Israeli or Hamas attack. Is that really possible? Is it plausible? Do Palestinians have a "military" at all? One report in the article ominously held that one Hamas-launched rocket made it almost seventy miles into Israeli territory. No mention was made of exactly what kind of navigation/aiming system those rockets use and what kinds of explosives are attached. The previous evening, CNN's Erin Burnett interviewed Israel's Ambassador to the US, who described the near-total precision of Israeli strategic capabilities. His description served, at once, as assurance about limited "collateral damage" and also as a bold declaration of unassailable Israeli power. The

Ambassador's interview stood alone as CNN's report on the increasing violence that evening. The scorekeeping continued. In the war.

After the jump to page 8 in the *Times*, about the "military confrontation," we're told: "Israeli military said . . . that more than 150 rockets had been fired at Israel." Meanwhile, the military reports that "Israel hit some 150 targets" in Gaza. So, at a glance, it's a tie?

No scorecard was offered for how many targets, if any, in Israel were actually hit. One guesses that, had there been hits, we'd know. Later in the story, confirming the Ambassador's comments as to Israeli accuracy, or not, we're told that

targets hit in Gaza included "five senior Hamas officials, ten smuggling tunnels, ninety concealed rocket launchers, and eighteen weapons storage and manufacturing sites." That's one hundred and twenty-three. No mention of the other twenty-seven hits in Gaza. No mention of how many firings were required to hit one hundred and twenty-three targets. Elsewhere in the article the tie score diverges, "Palestinian officials said that at least twenty-three people were killed in Gaza on Tuesday" while Israel reports "two people were wounded in rocket attacks on Monday" though it doesn't say exactly how these injuries occurred or note their severity. If you're willing to actually follow the news out of the region in American media, these are the kinds of feigned attempts at balance that portray an evenly matched "military" struggle on one hand and, on the other, assure that one side has the unassailable upper hand and, of course, the unquestioned right to secure its territory.

So it is that equality, supremacy, and security all go together. Just don't try it at home, these are trained professionals at work. Even so, exactly the same thing is happening at home, which is the whole point. Middle and upper class Americans are assured that everyone's equal in the eyes of the system; meanwhile, they insist that their privileges and comforts (supremacy) are secure and that their right to safety is ensured.

When it comes to sports we're free to feel the elasticity of the facts in pursuit of deeper truths; 7 to 1 felt like 70 to 1, we say, adding that "it wasn't as close as the score suggests." Such elasticity is delightful. No wonder ESPN is what it's become. Inches away, however, a story about an occupying power (one in violation of scores of international laws and accepted rules controlling political occupations) is told in ways that preempt and even invert a reader's freedom to extend the facts into coherent feelings in order to understand the world. That elasticity is dangerous.

As I wrote this piece, on the morning of July 10, NPR reports, now, eighty Palestinian dead. Then, I woke up to reports of one hundred dead and a report of one Israeli seriously injured at an exploded gas station. Now there's been a fatality; an Israeli man delivering food to troops at the entrance to Gaza. Soon, there'll be more. The numbers roll along, each a life, a death, each a blurring cloud of grieving and terrified people. In my morning brain, Baby Suggs playing checkers with June Jordan, "king me, honey, will you please."

Fully awake, it's clear to me that when it comes to Israel and Palestine, for Americans, it doesn't matter if the careful phrases contradict the most basic facts or if numerical equivalences depict "military" parity in one paragraph and describe unassailable supremacy in the next all the while affirming a people's (one can't but think, "all people's?") unquestioned right to security. No one's looking that closely. They can't. Close examination of Israel's relationship to the Palestinians under their control, its quest for simultaneous supremacy, security, and the semblance of democracy or equality, would reveal more than Americans are willing to admit about our own towns, schools, states, and the filmy mythology that coats—whether with security or numbness no one investigates too far— our experiences of our own and each other's lives.

Excerpt from "Verbaţim Palesţine"

VIII.

On June 14, 2014, on a plane, Robert, a retired doctor from Winston-Salem, North Carolina will ask, "where have you been?" In the conversation that follows you'll realize, again, how one's vision of home, of life, impels one's vision of everywhere else. You'll briefly describe the "wall," the "checkpoints," the division of Palestinian sovereignty into cages within cages depending on the (most often illegal) whim of an occupying power, one's right to movement, among other rights, converted into privilege conveyed by the color of one's ID card. Slipping his folded copy of *Time* magazine into the seat pocket, Robert will say, "Well, Israel has a right to secure its territory." You'll feel an ache in your hands; you realize that almost every word he said needs redefinition. Ricochets. Will imagine this doctor's territory in North Carolina, the life with which he's listening to you: swerving streets and sloping lawns. Secure. Will remember yourself, age twenty, with Riccardo Williams and Eric Lassiter, handcuffed to an iron railing and questioned on the Northside of Chicago—North Central Park Ave and Irving Park Road—for sitting on the porch in mixed racial company. Will know you can't tell him that, much less this. At the time, early days in the final quintile of the twentieth century, you'd never heard a word for "mixed racial company." You all knew you all were cuffed because you were black—you knew, at times, it made no difference that your parents weren't. One chrome thing cuffing your wrist to Ric's, another cuffing your other to Jock Barr's porch railing. Metaphors. Echoes. In row fifty-six of an aging 747, far enough back so that turbulence doesn't jolt up and down but swings back and forth like a fish tail, will attempt—and fail—to speak to Robert about Palestine from a life in a city of racial checkpoints. It was the same on the South Side, a grid of detainments, false questionings, and harassment. Since 2011, the commander in charge of that regime is in prison—Time might have mentioned it. When we were young, all we knew was that it was the law. And Time can only ricochet—has no metaphor for—that. You'll remember that Lorca said that, at times, the duende is supplied by the listener. Will remember three years ago, age forty-four, the

Principal of Clarke Central High School in Athens, GA, where your son, Milan, will go to school the next year, saying "This is a city school, we've got all kinds of kids. I like to say, 'we send them to Yale and we send them to jail.'" Will realize that it's not possible to tell this retired doctor, on his way back from a vacation hiking in Italy, much at all about Al-Khalil/Hebron given what he knows and doesn't know—will admit and won't admit about the life he listens with. His ricochets and your echoes. On the plane our bodies contain a level of energy, of power, none could survive for ten seconds; we breathe a metaphor—one too dry to breathe for too long—for air.

Getting the News

CHANA BLOCH

> *It is difficult*
> *to get the news from poems*
> *yet men die miserably every day*
>
> *for lack*
> *of what is found there.*
>
> – William Carlos Williams,
> from "Asphodel, That Greeny Flower"

How do you get the news? I read the papers, the blogs, listen to the latest, and what do I know? In my poem "Power," my neighbor asks about the intractable conflict of the Israelis and the Palestinians as if he were grousing about kids in a sandbox. His answer is as superficial as his question. The headlines won't tell him what's happening or why, so he's irritated, this man who has only the power to irritate. The former Israeli Chief of Staff, Gen. Dan Halutz, whose words end the poem, had the power to kill. I have taken his remark almost verbatim from the *New York Times*, paraphrasing it slightly to point out the irony.

According to the *Times*, Halutz was being questioned about an incident in July 2002, when an Israeli warplane dropped a one-ton bomb on a Gaza apartment building in a densely populated residential neighborhood, killing a senior Hamas commander, Salah Shehadeh, his family, and a dozen others. Halutz was then Commander in Chief of the Israeli Air Force. For his bomber pilots he had only praise: "Guys . . . you can sleep well at night. I also sleep well, by the way. You aren't the ones who choose the targets, and you were not the ones who chose the target in this particular case. . . . Your execution was perfect. Superb." Then he offered his deadpan response about dropping a bomb:

> "And what did you feel," the reporters ask,
> "when you dropped a bomb from an F-16?"
> *I felt a slight lift of the wing*, he says.

After a second it passed.

To "feel" is to experience a sensation or an emotion; Halutz's answer turns on the two senses of this word. He chooses to mention only a physical sensation. Is he the kind of man who doesn't have emotions, doesn't *feel* his feelings? A living automaton, who can dissociate feeling from conscience? I am trying to imagine what it means to have power. The subject interests me because I cannot understand it: why would anyone want to have power over someone else?

To have insight into what is happening, we need the kind of "news" that is found in poetry. "Men die miserably every day / for lack / of what is found there," Williams wrote, connecting poetry with the kind of news that stays true and illuminating. Those are the qualities I look for and find in the work of Dahlia Ravikovitch (1936–2005), one of the leading Israeli poets of her generation.

Power and powerlessness is her defining subject: the devastating consequences of unequal power relations for the individual and for society. Her early work reflects the asymmetries of power in poems about fathers and daughters, men and women, kings and their subjects. The later work focuses more intently on the precarious position of women and, with increasing directness, the plight of Palestinians under the Occupation. In a 2004 television interview Ravikovitch said of her political poems: "Because I hold an Israeli passport, I have a share in all the wrongs that are done to the Palestinians. . . . I want to be able to say that I did all I could to prevent the bloodshed." She is not concerned with simply replaying the literal facts. With great imaginative skill, she enters into them so that the reader can *feel* what they mean—perhaps the deepest form of knowing.

In "The Fruit of the Land," Ravikovitch ventriloquizes the voices of a gang, a political force, an army. She lets us hear them laughing and boasting about their stockpile of military hardware, relishing its power to destroy. *Zimra* in the title means "singing" in modern Hebrew, but in biblical Hebrew it can mean "produce, bounty" and "power, might." The biblical meanings come together in Ravikovitch's shockingly ironic metaphor of Israel's military might as its bumper crop:

> crates of napalm and crates of explosives,
> unlimited quantities, cornucopias,
> a feast for the soul, like some finely seasoned delicacy. . . .

Gathering force through an accumulation of detail, the poem hurtles toward its apocalyptic climax.

The ending alludes to a poem written in 1944 by the partisan Hannah Szenes, praising the match that ignites the hearts of others even as it is consumed:

> Blessed be the match consumed
>   in kindling flame.

Blessed be the flame that burns
    in the secret fastness of the heart.
Blessed be the heart with strength to stop
    its beating for honor's sake.
Blessed be the match consumed
    in kindling flame.

Szenes was parachuted into Europe by the British Army during World War II to aid in the attempted rescue of Hungarian Jews, and was apprehended, imprisoned, tortured, and executed by a German firing squad the year she wrote that poem. Ravikovitch inverts the "Blessed be" of noble self-sacrifice into a raucous celebration of carnage, playing on both the cliché of the Middle East as a keg of gunpowder and Ariel Sharon's terrifying quip, "The Arabs have the oil, but we have the match."

Through her skillful orchestration, Ravikovitch certainly knows how to dramatize the horrors of brutality, though she is best known for the empathy with which she regards the suffering of the powerless. "A Mother Walks Around" enumerates a newborn's first moments, a mother's care and concern. At first it isn't clear why the poem is built on a series of negations—"he won't, they won't, she won't"—though an informed reader would probably guess that the unborn child is Palestinian. It is surprising, then, to hear her describe the fetus in unmistakably Jewish terms:

The child is a perfect *tsadik* already,
unmade ere he was ever made.

A *tsadik* is a saintly Jew; "*unmade ere he was ever made*" alludes to the medieval hymn *Adon Olam* ("Master of the Universe"), one of the most familiar in the Jewish liturgy, where God is said to have reigned "before any creature came to be made." Ravikovitch keeps the identity of the child unresolved at this point in order to allow the final line its full sardonic force.

That detached impersonal statement, spoken in the voice of a military reporter—"under circumstances relating to state security"—is completely at variance with the rest of the poem. In our translation, Chana Kronfeld and I kept the Hebrew *tsadik* and the archaic phrasing of the hymn in the lines quoted above in order to emphasize how surprising they are in context. And in the final line we chose to add quotation marks which do not appear in the Hebrew to convey the abrupt shift in tone, something that would have been clear to an Israeli reader.

"A Mother" may reflect Ravikovitch's own experience of motherhood, but "The Story of the Arab Who Died in the Fire" draws only on her empathic imagination. She spoke about the impetus behind "The Story of the Arab" in an

1996 interview with the news daily *Yediot Acharonot*: "As to the [poem about the Palestinian] day-worker [from the Occupied Territories], when Jews nailed shut the door of the warehouse where he was sleeping, so he couldn't get out when it was set on fire—I wrote that poem because I understand the fear he felt before he was saved by death." Her restraint of tone keeps pathos in check through elevated diction ("such a thing hath not its likeness") and biblical allusion ("as if he were bound and laid on the altar"), along with the use of scientific language ("the pain transmitted in electrical pulses / along neural pathways to pain receptors in the brain"). Still, "The Story of the Arab" is excruciating on the page and nearly unendurable when read aloud.

The news we find in Ravikovitch's poetry is as harrowing as it is essential; it is the kind of news we need to keep from dying miserably and killing ignorantly. Its very painfulness has a healing force. Ravikovitch might have said that her beloved country, Israel, hurt her into poetry, to paraphrase Auden's elegy on Yeats. Through her art, she hurts her readers into empathy—the first condition required of the powerful if they wish to make peace with the powerless.

Power

"Why can't they just get along?" he protests
when he hears the numbers on the morning news.
Then he's got the answer:
"They're people, that's why."

Thus saith my neighbor
who lets his Doberman out to bark at midnight
and grumbles "Yeah, yeah"
when I call to complain.

Meanwhile, in the precincts of power,
the new Chief of Staff
who learned his trade as a fighter pilot
is fending off questions from his swivel chair.

"And what did you feel," the reporters ask,
"when you dropped a bomb from an F-16?"
I felt a slight lift of the wing, he says.
After a second it passed.

The Fruit of the Land *a farewell song to the good old days*

by *Dahlia Ravikovitch*

(Translated from Hebrew by Chana Bloch)

You asked if we've got enough cannons
They laughed and said: More than enough
and we've got new improved anti-tank missiles
and bunker busters to penetrate
double-slab reinforced concrete
and we've got crates of napalm and crates of explosives,
unlimited quantities, cornucopias,
a feast for the soul, like some finely seasoned delicacy
and above all, that secret weapon,
the one we can't talk about.
Calm down, man,
the intel officer and the C.O.
and the border police chief
who's also a colonel in that hush-hush commando unit
are all primed for the order: Go!
and everything's shined-up like the skin of a snake
and we've got chocolate wafers on every base
and grape juice and Tempo soda
and that's why we won't give in to terror
we will not fold in the face of violence
we'll never fold, no matter what
'cause our billy clubs are nice and hard.
God, who has chosen us from all the nations,
comforteth with apples
the fighting arm of the IDF
and the iron boxes and the crates of fresh explosives
and we've got cluster bombs too,
though of course that's off the record.
Serve us bourekas and cake, O woman of the house,

for we were slaves in the land of Egypt
but never again,
and blot out the remembrance of Amalek
if you can track him down, and if you seek him in vain,
Blessed be the tiny match
that a soldier in some crack unit will suddenly strike
and set off the whole bloody mess.

A Mother Walks Around

by *Dahlia Ravikovitch*
(Translated from Hebrew by Chana Bloch)

A mother walks around with a child dead in her belly.
This child hasn't been born yet.
When his time comes the dead child will be born
head first, then trunk and buttocks
and he won't wave his arms about or cry his first cry
and they won't slap his bottom
won't put drops in his eyes
won't swaddle him
after washing the body.
He will not resemble a living child.
His mother will not be calm and proud after giving birth
and she won't be troubled about his future,
won't worry how in the world to support him
and does she have enough milk
enough clothing
and how will she fit a cradle into the room.
The child is a perfect *tsadik* already,
unmade ere he was ever made.
And he'll have his own little grave at the edge of the cemetery
and a little memorial day
and there won't be much to remember him by.
These are the chronicles of the child
who was killed in his mother's belly
in the month of January, in the year 1988,
"under circumstances relating to state security."

The Story of the Arab Who Died in the Fire

by *Dahlia Ravikovitch*
(Translated from Hebrew by Chana Bloch)

When the fire seized his body, it didn't happen by slow degrees.
No burst of heat to begin with,
no stifling billow of smoke
no prospect of a room next door where one could escape.
The fire took him all at once,
such a thing hath not its likeness,
it peeled away his clothing
seized upon his flesh,
the first casualties were the nerves in the skin
then the hair fell prey to the fire,
God, they're burning us, he screamed,
that's all he could manage in self-defense.
The flesh was blazing along with the planks of the shed
which sustained the fire in the primary phase.
By that point his mental faculties were gone,
the firebrand of the flesh
paralyzed any sense of a future,
the memories of his family
the links to his childhood.
He was shrieking, no longer constrained by reason,
by now all the bonds of family were broken,
he did not seek vengeance, redemption, the dawn of a new day.
All he wanted was to stop burning
but his own body kept feeding the blaze
as if he were bound and laid on the altar
though he wasn't thinking about that, either.
He went on burning by the sheer force of his body,
flesh and fat and sinews.
And he kept on burning.

From his throat issued inhuman voices
since many human functions had already ceased
except for the pain transmitted in electrical pulses
along neural pathways to pain receptors in the brain.
All of this lasted no more than a single day.
And it's a good thing he breathed his last when he did
because he deserved to rest.

RAMOLA D

In December of 2008 and through January 2009, when Israeli bombs dropped on Gaza, my daughter was four, as old as some of the children being slaughtered. Each time I watched the footage, I felt the insane terror at the thought of one's own child being exposed to such open brutality in one's own home—right where one lived. These children and families who were killed were denied all sanctuary.

Barack Obama had won the election but was not yet inaugurated. He refused to make any statement about the carnage. My first disbelieving disappointment in this new presidency. Change? I wasn't seeing it.

Several years earlier, despite the anti-war marches and rallies I too had joined, when the US dropped bombs on Afghanistan, and later Iraq, and the news reports of the carnage came through, with sounds and sights of shells, tanks, bombs on television, and the steady stream of numbers killed, maimed, of Iraqi civilians and US soldiers, I started to write a series of stories about war, babies, soldiers, children.

I wrote this story on Gaza, after reading about the deaths of several members of one family killed together. I considered this question: what is it these soldiers are not seeing that permits them to engage in such insanity of aggression? During the unforgettable summer of 2014, the same thing happened again. The same attack on civilians, the same massacre of whole families.

From what has happened in Gaza, and what is happening now in the US, it is clear that we are at a tipping-point, facing the danger of coldly imperialistic, militarized, corporatized, technocratized governments. Speaking out on Palestine is speaking out for us all.

Excerpt from "Constant Comfort"

TENDER SPACES

Daniyah was sucking a sweet red cherry lollipop when the ceiling caved in on her, the weight of several stories of concrete, brick, mortar, and steel whistling down to avalanche on her skull, so her hand involuntarily released the lollipop stick and her lungs, choking with fine grey dust, released the world. A breath had passed, maybe two, in which, believing she was still alive, she had raised her lollipop hand to the back of her skull where the wrenched concrete slab which had once held up a bedroom wall had impacted, and incomprehensible wads of tissue and blood leaked onto her fingers, and dripped into the tender spaces between her fingers. She withdrew her hand, marveling at the stickiness of life, the ease with which parts of the body could crack blindly open, spill their most secret contents, even the youthful crimson glaze streaming out of her five-year-old self thick with its own burden of wants and unwants, long threads of memories, viscous friendships, slow pools of regret.

The Bomb had arrived like a freight train, a tornado, from deep inside a fighter jet. She had heard it ripping through the cauldron of space just above their building in Gaza, hissing its intent as it tore open the walls. For comfort, she had been sitting on her sister Aaliyah's bed.

Beyond the sound, beyond the ungainly explosion of brick and concrete in large, unmanageable confetti all around her, streamers of ash rose like cirrus and floated. Now she noticed she was still sitting on the bed although the room had been demolished. Debris had torqued her feet inextricably into a devil's arabesque. Ash still rose. It feathered the shattered brick, stopped up childish nostrils, climbed the torn-open curtains, sought out the glottis of every child and settled inside the moist alveoli of little lungs.

COME TO THE BALL

Her sister Aaliyah had been reading a book, lying on her back in bed, flipping through pages of illustrations: fairies rising out of flowers, their legs stemmed and petaled, thighs subsumed in bright corollas. Laboriously, words being sounded: *She whispered to him, it was permitted, he could come to the ball.* Aaliyah held inside her mouth like an unbreachable crevasse a learning disability which had once held her back in school. Words she could not pronounce pirouetted inside her. Words whose meaning eluded her flickered like constellations visible on rare occasion through blowing cloud. Some phrases and juxtapositions flummoxed her. Often she slipped into verbal transpositions and transgressions lucid only to those, like herself, who could not read in straight lines, word upon word. Because of these matters, she had only recently learned how to read in ways that could infallibly disperse inside her the certain seeds of story. This, astonishingly, had excited her to the point of undiminished hunger. Now all she wanted to do, in between eating, sleeping and going to school, was read.

Seven-year-old Aaliyah was reading when the Bomb tore through the upper stories of the building and exploded in a fireball that set fifty-six rooms above them ablaze, collapsed hundreds of walls, shattered windows, and tossed numerous body parts and dreams along with lullabies for infants, fabric from curtains and clothing, house pets, once-enclosed bricks, and just-made evening dinners into the pulverized air. The book was dragged from her hands, as were her hands from herself. Parts of her limbs scorched and melted, parts of her limbs disintegrated. Her eyes, still scanning a line of text, followed the exit of her unclad feet through the newly exploded window, into the night-lit air, into the shuddering vibration. Black smoke and white ash plumed abruptly around her, obscuring vision. Coughing, she leaned forward to tilt a cup of bedside water to her mouth, her reachings with a phantom hand suddenly visible even to herself. Bone stood out white inside a shell of macerated flesh scorched to coal on the skin. Burning dreams from floors above fell with building debris on her desecrated limbs. In the whitening that ensued, of skin, lungs, and breath, a part of her still floated on butterfly wings, wrapped in diaphanous silks and glittering with rare crystalline stones, toward a fairy ball in an enchanted forest. Other parts of her reached for parts forever gone with an unregistering insistence.

CONSTANT COMFORT

A long time ago, their thirty-seven-year-old father, asked by a visiting Dutch journalist, what his children meant to him—he had five of them then, and the sixth on the way—said, tentatively (he was a shy man, unwilling to draw attention to himself) in his usual, retreating way: they were a constant comfort to him and his wife. They were the creation of family succeeding the death of his own parents. Children, he explained, were the meaning of home.

WOMB-LIKE

In the moment the Bomb hit, their mother, holding the seven-month-old baby, in the room furthest from the one in which the children played, had bent down to rummage beneath the bed for a new blanket for the baby's crib. Joists crashing around her miraculously shaved a womb-like space surrounding her bent-over body. In this she froze, bent-over. The screech of matter ignited abruptly to oblivion around her cascaded, rippled, echoed. Walls crashed and fell, smoke and ash rose. The baby choked, she coughed, for a moment she held a still-whole hand to a still-whole mouth, deathly afraid for her children's lives.

AN INSTANT'S RAVAGING

The second-youngest, three-year-old Isra, was on the carpet playing with her doll, a gangly mini-skirted Barbie with unruly golden locks, narrow lips, blue eyes, and red Mary-Jane stilettos, combing the knotted hair with a doll-brush, bending the legs sideways and forwards, backwards and back, readying her for school, she said, smoothing down the upturned sequined collar, when, in an instant's ravaging, concrete confetti from the explosion needled through her spine and out her abdomen, crushing vertebrae, slushing together spinal fluid, blood, muscle, intestine, and intestinal contents in one gory mass that extruded beneath the doll's golden hair and lay, for a brief moment, steaming before her eyes as the greater mass of the ceiling pounded all over her.

The oldest, Hadiya, was sitting by the window, staring into the deepening dusk, yellow window lights coming on all around them, dim swathe of stars above, dreaming of lean, handsome Fuad, the brother of her friend Mariam, with whom she had recently exchanged a series of letters, tentative and breathless, when she noticed the ominous congealing of sound around them, saw the fighter jet plummet and loosen its dark, silvery load of terror directly above, heard the raw Doppler crunch of its coming and going, and half-rose, shaken from her window seat, when the end of the world sliced her sideways and with glass and metal she was blown to the center of the room, bleeding profusely from head and neck, legs paralyzed in one instant, and covered the next in the flaming, smoking debris that descended from above and kept on descending.

Her seventeen-year-old body slammed into the second-oldest, Malaika, the sleeping one, who had been sick that day and not ventured to school, curled in a ball on her bed, a single cotton sheet over her fourteen-year-old limbs, which boiled instantly to flame and sealed her skin at roiling temperatures into its fibrous threads, delving deep through layers of epidermis, dermis, muscle, to reach the hidden bone and surge against it. Flame, ash, bone, and shards of metal embedded. The weight of the rooms and objects above thrust onto shoulders, ribs, ankle bones. When she opened her eyes, blinking past the ash coating her lashes, weighting her lids, Malaika believed she had transformed in her dreams into a caterpillar's tight cocoon, so fully was she encased in ashen, fallen plaster, and brick.

ONE MOMENT TO THE NEXT

Except for Hadiya, who had, for an instant, observed the blinding arc of terror dislodged from the roaring fighter jet, none of the girls had had an inkling of the enormity of what was about to happen to them. None comprehended what had occurred after it happened either. The desire to move, from one moment to the next, within one's own footprints, is rife in all of us. The girls blinked their eyes, touched their heads with shattered fingertips. Aaliyah wished to turn the page. Isra wished to clean the doll's suddenly bloodied hair. Hadiya longed for Fuad, to reach down and lift her up to her feet. Daniyah wanted the sweet lick of cherry once more on her tongue. Malaika wanted merely to go back to sleep.

SUPERNATURAL LIFT
Instead, they rose, five slaughtered sisters, holding their parts together, or striving to, Daniyah pushing back the mass of extruded brain and blood as best she could, Isra tucking in stringy layers of intestine, Aaliya grateful for the supernatural lift which obviated the need for limbs, the burned Malaika still able to smooth scraps of burnt skin away from mouth and eyes, Hadiya, floated above the bed with its cover of smoke cloud, still paralyzed but able to see, rotating her head, where they were heading. Stars drifted loosely above. Smoke occluded parts of the nighttime sky. Lights in buildings below flickered, went out. Other bombs were flaring fiery mushroom clouds into the sky. Other balls of smoke rose, other streamers dissipated into the weedy blue of dusk the ashen white of burning phosphorus. Low, violet hills duned to a dim horizon from where artillery shells arced destruction. Missiles flew about them, bodied and silvered, making the air sing. Everywhere, cries could be heard, of people attacked or bereaved, of fear or terror, of unstoppable grief, first plainly, then muffled, as great heights intervened between their bodies and the earth. Date palms and olive trees, for a moment so close, diminished in size steadily until miniscule rivets of green waving timidly from below were all that was left.

Now clouds approached, and more of them, fluffed-up columns and roofs and porticos of silk-shower cloud, endless galloping battalions of styrofoam cloud, stained the colors of battle—blood red, earth brown, gunmetal grey. Cool mist dampened burned skin as swiftly the ascending children pierced layers of soaring cloud, into a sudden vertical sea of calm. Night skies stretched out here, starry and clear. Now they could hear the thrum of the speeding jet, the singular roar of powerful engines already past the sound barrier and booming their shifted velocity into the violet atmosphere. Their bodies lifted naturally toward the sound and dusk-lit metal sight of it, sleek, tearing beauty of the long-nosed jet, the very one which had discharged its artillery over their building, and so easily secured their death.

PAPER HOUSES
From the sheer glass of his bubble canopy in the speeding F-16, the thirty-eight-year-old IDF pilot, Raphael Even-Zahav gazed steadily into the future: clear navy skies to left and right, starry foam of the Milky Way above, distant surround of

coastline, dune, city lights, white memories of clouds below. These long-gone clouds had come already between his past and his future, or so he believed. He was flying at thirty-six thousand feet and climbing. Behind him sat his buddy, thirty-nine-year-old Doran Ben-Ami, with whom he had grown up on the same street in Tel Aviv and with whom he had trained once at flight school. A long time ago, they had been boys together, flying paper houses on strings. Now they were IDF men in fighter planes, several years of frenzied adulthood behind them. Many things having happened in those years.

Raphael had married, had one child, divorced. A bitter divorce, with his wife refusing joint custody, citing abuse. In the throes of ego and passion, he had hit her once or twice. Raised his voice to her, that was only as much as he had grown up with, from his father. Never hit the child. Didn't drink that much. Combat pilots had more sense than that. But he'd come home late a couple times, drunk. After the baby, things had wrenched apart between them. She said she had no time to herself, all day at home with the baby. He had laughed. After the baby, he thought, she'd had no time for *him*. She had gone off to America, to live with her mother in New York. From seeing his baby girl everyday, he saw her once in two or three years. His wife remarried, had other kids. He had never wanted to marry again. He lived in a one-bedroom apartment and changed his girlfriends when they mentioned any possibility of future. Raphael, whose name meant Angel, did not practice being angelic.

Doran was not that much different, although he had not married young, like Raphael. He married in his early thirties and his first child, Aviva whose name meant Springtime, had been mown down at age six by a bunch of drunken men in an oversized SUV on New Year's Eve, two streets from their home, near a neighbor's house. He had a second child, she was two then. But the marriage cracked and splintered. Too much grief can paralyze, he learned. His wife became depressed. He stayed out with Raphael in bars. There were nights the two-year-old was not fed, nights he came home to nonstop crying and frantic searching in the refrigerator for something to give the child. It was a relief when his wife's sister took the child and his wife in to live with her in Haifa.

CHILDREN, SITTING

Raphael did not witness the steady rising because his eyes were on the upper skies. But he was the first to notice the motley crowd of figures on the nose of the fighter jet, as the girls sailed onto the smooth curved fuselage and wedged themselves in upon its metal curve. He rubbed his eyes, he had been awake until the wee hours the night before, prey to his latest curse, insomnia. The round, childish figures did not dissolve or disappear. A mirage of paper lanterns, he thought at first. Light reflected into shapes of conch shells. Desert pottery. Dolls. From this he progressed. Not mirages of dolls but dolls themselves? The figures had childish limbs. Children, he saw finally, his mouth inside the oxygen mask agape. Small children. Teenagers. And the masses attached to parts of their heads, stomachs, chests, were body parts, extruded. That was blood, in jagged streams. That was skin, burnt and mixed-in with flesh. That was bone he saw, and brain, and the insides of a person's guts. That was stiffening and rigor mortis, the waxen look of death.

That was a small group of children, sitting where no one could sit, forty thousand feet above the earth's crust, in icy cold, thrust forward at tremendous speed, on the nose of his fighter jet. All dead.

His hands slipped on the throttle then, disbelief pocking holes in him. His entire body, clad in his heavy G-suit, tingled. But he was a combat pilot, trained to take evasive action. Doran, he called. Doran!

Doran, who had been momentarily asleep and dreaming of space travel, white-hot neutron stars, cold burn of space, jerked his head up and saw Aaliyah, reading a book, streaks of red pouring down her forehead. Behind her, stars glittered. Aviva, he whispered. Are you here?

PARALLEL/IDENTITY

I Have Seen the One Who Sees Me

TIPHANIE YANIQUE

The great story goes that they met and fell in love. It was ill-fated, ill-advised—a desperate passion. In this story we will call him Andre. The woman, we will call Ms. Harrigan. For those were their names in real life. They did what people in love do. They made love. In doing so they begat Eva. But Andre and Ms. Harrigan did not marry. Eva was born a bastard, despite being firstborn. She was treasured by her father, so I am told, despite her parents lack of official union.

But then Andre begat again. Sons. Many sons. This time legitimate. And so Eva and her mother were cast out to the island of St. Thomas . . . away from the legitimate children who settled with Andre and his wife on the island of St. Croix. Andre became wealthy. Ms. Harrigan did not.

In this narrative the Arabs are the St. Thomians, and the Jews are the Crucians, and maybe the St. Johnians go on to become the Christians . . . though of course they are all the same people at the root. If you know the Virgin Islands, you will see that this metaphor is no stretch at all.

So Eva grew up with her mother and her mother's people. Eva became a wild woman. Perhaps that was the prophecy. Perhaps it was what any firstborn would do when left out of the legacy. Eva knew her father, and her father's children knew her. And yet, she appears not in one of Andre's family pictures. She is there in desert, it seems. One of the legitimates tells the tale of Eva visiting them . . . as Ishmael did. Eva sang at the piano for their entertainment. Supper, perhaps, followed and Eva was allowed to join them at the table before leaving again for the rocky island.

There is a story that goes like that. It is my story.

Even in history there is always a mystery. It is not hard to imagine that Andre is Abraham. And Ms. Harrigan is Hagar. The magic of the names makes it easy. In which case, Eva is, of course, Ishmael.

Eva is my mother.

So then it is clear where I land in the narrative. I am Nebajoth and Kedar and Abdeel. I am Mibsam and Mishma and Doomah. I am Massa and Tayman and

Yathur. I am Nafees and Kedemah and Mahalath. Do you remember these names? I am the cast out. I am the Arabs to the east.

Oh, it is true that I grew up Catholic in the Caribbean. And yet. And yet . . .

In this terrible story I am the Muslim. I am the people of Palestine. Me and all my progeny. The details are different. The details are always different. The narrative may not be true, but nor does it lie. And who, if they placed themselves in the story, as we all must to make sense of it, wouldn't see clearly what is? Father Abraham, grandfather Andre, lived to a great old age. And I was there. As were all the brothers. There to bury and honor him.

Oh, but did Andre help pay for Eva's college education? He gave parting gifts, yes. But Eva did not inherit from Andre's house. So the covenant insisted. And so it was. In exchange, the children of Ms. Harrigan were promised a line of princes. Is that me again? In a surprising twist, I myself teach college now. Professor and prince share an initial letter. Let me be satisfied with that, then. We will multiply and we will be fruitful.

But how does the story end? To whom and to where do we belong? We wonder and wander. We have the patience and endurance of Job. He, too, was of the disinherited, a man of the east. One of us, remember.

The Story of Joshua

ALICIA OSTRIKER

And Joshua said, Hereby ye shall know that
the living God is among you, and that he will
without fail drive out from before you the
Canaanites, and the Hittites, and the Hivites,
and the Perizzites, and the Girgashites, and
the Amorites, and the Jebusites.
    —Joshua 3.9

The New Englanders are a people of God settled in those which were once
the devil's territories.
    —Cotton Mather, The Wonders of the Invisible World, 1692

We reach the promised land
Forty years later
The original ones who were slaves
Have died
The young are seasoned soldiers
There is wealth enough for everyone and God
Here at our side, the people
Are mad with excitement.
Here is what to do, to take
This land away from the inhabitants:
Burn their villages and cities
Kill their men
Kill their women
Consume the people utterly.
God says: is that clear?
I give you the land, but
You must murder for it.
You will be a nation

Like other nations,
Your hands are going to be stained like theirs
Your innocence annihilated.
Keep listening, Joshua.
Only to you among the nations
Do I also give knowledge
The secret
knowledge that you are doing evil
Only to you the commandment:
Love ye therefore the stranger, for you were
Strangers in the land of Egypt, a pillar
Of fire to light your passage
Through the blank desert of history forever.
This is the agreement.
Is it entirely
Clear, Joshua,
Said the Lord.
I said it was. He then commanded me
To destroy Jericho.

"The Story of Joshua" appears in my book *The Nakedness of the Fathers, Biblical Visions and Revisions* (New Brunswick, NJ: Rutgers University Press, 1997). It is in the voice of Joshua as he is about to conquer "the promised land" on God's command. The land is called Canaan in the Bible; we call it Palestine now. Joshua's voice in the poem is matter-of-fact about what has to be done "to take/the land away from its inhabitants." Our modern word for it is genocide. I hope it is clear from the twin epigraphs that the motive of conquest in God's name was also the motive of the American Puritans. Every nation is founded on blood, perhaps. Certainly as Americans we cannot claim moral superiority, as we too inherit land once inhabited by others. But for me the story of Joshua is a story of what Blake might call "double vision." For the God of the Bible is self-contradictory. He commands genocide. He also commands, "love the stranger, for you know the heart of the stranger, for you were strangers in Egypt." I wish my footnote to be read as attentively as I wish the poem to be. The absolute tension between these opposite divine commands has produced (I believe) a deep, probably mostly unconscious split within the Jewish soul. We are compassionate. We are also ruthless.

Israelis today get both messages. According to David Remnick in the *New Yorker* ("Letter From Jerusalem," November 17), one of the Israeli boys who beat and burned alive a Palestinian boy in retaliation for the murder of three Israeli boys by Gazans, makes this clear:

> "The Israelis then drove to a nearby park. Ben-David confessed that they began to feel remorse. "I was in shock," he told the interrogators. "We're Jews, we have a heart. Afterward we talked about it and . . . each one poured his heart out and we regretted doing it. I told them . . . 'This is not for us. We erred, we're compassionate Jews, we're human beings.' Then we got depressed."

Depression does not undo murder, and telling ourselves that we are compassionate doesn't make us so. As an American Jew for whom Israel/Palestine is like a weird doppelganger beating and beating alongside my own heart, my hope (I can't use the word "faith") is that the sooner we all recognize our own doubleness, the sooner we all will be able, as Deuteronomy commands, to "choose life."

East Jerusalem

DAVID GORIN

lord it is not your silence that bulldozes but promiscuous thunder
    not for one only, the pillar of cold butter   the paper crown and infinite tokens

land that I will show you   sayeth the billboard to the highway
    each prophet turned to the other and said   what was the question?

the house I built with my teeth is   become your sandcastle   blessed
    is he who dashes his head on the wall   a newborn child

my heart is no boombox   though I shoulder it from beach to beach
    though its lo-fi speaker bleats   a phoned-in vulgate of your sickest jams

volume lower than the lowest of the earth   lord of waves therefore
    end this lip-to-lip service   these remixed messages

in the school yard we put out with a fire-extinguisher that fire
who was a boy, who said your name before he started screaming

hear us O lord and shut your fucking mouth   you who have given
    your word to every mother like a business card

like sunlight   a child in every town   we are not asking for the moon

A NOTE ON WRITING EAST JERUSALEM

Many psalms plead with God not to be silent. The poem I have written is a psalm, but it imagines God's silence is not a problem. In fact, it thinks God's silence would be a solution to a problem. The problem with God is that he talks too much.

    This poem imagines that God is one possible (and historical) name for that teacher of mortal arithmetic who helps us tell murder from "collateral damage," the lives worth caring for from those which can not matter. God, in this sense, is one name for whatever underwrites what the political philosopher Carl Schmitt has called the "friend/enemy distinction." He tells you how to sort Gentile from Jew, German from Jew, Palestinian from Jew, Sunni from Shiite, Hindu from Muslim, believer from heathen, American from un-American, civilian from combatant, terrorist from revolutionary, black from white, brother from other. Even when the identities in play have nothing to do with theology, the actors are in the presence of this God. He is the God of social distinctions, the zero-sum economy of love. And he makes exclusive promises to everyone.

On a fundamental level, this psalm is a cry against the occupation of Palestine by the State of Israel. The genre of the Hebrew psalm seemed to me uniquely appropriate for this cry, or appropriately inappropriate. Like so many psalms, it laments the condition of a people who dwell in exile from that literal and conceptual refuge called a "home." As a Jew—and as someone who has spent his life feeling personally implicated in the activities of Israel, concerned for the safety of its people and complicit in the violence done in the name of that safety—I wanted to use a historically Judaic genre to speak against the suffering of those for whom Israel remains a Babylon. Its last words are those Yasser Arafat used in the year of my birth to insist that East Jerusalem should belong to the Palestinian state to come—though in the poem they speak for other things as well.

I wrote this poem in 2008, two years after retuning to America from a year on a fellowship in Jerusalem. My apartment in Jerusalem was about 1,000 feet west of the Green Line, the line of the "1967 borders," dividing East Jerusalem from West. While I was living there, a young religious Jewish man set fire to himself at a nearby Hebrew language school to protest Israel's (so-called) disengagement from the Gaza Strip—a disengagement I very much supported. He was a Jew like me, yet on the question of Gaza I was his other. I included his story in the poem without reference to his Jewish identity because I wanted his suffering to speak for more than merely those identified with him. But I also wanted to preserve in the poem, for myself if no one else, that uncomfortable act of erasure. I liked this poem for its secret: that a Jewish boy occasioned those lines which the poem might encourage you (did it?) to read as speaking for a Palestinian.

The poem was scheduled to appear in the January 2015 issue of the *Boston Review*, but was published early by the magazine shortly after Israel began "mowing the lawn" again in the summer of 2014. Six days before or after the poem appeared, I saw reports of four Palestinian boys—Mohammad, Ismail, Zakariya, and Ahed Bakr, ages seven to twelve—who were killed on a beach in Gaza by an Israeli missile strike. Their deaths have become part of what this poem means by "beach" and "that fire / who was a boy." Such deaths erode this poem's capacity for universalism and pressure it to choose a side, a highly particularized "we." And obviously, these deaths are not the first to do so.

That "we" must be defined to some extent if "we" are to stand against what we feel is injustice. But if that "we" becomes strongly defined enough, this psalm would become, against its will, like the one that goes this way: *By the rivers of Babylon we sat down and wept when we remembered Jerusalem. [. . .] O daughter of Whomever, doomed to be destroyed, / blessed is he who repays you / with what you have done to us! / Blessed is he who takes your little ones / and dashes them against the rock!"* It would become, in other words, the word of God.

PHILIP TERMAN

What often moves me to write is Jewish-related: from childhood to ancestry to Jewish figures in poems that celebrate and critique the tradition—but I'd never written a poem about Israel. For my parents, Judaism was at the center of their lives. They taught me that Judaism was not just a "religion," but a way of life, which included celebrating the miracle of existence as well as being a "mensch"—a responsible person who cares about others. Central to all Jews of that era was the Holocaust. As a child, learning about the concentration camps was intricately related to the commitment to the state of Israel as a Jewish homeland.

Like many others, as I grew older, I learned that the situation was more complicated, and that, in order for Palestine to become the Jewish homeland, many others had to be displaced. In my first trip to Israel, I was moved by the passion of the Jews praying at the Wailing Wall, but I also took notice of the Arabs who were struggling in the market place. The tour guide spoke of the land as "ours," and the "Arabs" as the enemy. Ironically, the "prophetic" part of my Jewish upbringing forced me to understand the unfairness of that separation. There were instances that brought the political unfairness to the forefront, including meeting my Jordanian student Emil, who told me about how his father lost his house in Jerusalem.

I decided to return to the journal entries I made during my two journeys to Israel, which reflected my early "innocence" and my growing awareness of the issue's complexities. In my collection of poems, *The Torah Garden*, "Our Jerusalem" appears directly after a poem about a visit I made to Auschwitz. I wanted to honor both my mother's and Emil's passion and claims. Perhaps if we understood the poetry of each other's passions more fully, we would go deeper into healing the separations, where peace might reside.

Our Jerusalem

1: *Next Year in Jerusalem*

Where was that place?

Was it on the tree-lined street
we drove down Sunday mornings
to look at mansions?

Was it on the basement shelf,
too high for me to reach
to see what was stored there?

Or was it like that horse
that cantered across the white fields
when no one was watching?

Or like the word *death*
I thought about in bed
after my mother whispered the story

and my body shook
and she explained it's a place
we all go?

Would it be next year?

Or perhaps it was like
that diagram she drew
when I asked how I was born:

the man's part,
then the woman's:

This goes into this.
When would I understand?
Next year?
In Jerusalem?

On Passover
she gave me a piece
of rock candy to suck on

as we sat through the seder—
the sugared cherry sweet
on my tongue as we sounded the words:

Next year in Jerusalem, mine,
she said, as God commanded,
forever.

2. *Planting Trees*

In Hebrew school,
on the teacher's desk,
the blue and white *tzedakah* box,
its map of the holy land beside the words:
Your direct link to the land of Israel."
Between the aleph and the bet
we're told to slip our loose change
into the slot.
We're planting trees.
How many will I own?
A few for my birth,
a few for my manhood,
a few for my marriage,
a few for my death.
A small forest
in a country they say is mine.

5. *For Emil*

Mediterranean among the Midwestern
fair-skinned, you come into my office
from the snow that swirls in pockets,

sit down and say you are sad
because the oranges are not so good,
then you notice the picture of my mother
posing in front of the gold dome of the Al-Aqsa Mosque.
Al-Quds, you say. *Where my father was born.*

6. *"Rachel, She Came for the Tanks"*

[Rachel Corrie was a twenty-three-year-old peace activist who was killed on March 16, 2003 when an American-made bulldozer crushed her as she protested the destruction by the Israeli government of an Arab house in the Gaza Strip. Below are fragments from the last emails she sent back home.]

2/7/03:

They shot an 8-year-old boy and the children murmur his name.

I have a home. I'm allowed to see the ocean.

Today I walked on top of rubble where homes once stood.

We are all kids curious about other kids.
Palestinian kids shot from tanks by Israeli kids.

2/27/03:

The bulldozers come and take out people's vegetable farms and gardens.
What is left for people?
Tell me if you can think of anything.
This is not what I asked for
when I came into the world.

This is not what I meant
when I looked at Capital Lake and said:

"This is the wide world, and I'm coming into it."

From the last email (undated):

Dear Papa—

Let me know if you have any ideas

about what I should do for the rest of my life.
To make things easier here I utterly retreat
into fantasies that I'm in a Hollywood movie or a sitcom
staring Michael J. Fox.

So feel free to make something up,
and I'll play along.

7. At the Wailing Wall

That last night, after everyone
in the hotel fell asleep, you
led me down the rough stones,
whitened by stars so close

we could touch them, to the square
in front of the old temple. You wrote
your message on a scrap of paper,
placed it in a fissure with thousands

of others, forced it in tight
and hoped it would stay. My secret,
you whispered, you write one, too.
The cracks were crammed

with petitions folded and packed in,
sealing the stones with pleadings
in that puzzle of boulders caulked
with tears and words and breath

whispered into the crevices.
We'd passed through checkpoints,
our bags searched, our bodies
scanned and measured and judged

for that fragment, that chamber
of the original heart, that constellation
of oddly shaped stars fixed
in our shared sky, that calendar

that held all of our next years.
A flock of black-robed figures
requested us to follow them
down the stone steps into

a chamber beneath the wall,
thrusting shadows of books, pulsing
birds, into our quivering palms,
their eyes penetrating our flesh,

an obscure longing for us to take up
their responsive chanting, in that place
your tongue spoke of all your life with promise,
in that language you blessed me in.

8. *Shalom is My Middle Name*

What my mother left me with—
the word we should mean
when we say every other word,

the word we want to be more
than a word, the word I carry
tucked between other words,

from my birth to my death,
the word embarrassed
by its public display, preferring

its privacy, perhaps lifting
its first letter then retreating
back into the silence. But

there it is, stamped on my passport,
risking itself each time
it passes through security,

each time it wants to haul
its baggage from one country
to the next. Why, after all

these journeys, does it suddenly
step outside and assert itself,
aware as it is of the separations?

Why—
this hello, this goodbye
this peace?

NAOMI SHIHAB NYE

I grew up in Ferguson, Missouri. No one ever heard of it, unless you lived elsewhere in St. Louis County. Then my family moved to Palestine—my father's first home. A friend says, "Your parents really picked the garden spots."

In Ferguson, an invisible line separated white and black communities. In Jerusalem a no man's land separated people, designated by barbed wire.

My father and his family became refugees in 1948 when the state of Israel was created. They lost everything but their lives and memories.

My dad found himself in Kansas, then moved to Missouri with his American bride. He seemed a little shell-shocked when I was a child. My father was the only Arab in Ferguson. But he ran for the school board and won. I attended the red brick elementary school called Central.

At twelve, I took a berry-picking job on "Missouri's oldest organic farm" in Ferguson. I wanted the job because I had noticed the other berry-pickers were all black boys. This seemed my only chance to meet them; Ferguson would not be integrated until 1968. By that time we were gone.

In 1966, my father took our family to the West Bank. I was the only non-Armenian attending the ancient Armenian school in Jerusalem's Old City. Our father said, when he was a boy, Jews and Arabs had been mixed together, neighbors. Now there was power and domination at stake.

Dominate—to exercise control over. Black kids in streets. Thousands of Palestinian families.

In 1967 with the Six-Day War brewing, my family left Jerusalem. We settled in San Antonio, a majority Latino city, which felt like a relief.

Back in Israel/Palestine, nothing improved for the Palestinians and they were always blamed for it. A gigantic "Separation Wall" was built. Americans elected a half-and-half president twice, which gave many of us great hope.

Summer 2014, the news exploded. Massacres in Gaza—not the first time—people who looked exactly like our Arab family. Regular people. Kids. Sleeping kids.

A Jewish friend sent a one-word message: stop!

Of course we wished Hamas would stop sending reckless rockets into Israel, provoking oversized responses. But why didn't the news examine back-stories more? Oppression makes people do desperate things. I am frankly surprised the entire Palestinian population hasn't gone crazy. If the US can't see that Palestinians have been mightily oppressed since 1948, they really are not interested in looking, are they? And we keep sending weapons and money to Israel, pretending we'd prefer peace.

But help came to Ferguson!

After unarmed teenager Michael Brown was shot, quiet old Ferguson took over the news. Citizens marching, chest placards, "I'm a man too" and "Don't shoot!" It's easy to see how a white officer raising a gun against an unarmed black kid is simply wrong. Why is that harder for people to see about Gaza?

People in Gaza sent messages of solidarity to Ferguson. I thought I was hallucinating. What if they could all march together? 1.8 million Gazans would really clog old Florissant Avenue.

Israelis have never been called militants by the American press, even when they blast whole families to oblivion. It's just "defense." A newscaster described Ferguson as "a series of stings and hurts." Try the open-air prison enclave of Gaza for stings and hurts.

Things will change again in Ferguson. But will things change for Gaza? Will the United States ever speak out in solidarity with scores of exhausted people burying their dead, staring up with stunned eyes, mystified?

Before I Was a Gazan

I was a boy
and my homework was missing,
paper with numbers on it,
stacked and lined,
I was looking for my piece of paper,
proud of this plus that, then multiplied,
not remembering if I had left it
on the table after showing to my uncle
or the shelf after combing my hair
but it was still somewhere
and I was going to find it and turn it in,
make my teacher happy,
make her say my name to the whole class,
before everything got subtracted
in a minute
even my uncle
even my teacher
even the best math student and his baby sister
who couldn't talk yet.
And now I would do anything
for a problem I could solve.

Everything Changes the World

Boys on a beach,
women with cook pots,
men bombing tender patches of mint.

There is no righteous position.
Only a place where brown feet
touch the earth.

Maybe you call it yours.
Maybe someone else runs it.
What do you prefer?
We who are far
stagger under the mind blade.
Words, lies.

Every shattered home,
every story worth telling.
Think how much you'd need to say
if that were your kid.

If one of your people
equals hundreds of ours,
what does that say about people?

RICKEY LAURENTIIS

I feel the fault line that runs through Palestine to Ferguson. It's one that's been running beneath us a long time, through several borders, across many ages, linking one injustice to another, one set of historical violences to its cousins. Though it's important to note that to "link" injustices isn't, necessarily, *importantly*, to "conflate" or "equate" them. I can recognize, for instance, the logic that leads to a Palestinian child being killed, unsentimentally, by a drone attack (a lynching) as *linked* to the logic that would also have policeman's bullet enter a black American child's head (a lynching), without ever once having to claim that the cries both children made—that their mothers made—were the same. They are not the same. They carry different weights, different colors, but have some kinship, I think. When I say "logic," I guess I mean all the discourses that would have these events make "sense" (even as they are senseless) and, therefore, continue to propel these events outside the arena of the imagination and into bald reality. The imagination—that's what I'm always thinking about: how it is that thing both uniquely, paradoxically, responsible for the ways we can bring harm to each other, and the all the other ways we can love and heal.

Excerpt from "Of the Leaves That Have Fallen (Stevens, Like Decorations in a Nigger Cemetery)"

1.
In the imagination there is no daylight and,
Like Wallace Stevens, I know the dark is crucial.
I sing, I grieve in it, I dream what haunts each night:
These bodies, even lynched, still are thinking.
Nothing is final, I'm told. *No man shall see the end—*
But them, my fathers, lifted into fire, like tongues.

7.

Sometimes they skinned the faces so the tongues,
When they fell, fell. Sometimes they yanked and
Hacked away, detaching limb from limb, upending.
Not Death, sometimes it was the dying that was crucial.
Seven hours once for the torture: I read this, thinking
About that body's slow unblooding union with the night.

14.

This was the American South, American night,
The Medusa, the live head with the many tongues,
The live tongues with the many minds, and the thinking
That through a kind of swank violence and
Through a kind of steel, a beauty, a pure and crucial
History, could be found, be restored and made endless.

21.

When did you decide to try your endurance,
To turn back on this world dressed in a spectral night?
You know it by the ash, the wake of the crosses,
How "Shut up, Boy" burns beneath every tongue.
I wonder whose eye can resist looking back and
Not swallow them, these men: muted, gray, thinking.

28.

What will the mind do for thinking
When a body stalls, slows, diminuendos
But continue? The thinking gone on and,
Like grief, grown as pregnant as the night?
Imagine: his body, like a pendulum, a tongue,
A fever that won't break, gorgeous, that furious core.

35.

History, here is my muscle, my skin, my crucial
Blood, my heart, my stubbornness, my thinking,
My hauntedness, my ghosts, my American tongue:
I give it up. I give it all away. Here is my ending,
My making, a tableau of me traced against the night.
Take my unworthiness, my privilege. Take my hand.

KIESE LAYMON

My grandmother taught me to read. My mother, a political science professor at Jackson State University, taught me to write. My mother gave her life to educating young black women and men about the importance of reckoning with individual, communal and structural terror. When I was in high school, she started doing this work that connected poverty and structural oppression in the Mississippi Delta to poverty and structural oppression in places like Cuba, Palestine, and Zimbabwe. Whenever she went to these places, she'd tell me because she wanted to understand the connectedness of love and struggles for land and dignity. I wrote this piece in response to one of her last trips to Palestine.

My Mama Went to Palestine

My mama went to Palestine when I was thirty-one years old. I was afraid. My Grandma thought she was in St. Louis. My Auntie thought she was in the Mississippi Delta. Her boyfriend thought she was in Boston. Her students thought she was in Baltimore. My mama knew her sister and her mother and her boyfriend and her students would be so afraid if they knew why and how she flew to Palestine.

So she lied to them.

My mama went to Palestine when I was thirty-one years old. My mama knew I would be so afraid if she, a beautiful black southern woman committed to fighting and truth-telling and screaming the loudest when she's afraid, went to St. Louis or the Mississippi Delta or Boston or Baltimore or anywhere on earth there were plain men propped up by structural violence.

So my mama told me the truth.

My mama went to Palestine when I was thirty-one years old. I was afraid. Then she came back. Then she told everyone the truth about Palestine. Then she went again. And she went again. And she lied to everyone who she loved about going every time she went. But she never lied to me. Not about Palestine. She never lied to me.

PHILLIP B. WILLIAMS

I want this poem to reflect the fragmented nature of my own thoughts and fears about this conflict. What terrified me the most were the parallels I found between police violence in the US and the politics held by those against a two-state resolution for Israel and Palestine. Just when I thought I had it all figured out, I understood that my own long-distance witnessing was like looking into a mirror, one that I wish broken for both myself and my reflection.

Homecoming

Words are heavy and loaded, cold
when unspoken and when spoken: political

climate, agitators, riot, war, smoke bombs, genocide.
The nation has a name and is populated,
the city looking up through window glass
that burst along the ground. This lens is not new.

In photos, it is hard to tell the shape of things
through all the smoke, the brown faces
carrying bodies from where bullets found rest

inside a lung. When the living complain
they are called immigrants. Imagine that, a home

made of immigrants suddenly uninhabitable
by immigrants. Bombs that are not yours put in
your hands by the news. Your churches, mosques,
basements changed into places for bandaging shut

a woman's missing eye.
Bodies are left visible as a warning
that apathy can be a kind of shrapnel.

◆　◆　◆

When the cease-fire happened for the last time, I celebrated. No more anti-Arab
policing of bodies. No more fear of anti-Semitism. But a truce, what I assumed a
ceasefire to be, may break.

It was easy to think all Muslims are terrorists and all terrorists Muslims. Easy to
think only one side with weapons is a true enemy. It makes sleeping easier, makes
drinking a latte even when you hate lattes easier.

Then Stokely Carmichael visits you in a dream and says that no one feared anyone having weapons until the Blacks had weapons. But I wonder when have Blacks never been considered weapons?

Have the Palestinians always been considered this way, too? To want an entire people erased, I know both sides: to be erased, to want the erasure of others. It always feels like safety though it is always only hatred.

• • •

When I say people I mean any people
in a nation of many people split
like a pig down tender seams
no one remembered creasing into existence.

On the news a young boy is left for dead
and it is everyone's betrayal and it isn't.
We have a need for common words: war,
borders, justice. The officer with the weapon

said he had to defend himself, the offenders'
shields of blood-bone flat in the road,
whom they protected nowhere, nowhere.

• • •

In the comment section:

"But how can we care so much about their Holocaust when they care so little about ours?"

"We stand with those who stand with us. Gay rights are human rights. They get that. They are for humans."

"They attacked first. This is the price of lifting your hand against an army!"

I could not tell who was speaking to whom, for whom.

• • •

1. Terms to look up:

Israel, Palestine, nation, Hamas, Gaza Strip, Prime Minister, refugees, home, United Nations, treaty, Gaza Strip, Article 51, Hague Regulations, territory, terrorist, ally, unilateral withdrawal, anti-Semite, West Bank, 700 dead, River Jordan, Fatah, cease-fire, extrajudicial, blood, Hebron, Operation Brother's Keeper, 300 dead, rocket, faith, Gilad Shalit prisoner exchange, Dahiya Doctrine, 3 dead, 1 dead, military base, civilian.

2. What are the terms of engagement?

"What happened in the Dahiya quarter of Beirut in 2006 will happen in every village from which Israel is fired on. . . . We will apply disproportionate force on it and cause great damage and destruction there. From our standpoint, these are not civilian villages, they are military bases."

—Maj. Gen. Gadi Eizenkot as quoted in "Five Israeli Talking Points on Gaza—Debunked" by Noura Erakat, *The Nation*, July 25, 2014

"Since 2006, according to an analysis by the *New York Times*, police departments have acquired 435 armored vehicles, 533 planes, 93,763 machine guns, and 432 mine-resistant armored trucks. Overall, since Congress established its program to transfer military hardware, local and state police departments have received $4.3 billion worth of equipment. Accordingly, the value of military equipment used by these police agencies has increased from $1 million in 1990 to $324 million in 1995 (shortly after the program was established), to nearly $450 million in 2013."

—"The Militarization of the Police" by Jamelle Bouie, *Slate*, August 13, 2014

To choose a side. To be forced
to choose a side and assumed, always,
that you have chosen incorrectly.

◆　◆　◆

In high school I was called the "Little Indian Boy" because of the way my hair lies flat when cut low. There was a guy we always mistook as Indian but he proudly proclaimed he was Pakistani. We looked nothing alike.

But I felt with him a small camaraderie, to be called something you are not and speaking vehemently against it in order to retain control of your identity. "I am Black." "I am Pakistani." To be seen as what you are.

Civility and civilian are not the same thing, though to remain neutral seems to be how many people feel one must practice their civilian status. To defend oneself makes you an active soldier. Though, civilians do vote.

The act of voting can been seen as an act of freedom and terrorism. Consider the advent of democracy in the USA post the Revolutionary War. Who suffered or strived under whose laws? When Hamas was democratically voted into power in Palestine, was that an act of war?

◆ ◆ ◆

A friend was called a foul name for believing
in peace. Peace is called so many things
and the cameras add static to words
that would otherwise be clear. It is difficult
to know how to speak with a mouth
flexed like a crosshair, seeming that way
to so many. A photo of someone holding
the American flag such that the fabric licks
the ground: "Never let the flag touch the ground.
And never dispose of a flag by burning it,"
was a comment left beneath the photo.
Allegiance, is another word
we do not have in common. Here
in a nation of two flags, in a nation
where effigies of the president are tortured
surrogates, where everyone who looks
like him becomes his proxy. It is difficult
to hear of two Satans, two nations hated
by a single source outside of themselves
when inside, one nation has always had
a way with dark rituals. "Stop being
so violent" when hands are up. We see
hands are up. We see the weapons are not
our own, the armies not our own, the terror
somewhere over there. It has infiltrated
where there was no terror. It was given
hands and feet and eyes by its Michael,
but the Sword is poorly aimed, like a bomb.

◆ ◆ ◆

When I ask questions about Israel and Palestine's conflict, people think I am asking rhetorical questions. Rhetoric is not useful to me and even a rhetorical question, when asked in error, can be dissected.

I wanted to know who bombed whom first. Surely, that would get me the answers I needed. Surely, the timetable told all. And as I sat waiting for the answer, more rockets went flying.

In Gaza, the children flew kites to break a Guinness world record. In photos, the kite strings sit taut against the blue of the sky. I wrote, "Kites like bodiless shirts haunt the sky." I did not allow them a deserved beauty.

How even in empathizing with those under constant military pressure one can also refuse to see people as human. Children flying kites becomes an overt political statement and not simply children having joy.

◆　◆　◆

Or like a word, a phrase. The photo
of brown people holding a banner
while all around them their hospitals

go up in smoke. That they could still heal,
in all that ruin and across the ocean
of their own eradication, strangers.

To be called an anti-Semite when you say peace.
To be called a racist when you reject police brutality.
Called Cop-hater. Terrorist. Diatribe the first

weapon. To wonder about the Middle Passage,
the Trail of Tears becoming the Triangular Trade
and Manifest Destiny and gentrification.

I watched videos of Sudanese immigrants
and refugees attacked on Israeli streets.
Jim Crow, Tulsa Riots, Apartheid, settlements.

"Go back to___! This is our land! Go home!"

Home makes a crosshair, too, of the mouth.
Sometimes it is difficult to tell
which way it is pointing.

JASON SCHNEIDERMAN

In seventh grade, my Hebrew School teacher asked our class on which side we would fight if Israel and the United States went to war. Being the son of a United States Air Force Officer, the question struck me as absurd. In the first place, military service was a fairly mundane fact of my life (even though I wasn't serving), so it had no real romance or intrigue or association with freedom or adulthood. In the second place, it was a question without context. I wanted to know why these countries were going to war. Any war between the US and Israel would require a principled choice over moral position, not an easy question of loyalty. In a certain way, it was like being asked if you would live with your mother or father if they got divorced. Not that they're unhappy, or anything, but just for fun, take sides.

The question also struck me as incredibly stupid on a fairly practical level. The US would wipe Israel off the map if there were to be an actual war. Romantic notions aside, I have no interest in dying for a cause. Certainly, Israel's founding returned Judaism to the kind of heroic, martial, nationalistic ethos one finds in the Torah and in stories like Masada. But let's not forget that Talmudic Judaism was essentially founded by two rabbis who—depending on your view—were highly pragmatic cowards, or wisely self-preserving heroes. 40 years of heroic Zionism versus 2,000 years of self-sustenance and preservation? Only the Holocaust makes that one a hard choice.

This total failure of a pedagogical thought experiment from the '80s stands out to me because it marks the first time I found myself in the midst of an impossible conversation about Israel, with the terms and conditions already determined far in advance. The question was a loyalty test, and my reaction was essentially to opt out. I wouldn't discuss it. I shut down.

I do not subscribe to what I have seen called "communication ideology," which is basically the idea that any discussion of a topic is inherently good. "At least we're talking about it now," someone will say, or "We have to start a national conversation about this." Really? I care a great deal about what Ta-Nehisi Coates has to say; ditto Paul Krugman; ditto Hannah Arendt. But what passes for "conversation"—particularly on Facebook—looks more like a centrifuge for determining the most extreme versions of any position before partitioning everyone to like-minded thought bubbles.

I frequently quip that Facebook is the new poetry: it makes nothing happen. But the truth is that Facebook is the new affirmer of a trend; we know how to take sides, and agree with one side, not how to consider a question. There was a generation in the 1930s who thought that their choice was between Fascism and Communism. When Hitler and Stalin go to war, is there really a right side to choose? I find myself falling into this trap every four years. I started going door to door for the Kerry campaign in 2004 because I wanted to meet undecided voters. In my imagination, they were credulous, mouth-breathing morons, destroying the country through their lack of engagement. What I found in reality were fascinating people with legitimate questions and reasonable positions (with the occasional delusional nut job thrown in). It returned me to sanity in a very real way.

My husband and I are members of Congregation Beit Simchat Torah, the largest gay and lesbian synagogue in the world, and our rabbi, Sharon Kleinbaum, gives a report when she returns from her annual trip to Israel. A few years ago, we attended the report, and my husband and I were relieved to hear a nuanced and complex discussion of the various issues. Rabbi Kleinbaum had visited the occupied territories; she had gone through checkpoints; she discussed differences between Israeli and Palestinian and Arab perspectives and experiences. The questions during the Q&A followed one of two tracks. Either "Israel is a colonial project that has no right to exist and you are colluding in oppression by supporting it," or "The Arabs are our enemies, and you are bringing about the destruction of Israel." Rabbi Kleinbaum is especially good at facing hostility without compromising her integrity or simplifying her position. This is not a skill that I have. It's why I simply don't enter the conversation. I don't believe I can do any good in the face of a made-up mind or an extreme position unless I'm in front of a classroom—but college classrooms are not democracies.

Based on all of my other political, intellectual, and personal sympathies, the easiest position for me to take would be a simple pro-Palestine/anti-Israel one. Pinkwashing is fairly well documented, I have never been to Israel, I don't speak Hebrew, and I'm generally appalled by the conduct of Orthodox Judaism. I recognize that many of the myths that I was taught about the creation of Israel are myths. But the fact is that I think that the state of Israel has a right to exist. It was brought into being by world historical forces that include thousands of years of anti-Semitism, and in the past five years or so, I've been surprised at how very quickly anti-Israel sentiment slips into anti-Semitism—or rather reveals it. Caryl Churchill's play "Seven Jewish Children: A Play About Gaza" struck me as infuriatingly anti-Semitic.

Last summer, the spiral of violence was set off by the murder of three Israeli teens. Israelis responded by killing a Palestinian teen. What is needed here is neither a simple condemnation of violence, nor a simple taking of sides—but a re-humanization of each side to the enemy. The efforts to do just that (the Daniel

Barenboim/Edward Said project of a combined Israeli/Palestinian youth orchestra springs to mind) seem to have disappeared. I don't think that "re-humanization" will happen. I never thought it would happen. I have no hope for a solution. I think the people there are locked into a cycle of retribution and violence, which is what most foreign relationships have looked like for most of human history.

And worse: having this conversation in the United States! You want to talk about a place that has a "right to exist"? You want to talk about a "right of return"? The US has put forth the myth of "A land without a people for a people without a land" far more effectively than any Zionist ever has. But I like my house in Brooklyn. I'm not giving it up any time soon. I'm even in the midst of a renovation so I can have warm floors on cold winter mornings before I go off to teach my Freshman Composition class about how the Cherokee system of writing was developed in order to resist genocide. You see why I refuse to talk about this?

I fear that my contribution is a non-contribution. Can I really say: I won't talk until I like the terms of the conversation? It's like the old joke about the French politician's response to a proposed solution. *Yes, it works in practice, but will it work in theory?* In the poem that forms my contribution—as much as I hate to explain my own work—I tried to attack the easiness that often informs political decisions, as well as the smugness that comes from being right. My frustration is both with the pieties of the students and with the way that knowledge tends to fail us in the real world.

The Sadness of Antonio

"In sooth, I know not why I am so sad"
    —The opening line of *The Merchant of Venice*, spoken by Antonio

"We come to the text with a question: why is Antonio so sad?"
    —James Longenbach, *The Resistance to Poetry*

"I will argue here that *The Merchant* deliberately frustrates any possibility of identification with its characters . . ."
    —James O'Rourke, "Racism and Homophobia in *The Merchant of Venice*"

Antonio, we should remind ourselves,
    is not real.

He is not in the body of the actor
    or the words on the page,

and yet we return to the question:
    Why is he sad?

There is no Antonio in the way
    for instance

there is a homeless man
    outside the subway,

his clothes made out of
    newspapers, folded

to ribbons and tied into bows.
    We would not

call him sad.
        We would call him crazy.

We avoid his eyes,
        We avoid his stench,

But he is there.
        He is there.

There is no Antonio
        in the way

that there are ten fifth graders
        placed under my tutelage,

and brought to a production of
        Merchant of Venice

because the younger drama class
        always sees

whatever the Manhattan Summer Shakespeare Group
        is putting on.

The next morning,
        writing earnestly in their journals,

they find themselves
        entirely offended.

As a Jew
        one writes

I was deeply offended
        by the behavior

in the play
        toward Shylock.

The quality of self-righteousness
        is not strained.

I think it was wrong
        writes an athletically-gifted blond boy

To be mean to someone
        for his race.

Then he crosses out *race*
        and writes in

religion. Oh, children.
        This is an easy one.

Not one of them notice
        that Antonio is sad.

Antonio is entirely ignored
        in their journals.

He holds no interest
        for them.

Fine. We can do this.
        I ask what

Shylock is ridiculed
        for calling out

when Jessica elopes
        and steals her father's money.

They don't remember,
        So I direct them in their scripts.

Finally they find it:
        my ducats and my daughter.

I ask them what Lorenzo has taken
        and as the light dawns

one girl answers,
        His ducats and his daughters!

I say,
        so the Christians want

what they ridicule Shylock
        for wanting

and slowly,
        they see the light.

Fifth graders of the world
        unite!

This is their first experience
        of what we used to call

reading against the grain.
        They have never

read against the grain.
        They have never

Felt so smart. They have never
        Realized that a text

Can contain it's own critique.
        Fifth graders of the world,

Do not spend your summer
        at school camp.

The most childlike of my children
        looks like a porcelain doll

and cries at the drop of a hat.
        He cries because the other children

are mean to him and the children
        are mean to him because

he treats them with disdain
        and is always about to cry.

As I comfort him
        for the third time that day

I realize how much less real
        he is to me than Antonio.

At the end of six weeks
        I will deliver this boy

Back to the incompetent arms
        Of his socially awkward parents

And never consider him again.
        The girl who is being possessed

By puberty, whose legs are ready
        for shaving and whose armpits

are ready for deodorant,
        who hides her face in a stack

of novels that are thinly veiled
        rape fantasies for the barely

pubescent, she too is less real to me
        than Antonio.

I try to ask about Antonio,
        but their interest

Is only in Shylock. When I was
        in fifth grade,

we also read
        Merchant of Venice.

I was the only Jew in class,
        and the only student,

who given the choice,
        memorized "The Quality of Mercy"

rather than "I am a Jew."
        I read the introduction

to our Bedford or Dover or
        Oxford edition

and learned about how Shakespeare
        gave Shylock a humanity

that no other Jew in Renaissance
        Drama even comes close to,

even if that humanity is not entirely
        complete. I learned a passage

that was twice as long,
        and secretly,

I learned the "I am a Jew" speech
        to see what it feels like

to say. When we read
        the play out loud,

I read Antonio, so I felt it more
        than the others,

his sadness. Under everything
        you can feel how

he would do anything
        for Bassanio,

And yet, he knew not why he
        was sad.

These children all love
        Shylock. They can't see

his racism or his cruelty,
        or rather they think

that powerlessness is panacea,
        because they are powerless

and they believe
        that to be unable

to hurt another person
        is the same as being good.

My assistant tries once more
        to interest

our children in Antonio,
        to start the conversation

that might lead to Elizabethan
        perceptions of sodomitical

subcultures as they existed
        In early modern Venice,

but without luck.
        We wonder if our students

Notice how queer we are,
        and that night

we joke about creating a 1990s version
        of *Merchant of Venice*

that could open with Antonio
        breaking the silence

and conclude with an ACTUP
        demonstration

in which a gender-queer Portia would insist
        on her right to body modification surgeries,

and a Derridean Jessica
        would deconstruct

the Jewish/Christian binary,
        in addition to dredging up

recovered memories
        of satanic abuse,

at the hands of Shylock.
        We make ourselves laugh,

smug in our knowledge,
        but sad in its failure,

though even that
        doesn't quite

resolve the question of why
        Antonio is sad.

Do you remember the homeless man?

He doesn't ask me for money,
        nor does he ask anyone.

He sits on the grate, and talks to himself.
        His elaborate costume

is ineluctably real. He is
        real, but he is not

my object of study. He resides
        in himself, and he cannot

be read with or against the grain.
        I do not talk to him.

He occupies my mind
        for as little time

as he is in front of me.
        Poor Antonio.

As I return to my home
        by train

Antonio occupies my mind.
        He is nowhere at all:

not in the past,
        not in the body

of the actor,
        not in the history

of Venice
        or England

or America.
        And still

the question returns:
        Why is Antonio sad?

I look around
        my train,

and there is no one
        to ask.

LAWRENCE JOSEPH

Born in 1948, I am of a generation of American poets whose entire life has been lived in a period of continuous violence, a series of successive, now permanent, foreign wars, and, domestically, the equivalent of class- and race-driven civil wars. In each of my books of poems, I have written of this violence and its transmogrifications inside and outside our geographical borders. It is a violence which, in different forms, has been a fundamental reality of the United States of America from its beginnings. It is a violence that is also in our literature from the beginning—in our poetry and in our prose—a fundamental part of our language, our sensibilities, our imaginations, our aesthetics.

There is, for me, an additional, biographical dimension to it. My grandparents, Lebanese and Syrian Catholics, emigrated to the United States over a century ago, when Lebanon was still a part of Ottoman Syria. They were among the first émigrés from the Arab world to Detroit. My mother and father were born in Detroit and lived their entire lives there. I was born and raised in Detroit and was, from childhood, a part of Detroit's Arab American community. My Lebanese and Syrian identity, and heritage, and the imperialist, colonialist, post-colonialist, corporatist, techno-capitalist, militarist war-making by the United States in Southwest Asia and North Africa during my lifetime, have also been a part of my poetry from the start.

"News Back Even Further Than That" is situated in these, among other, contexts. It was written during and in the aftermath of the invasion and occupation of Iraq by the United States in 2003.

News Back Even Further
Than That

I
Dust, the dust of a dust storm;
yellow, black, brown, haze, smoke;
a baby photographed with half
a head; the stolen thoroughbred
a boy is riding bareback attacked
by a lion; the palace, fixed-up
as a forward command post—"This,"
says Air-War Commander Mosely,
"would make a pretty nice casino";
why is such a detailed
description necessary?;
that smell in the air is the smell
of burned human flesh;
those low-flying A-Ten Warthogs
are, each of them, firing
one-hundred bullets a second.

II
The president refuses to answer a question
he wasn't asked. The president denies
his eyes are the eyes of a lobster.
The map is being drawn: Mosul in the north,
Baghdad in the center, Basra in the south.
The news back even further than that:
"He Says He Is the Prophet Ezekiel.
In the Great Mudflats By the River Chebar,
He Has Seen, He Proclaims, Four Angels,
Each With Six Wings, On a Fiery Wheel."
Collaborators cut into pieces and burnt to death
in public, on spits, like lambs . . . In spray-paint

across the armored personnel carrier:
"Crazy Train," "Rebel," "Got Oil?. . ." There,
on Sadoun Street, in a wheelbarrow, a coil
of wire, a carpet, rolled, Persian, antique.

III
"I've just been to see her. It's made her
Mad—angry, yes, of course, but I mean mad,
truly mad. She spoke quietly, quickly—
maniacally. 'Wargame, they're using wargame
as a verb, they didn't wargame the chaos—
chaos! Do you think they care about
the chaos? The chaos just makes it easier for them
to get what they want. Wargame!
What they've wargamed is the oil,
their possession of the oil, what they've wargamed
is the killing, the destruction,
what they've wargamed is their greed . . .'
Had I noticed that Lebanon had become
an abstract noun, as in 'the Lebanonization of'?
'It may just as well have been two or three
atomic bombs, the amount of depleted
uranium in their bombs, the bombs
in this war, the bombs in the war before this—
uranium's in the groundwater now,
uranium is throughout the entire
ecology by now, how many generations
are going to be
contaminated by it, die of it, be poisoned by it? . . .'
War, a war time, without limits.
Technocapital war a part
of our bodies, of the body politic.
She quoted Pound—the *Pisan Cantos*—
she couldn't remember which—
there are no righteous wars.
'There is no righteous violence,'
she said, 'it's neurobiological
with people like this—
people who need to destroy and who need to kill
like this—and what we're seeing now
is nothing compared
to what we'll see in the future . . .'"

Our Children Will Go to Bed With Our Dream

FARID MATUK

I am sitting high in the stands of the basketball stadium on the campus of the public university where I teach. The game begins with the players, their effort to make
and then stay in a field of understanding that stretches as far as their peripheral
vision allows, and as far as their trained memories' projections of where each
should occupy space in the next moment. In one of the laws criminalizing the
public sociality of blacks, the Pennsylvania colony in 1700 legislated that "over
four Negroes meeting together on Sundays or other days 'upon no lawful business of their masters or owners' were to be whipped" (Dubois, 411). But today, the
boys on the court, many of whom are black, enjoy an intimate and public sociality
sanctioned by its aim at winning, and by its calling together of a broader collective attention considered a market. At a break between periods an announcer
calls onto the court "the hero of the game," a lance corporal not much older
than the athletes and the crowd pitches their cheers, standing. Exactly a week
before, the Senate Select Committee on Intelligence released its 528-page executive summary on the CIA's "detention" and "enhanced" interrogations of "enemy
combatants" after 9/11. Those are the terms—detention, enhanced, enemy combatants—many news outlets use in earnest to articulate the story. There's a calcu-
lus there, maybe, about how few scare quotes one should use around the state's
obfuscations so as to avoid sounding shrill or conspiratorial, which is another
way of saying that the measure of our journalism's objectivity is the degree of its
alignment with state discourse. I wonder if Americans only remember our war in
Vietnam now as a vague imperative to support our troops, at least with our affect.
The lance corporal corseted in his dress uniform and looking a little confused at
the bottom of our basketball agora stands as another piece of official state diction.
Maybe perfected ideology looks like this: a public gathered to clap and cheer with
feeling that resists interpretation. We can't know if our cheers affirm state power
or mark whatever innocence the lance corporal might, like a local martyr, have
forfeited for our sake, let alone which cheers are for both positions simultaneously, which is to say for the perfect ambivalence of the first world.

Many of us in the US now acknowledge the militarized police responses to protests and acts of outrage inspired by the most recent police killings of unarmed black boys and men. We understand how manufacturers of military equipment want to expand into new markets, and how politicians can pose as protectors by increasing the budgets of police departments. By "understand" I mean "accept," "rationalize," but also "support" because we seem to like the thought of keeping such force at hand, at least when we assume it won't be used on "us." Indeed, the response to the militarized hunt for the Boston Marathon bombers in which a major US city came under a voluntary "shelter-in-place directive" was largely celebratory and grateful. In 2010 legal scholar Michelle Alexander published her study on how biased enforcement of drug laws, mandatory minimum sentencing, and the vulnerable legal status of released felons collude to enact what she calls a "new Jim Crow" state that keeps poor black populations in misery, contained, incarcerated, or dead. Part of Alexander's point is that we tend to notice the force of domestic policing only when it impacts white communities or integrated protests. I am pessimistic about Americans' occasional flare for synthesis. We expend ourselves in it. Nonetheless, it seems clear to me that the militarized and legislative confinement of Palestinians is a macabre refinement of the militarized and legislative confinement of blacks in the US, and that vulnerable populations worldwide serve as grist for the imbricated work of governments and global corporations. As the British poet Stephen Willey recently reminded an audience here in Tucson, one of the two lead contractors for Israel's apartheid wall in the occupied West Bank, Elbit Systems, won a $145 million contract from the US Department of Homeland Security to construct similar structures on the Mexico–US border.

Here in the US it seems the only anti-racist civil action that eludes confrontations with heavily armed police is our donning of slogans on t-shirts. "We are Michael Brown" is a popular slogan of identification with the young black man killed by a police officer in Ferguson, Missouri. "We can't breath" is a slogan of identification with the last words spoken by Eric Garner while being restrained by several NYPD officers alleged to have used a chokehold on Garner. While these slogans can mobilize protests, some argue they offer equivalencies too cheaply. Years before the notoriety of the Brown and Garner killings, a black friend told me that for the racial caste system in the US to change white families would have to put their children on the same corners in every neighborhood in the US where black kids are routinely killed by stray or aimed bullets, by panicked cops and panicked vigilantes. I wondered if he meant something like the US activists who placed themselves, like human shields, among street demonstrations in El Salvador in the early 80s to dissuade government snipers who would not want to shoot first-world citizens. No, he meant the bodies of white children would need to pile. I think, too, of my cousin's husband, a white Vietnam vet, a retiree who drives a new Porsche, bikes every day along the California coast, and dreams most nights of the time he was sitting on a wall with a friend overlooking the green fields of Vietnam, both of them eating lunch out of their helmets. The moment was an idyll even as he bent down to take a spoonful of ration and suddenly it wasn't when a Viet Cong sniper's bullet pushed the friend's brain matter onto his food, onto his uniform, onto his hair, and onto the side of his face he had allowed to be seen by anyone, as if nobody wanted to kill him, as if nobody could imagine the right.

My poems here are part of a series that addresses my daughter. I don't want her to die and I do not lay her body on anyone's scale of justice. Such common feeling should be a point of global solidarity, though it never has been. She and I have been training these four years she's been alive to make a sociality of two every bit as attentive and calculating as that of the basketball players. Our sociality is not only sanctioned, it's privileged, partly because our shared Syrian ancestry, mixed as it is by desires that crossed nations and ethnicities, sometimes gets read in the southwest US where we live as white and sometimes as ambiguously ethnic. First-world whiteness atomizes us into intimate tribes of nuclear families who get along in an economic system of socialized risk and privatized profit where most forms of large-scale mobilization are deemed suspect. For all our sympathies, for all our emails to elected officials, for all our wearing of slogans and walking in front of police, we are a far step from working to liberate black America let alone Palestine in any serious material way. "I have seen this swan and / I have seen you; I have seen ambition without / understanding in a variety of forms" wrote Marianne Moore in her poem "Critics and Connoisseurs," and though the poem seems to place efforts expended without understanding in its crosshairs, it goes on to drape the swan and the ant who expend themselves thus in the tinsel of its gaze. What do our various forms of lyric poetry have if not a little tinsel and the need to keep looking? These poems imagine first what I love most, my small tribe, and there train their gaze. My daughter enters these verses as a figure through which I imagine attention itself as an indigestible remnant, a promiscuous solidarity, and an array of perverse failings. My hope, my ambition without understanding maybe, is that attending so, holding each other in an intimate sociality, can help us be perverse to our own privilege, to resist the bargains offered us as people of the first world. Maybe our flare for synthesis will sustain itself beyond the first blush of critique when we walk away from what we think we know and who we think we are.

Years before my daughter's birth, I read an article about the Thai people's reverence for their king, Bhumibol Adulyadej. One subject explained, in words for which my memory is likely somewhat responsible, that people in the US could never understand a love for a king, for we only had a president who died in the street and our children would go to bed with our dream. This short sequence of three poems ends with an image of the dead looking down on grains of sand in our desert and wishing to be whole, complete, "simple / and done." The poem imagines that wish, not its fulfillment. Our children carry us forward, most often unwittingly maybe, but they carry our phenotypes, our commitments, our privileges, and our ignorance. What are we carrying? What can we put down? Who would we be if we did?

WORKS CITED
Dubois, W. E. B. *The Philadelphia Negro: a Social Study*. Philadelphia: University of Pennsylvania Press, 1899, 1996. Print.

My Daughter Davis-Monthan Air Force Base, Tucson, Arizona

Cared for, laced
into a sequence three
pipe bombs gave themselves
to the streets about your school
hardly making local news

There is a light that neither
of us will absorb

winking in it all the while
by its known waves the state's
cargo planes keep from folding into our streets

Maybe you're the steady
light impulse to start a new
spinning in the privileged
soft heads of everyone so when we wake
we are each the queen, the happy
ghost in the halls of the old cruise ship
maybe I am

The martyr takes her own state
and her own neighbors inside herself
making an imbalance of terror

How will you, in your years, account for the victimhood of which we were
bereft?

They were little things
in the hollows in a matrix of demands
and performance reviews

we did to make wall and sky
sway like long wheat in a wind
about you like something
that wasn't continuous

If this talk could go on
the dead
might lay a little deeper in the air

My Daughter Not You

Maybe mirrors are not our only hosts
a turning in your eye
and you look up

far behind the dead there are many mistakes
whole nations we can't handle
make their rustling

Colors, furloughed
visit your head

they can't help themselves

and on this sidewalk
cellophane and foil
brighten your arrival

What inscribes itself in your eyes
is a small canyon—
and in its bottoms the chattering speech?

It isn't enough to say images

Seen, the still pine needles
a tarp billowing at the lower winds
are a weather

How long could you look?

In the foreground a wet child appears
who isn't you

The two bits of peeling white light
she tossed into us

are a gain, a weight

water falling down
your back in the shower

an edge
you can join

My Daughter Emily Dickinson

To wipe away
the track of your next minute
your little voice claims the mountains go on forever

They really do
in a funny wave
white cityscapes of sand poised at our heads
looped, a kind
delay of form

To turn fast and clean in that line
dust gray and feeling
laid out on the dusty plains

The light makes words in the room

so un-American in its humors
and hugging near death
as stars and the dead
perch, awaiting your glance

Hovering new your hands turn about
themselves as the dead laying a little deeper in the air

It's not a word
but their anger will be

Gooselight and pines from one desert
stand here in the rain of another

at every roof and run-off a wind notes

each drop's leaf and needle touch

a turning over of paper
lacquered, thinnest
layers of our habits

in their excess drops bound
down crevices
Aleppo and France, what thirst and turning
of skirts, Puno and Spain what
resistances of mountain planes
are made, child, in your face

resins in time
the better to move over the waters of this desert
reservoir at whose edge we take our walk

What of this American
faith in artifice?
Dickinson's butterflies
plashless in the, what
the coined word?

Clean-
edged, dry
this plain opens
under a mirroring
sky its

available dead
look down to each grain of sand

those sharpest edges
their binding
single selves
in facets

in such futures
to be simple
and done

THE RIGHT TO SPEAK

Circle Dancing

PETER MOUNTFORD

Fundamentalism, religious or ideological, liberal or conservative—whatever its condition, the allure of fundamentalism is that it provides a reassuring order to things that are, in fact, disorderly.

Even among non-fundamentalists, we require a digestible story—something not much more morally complex than *Die Hard,* or *Indiana Jones.* Friendships I've had—we've all had—grow stronger when we convene and cast judgment on shared acquaintances. Few conversations bind people quicker than when we can align ourselves on the "correct" side of a thing, anything, and observe someone else over there, on the wrong side. We crave, desperately, the simplicity of those clean lines: the bad guy and the good guy, and we seek out a plain binary everywhere we look.

In my life, I have met genuinely good and genuinely bad people. Taken together, I suspect that these purely good or bad people account for about 1 to 3 percent of the people I've known. Everyone else is another kind of person. I am another kind of person. I am flawed, meaning well, more or less, trying to do right by the world, and myself, and by the people I love, but often failing in one or more of these categories. Most of all, I don't have the necessary information to make a good choice, I find.

Should I give a few dollars to that woman who appears to be pregnant and is begging beside the on-ramp of this freeway? It could miraculously change her life for the better, maybe. It could help her baby, which would be nice. Maybe she's not really pregnant? Maybe this gift will somehow damage my life—some freak circumstance involving me needing a few dollars? Maybe, more likely, it'll damage her life in some way? Probably nothing will change. But I really don't know what will happen. I have no idea. I have no useful information, none at all, so I make the choice based on a vague feeling I have, and if I do give her money, I feel good about myself for a minute or two, and then I accelerate into heavy traffic and I forget about her forever.

This is how we are. We are all fumbling, insanely, in the dark.

We join a party, pick a side, and then we're in a team. We have a uniform, a vocabulary. We are not alone.

I am of a certain political tribe—Jon Stewart and Paul Krugman are a couple of our notable leaders—that is quite common here in the United States. We tend to be educated, upper-middle class, and liberal. We like Trader Joes, and Rachel Maddow, and claim to disapprove of Starbucks although we drink their coffee pretty often. About Palestine, we tend to know a certain amount, and we have opinions. Most of us believe in a two-state solution, and that Israel is treating the Palestinians with atrocious brutality. Mostly, the intricacies of the conflict, the history, and the proposed peace plans appear, to us, impossibly detailed and esoteric.

Nonetheless, like all political tribes, or teams, we are confident of our superior position on this and most other political matters. Whether or not you are on my team, I would wager that you, too—whatever your team—you are confident of your superior position on these and most other political matters.

If you want to engage in a meaningful conversation about a way to peace in the Middle East, you should bring with you a working knowledge of the geography of the region (including changes from the last hundred years), familiarity with the 1947 Armistice Agreements, the complex roles of Egypt, Iran, Syria, and the history of Hezbollah, Hamas, the intifadas, a keen understanding of the 1967 borders and their origins, a rudimentary (or better) sense of the thousands of years of history describing Israel and Judah, and the persecution of the Jews, in particular in the twentieth century. Now, assuming you're still with me, try this question on: Should a new Palestinian government invite the Palestinian Diaspora to repatriate the territory, and if so how would that look? It is a question that blooms, ever more ornately, the closer you look at it. Most of the questions around Palestine bloom, endlessly, in this manner.

I do not live within these questions. They are not *mine*. I have never lived in the region—I haven't even visited. I am not religious, at all. So what do I do? Nothing? Am I not entitled to an opinion? I think a great many people would say yes, I am not entitled to an opinion, or if I have an opinion I should shut up about it.

Fine, but I do not know *nothing*. I do know *something*. I did, after all, get a degree in international affairs, and I was briefly an adjunct scholar in a public policy think tank. I am not as out of touch as some (see how I'm trying to put myself into a elite subgroup of my political tribe?). But yes, I am not an expert. I have merely watched it unfold on TV, or read about it in *Foreign Policy*, *Al Jazeera*, the *Economist*, *Harper's*, the *New York Times*, etc. And it *is* arcane, regardless how much I pay attention, it remains stubbornly arcane.

I think there is a good case to be made that I should shut up about this question.

But if everyone who doesn't have a place to talk—who hasn't earned the right to have an opinion because they haven't done the required research, or been touched personally by these questions—remains quiet, then most of the world will sit silent. We will all sit quiet not only on Palestine, but on most of the world's questions.

What is more dangerous? A world where the ignorant rally together in loose teams, based on vague emotional impulses, or a world in which everyone respects the full complexity of things, and therefore do not rally into teams that have thoughts about things that we don't fully understand? Who among us has time to research everything so exhaustively before we go sign that petition, or join in the warm embrace of our protesting brethren?

Consider this: for some reason, a lot of dedicated potheads pleaded with voters in Washington State to vote *against* legalizing marijuana in 2012. I never paid attention to these activists—I have no idea what their argument was. I voted for legal marijuana, and my team won. And I haven't thought about it again since.

In democracies, we have political parties. Notice that word: *Parties*. These things are parties as much as they are political. Welcome to the party, my friend, please make yourself at home.

◆　◆　◆

"Circle dancing is magic," wrote Milan Kundera in *The Book of Laughter and Forgetting*, and he went on to describe a group bound together by ideology joining hands and dancing and laughing until they ascend heavenward.

For Kundera, all spiritual and ideological movements are circle dancing and the circle, crucially, is a *closed* shape, one that creates magical love between members, but if you leave the circle it will close behind you. Whereas, if you leave a row, you can return to it, because it isn't a closed shape. But a row isn't *magic*. A row does not induce levitation or love, it does not solve the problem of not belonging. There is no shape like a circle to create the illusion of belonging, and there is no act like laughter to create the illusion of happiness.

◆　◆　◆

My father was an executive at the IMF—which he once told me, with wide-eyed exasperation, was sometimes called 'the international murder fund' by protesters. For him, it was insane that people didn't understand that the Fund was a force for good in the world. I don't agree with him about the IMF, but I know that he believed that absolutely.

We had a difficult relationship, which had nothing to do with our opposing politics. He lived and breathed global economics. I, on the other hand, liked slam dancing at Bad Brains concerts.

When I was a teenager, the *Financial Times* would arrive at our house, and I'd scan the headlines, but I understood almost nothing. Was NAFTA good or bad?

What about this subsidy on natural gas in Brazil, or the recent election in Turkey?

My mother died when I was eleven, and my father was abruptly not just the breadwinner and advisor to the main parent, he was a single dad with four children and a full-time job. So things were hard in various ways that are irrelevant to this essay. What is relevant is that although my politics have always leaned to the center left, I was forced to see his humanity in a harsh and extremely vivid light. And, as a result, I was forced to recognize the fantastic complexity within the IMF and World Bank. Carolyn Forché has argued that any worthwhile "political" literature erases the distinction between personal and public discourse. That's what was at play in my life, the conflation of the personal and the political was inevitable, they were inseparable.

My friends who have protested outside the IMF will tell you that the organization is trying to rob poor countries of their natural resources. You may well agree with them—it's a popular belief.

That said, it's now widely accepted that the reason that the IMF didn't do more to prevent the Argentinean crisis in 2001 was that too many of the Fund's senior staff at the time were Argentinean. They didn't want to chastise their own country. So, the problem wasn't that the IMF was trying to loot Argentina, the problem was that they were feeling protective of Argentina.

To be clear, I think the IMF has directly hurt hundreds of millions of people. The first piece of writing I ever published was an op-ed for the *Christian Science Monitor* in 2000 criticizing the IMF's policies in Ecuador. I also think—no, I *know*—that the people who work at the IMF believe they're helping the world.

And I know that the IMF and World Bank fail most of the time, and the consequences of their failures are shouldered by the poor. They fail because their staff is harried, and busy, and they are as unimaginative as everyone else on the planet, and they are stressed, they have long commutes, and their mathematical models are flawed, and they are mired in dysfunctional office politics just like everyone else.

So maybe they shouldn't exist at all? A simple solution to a complex problem. But what happens the next time Greece or Mexico or Thailand is facing economic Armageddon? We just let them go? That was the attitude toward Germany after the First World War. If the Germans hadn't been wheelbarrowing cash to the bakeries in the 1920s, Hitler probably wouldn't have found a foothold. The IMF and the World Bank were created in 1944 in an effort to prevent another World War.

Moral clarity—that kind of plangent outrage that I heard in the Dead Kennedys songs I loved as a teenager—is emotionally satisfying, but it is impossible to sustain once you truly see the other side. Then things get difficult, as difficult as reality. We are not living in *Die Hard*. We're living in *The Wire*, but even that is too simple.

The best antidote to prejudice is knowledge, a full and intimate view inside the life of your enemy, whoever your enemy is.

• • •

Despite considerable due-diligence—I know more about the issues at play in Palestine and Israel than I do about, say, the track record of my own city's mayor—I remain trapped in a kind of ideological paralysis about Palestine. I feel incapable of becoming un-ignorant about the Middle East. When I think of Palestine, I am forever that sixteen-year-old scanning the *Financial Times*, finding that he doesn't understand what is good or bad or why it is good or bad.

On the surface, there's a reassuringly simple story about the poor underdog getting beat down by the wealthy overlord. But you don't need to dig deep to discover the anti-Semitism lurking inside of some of the more strident pro-Palestine voices. Also, I've looked into it, and none of us are demons or saints. I do think people mean well, by and large, but I also think no one, or almost no one, is doing a good job of being a saint.

John Oliver recently did a segment on Net Neutrality in which he cut away a couple times to the congressional hearings about Net Neutrality. The monotonous and arcane ramblings seemed designed to prevent a clear understanding of the question. The issue wore its jargon, its obfuscating powers, like a protective coat—and all the while powerful forces were pressing their case behind the scenes. The public stood by, scratching our heads, baffled into complacency.

Of course, the Middle East isn't engaged in a conspiracy to obfuscate, but I do often feel baffled into acquiescence.

• • •

When Trayvon Martin was killed, we all rushed onto Facebook and linked arms virtually and cast our confident scorn at George Zimmerman and his ilk—they made very easy targets, those evil-doers. To this day, I still feel a little spike of glee whenever I hear some story about how Zimmerman's life has been ruined. Fuck him! I wish the worst upon him. I would fire a laser-guided missile at him, if I had one.

Then there was Michael Brown and Ferguson. We were chanting on Facebook, it seemed, and we were together. And we were right—we *are* right!—I know we are right. But are we here and were we there because we are right, or because we want to be together, glaring across that bright line at the wrong people? At abortion clinics, the pro-life protestors must stand back behind a literal line, a barrier, and they embrace each other and weep and yell and chant and they feel alive, and they are not alone, and they will never be alone.

At brunch, if Palestine comes up, I might talk about how I am appalled that my politicians have been co-opted by Israel. These are people I voted for!

People will nod, or shake their heads—either way they want me to know they feel the same, or maybe they're going to take it further. Or maybe they're going to walk it back, but we're just nudging ourselves around on the safe side of that bright line.

In the United States, our politicians can be bought, someone might point out.

And I will agree, wholeheartedly.

I won't talk about how I believe that the issue is much more boring and arcane and confusing. Money does lead politicians around, yes, even principled and generous-hearted politicians are navigating through a complex network of cash flows. If they *really* escaped from the cash, they wouldn't be politicians, they would be people who tried to become politicians and failed. The problem is systemic. But now I'm ruining everyone's brunch, so I won't say that.

At brunch, I'll say that while I can't control forces at work in the Middle East, I can take ownership over what my own congressperson does, also my president, also my senator. Maybe, if there have been some mimosas, I'll talk about sending a letter to my elected officials. More likely, I'll leave it there.

But here, in this essay, for you, I'll go on.

I have never voted for or against someone because of their stance on Palestine or the Middle East. If I'm going to be honest (and why stop now?) these issues do not even rank in my top ten pressing issues when I consider a candidate for office. I might let them know that I disagree, if I get around to sending that email, but I do not expect they'd be surprised by my message, and I do not think they will change. Because I'll still vote for them again, even if they don't change, and they know that. And Israel knows that. And Palestine knows it.

People in my tribe do not seem to want to talk about this dissonance, and I sympathize. I don't really want to talk about it either.

This Is My Fight Too

DURANYA FREEMAN

I shy away from political discussions. My Facebook status is usually an article from *McSweeney's*, or the frequent update that I've lost my phone. When I do post a link to something controversial on social media, I spend far too long perseverating over the exact wording of my comment. Usually I settle for a quote; it's always safer to hide behind someone else's opinions.

I avoid politics because of this: I am nineteen years old and I am terrified of sounding stupid.

You can imagine then, that it was quite a journey for me to write a full-page article in my high school newspaper, my college admissions essay, and a college newspaper article, all on Palestine.

Three years ago, I sat in a lecture hall at the University of Pennsylvania listening to Omar Barghouti speak about the Boycott, Divest, and Sanctions (BDS) movement, and associated campaign. I listened carefully I but I struggled to follow his ideological points and at one point asked my mother, who was with me, what he meant by "Tel Aviv." This is where you might begin to question why I would be listening to one of the leaders of the largest international campaign in support of the people of Palestine when I didn't know the most rudimentary of facts about the force that is occupying that country.

Backtrack: I lived in Bala Cynwyd, Pennsylvania, where there are fifteen synagogues and Jewish community centers within a five-mile radius of my house. My middle school years were a ceaseless stream of Bat and Bar Mitzvahs. My school district observed holidays on Rosh Hashanah and Yom Kippur. Despite my last name, which is often misspelled Friedman, I am not Jewish, but most of my friends attended Hebrew school and spoke about their religion and holidays as though I ought to know what they were talking about. At school, we learned a great deal about the Holocaust, yet never mentioned Palestine.

Palestine did not exist. Hamas did. It made me think.

I lived in a house that forced me to do so. I couldn't just know there were elections happening, I had to pound the pavement and register voters and hand out flyers when I was barely old enough to know the difference between the Senate and the House. The Thanksgiving feast was annually edged by the mention of smallpox. Whatever happened—9/11, burning Qur'ans, abused prisoners, Guantanamo—I was never allowed to look at things from just one side. And so I thought about the country behind Hamas. And, as an editor of the opinion pages of my school newspaper, I decided that I would write about Palestine.

After I sent in my first draft, there was a backlash of unpleasantries from my (Jewish) coeditors. I fought the urge to chalk it up to lessons learned and retract my good intentions. I decided to take the chance to really say something. I edited relentlessly, scouring for inflammatory phrases, inflammatory words, inflammatory semicolons. I triple-checked every statistic, fact, and source.

I wrote about the creation of Israel as compensation for the persecution of the Jewish people by those unrelated to the Palestinians whose land was unilaterally taken to create this home. I wrote about how though that first act was neither acceptable nor diplomatic, generations of Israelis have been born now on "Israeli" soil and, understandably, call it home, and how home, however, is a word that Palestinians have had to relinquish, because of the occupation of their land, the permitting of settlements, and the systematic imprisonment of Palestinian refugees. How could we deny that these were flagrant violations of human rights? I asked why, in American media, Israeli casualties were given names: Yitzchak Amsalem, Mira Sharf, Aharon Smadja, while Palestinians were presented only as numbers? Why were we made to look on them as unimportant, a faceless group whose people bore no resemblance to our faces? I quoted *New York Times* reporter Jodi Rudoren, who wrote, shamelessly, that "Israelis are almost more traumatized," and that the Gazans, "have such limited lives that in many ways they have less to lose," and that Palestinians are "ho-hum about death."

I wrote also about Israelis like Dov Khenin, and liberal politician Zehava Gal-On, and writers such as Amos Oz, who raise their voices on behalf of the Palestinians, of Jewish American journalists like Phillip Weiss, a veteran *New York Observer* reporter who sympathizes with the Palestinian perspective. I argued that, there need to be many more such voices in order to counter those of people like Israeli politician Eli Yishai who said that, "we must blow Gaza back to the Middle Ages destroying all infrastructure including roads and water."

I concluded my high school article this way:

It is my belief that a two-state solution will never lead to peace for, so long as there are two "kinds" of people, there will always be conflict. The only solution is a single state, one that treats both Palestinians and Israelis as human beings and accords each the same rights and dignity. For that to come to pass, we need Israelis to speak up, and we need Americans to make sure that in supporting the battle for Israel we are not losing the war of ideals on the global stage.

Predictably, allegations of anti-Semitism followed. Even my friends criticized me: *Why would you write about Palestine when our school is mostly Jewish?* they asked me. My worst fear, that I was stupid, was a given.

One year later, I sat at my computer, trying desperately to think of 650 words that would somehow define the person I was, and had the potential to become, that would get me into college. I wrote five different essays to five different prompts, including ones about my running (I was very good at it), my life in Maine (which I missed greatly), Outward Bound (where I learned that the essence of who I was had a lot in common with the essence of my peers from the projects of NYC who hailed from broken homes, had gang names, and undergone hardships that I had not), and my eating disorder (which had plagued me throughout my years as an athlete).

I had studiously been avoiding one of the prompts: "Reflect on a time when you challenged a belief or idea. What prompted you to act? Would you make the same decision again?"

My dabblings in politics junior year had left me exhausted, scared, and fed up, but the more I thought about it, the more I realized that I would absolutely make the same decision again. Here is what I wrote, in closing, on the one-year anniversary of my newspaper article:

> I didn't decide to take a stand to make some huge impact on my community; in the end, I didn't, really. I learned that the reason you tell a story is because it needs to be told. You tell it because you can and there are people who can't. No matter how hard it is, you tell it because someone—whether it's a nation, a community, or a lone high school student—needs you to tell it.

The summer before college, I was in Port Angeles, Washington when I got wind of the newest round of attacks, watching in horror as the casualties grew by the hundreds every day. I attended two protests in Seattle organized by local chapters of Voices for Palestine and the Palestine Solidarity Committee. During the second day, we faced a pro-Israel rally separated from our group by the first police barricade I had ever experienced. Although they shouted insults and profanities at us, and we remained calm, and stood in silent protest, our mouths taped shut, the entire row of police, one by one, turned to face us, with their backs to the real aggressors. It was both surreal and chilling.

Today, I keep an active presence on Facebook, sharing posts about Palestine, beginning with those attacks on Gaza in July of 2014. I wrote an article that was a call to action for my peers, as a staff writer for the college newspaper during my first semester there.

I believe that this is the biggest issue of our generation, in the same way that protesting against Vietnam, the Berlin Wall, and Apartheid South Africa belonged to generations before us. Like those struggles, this is not a conflict of religion, or politics, or nationalism. It is a question of humanity. One doesn't have to be the leader of the debate team, a powerful dignitary, or a scholar to feel for the thousands of Palestinians who live in fear and under oppression every second of every day. One simply has to have a basic set of morals that says that such suppression of human beings, of the human spirit, is wrong.

Looking back on my series of small actions, I realize that I am only another face in the crowd, another article attached to my name on Facebook that 90 percent of my friends probably will scroll past. And yet, I am one of the parts who combine to make that larger group, that larger voice that *can* and *does* and *will* change the course of history. I have learned that the only kind of stupidity is that which results from being aware of an injustice, knowing one should speak, but choosing to remain silent.

All Day the Light is Clear

TESS GALLAGHER

Today I wished without mercy
in the bloodless nations of the mind
that a city had gone down with you
as in a war fought—not
on foreign soil, but here
in the part of the country I can't
do without. Then, if I wept for you
inexplicably, as I have
on street corners, I could say the name
of that city and ignite in the memories
of strangers, a companion
sorrow. "Yes," they would say, "Yes,
we know," giving again that name
like a fountain
in some dusty village where the women pause,
dash water across their brows,
and pass on.

And though I shame such power and force it
from my mind, you enter this street
as a touch on the shoulder, a stare that
speaks, or in the brief nods
between workers at change of shift.
I lean on their conquering faces.
I add you to the heap, to the beautiful
multitude for whom only singing
and silence may serve—those
of our city, city of the unmiraculous,
undiminished belonging, toward which
in the green fields—as did the women
of Leningrad—I bow, bow again
and make no sound.

Love Poem to be Read to an Illiterate Friend

I have had to write this down
in my absence and yours. These
things happen. Thinking
of a voice added
I imagine a sympathy outside us
that protects the message
from what can't help
being said.

The times you've kept
your secret, putting on
glasses or glancing into a page
with interest, give again
the hurt you've forgiven, pretending
to be one of us.
So the hope of love
translates as a series of hidden moments
where we like to think
someone was fooled
into it.

Who was I then
who filled these days
with illegible warnings: the marriages
broken, the land
pillaged by speculators, no word
for a stranger?

This island
where I thought the language mine
has left me lonely

and innocent as you or that friend
who let you copy his themes
until the words became pictures
of places you would never go.

Forgive it then
that so much of after
depends on these, the words
which must find you
off the page.

I Have Never Wanted to March

Or wear epaulets. Once I walked
in a hometown parade to celebrate
a salmon derby. I was seven, my hair in
pigtails, a steel flasher strapped diagonally
across my chest *bandolier*-style
(in Catalan *bandolera* from *banda*—band
of people—and *bandoler* meaning bandit).
My black bandit boots were rubber
because here on the flanks of the Olympics
it always rains on our parades.
I believe I pushed a doll buggy.
I believe all parades, especially military
parades, could be improved if
the soldiers wore *bandoliers* made to attract
fish, and if each soldier pushed a doll buggy
inside which were real-seeming babies,
their all-seeing doll-eyes open
to reflect the flight of birds, of balloons
escaped from the hands of children to
hover over the town—higher than flags, higher
than minarets and steeples.
What soldier could forget
collateral damage with those baby faces
locked to their chin straps? It is
conceivable soldiers would resist
pushing doll buggies. Bending over
might spoil the rigidity of their marching.
What about a manual exhorting the patriotic
duty of pushing doll buggies? Treatises
on the symbolic meaning would need to be
written. Hollywood writers might be of use.
Poets and historians could collaborate,
reminding the marchers of chariots, of

Trojan horses, of rickshaws, of any wheeled
conveyance ever pulled, pushed or driven
in service of humankind.
I would like, for instance, to appear
in the next parade as a Trojan horse. When
they open me I'll be seven years old.
There will be at least seven of me
inside me, for effect, and because it's
a mystical number, I won't understand
much about war, in any case—especially
its good reasons. I'll just want to be pushed
over some border into enemy territory, and
when no one's thinking anything except: *what
a pretty horse!* I'll throw open myself
like a flank and climb out, all
seven of me, like a many-legged spider
of myself. I'll speak only
in poetry, my second language, because it
is beautifully made for exploring the miraculous
ordinary event—in which an alchemy
of words agrees to apprentice itself to the possible
as it evades the impossible. Also poetry
doesn't pretend to know answers and speaks best
in questions, the way children do
who want to know everything, and don't believe
only what they're told. I'll be seven
unruly children when they open me up,
and I'll invite the children of the appointed enemy
to climb into my horse for a ride. We'll be seven
together, the way words are
the moment before they are spoken—
those Trojan horses of silence, looking for a border
to roll across like oversized toys
manned by serious children—until one horse
has been pushed back and forth
with its contraband of mutually pirated children
so many times it will be clear to any adult watching
this unseemly display, that enemy territory
is everywhere when anyone's child is at stake, when
the language of governments is reduced to ultimatums,
when it wants to wear epaulets

and to march without
Its doll buggy.
But maybe an edict or two could be made
by one child-ventriloquist through the mouth
of the horse, proposing that the advent of atrocities
be forestalled by much snorting, neighing, prancing and
tail swishing—by long, exhausted parades
of reciprocal child-hostages who may be
rescued only in the language of poetry
which insists on being lucid
and mysterious at once, like a child's hand
appearing from under the tail
of the horse, blindly waiving to make sure that anyone
lined up along the street does not submit entirely
to the illusion of their absence, their
ever-squandered innocence, their hyper-responsive
minds in which a ladybug would actually fly away,
with only its tiny flammable wings,
to save its children from the burning house.

Life hands us lessons in circuitous ways. On a recent visit to Dublin via Paris from Seattle, I was assigned a seat next to a young man. After five months of study in Portland he had been called home because his father was ill. He was intensely sad about his father, whose dilemma wasn't clear to me, though it seemed serious. He had limited English but we spoke. At one point he reached for his rucksack and pulled out a book and handed it to me. It was my language—an American dictionary! It seemed to be almost the only thing in his bag. I tried to comfort him, probably futilely, about his father.

Finally we closed our eyes and slept, side by side. When the plane landed I became involved getting my companion ready for his wheelchair to manage the huge distances of Charles de Gaulle Airport and to find our Dublin flight. I was carried away from my seat-companion without bidding him a proper "good journey," for he had told me he had a very involved passage still to make in order to return to his home in Palestine. Somehow he came and found me as I was struggling to get my companion into a wheelchair. He reached out and took my hand, and said in glorious English: "I am so glad to have met you!" We smiled and I said—"Me too! I hope you stay safe and your father will recover." The pulse of travel carried us apart but our hands were raised, and I thought how fortunate I had been to at last meet my Palestinian grandson.

That interaction reminded me of a poem I wrote, "Love Poem to be Read to an Illiterate Friend," which takes on the story itself, (little "language" but much understanding), and the way that our words have power beyond the pages they occupy, and our words are given weight by our actions. To these I add two others that round out the way I look at Palestine from the far northwestern corner of the United States. "All Day the Light is Clear," though not written about that country or the young man, as poems are writ and live on to speak to other circumstances, I feel it could be so. It addresses, in its way, the distance between where we are, as Americans, and where they are, as Palestinians. The second, "I Have Never Wanted to March," focuses on the innocence of children as they face "the language of governments reduced to ultimatums," and soldiers who put on disguises so they can unsee the children before and within them.

Borderland

DIEGO VÁZQUEZ JR

I am a survivor of the border between the United States and Mexico. I was raised in El Paso, Texas, and discovered the joy of life in Juarez, Mexico.

My heart and soul is conditioned from living in turmoil among those whose lives are prosperous, and peacefully secured with military power. The heart within me is from a borderland of racist backhanded slaps against the language that my family spoke. The rhythm of my soul is tuned from a land where the haves look casually across a political divide at the misery of the have-nots. Stand on any overlook from the United States side of the border and take in the sprawl of brutal poverty and dusty misery, a massive survival that stretches the limits of the sky.

Pick any border with immense poverty on one side and power and prosperity on the other side and there will be cruelty so commonplace as to almost be acceptable. The basic human instinct to offer a sip of water to a parched immigrant too often is seen as traitorous by those in control.

A powerful government, a powerful banking system, a powerful and biased policed force, a powerful and unjust immigration border patrol, a powerful and deeply scarred and abusive church, they combine to nurture an unjust system that turns away from those who seek a future that promises something better than just more tragedy. And we the people hold the weapons of mass destruction within ourselves—our hatred, and our disregard.

I lived with my extended family on the border of El Paso y Juarez. I grew up having to refer to myself as "American," in order to return from two towns zero miles apart. I was interrogated until proven legal. During the rise of the Chicano movement, to declare oneself Chicano at the border became a suicide mission, without explosives.

Immigration is my blood. Abuelo y abuelita immigrated first. Immigration meant four uncles, a father, numerous cousins, and myself, all serving in the armed forces of the United States. The day I was inducted into the United States Army I swore an oath of allegiance to this country.

I don't believe in annihilating people. I am for the right of any people to protect themselves against older men who turn the young into weapons for the elite.

I do not accept the complacency that is thrust upon us by any government that tells us that we can't understand "the situation," because they don't live there. No genius or acquaintance is needed to understand intolerable cruelty.

It is a simple thing to know that walling in Gaza is to imprison an entire population.

LESLIE JAMISON

I remember walking into my seventh grade history class one day and finding that my teacher had drawn a house in chalk on our board. He told us that two different families believed this house was theirs. What would be a fair way to decide who should get to live there? It was an interesting Rawlsian exercise—behind the veil of ignorance, the gauze of parable, what would we see? Make it a duplex? (The two-state solution.) Figure out who'd lived there first? This was 1994, just after the First Intifada, now more than twenty years ago. I wish I could say there is peace in the house today. But there's not.

The piece I've chosen to include is an excerpt from an essay I wrote after attending a literary conference in Tijuana and Mexicali, Mexico in 2010, where I had the chance to speak to several Mexican poets and writers who—in their art and in their daily lives—were reckoning with the enduring impact of the Mexican narco wars. This piece is less an act of witnessing in its own right and more a meditation on the ways in which other writers—much closer to the violence—were finding a language for the breadth and ferocity of its impact.

Surveying or excavating the history of the Israel-Palestine conflict can feel like a series of endless trapdoors: each time you look for a beginning, you find another beginning that precedes it. Many of these beginnings had their origins elsewhere—the McMahon-Hussein Correspondence, the Balfour Declaration, the white papers—just like so much of the history that inflects and perpetuates the narco wars has happened, is happening, elsewhere as well, the result of policy decisions in states whose citizens aren't suffering the chronic consequences of the ongoing violence so deeply. I live in the elsewhere. But that doesn't mean that the people who keep dying aren't my concern. What does it mean to be a writer-citizen living in the midst of violence: in Gaza, in Syria, in Ferguson? I wanted to submit a piece of writing here that did justice to the complexity of violence—how tangled in its lineage and ramifications—but also proposed that we shouldn't shut down or turn off in the face of this complexity: shouldn't stop trying to parse what we can, recognizing the limitations of our perspectives, and shouldn't stop bearing witness to what we see, asking questions of what we can't.

La Frontera

If the road I take into Tijuana is clogged with guns and cars and men in uniform, the pageantry of American panic, the highway I take out is dust-ravaged and ghostly, snaking from the outer barrios to the gaunt hills of a frontier desert. Beyond city limits, shacks perch on muddy slopes strewn with bits of wall and fence. Many have been wrapped or roofed in billboard posters. They look like presents. Their sides show the giant toothpaste tubes and human smiles of advertisements. Eventually, the slums give way to an infamous highway known as the Rumorosa, a roller coaster that twists and dips through the hairpin turns and rockslide slopes of bleached red mountains.

At a lookout point halfway to Mexicali, where the road drops off raggedly to our left, we emerge around a bend to see the partially blackened wreckage of a semi truck. The cab is inches from the edge of the cliff. A man is curled fetal on the ground, bleeding from his forehead. He doesn't look dead. There isn't an ambulance in sight, but a priest stands over the man's body, blocking him from the noon sun and muttering words of prayer, waving at the passing cars: Slow down, slow down. It must be 90 in October and this man wears black vestments that soak up the whole of the heat. His cross glitters silver. The grill of the truck glitters silver behind him.

It's not just that violence happens here—intentional, casual, accidental, incidental—it's that the prospect and the aftermath of violence are constantly crowding you from all sides: men with machine guns on the Avenida Revolución, growling dogs leaping into SUVs to sniff for drugs, a drunk passed out in front of the panadería, a driver so tired or tweaking he barrels his semi into a cliff. We pass a soldier standing alert with a semiautomatic in his hands, apparently guarding the giant pile of scrap tires behind him. There's nothing else in sight. The soldiers of the country stand ready against an uncontrollable violence, perched on trash, their guns pointed at thin air.

In a 2010 op-ed in the *New York Times*, Elmer Mendoza reports that when a troop of Niños Exploradores (something like Boy Scouts) was brought to welcome officials visiting Ciudad Juárez, their scoutmaster took them through a call-and-response routine. "How do the children play in Juárez?" he called. The boys all dropped to the ground.

At a drug checkpoint, our entire van is emptied out. Larger vehicles inevitably attract more suspicion. The soldiers empty our bags. It all feels pro forma, but

173

still—of a climate, of a piece, setting a tone. As we drive away, I glance back and notice that another soldier, this one standing on a truck, had his machine gun trained on us the whole time.

There are no flashy clubs in Mexicali, no zebra burros, no drink specials. You couldn't find a smoking frog to save your life. You can get plastic bags full of chopped cactus or cigarettes for $2. The closest thing to a Spanglish shot glass is the soundtrack at a club called SlowTime, where a woman's voice moans over and over again: "Oh, you fucking me makes me bilingual."

The light is harsher in this city than it was in Tijuana, everything dustier. The hotels advertise rates for four hours instead of one. I don't know what this means, but it seems to mark an important difference in civic culture. In Chinatown, the restaurants serve bean curd with salsa and shark-fin tacos. I eat lunch at Dragón de Oro (the Golden Dragon), whose parking lot runs up against the border itself, a thick brown fence about twenty feet high. The stucco homes and baseball diamonds of Calexico are barely visible through the slats.

At the conference, I meet Oscar, a poet who tells me his vision of Heidegger over chilaquiles one morning, and Marco, who tells me he walked across the border to buy a new pair of Converse in Calexico. Marco also tells me that he abandoned his "lyric self" about a year ago, once his city grew so violent he got scared to leave his house. He needs a new poetry these days. He's interested in repurposing in general and Flarf in particular. Marco teaches college students. His life sounds a lot like mine until it absolutely doesn't. The night before coming to Mexicali, he stayed up till 1:30 to finish grading a batch of papers, then decided to reward himself the next morning by hitting the snooze button. As it turned out, a grenade explosion woke him anyway, two minutes later, followed by a volley of machine-gun fire. "Like a conversation," he says, "one voice and then the response." He says it wasn't anything unusual.

I meet a man named Alfredo, a bearded hedonist and founder of the Shandy Conspiracy. Every time Alfredo sees me, he asks if I'm ready to be Shandyized. All I know about this process is that it will involve "subtlety" and "darkness." He puts out a magazine (the epicenter of his "conspiracy") whose masthead features a lion attacking a zebra. Instead of blood, the zebra's neck issues jets of rainbow fluid. It's Darwin on acid. I catch myself looking at all the artwork here in terms of sociopolitical fractals: How can I see the narco war contained in every illustrated zebra? It's a strange feeling, watching quirk spew from the jaws of war—like a guttural cry, flayed and searing, this absurd fountain of rainbow blood. I bend everything according to the gravity of conflict.

More accurately put, I bend what I can understand. There's so much that eludes me. In a crowd of bilingual writers, my Spanish is embarrassing, and this embarrassment starts to shade into a deeper sense of political and national shame. I'm afraid to talk about the current landscape of the narco wars because I'm afraid of getting something wrong. Americans are known for getting things wrong when it comes to conflicts in other countries. So I listen. I gradually get a sense of the terrain. The Sinaloa Cartel controls much of the Western Seaboard—where most of the weed is grown, and a frontier mythos maintains the drug dealer as outlaw—while the Gulf Cartel operates along the Gulf, trafficking coke and Central American illegals called pollos, peasants whom they either smuggle or extort.

Reading about the drug wars is like untangling a web of intricate double negatives. One cartel pays a prison warden to set prisoners free at night so they can act as assassins targeting the key players in another cartel, then the targeted cartel captures a police officer and tortures him until he admits to this corruption. They tape and broadcast his confession. The authorities step in, the warden is removed, the prisoners riot to bring her back; the reporters who cover the riots are kidnapped by the rivals of the cartel that released the videotape of the tortured officer. They counter-release their own videotapes of other tortured men confessing to other corruptions.

Got it?

Tracking the particulars is like listening to a horrific kind of witty banter in a language built for others' mouths, finding yourself participating in a conversation in which you have no ability to speak. "Conversation" means something new in this place: a flood of words I can't understand, the call-and-response patter of semiautomatics I've never heard.

I get to know another cast, not authors but killers: There's El Teo, vying for control of the Tijuana Cartel, who likes to kill at parties because it makes his message more visible; and there's El Pozolero ("the Stewmaker"), who dissolves El Teo's victims in acid once their message needs to turn invisible again. The most famous drug lord in Mexico is El Chapo ("Shorty"), head of the Sinaloa Cartel and currently ranked 60th on Forbes's list of the most powerful people in the world. That puts him behind Barack Obama (2), Osama bin Laden (57), and the Dalai Lama (39), but ahead of Oprah Winfrey (64) and Julian Assange (68). The president of Mexico didn't make the list at all. In Mexicali, I find myself learning the statistics of two economies—authors don't get paid advances for their work, hit men in Ciudad Juárez get 2,000 pesos a job—and the contours of two parallel geographies, one mapping the narco wars and another the landscape of literary production. This first topography is tissued like a horrible veil across the second. Durango, for example, is where El Chapo found his teenage bride, but it's also home to a poet who wears combat boots and spits when he reads his poems, which are mostly about tits. Sinaloa is home to its namesake cartel, obviously, but it's also home to Oscar and his Heidegger study groups. The capital of Sinaloa, Culiacán, has a cemetery full of two-story drug-lord mausoleums, impeccably furnished and air-conditioned for the comfort of mourning friends and family. Across town from these palaces, Oscar lives in a house with his kitten, Heidie.

I imagine an entire menagerie: a dog named Dasein, two birds named Tiempo and Ser. I imagine an air conditioner humming quietly next to the ashes of a man. I am trying to merge these two Sinaloas, to make them the same.

The geography lesson moves east: Tamaulipas is a region famous for the August massacre of seventy-two illegals who wouldn't pay up when the Cártel del Golfo asked them to. Wouldn't. Right. Couldn't. But Tamaulipas is also home to Marco, the poet interested in Flarf. When I think of Flarf, I think of poems that deconstruct and splice together blog posts about Iraqi oil and Justin Timberlake's sex life. It's true that Marco is up to something like this, but his project is made of different materials and perhaps a bit less irony. He is repurposing the language of the conflict for his poems. He trolls Internet message boards full of posts from people sequestered in their homes. He takes phrases from the signs that cartels leave on the corpses of their victims, and scraps from the messages they scribble onto the skin of the dead. He cuts up quotes; fits the puzzle pieces of fear back together to make his poems. This is a new iteration: Flarf from and for and of the narco wars. Narco-Flarf. I wonder how this kind of work preserves that part of Flarf that feels so central: its sense of humor. I wonder whether this matters. To judge from how often Marco laughs (very), it matters a lot.

The whole encuentro is an odd mixture of revelry and seriousness. People speak constantly and painfully about the narco wars but they also do a lot of coke. They do it off one another's house keys, just like I imagined they would, and I find myself wondering about those keys and the locks they turn. How many locks do people have in their homes? More than they did before? How often do they go to sleep afraid?

Just a few weeks before coming to Mexicali, Marco presented his work at an American gallery called LACE (Los Angeles Contemporary Exhibitions). Marco named his piece SPAM. It was a wall hanging that showcased a poem he'd made from message board fragments—in this case, posts from residents of Comales, a barrio on the outskirts of Tamaulipas that had essentially become a cluster of hideout bunkers.

Marco called the neighborhood zona cero. Ground zero.

On the internet, and in Marco's work, these zona cero voices find a mobility their bodies have been denied: "no se trabaja, no hay escuela, tiendas cerradas . . . estamos muriendo poco a poco" ("there isn't work, there isn't school, the shops are closed . . . we are dying little by little"). The language isn't "poetic" because it didn't start as poetry. It started as a cry. And now it's something else. Marco, of course, abandoned his lyric self a few years back. Now his poems have no single speaker but a mass of ordinary voices that speak these desperate words, coaxed into cadence by his own sequestered hands.

SPAM was made in Tamaulipas and shown in Los Angeles, but it's composed of materials from an immaterial network (the internet) that hangs suspended, contrapuntal and infinite, in between these places and essentially in no place at all. The piece has some faith in the internet but also understands how it abstracts experience into something nonsensical or illegible (spam!). The piece mocks borders but speaks explicitly toward them: "La pieza intentará crear diálogo más allá de las fronteras . . ." The piece is not simply a dispatch, Marco writes, but rather part of a conversation—the same conversation that includes the grenade explosion on his street.

CORBAN ADDISON

I wrote the article below for the *Huffington Post* after the publication of my second novel, which addresses human rights in Southern Africa. I chose it for this anthology because the underlying theme of the piece—the essential role of empathy in promoting human dignity—is relevant to every conflict, whatever its source and particulars. Whereas conflicts proliferate where difference, misunderstanding, and prejudice mix with historical pain and present fear, empathy begins with the unqualified affirmation of our common humanity.

All of Us Are African

There's an exchange in the film *Beyond the Gates* that transcends the script, transcends even the Rwandan genocide. It illumines a subtle mood in the West, a deficit of empathy toward Africa that persists twenty years later. Rachel, the BBC reporter, tells Joe, the schoolteacher, that she cried every day covering the Bosnian genocide, but in Rwanda, "not a tear." Then she makes an unforgettable confession: "Any time I saw a dead Bosnian woman, a white woman, I thought that could be my mum. Over here, they're just dead Africans."

What is it about Africa that makes so many of us tune out and turn away? Is it guilt about the devastation our ancestors wreaked through colonialism and slavery? Is it subliminal racism (among Anglos, at least) toward the millions of Africans who are black? Is it the impression that the continent is hopeless, that the wars and coups and corruption and famine and disease we've seen in the headlines prove that Africa is a problem without a solution? Or is it, as Rachel puts it in the film, that, "we're all just selfish pieces of work in the end"?

Whatever the source of the poison, there is an antidote. The human heart is moved to empathy when we see our own faces in the faces of strangers. What we need is an undistorted lens of perception—part prism and part mirror—that can separate our prejudices from the truth at the core of our humanity: that the blood that runs in my veins is the same blood that runs in the veins of a Rwandan, a Zambian, a South African, and so on; that beneath the epidermis of ethnicity and culture and language and history we are all the same.

One might think that experience is the lens. But sense knowledge is insufficient. We can see something with our eyes, hear it with our ears, and still shrug it off with our hearts. For empathy to happen, experience must connect with feeling.

The lens we need is story.

There is a reason that story is the world's oldest language. It teaches us who we are. It awakens the conscience to right and wrong. It conveys truth in the vernacular of the heart. As a novelist, I admit I am biased, but I have seen the humanizing effects of story in my own life, both in the works of others and in researching my own work, including my recent novel about Southern Africa.

It was a story, in fact, that inspired the novel—the story of a Zambian girl with Down syndrome who had been raped by a neighbor and whose abuser never would have seen the inside of a jail cell if not for a team of courageous non-profit lawyers who intervened and ensured that justice was served. I traveled to Zambia and spent time with these lawyers and with their colleagues in medicine, law enforcement, and development, investigating the epidemic of gender-based violence in their community. I went into the compounds and met kids with intellectual disabilities—a little boy with cerebral palsy whose parents weren't feeding him, a child with Down syndrome who loved to laugh. I spent time in South Africa with epidemiologists and health workers who care for people living with HIV. The stories I heard broke my heart and made me fall in love with Africa.

My goal as a storyteller is simple—to evoke empathy in my readers. In writing about Africa, I hoped to bring the continent alive in all its splendor and brokenness; to give faces and names to women and girls who suffer in distant lands but who are no different from our own mothers and daughters; to remind us that gender-based violence is a human problem, not an African problem—that rape and abuse happen all around us; and to inspire us in the West to extend our efforts to protect the most vulnerable in Africa and the developing world from exploitation and provide life-saving medical care to those who cannot afford it.

It doesn't take a celebrity like Bono or a philanthropist like Bill Gates to care about the future of Africa. All it takes is a person honest enough to admit what science and religion already tell us: we all come from the same womb. In the end, all of us are African because all of us are human.

Shadowboxing: Eyeless in Gaza and Ukraine

ASKOLD MELNYCZUK

Who has power enough to proclaim that the defenders are doing the attacking, that the sentinels sleep, the trusted plunder, and those who watch over us are killers?

—Cervantes

The Italian philosopher Franco "Bifo" Berardi blames the financial crisis of 2008 on the poet Arthur Rimbaud. Not in so many words—but that's the implication of his recent book *The Uprising: On Poetry and Finance*. Briefly, Berardi translates Rimbaud's celebrated expression "deregelment de tous les sens" not as it's traditionally rendered in English, "derangement of all the senses," but as their "deregulation." Once common sense has been overthrown and the familiar relationship between word and object severed, all hell breaks loose too—first in the mind, and subsequently in the realm of the senses. All kinds of financial shenanigans become possible. Financial instruments such as derivatives, whose ostensible worth derives from the valuation of objects already de- and re-contextualized from their natural states, grow ever more powerful even as they become more ethereal and abstract.

I'll let others whistle Ockham's razor through the argument. What intrigues me in Bifo's theory is his corollary: just as poets helped destabilize our world, so too can they contribute to its transfiguration. Poetry, in Bifo's view, is "the sensuous body of language," with resources capable of compelling a linguistic realignment until word and object recover a more direct relationship. "A lemon is not an oboe / because I say so," wrote poet James Galvin. Yet we are invited to believe that the slaughter of children is somehow leading us toward peace.

Like Bifo, I have hopes that poetry might help set the world back on its axis. But can we really fault poetry if it fails to find a vocabulary adequate to our bewildering moment? Is it possible that our language, and all the work it does, not merely in aesthetics, but in the fields of law, policy, and human rights, has spun too far out of control ever to recover? Can words possibly reclaim their purchase on the real, and thereby restore us to our senses? Or have we been deranged too long? Have the torture memos issued by members of the Bush administration and the relentless lies streaming out of this White House—about the NSA, the CIA, drones, the economy, the situation in Iraq and Afghanistan, about Syria, about Israel—forced on us such radical doubt that we will never again trust a word spoken by anyone in authority?

Earlier this month, the world briefly achieved a fearful symmetry when the number of casualties in both Gaza and Ukraine topped 1,000, with 800 of these presumed to be civilian dead. Since then, the numbers have risen. As I write this, Palestinians are digging mass graves for the nearly 2,000 dead in Gaza. They're unable to offer proper burials because cement isn't allowed across the border. Children's bodies are being stored in ice cream freezers. According to the *Huffington Post*, one in four of the dead are children. Nearly half a million people—a quarter of the population of Gaza—have been displaced. Imagine a quarter of the US population rendered homeless. Israelis shelled UN schools sheltering refugees. Human Rights Watch notes that civilians in the village of Khuza, near the Israeli border, were not only shelled: they were shot trying to escape the fighting. The numbers suggest a point I've made here before: these days, in a war, the safest place to be is in uniform. Why anyone would want to thank people for such service beggars the imagination.

The murder of children by Israeli forces is as dumbfounding as the image of Russian separatists on Ukrainian territory robbing the corpses of the passengers of the downed Malaysian plane right in Gogol's back yard. The Russian leader of the separatists speculated on social media that the plane was in fact carrying only corpses—that the separatists had been set up. Never mind that they consistently claimed they didn't do it. Chichikov, the protagonist of *Dead Souls*, traveled across the countryside buying up dead serfs in a get-rich-quick scheme that made better sense than many of our current policies. Chichikov, purveyor of dead souls, may be the prototype for politicians worldwide. The war crimes committed both by the previous US administration and this one go unpunished. The criminal conduct of our bankers and the suits on Wall Street goes unpunished. If, by the old definitions, money laundering, fraud, and cheating were once regarded as crimes—and, as Matt Taibbi and others have demonstrated, countless bankers and Wall Street operators indulged in such behaviors yet have never been punished for them—then maybe we need to change the definition of the word *crime*. Maybe the crimes of the past should be reclassified as the business practices of the future.

Like Bifo I believe in the power of poetry. But let's admit, the task before it is daunting.

Returned from Long Travels

JANE HIRSHFIELD

Author's note: This piece is adapted from a column first written for the *American Poetry Review*'s "The Poet About The Poem" feature. The poem here included appeared in the book *Come, Thief* (Knopf, 2011), retitled "Izmir."

In the spring of 2007, I was invited to join the New Symposium, a conversation on the island of Paros sponsored by the University of Iowa's International Writing Program. The subject that year was "Justice." A group of writers would gather from Russia, Burma, India, South Africa, Peru, Nigeria, Algeria, Turkey, and elsewhere to spend some days exchanging ideas, disappointments, analyses, anecdotes, hopes. One man had spent his boyhood under apartheid, another had experienced Peru's Shining Path. A woman sat at a café table by the Aegean mixing for us, with ingredients taken from a large straw bag, a traditional Burmese salad of dried tea leaves and ginger. She described calmly, without any visible residue, her near-death in prison in the country still her home.

Not long before the trip, there was a phone call. Might the American writers want, before and after the larger conversation, to see some of the nearby places where issues of justice might be recognized as particularly pressing? In Iraq then (as still, at the time of this writing), the counted and uncounted losses were climbing a night-fever ladder. Gaza was nearing its shift from Fatah to Hamas. In Istanbul, Hrant Dink, the editor of the tiny Turkish-Armenian newspaper *Agos*, had been assassinated a few months before, just outside the paper's walk-up apartment offices; a million people had marched soon after, in solidarity and protest. Yes, I would very much like to go to Syria, Jordan, Israel, Ramallah, and Turkey, in addition to Greece.

We met with Syria's Grand Mufti and Damascene Christians; with the new editor of *Agos* and the editor of *Zamman*, the Turkish ruling party's paper, 100 times larger in circulation. An Istanbul baker, practitioner of what can only be called baklava diplomacy, gave instructions to dip the pieces into bowls of whipped sheep's cream and chopped pistachios. We met with a blind Jordanian professor of English literature, a Tel Aviv filmmaking couple (recipients, a week later, of the Cannes Palme D'Or), and Afro-Palestinian social workers, their families originally from Senegal and Somalia, who were trying to save the last playground in East Jerusalem from conversion to settlers' apartments. "The lungs of the city," one called it. Looking out from that playground's fence, the Dome of the Rock glittered in the middle distance; on a wall mural, a painted dove lifted from thick barbed wire while behind it a woman's three-foot-high painted face dropped large, black tears.

Everywhere we went, we met with English-speaking university students, who gathered around each of us in the halls after the formal presentations and would not let us go.

I asked, "What would you like me to tell people for you, when I go home?" They answered, each place we went, "Tell them that we are just like you, we want respect, we want to fall in love, we want to study." In Syria, home by then to three-quarter million Iraqi refugees, where driving from Aleppo to Damascus we passed a green highway sign for Baghdad looking just like the turn-off for Sacramento when driving between San Francisco and LA: "Tell them we are Syrians, not 'Arabs,' not terrorists. Tell them we are afraid. Tell them we are wondering if this is what it must look like when democracy comes." What would I do, one young woman asked, if my brother were asked to bomb them? Tie him to his bed, I answered, though I don't have a brother.

At Ramallah's Bir Zeit University, a girl described her daily experiences crossing from Jerusalem and back. She never knew if navigating the guard post into the Palestinian Territory would take twenty minutes or six hours. Living in East Jerusalem brought rights and possibilities that made the trip worth making. She recounted being spat upon, shouted at in a language she didn't speak, prodded like livestock, humiliated in countless small ways. Then she added what became for me the most memorable sentences of the entire trip, "Mostly I feel sorry for the soldiers. I know what is being done to me. They don't know what's being done to them."

The Wall our group passed through so quickly, still under construction, was shocking, failure's concretization. No graffiti on the Palestinian side condemned it more loudly than its own existence.

"Returned from Long Travels" was written immediately after that trip. The 4:30 a.m. call to prayer in Istanbul haunting the ears one morning, California chickadees the next—we are not constituted to encompass such transitions.

Returned from Long Travels

Waking
after long travels

not recognizing the light

the windows

the calls of the birds of this place

not even your own planted roses

not knowing if this
is exhaustion
or failure

or transformation into
some changed existence
as yet
unacknowledged

like the fields
of red
and blue tulips
of stylized Izmir

painted now onto a bowl
now onto a vase

"The Poet on the Poem," this column is titled. OK then, something about the poem. It is unpunctuated, a relatively rare practice for me at the time I wrote it. I might say now of this choice that it was because the experience held by these lines was one of finding myself undone and, quite literally disoriented, stripped of context and markers. When I wrote it, though, I was not making a conscious aesthetic or semiotic decision. I knew only that any attempt at a guiding notation felt like both vertigo and lying. I knew I knew nothing, except that I had been translated from my prior life in ways I could not then name or objectively comprehend. I still cannot.

Maps separate what is continuous into fragments; fixed names harm. The admission of bewilderment and ignorance, the willingness to sit inside incomprehension and grief, may be at times what is most needed for the beginning of honest response. The editor of *Agos* said, in his crammed office, "It does us no good for the US Congress to pass a declaration that there was an Armenian genocide. That word is a red flag to a bull. What will help is that young people here talk to one another, and this has started to happen. What will help is that the stories be told."

We were asked to write afterwords for our papers for the New Symposium. Mine closed with this:

I feel increasingly, though, that even "remedy" is the wrong word. There can be healing, but no full cure. The broken bone will always ache in the rain . . . The effect on me of these days of conversation has been, perhaps surprisingly, an increase of grief. I've grown less optimistic and more sad. This isn't, though, a bad thing. When the arrogance of certainty loosens its grip, we loosen ours. Life is fragile, small, perennially vulnerable, and wants to be held softly. The statue of Justice, I now think, is blindfolded so we cannot see it is weeping. The scales tremble in its hand, and that is what we call balance.

TOMAS Q. MORIN

The three poems I've chosen are not what a purist might call true political poems. The moments in our history that inspired them (water boarding, drones, kidnapping) are not placed front and center for critique. The reason for this is because anyone with a moral compass knows these things are bad. Instead, I tried to examine how people react to these injustices. If my poems have a compass, it's my hope that it points toward decency.

Extraordinary Rendition

for Philip Levine

When the CIA said, *An extraordinary rendition
has been performed*, I knew Lester Young
blowing his saxophone in that way he did
when Billie Holiday was a few feet away
smoking, singing "I Can't Get Started,"
was not what they had in mind. No, the agent
at the podium talking to reporters
who spends most of his days staring
at computer screens riddled with numbers
and names and maps of places he's never been
probably thought of a man in a hood
far from home swimming
in a room flooded with questions.
If the agent had children
to pick up from school after work
maybe he thought, in spite of his training,
of the hooded man's daughter waking
to find her father gone, her mother
in pieces. What might never cross his mind
is how sometimes that same girl
or any one of a hundred others
might be imagining him
an ocean away, standing in a pressroom
in a charcoal suit, one size too big,
stammering to explain the state
of their nameless fathers one day, the wail
a drone makes the next. In her mind
and language "extraordinary rendition"
still means her mother humming
"Somebody Loves Me" with more heart
than anyone she's ever heard
before or since. If you think the agent

and daughter will meet at the end of this poem
for the first time, then you're wrong
because they met many years ago
when he closed his eyes
and the trumpet she presses against
her lips when she dreams entered his sleep
like a bird made of metal. Hungry
and not sure of what it saw, it plunged
toward the cut open chest
of our agent (it is always this way
in his dreams) as if diving into a lake
and then soared to a great height
from where it dropped his unbreakable heart
that whistled as it zipped past our windows
just before it hit the sidewalk.
Because this scene will repeat itself
for years, a therapist will one day say *guilt,*
forgiveness, and *pain* to our agent
to unsuccessfully explain how death,
when it comes from the sky, makes a music
so hypnotic you will never forget it,
a truth that has always been obvious
to the daughters of Honduras
and Ukraine, Palestine and St. Louis.

112ᵗʰ Congress Blues

Between those symbols of vision the pyramid
and eagle In God We Trust sits in sturdy
caps where it has testified since the 1955
Congress yoked Yahweh to the sawbuck,
which the nickel would say was about time
because it had been preaching the faith
ever since the last days of Lincoln, though
back then it carried a shield and not
the mug of Jefferson, he of the splendid
mind that cleansed the Gospels of Plato
by that miracle of miracles called reading
until all that was left was a Jefferson Jesus
who was wearing tye wigs when he ascended
to the dome of Monticello from where
on a day without clouds he could see
down from the little mountain past the apple
and peach trees all the way to the debating
loons on Capitol Hill who believed then and now
in evil, that there is a hell with a devil
two shades redder than Oklahoma
dirt, that you can know him by his goat
hoof, or his less famous chicken foot
which you can buy, nails intact, at the grocery store
where they are called chicken paws, not feet,
which is no doubt for the squeamish
who can't bring themselves to eat a foot,
though they have probably chewed
and ripped apart a fried leg or a breast
with such enthusiasm it would make a hen
or two probably faint at the sight and to
the good vegetarians wondering where
is the divine justice in all of this tearing

of flesh they have only to listen to the crunch
of the special recipe skin as it cuts the cheek
and gums of my brother carnivores
just enough for one of my kind to yell Goddamn
and call up his state rep. who knowing nothing
better to do proposes a law that already
exists when he should instead order
a two-piece special with a biscuit
and bleed a little, and run his tongue over it
until he can remember for our country
it's never really been about money
or God as about the pain in which we trust.

At the Supermarket

What have I forgotten? Milk for bones—
Salt for blood—A fresh loaf
for sleep. Outside, Sunday morning
has expired. The line is long
for this hour. When the doors open
the squawks of gulls blown too far inland
announce nothing is impossible. The cashier
vanishes again for the cigarette key
and the moment slows the way moments do
when the eye is fixed for too long—:
the man in front of me smells tart,
like solder; a woman's clutch
blurs into the business end of a rabbit,
while her blond son negotiates
a landslide of candy. Before my eyes
water and wash away the fog, a hand,
mottled indigo like a map of archipelagoes,
brushes my lettuce as the man behind me
leans forward to say, "Would you look at that?"
On the cover of a magazine, a man is bound;
above him, a white metal bowl
trimmed in navy, big enough to wash an infant in;
from within, a sheer, crystalline arm
reaches down the page to the pit of his mouth;
in the foreground, his stomach swells
pale over the words, manifest in a slanted,
judicial font: *What Can Water Cure?*
"Look, like a froggie," the boy giggles,
pleased to have discovered something familiar.
His mother, shocked, covers his mouth
and whispers about their box of ice cream,
praline I think, that is already sweating.

If we were trapped in a Rockwell,
the boy would be on his knees
with a ladder truck, imagining all the fire ants
he would douse and save from themselves.
And his hero's face would be grim and grave
like the gorilla slung from a pole
on the *National Geographic*.
And because love is better shared,
there would be a sister for the boy,
clutching her wooden doll, whose arms
join deep within her maple body
to a single peg so that she can only cheer
and mime *ra ra ra* with the thick red "o"
drawn where her nose should be.
An exotic cigar juts from a jeweler's mouth
—is this me? Or am I the carpentered parrot
clutching a ring, drawn toward the door
and the dull horizon that is always itself,
no matter how jungled his dreams?

"What?" I say, then, "Oh, yes, horrible . . ."
in that blunt, exasperated voice we perfect
during times like this. The counter resumes
with a jolt and my cherry tomatoes,
the last of the heirloom season, roll
from their bag toward the awful laser eye
we are taught to avoid lest one go blind.
(This must be what it's like to be seen
by God: a lidless light sunk in the dark
scanning the soul.) Now beer, now crackers—;
the girl totals and totals what we owe,
as we inch and inch toward the infinite.

Tunnels

MATT BELL

It is impossible to proceed without acknowledging my ignorance. I do not know where I am in this story. I have never been to Israel or Palestine. More than likely, I will never go. When I think of these places, what I summon are confabulations, fabrications, combinations of news reports, YouTube videos, propaganda both obvious and subtle. We see what we want to see.

Too often the real state remains hidden, inaccessible to us, beneath the state we have dreamed.

In 2014, Al Jazeera estimated there were over a thousand smuggling tunnels running underneath the border between Gaza and Egypt, and at first I thought that I would write a story about these tunnels, about the men who work them. Watching a documentary online, I learn how some of the tunnels begin in the basements of houses bought to mask their construction, but I cannot imagine the public portion of this tunnel-masking house, nor the house's exterior, nor the street where it's located. The tunnels are dug by hand, twenty-five meters deep, their walls and ceilings reinforced by wooden supports. A winch carries displaced dirt out of the earth, into the basement of the house, where it can be wheelbarrowed . . . where? The video does not show how the dirt is removed, hidden, kept secret. The workers explain that when they believe they have made it under the border and into Egypt, they push a marker up through the earth, where other men on the surface can see it and report back: have they gone too far or not far enough? Work resumes, and the diggers move forward by slow guesses, costly approximations.

These films do not give me the details I want to know so that I might write about these men, details I might only truly be able to learn firsthand: How do they mask the sound of their work? How do they explain the piles of dirt that must be left somewhere? Are they are stored in the rooms of the house which masks the hole, thick earth and clay clogging the rooms, ruining the house for any other purpose? Perhaps the house will never be inhabited again, but still food and medicine will come through the tunnels, vehicles and fuel and even livestock. I watch men dragging buckets of earth out into the sunshine, the outside of the tunnel surprisingly visible to the world. Where has the house gone? Is this the same tunnel? Are we still in Gaza or have we crossed over into Egypt?

As a fiction writer, verisimilitude is not everything but with certain topics it takes on a moral dimension: A reader cannot be expected to make sure interpretations from suspect information. I believe what I am told, but my surety vacillates. It is impossible to verify what I am seeing and hearing—the more I learn the less I know.

But perhaps I *don't* need dominion over this narrative to be useful. Perhaps I can still journey into this story in other ways, to bring back something true that can be given to others.

I watch more videos, taking notes, looking for the smaller details that might unlock this life for me. I watch gravel, cement, cigarettes, sugar, all manner of goods move through the tunnels, followed by car parts, canned food, livestock, medicine, everything else you might imagine, most of it plastic-wrapped, dragged on sledges through the underground. If there are weapons coming through the tunnels, as the Israeli military says there are and as these workers claim there are not, the videos I watch do not show them. Instead they show me markets stocked with products that could only have come through the tunnels and I think of how often I don't know where my food is made, where it is grown, how it is processed or moved to market. Here perhaps there would be less confusion, even though the routes are hidden beneath the earth. One Gazan market stall is stocked with corn flakes, canned goods, containers of juice, all their labels printed in English. How far have these familiar products journeyed to be here?

According to the *Economist*, prices in these markets soared after the new Egyptian government destroyed many of the tunnels in 2013, as shelves emptied, as basic utilities were suspended when fuel became scarce. If these necessities require an illegal infrastructure to exist, isn't that a humanitarian crisis? I can picture the empty market stalls that resulted from that destruction, I can even imagine the anxiety and fear of that emptiness as it lasted days, weeks, a month.

As a writer, I question the ethics of inhabiting a story that isn't mine, and in the past this has kept me from the attempt. Now, increasingly, I feel called to try, to risk saying the wrong thing, to go with my imagination where I might not go myself, in the hope of illuminating for others, that which concerns me.

I continue. I watch as cement and gravel and iron, all illegal to import, are moved through the tunnels and then by van "throughout Gaza," a phrase that highlights the imprecision of my imagination: from where to where, exactly? I know only the gross anatomy of this landscape, these cities, what I can glean from the internet, from overlaid satellite maps. I watch as horned cattle appear in the tunnel, then are lifted out of the earth and into the basement of a house in Gaza. I do not know where the cattle came from, except in the broadest sense. The video begins too late, ends too early to answer my questions. I do not know what is being left out, what might complicate the narrative I am being shown. If I had the names of these masked men it might change how I felt about them—they might come in out of abstraction, might become individuals instead of types—but for now, this is as real as these particular men will be to me. But is it real enough?

The political tactic that I have come to fear the most is doubt, in the way it is wielded by fearmongers of all types, at home and abroad. But how can I try to understand the lives of these men, the provenance of this cow, its ultimate destination, without being willing to pass through doubt at what I am being shown, without overcoming my skepticism at the interpretations suggested by the filmmakers?

In the next video a tunnel worker is lifted out by the same kind of winch the cattle rode, and the dirt rode. Seated precariously on a board suspended like a homemade swing, his bare feet press against the packed dirt walls as he disappears into the sunlit world above. A moment later, this man or another just as young appears on camera, speaking of his motivations for working in the tunnels. He says he is not a revolutionary or a terrorist, only a student who cannot afford his fees. "I have young siblings," he says, "but I have come here to survive."

"Fifty families live on the proceeds of this tunnel," another worker explains. "We have no other work but the tunnels." But for the depths of the tunnels, the plastic wrap on the goods, this could be a loading dock anywhere, and it is the familiarity that moves: this setting is novel and terrifying but the work is recognizable, but the motives are my motives, the same reasons I go to work every day, in my much less-dangerous job, in a city where I am allowed to move freely, where I am allowed to think and speak as I choose.

"Our lives are hard and bitter," the next man says. "Every day men die in the tunnel. Some are just children but they need to live." The documentary does not linger but I pause, go back, listen again, then check my impressions against other sources. According to James Verini, writing for *National Geographic,* over fifteen thousand people worked in and around the tunnels at the height of their operation, and their efforts created work for tens of thousands more. In 2014, the magazine estimated that two-thirds of the consumer goods in Gaza were brought in through the tunnels. Elsewhere in his article, Verini quotes a government engineer, who says, "We did not choose to use the tunnels. But it was too hard for us to stand still during the siege and expect war and poverty."

The tunnels used to bring in food and supplies and other materials into Gaza to undermine the border feel both necessary and inevitable, an obvious result of the blockade. The tunnels used by Hamas to hide and store weapons or to support attacks in Israel are perhaps also inevitable, but their presence complicates the existence of the other. Like so much else in Israel and Gaza, the actions of a few are often used to stand in for the actions of all.

But a tunnel isn't a bomb. It isn't by itself an act of terrorism, isn't an object with only one use. It is a kind of secret—a way of moving unseen—and of course it can be a violation, when it crosses a border, when it undermines a wall—but those actions can have their own moral might, in the right circumstance, done for the right reasons. And so a tunnel is by itself inert: It's what comes through the tunnel that makes all the difference to me. Any use of the tunnels to smuggle weapons—even though they are probably not the same tunnels as the ones used to smuggle necessary consumer goods—inevitably taints the other tunnels, their nobler uses.

It is not so different with language, which can be used to oppress a people, which can be used to help set them free.

I watch more videos, I read more articles, more op-eds. Despite my resistance, soon enough the tunnel workers begin to seem like representatives of types, their individuality subsumed into the arguments their bodies and their actions are made to participate in by journalists and politicians. The more I research, the further I get from the human beings at the center of these stories, and the more distant I feel from the lives I have just barely been allowed to glimpse. My empathy is replaced by doubt and confusion, coalescing around a feeling of helplessness. I don't know what to write next—and who does this feeling serve? Certainly not those most in need of our help. Silence, whatever its reason, serves only the status quo.

For now, fiction feels insufficient to the task of writing about these men, their tunnels. I have command only over these: my questions, my doubts, my worries, my fears. I fear that, given the state of the world, making art is not enough of an action, an anxiety that is beginning to underpin much of the writing I'm doing, as if the disease can be cured by another inoculation of the same sickness. For a person with all the privileges of time and energy that being a writer requires, what is the right response to clear and present injustices? A story will probably not stop a bomb from being dropped. A poem is unlikely to convince either a president or a freedom fighter to turn away from violence; neither is likely to read the poem. A poem or a story is neither bullet nor shield, neither rocket nor wall. Our art fights no wars. So what is the real power of the art we create? For whom do we write?

Perhaps the best we can hope is that our art might become another kind of tunnels, used always for the good of others, making connections between two walled-off parts of ourselves, between people who seem to defy reconciliation. Perhaps this art might take us into countries we could otherwise never hope to see, showing us what we are afraid to know, what it will cost us to know more. These works of literature would have to refuse mere cleverness, mere entertainment. They might be clever or entertaining but they would have to always be doing something more dangerous, harder, more lasting.

Is it possible to send a word to tunnel through a brick of prose? Perhaps we might send the most concrete words first: *shovel* or *bucket. Rope* or *winch.* They descend but they do not necessarily do better work than an abstraction. What about *justice.* What about *mercy.* Try pressing one of those words against the hard ground of hateful rhetoric and see how far you get. The lines and serifs of a word can only go so far. Put the blade of *forgiveness* against the hard language spoken on either side of the wall and sooner or later it will snap right off.

We will not give up. The task is difficult, the work slow but necessary. In the face of our failure to change the world in one try, what else is there for the writer to do but to design another tool, to build a better machine of words, one that might succeed less partially than the last?

In *Don't Let Me Be Lonely*, Claudia Rankine writes: "What alerts, alters," and I have been alerted and altered by great art as I have been by little else. I understand that it is a privilege to be able to be formed in this way, a gentler crucible than that which shapes many others. Nonetheless, it has left me wanting to engage with the world, because what good art does is wake us up, ask us to look again, to see more clearly than we had before, how our lives intersect with the lives of others.

The novel is my art of choice, in large part because it so perfectly provides what so much other media cannot, a long slow immersion in another person's life, allowing me to linger among their concerns, their emotions, their form of attention toward the world. By contrast, a news culture in which people rarely pause on a website for more than a few moments or where an expert might be given only fifteen seconds on television to state his or her opinion does not allow for much depth of thought, of emotion, of response. No amount of journalism could have convinced me of what I have been constantly reminded of by literature, that the lives of others are more complex than I imagined, that it is possible to simultaneously do good and evil; that many people often do harm in an attempt to do good, and that this is one of the central sources of grief and terror in the world; that the harmful righteous are so much harder to turn from their path.

Over a decade ago, Toni Morrison told an interviewer, "How can I get your attention . . . Unless I show you what can go wrong, with excesses?" I find it hard to imagine a world in which people are more acquainted with the excesses of what can go wrong than ours, and yet so many still turn away, unchanged by the horrors brought so clearly to our living rooms by twenty-four hour news. We turn away, too unwilling or too fatigued to dwell on such problems, and eventually we stop watching the news, or else we wait for some expert to interpret the news for us, to give us the world already wrapped in a familiar narrative, one that absolves *us* of any responsibility for further inquiry. It is as we always expected, we might think: The school shooter is an aberration, a monster unlike us, whose actions have nothing to tell us about who we are. The dead black teenager is a criminal so we don't have to think about his death at the hands of the police. The Israeli government argues that their harsh treatment of the residents of the Gaza Strip is justified at least in part because of the presence of *terrorists*, the one word that sets a people apart faster than any other in use this century. And as long as we keep the other so othered, nothing else is required. Those in power benefit from keeping us separate with language, and too often we more ordinary citizens benefit from the same walls and divisions: If the people in Gaza are not my brothers and sisters, I don't have to worry about their plight nor my hand in that plight.

But if a novel or a poem or a song could, like a tunnel, circumvent the systems designed to keep us apart, what would be left to prevent me from seeing us and them as one indivisible body? Perhaps the language we need most is not certain argument but an attempt at hopeful connection, or else an exploration of what prevents such connection, of what pushes us apart. The more I know that the borders that separate us are not impenetrable, the less I will be able to stand any injustice others suffer, or any injustices they might cause to be.

I want my writing to be a tunnel between myself and others. Though my effort may be inadequate, I know that it is not necessary to dig the entire tunnel in a single go. Like the physical tunnels that penetrate the earth below Gaza, any tunnel made of art will not be dug by one man or one woman but by many. What false steps there are along the way need not doom our efforts. The political discourse discourages complexity of public thought, preferring *us versus them*, where both the speaker and the listener know exactly where they stand, together against the other. As artists, we must insist on complexity anyway, tunneling through what is discouraged, to create spaces where we might move more freely, talk more slowly, and where we may sustain our speech as long as it takes to get things right. In the age of the sound bite and the hashtagged slogan, we artists know there are other ways to speak, to make our voices heard.

Where language is the problem—language of oppression, language of suppression—better language must be the cure. Poetry as shovel. Story as pickaxe. Novel as earthmover. Our voices are free and we can use them to bring attention to those whose voices are not. The ground of injustice and oppression is hard but surely there are those among us who are determined to break through. What is on the other side of every wall is another country whose borders exist on no map but whose citizens live everywhere. Every so often, a brave tunnel digger pushes a marker up through the earth from the subterranean world below, an attempt to get nearer to another. They say, *Look for me. I am so close. I am right here, nearer than ever.* We send our own signal back. We say, *Come closer. Keep digging. We need you to go further to breach the walls between us.* Soon so little separates us: a thin scrim of dirt, a little rock, a last bit of false rhetoric, hateful speech. We press our hands to the barrier. We push.

WHAT IS

Excerpt from "Galilee"

SUZANNE GARDINIER

4

On your side of the wall I hear there are oranges / But it's been so long I can't
remember
*On your side I hear unoccupied planes / keep you sleepless Staring from eyes in
their wings*
On your side there used to be a well / where my aunts passed messages Is it still
there
The eyed wings watch here too Where we pretend / we forget what a camp is

The restricted road where you live used to run / past my mother's occupied kitchen
I live on the road called Sheep Skin / Wrapped Around Whose Hidden Shoulders
The matrix of civilization over / the matrix of theft & the matrix of ruin
The taste of stolen recipes The stolen / hill's shoulder of stolen thyme & mint

The soldier with your accent Flecks of phosphorous / burning in the unwritten
vowels
My passport with the seal of a watchtower / stamped using burned blood for ink
Your language waking the babies screaming / Your star made a flare to light the
way to destruction
The vowel in your erased village's name / low every morning in the coffee pot's throat

7

The Special Night Squads were here again / breaking the doors & cutting the
pillows
*When we walked in the camp moonlight I could see / the holes cut between living
rooms to march through*
They're taking the firstborn of Galilee again / but gradually So no one will notice
*& after the artillery you showed me / the one child in the one chair in the one house
saved*

Can you hear the songs the night wind plays / on the buried bones of the
   extinguished animals

They say on the other side there's nothing / but dancing but hard to see that from
   here

The moon's lost names & the remnant songs / from the time before the
   settlements

Over there Before the castle garrisons / had found all these ways to destroy a tent

Their chainsaws smeared with the old matrix / Something like how you taste
   where you're softest

How we watched the storm petrels with no land to light on / walk on water in order
   to eat

Is that what we're both faithful to / The integrity of wandering

The creole of the sound of your eyelashes mixed / with the sound of a rooster just
   before we had to leave

10

Is it Friday Is today the day you pretend / we were never illegal together for a
   minute

The authorized Haifa falcons are chasing / the sans-papiers petrels over the waves

Is it true there are snipers in the lighthouses now / scanning the tired
   diaspora-drunk harbor

My yearslong embrace of someone else's city / One hand over my mouth until you
   moved it to kiss me

Nazareth won't look at us anymore / There's a bounty office that collects our
   absences

In the souk by the oud shop as the market was closing / The first place I heard your
   name

If I hadn't forgotten you I would remember / your eyes' quarrel between desire &
   compliance

The divided birds Migrant Resident Vagrant / still know their way to the inland sea

The lake police monitor the bits of ocean / seeping up from the underground
   networks

The boy they took yesterday was shouting something / but no one could hear what
   he was saying

My cousin says you can still fish there / & they only shoot on special occasions

It's written on all the gates now In code / To Destroy Is To Build To Build Is To

11

When I woke up I'd raised one hand / to defend myself against the charges

It's a moveable camp now It crosses borders / to escape the tribunals & replicate anywhere

Remember when the winter festivals / celebrated the earth that seemed dying but wasn't

Yes Hard to hear through canned festival laughter / but now it's the other way around

They told me to smear the doorposts & I couldn't / wash it out or put down the bucket

Was that where those three girls lived with their mother / With prices from Lockheed on their heads

And a boy tied with his arms apart / He couldn't breathe Something was wrong with his shoulders

Yes His name was Zakaria Sorry / for all the bodies clogging up your dreams

We will build a new Jerusalem someone said / Over here Your bones will make the cement

Little bits of your people's consent / stay in the trees after the soldiers go

& two choices of passport One with a flag / One an envelope of a burned village's ashes

Their favorite time to take someone / is when almost everyone is asleep

"Galilee" was written in Havana in the fall of 2014; the previous August I was standing on 59th Street with my phone at a demonstration, during yet another Israeli ravaging of Gaza, after the *Times of Israel* had published an article titled "When Genocide Is Permissible." Scrolling through my Twitter feed I saw a message from the US Holocaust Museum—hardly a radical organization, and not usually one with much to say about the ways those to whom evil has been done may do evil in return: "Genocide is NEVER permissible."

I stood on the sidewalk thinking about Soweto in 1976, when another long colonial killing of children became suddenly visible far beyond the communities of the victims, and counted on my fingers the years between then and the day Nelson Mandela walked free: 14. Then I looked out over the packed barricaded block—the Satmars with their arms linked, the boy with a Che Guevara t-shirt and a beret, the four teenagers with keffiyehs that said PALESTINE, the youngest with a sign that said Palestine Will Be Free; a woman holding up her baby as if he were a sign, a line of people with white hair & a banner, New York Jews Say Not In Our Name; a woman in hijab whose sign said SAVE GAZA, another whose said Stop Killing My Family, the young man with a ponytail who'd played the funeral drum in another demonstration, with a sign that said Jewish Israeli Citizen Against Gaza Massacre Siege Apartheid, and I thought, maybe it won't take that long this time.

TEJU COLE

I visited the West Bank in June 2014 as a guest of the Palestine Festival of Literature. It was, for me, a matter of witnessing and of thinking about one of the most important political issues of our time. But it was also an act of solidarity with a people whose sufferings often go unseen by the world. A few months after the trip, I was able to tell John Berger that reading his work had convinced me to visit Palestine. Berger told me that it was his Italian translator, Maria Nadotti (who was with us that evening) who had convinced him to go there. And so, we had a positive chain of influence. This perhaps is one of literature's roles: through the words of others, through the influence of their sympathies, we become awake to something we might have thought had little to do with us, and in our turn might influence others.

The Diary

June 6, 2014 1:11 pm
The Diary: Teju Cole

Saturday

What I realize, during our five-hour wait at the King Hussein border crossing between Jordan and the West Bank, is that there is a fine art to wasting people's time. Everyone in our group of writers and artists invited to the Palestine Festival of Literature has the correct visas, correct passports, and letters of support from the British Council. But the point is to make it difficult, mostly for Palestinians attempting to return home. There are forms to fill out, and hours of sitting around. A young official emerges, walks toward one of the waiting groups and hands out one or two stamped passports, or asks for more information, then vanishes for another 20 minutes. What should have been a two-hour journey from Amman to Ramallah takes seven. But we get there in the late afternoon, a beautiful town in spite of its history of conflict. A resident tells us that, compared to other West Bank towns, it is a bit of a bubble.

Sunday

Nigerians are fond of titles and to conventional ones like "Mr.", "Dr." or "Alhaji" (a Muslim who has been to Mecca), we have added many others: "Engineer", "Architect", "Evangelist". A more recent one is "JP"—Jerusalem Pilgrim—which denotes someone who has gone on pilgrimage to the Holy Land. As I follow a group around the Old City—there's the Via Dolorosa, there's the Church of the Holy Sepulchre—it occurs that, without quite intending to, I've become a JP. But there is, of course, also the matter of faith, which I do not have.

Our group of writers is here to give readings and workshops. More importantly, I hope to better understand things I've only known by rumor. Earlier in the day, we came through the Qalandia checkpoint on foot. There was a crowd of people from the West Bank, let in at a trickle. There was the great wall, still under construction, but already extensive at the Jerusalem sector. And there was the guard ordering some members of our group to delete from their cameras the photos they had taken of the checkpoint.

Monday

How does one write about this place? Every sentence is open to dispute. Every place name objected to by someone. Every barely stated fact seems familiar already, at once tiresome and necessary. Whatever is written is examined not only for what it includes but for what it leaves out: have we acknowledged the horror of the Holocaust? The perfidy of the Palestinian Authority? The callousness of Hamas? Under these conditions, the dispossessed—I will leave aside all caveats and plainly state that the Palestinians are the dispossessed—have to spend their entire lives negotiating what should not be matters for negotiation at all: freedom of movement, the right to self-determination, equal protection under the law.

The Augusta Victoria Hospital, on Mount Scopus, is one of the better hospitals available to Palestinians. It is easy for those in East Jerusalem to get to. For those living in the West Bank, a permit is needed, and usually one isn't issued unless there's urgent need: for radiation therapy, for instance, or dialysis. Dr. Tawfiq Nasser, who runs the hospital, tells us about a man from Gaza who had the wrong ID and thus for eight years couldn't see his son, whose ID was similarly restrictive. The man was diagnosed with cancer and finally got a permit to enter Jerusalem. He went to see his son in the West Bank, spent three weeks with him, came back to the hospital for one week of chemotherapy, and returned to Gaza and died.

Tuesday

This is a pilgrimage after all, but in reverse. We find erasures and disheartening truths at every stop, evidence everywhere of who or what God abandoned. Our guide points out villages and towns that are either currently being encroached on by new settlements, or that were simply razed or depopulated in 1948 or in 1967 and renamed, rebuilt, and absorbed into Israel. We arrive in Hebron, the burial place of Abraham and the other Patriarchs, a once beautiful city now strangled by aggressive new settlements (built in contravention of international law). The presence of the army, protecting these settlements, reminds me of what Lagos was like on mornings after a coup: scowling men with heavy weapons and a wary manner. Parts of the city center are empty, ghostly, save for the soldiers. There are streets in which all doors and windows have been welded shut. How does this thing end? I see some Palestinian children playing in a side street. Their innocent game of blindfold, a block away from patrolling soldiers, suddenly seems sinister.

Wednesday

The next morning we drive through beautiful country: Galilee and, briefly, the occupied Golan Heights. We stop at what is now the Bar'am National Park, which was established on what used to be the Maronite Christian village of Kfar Bir'im. The inhabitants of Kfar Bir'im were ordered to leave in 1949, and the Israeli Air Force destroyed the village in 1953, leaving only the church standing. The stony ruins of the village are still there. Now, more than 60 years later, some of the villagers come to the park for a daily sit-in. This has been going on for 11 months. They hope we will tell the world they want to return home.

I climb up a stone structure next to the church. Galilee: my inner JP remembers this is the landscape in which many of the events in the gospels unfolded. I see two white doves nesting. A beautiful boy of about eight, whose wavy brown hair falls to his shoulders, looks, I think, like the young boy Jesus must have been. Every mile of the journey dips into the vocabulary of parable: sheep, lakes, cliffs, vineyards, donkeys. I am lost in thought. Then I hear a cock's crow.

GEORGE SAUNDERS

When George Saunders published *Pastoralia* (Riverhead), it was hailed by the *Guardian* as a book that stuck to "plausible absurdities," with a title story that evoked a simplicity "enhanced by modern technology and superior management skills." It was the first book of his that I had ever read. Given that Saunders had already written in support of *Palestine Speaks: Voices of Life Under Occupation* (McSweeney's, Voices of Witness Series), it seemed to me that he would appreciate the way in which this work of imagination—set in a different time and place, much as Colum McCann's 'Cathal's Lake' was set in Northern Ireland—might speak to the purpose of this anthology. The conditions of occupation are no less surreal than the characters in the title story from *Pastoralia*. Palestinians are manipulated into behaving in ways that are not unlike the behavior of the "cave creatures," their reality as well as how they are perceived is managed by their captors, and for most of the world, they are, truly, a show. The following excerpt, reprinted with his permission, focuses on the way Management manipulates the workers, dictating not only how they perform, but the narrative about the conditions under which they do so, as well as what is hoped for by those trapped within and what arrives (useless questions, and then nothing at all), and it provides an instructive parallel to the power dynamic between the government of Israel and the people in Occupied Palestine.

Excerpt from *Pastoralia*

1.

I have to admit I'm not feeling my best. Not that I'm doing so bad. Not that I really have anything to complain about. Not that I would actually verbally complain if I did have something to complain about. No. Because I'm Thinking Positive/Staying Positive. I'm sitting back on my haunches, waiting for people to poke in their heads.

. . .

5.

Once, back in the day when people still poked their heads in, this guy poked his head in.

"Whoa," he said. "These are some very cramped living quarters. This really makes you appreciate the way we live now. Do you have call-waiting? Do you know how to make a nice mushroom cream sauce? Ha, ha! I pity you guys. And also, and yet, I thank you guys, who were my precursors, right? Is that the spirit? Is that your point? You weren't ignorant on purpose? You were doing the best you could? Just like I am? Probably someday some guy representing me will be in there, and some punk who I'm precursor of will be hooting at me, asking why my shoes were made out of dead cows and so forth? Because in that future time, wearing dead skin on your feet, no, they won't do that. That will seem to them like barbarity, just like you dragging that broad around by her hair seems to us like barbarity although to me, not that much, after living with my wife fifteen years. Ha, ha! Have a good one!"

I never drag Janet around by the hair.

Too cliché.

Just then his wife poked in her head.

. . .

"Okay, so where do you poop?" asked the husband, poking his head in.

"We have disposable bags that mount on a sort of rack," said Janet. "The septic doesn't come up this far."

"Ah," he said. "They poop in bags that mount on racks."

"Wonderful," said his wife. "I'm the richer for that information."

"But hold on," the husband said. "In the old times, like when the cave was real and all, where then did they go? I take it there were no disposal bags in those times, if I'm right."

"In those times they just went out in the woods," said Janet.

"Ah," he said. "That makes sense."

. . .

8.

Next morning in the Big Slot is a goat and in the Little Slot a rabbit and a note addressed to Distribution:

Please accept this extra food as a token of what our esteem is like, the note says. *Please know that each one of you is very special to us, and are never forgotten about. Please note that if each one of you could be kept, you would be, if that would benefit everyone. But it wouldn't or we would do it, wouldn't we, we would keep every one of you. But as we meld into our sleeker new organization, what an excellent opportunity to adjust our Staff Mix. And so, although in this time is scarcity and challenge, some must perhaps go, the upside of this is, some must stay, and perhaps it will be you. Let us hope it will be you, each and every one of you, but no, as stated previously, it won't, that is impossible. So just enjoy the treats provided, and don't worry, and wait for your supervisor to contact you, and if he or she doesn't, know with relief that the Staff Remixing has passed by your door. Although it is only honest to inform you that some who make the first pass may indeed be removed in the second, or maybe even a third, depending on how the Remixing goes, although if anyone is removed in both the first and second pass, that will be a Redundant screw-up, please ignore. We will only remove each of you once. If that many times! Some of you will be removed never, the better ones of you. But we find ourselves in a too-many-Indians situation and so must first cut some Indians and then, later, possibly, some chiefs. But not yet, because that is harder, because that is us. Soon, but not yet, we have to decide which of us to remove, and that is so very hard, because we are so very useful. Not that we are saying we chiefs are more useful than you Indians, but certainly we do make some very difficult decisions that perhaps you Indians would find hard to make, keeping you up nights, such as Which of you to remove. But don't worry about us, we've been doing this for years, only first and foremost remember that what we are doing, all of us, chiefs and Indians both, is a fun privilege, how many would like to do what we do, in the entertainment field.*

. . .

20.

Next morning in the Big Slot is no goat, just a note:

A question has arisen, it says. Hence this note about a touchy issue that is somewhat grotesque and personal, but we must address it, because one of you raised it, the issue of which was why do we require that you Remote Attractions pay the money which we call, and ask that you call, the Disposal Debit, but which you people insist on wrongly calling the Shit Fee. Well, this is to tell you why, although isn't it obvious to most? We hope. But maybe not. Because what we have found, no offense, is that sometimes you people don't get things that seem pretty obvious to us, such as why you have to pay for your Cokes in your fridge if you drink them. Who should then? Did we drink your Cokes you drank? We doubt it. You did it. Likewise with what you so wrongly call the Shit Fee, because why do you expect us to pay to throw away your poop when after all you made it? Do you think your poop is a legitimate business expense? Does it provide benefit to us when you defecate? No, on the contrary, it would provide benefit if you didn't, because then you would be working more. Ha ha! That is a joke. We know very well that all must poop. We grant you that. But also, as we all know, it takes time to poop, some more than others. As we get older, we notice this, don't you? Not that we're advocating some sort of biological plug or chemical constipator. Not yet, anyway! No, that would be wrong, we know that, and unhealthy, and no doubt some of you would complain about having to pay for the constipators. expecting us to provide them gratis.

That is another funny thing with some of you, we notice it, namely that, not everything up here, in our shoes, you always want something for nothing. You just don't get it! When you poop and it takes a long time and you are on the clock, do you ever see us outside looking mad with a stopwatch? So therefore please stop saying to us: I have defecated while on the clock, dispose of it for free, kindly absorb my expense. We find that loopy. Because, as you know you, Remote Locations are far away, and have no pipes, and hence we must pay for the trucks. The trucks that drive your poop. Your poop to the pipes. Why are you so silly? It is as if you expect us to provide those Cokes for free, just because you thirst. Do Cokes grow on trees? Well, the other thing that does not grow on a tree is a poop truck. Perhaps someone should explain to you the idea of how we do things, which is to make money. And why? Is it greed? Don't make us laugh. It is not. If we make money, we can grow, if we can grow, we can expand, if we can expand, we can continue to employ you, but if we shrink, if we shrink or stay the same, woe to you, we would not be vital. And so help us help you, by not whining about your Disposal Debit, and you don't like how much it costs, try eating less.

And by the way, we are going to be helping you in this, by henceforth sending less food. We're not joking, this is austerity. We think you will see a substantial savings in terms of your Disposal Debits, as you eat less and your Human Refuse bags get smaller and smaller. and that, our friends, is a substantial savings that we, we up here, will not see, and do you know why not? I mean, even if we were eating less, which we already have decided we will not be? In order to keep our strength up? So we can continue making sound decisions? But do you know why we will not see the substantial savings you lucky ducks will? Because, as some of you have already grumbled about, we pay no Shit Fee, those of us up here. So that even we shat less, we would realize no actual savings. And why do we pay no Shit Fee? Because that was negotiated into our contracts at Time-of-Hire. What would you have had us do? Negotiate inferior contracts? Act against our own healthy self-interest? Don't talk crazy. Please talk sense. Many of us have Student Loans to repay. Times are hard, entire Units are being eliminated, the Staff Remixing continues, so no more talk of defecation flaring up, please, only let's remember that we are a family and you are the children, not that we're saying you're immature, only that you do most of the chores while we do all the thinking, and also that we, in our own way, love you.

. . .

25.
A memo, to Distribution:
   Regarding the rumors you may have lately been hearing, it says. *Please be advised that they are false. They are so false that we considered not even bothering to deny them. Because denying them would imply that we have actually heard them. Which we haven't. We don't waste our time on such nonsense. And yet we know that if we don't deny the rumors we haven't heard, you will assume they are true. And they are so false! So let us just categorically state that all the rumors you've been hearing are false. Not only the rumors you've heard, but also those you haven't heard, and even those that haven't yet been spread, are false. However, there is one exception to this, and that is if the rumor is good. That is, if the rumor presents us, us up here, in a positive light, and our mission, and our accomplishments, in that case, and in that case only, we will have to admit that the rumor you've been hearing is right on target, and congratulate you on your fantastic powers of snooping, to have found out that secret super thing! In summary, we simply ask you to ask yourself, upon hearing a rumor: Does this rumor cast the organization in a negative light? If so, that rumor is false, please disregard. If positive, super, thank you very much for caring so deeply about your organization that you knelt with your ear to the track, and also, please spread the truth far and wide, that is, get down on all fours and put your own lips to the tracks. Tell your friends. Tell friends who are thinking of buying stock. Do you have friends who are journalists? Put your lips to their tracks.*
   Because what is truth? Truth is that thing which makes what we want to happen happen. Truth is that thing which, when told, makes those on our team look good, and inspires them to greater efforts, and causes people not on our team to see things our way and feel sort of jealous. Truth is that thing which empowers us to do

even better than we are already doing, which by the way is fine, we are doing fine, truth is the wind in our sails that blows only for us. So when a rumor makes you doubt us, us up here, it is therefore not true, since we have already defined truth as that thing which helps us win. Therefore, if you want to know what is true, simply ask what is best. Best for us, all of us. Do you get our drift? Contrary to rumor, the next phase the Staff Remixing is not about to begin. The slightest excuse, the slightest negligence, will not be used as the basis for firing the half of you we would be firing over the next few weeks the rumor you have all probably heard by now about the mass firings were true. Which it is not. See? See how we just did that? Transformed that trashy negative rumor into truth? Go forth and do that, you'll see its pretty fun. And in terms of mass firings, relax, none are forthcoming, truly, and furthermore, if they were, what you'd want to ask yourself is: Am I Thinking Positive/Saying Positive? Am I giving it all I've got? Am I doing even the slightest thing wrong? But not to worry. Those of you who have no need to be worried should not in the least be worried. As for those who should be worried, it's a little late to start worrying now, you should have started months ago, when it could've done you some good, because at this point, what's decided is decided, or would have been decided, if those false rumors we are denying, the rumors about the firings which would be starting this week if they were slated to begin, were true, which we have just told you, they aren't.

. . .

26.

. . .

No one pokes their head in.

Burnt Offerings

ALICE WALKER

Some realities drive us to our knees
and since I was there
already
before my altar
I unwrapped and lit
the beeswax candles
I acquired for you.
My hope is you have never heard
the story of Hansel & Gretel
the trail of bread crumbs
the witch's cages
filled with children;
the big black pot
and the cooking fat.

Never overheard elders
whisper of foreign customs
that honor
capture of children
and their sacrifice.
The lump of terror
I feel in my own heart
must be magnified
in yours.
In this cage,
seeing how many there are of you,
where would you sleep? And how?
I ask myself this, as I toss and turn.
Remembering too, the great Winnie Mandela
who endured almost a year
of solitary confinement
in a South African prison.
Three ants became her friends
as she used a bucket
like the one I see you have
for night waste (the bottom)
and for food (the lid).
When she emerged from prison
a frightfully different woman,
few South Africans
appeared to consider
the isolation, the humiliation, and the company
she had kept.
What must you think
of us, little ones?
Grownups powerless
to get you out.
What must you feel
as day by day goes by
without parents or community
(a burnt offering that perhaps you witnessed;
as fire rained from the sky)
coming to claim you.
Until
now it is only
awareness

of the
utter
brokenness
of your small lives
that regularly
comes
to visit you.

What is missing from this photograph are the grownups who forced the children inside the cage. Let us consider them, and send them collectively, around the planet, all our thought. Recognizing as we do so that this was not necessarily their idea. What would we do?

Talking To Hamas

Huda Naim, democratically
elected official,
I do not know how it goes with you
and your children
but every day I am thinking of you.
Did you know that before we left the US
our government spokespeople
told us: you mustn't speak to anyone
from Hamas
as if we were little children
who must be warned
not to speak to strangers.
However,
the moment we heard:
someone from Hamas is here
to talk to us
every single woman
rushed to see who it was.
I had to laugh, we were so typical
in that way. One of the reasons I have enjoyed
so much
being what I am. Curious. A woman. Forgetful of advice.
And imagine our surprise
our delight,
when the dreaded "terrorist" we were warned
against—that we envisioned in battle fatigues
and shouldering a long black
rocket launcher—
turned out to be you:
portly, smiling, your eyes looking
directly into ours.
And what did we talk about: mostly
our children. Your five. Our twos and threes.

Or one. How we wanted, all of us, a sane world
for them.
Ah, Huda Naim, how I hope one day
that you will meet
our Israeli sister, Nurit, and our brother,
Miko. I know you will like them, as I do.
And the young ones refusing to join
the occupation army
but going instead
to jail
and the old ones, like Uri, somehow
holding on.
There are so many good people
in your tortured land.
And I wonder if you know
Natalya,
the poet who was with us
later
in Ramallah.
Our Natalya who writes poems to the world and emails to me
as the bombs fall around her sheltering
place: "Alice, I cannot breathe. Our hearts
have stopped."
I sit, and wring my hands,
at last old enough and sad enough,
and pathetic enough in my impotence
to do this.
Huda Naim, I pray you and your children
your whole family
all your worlds
are safe.
Yet how can it be
with Israeli bombs
and now assault rifles
and tanks
demolishing
your neighborhoods?
I would weep
but tears seem dried out
by the terror and love
I feel for you.

The world has awakened at last
to your true face, Huda Naim.
The world has woken
up. Though it is so used
to being asleep.
The whole world is standing, shouting its rude awakening
in the street.
That is the profit
I see, so far,
from the globally witnessed
fire sale
of your people's
pain.

Still, I have seen the world wake up
before. When it has woken up before
it has moved.

These poems represent some of my feelings about the ongoing genocide of the
people of Palestine by the people and governments of Israel and the United
States.

When I was in Gaza in 2008 I met Huda Naim. Once we meet people whose
neighborhoods are later bombed and razed it is impossible to forget the brief
moment of meeting. I will never forget this woman, so dignified and calm, and
I feel concern for her children, who, for all we know, may be no more. She loved
them with her whole being and gave all her strength to their survival. To us she
was hospitable and warm. Even though we, as Americans, and though unwill-
ingly, were part of the oppression of her people.

The kidnapping of children, the arrest of children, the scaring and tortur-
ing of children, the murder of children, all of which is happening, is of concern
to every adult. We know how delicate young beings are, and can easily imagine the destruction of goodness and joy in them that is a result of unfathomably
cruel behavior. We must take responsibility, at least for knowing what goes on. In
Gaza there is arrest of children in jails and prisons but also there is house arrest.
Presumably Israelis enforcing the occupation of Palestine made the decision to
break the spirits of the children before they become adult. It was the same in the
American South when I was growing up, and in Africa, and in other colonized
parts of the world.

CHRISTOPHER MERRILL

The following scene is drawn from *The Tree of the Doves: Ceremony, Expedition, War* (Milkweed Editions, 2011), an account of my travels in the wake of 9/11, in Malaysia, the Middle Kingdom, and the Middle East. The sad fact is that in the conflict between Palestinians and Israelis, now in its seventh decade, names and dates may change in the political arena, but the occupation continues and the mechanism of oppression remains the same, with predictable results: regular outbreaks of violence and war marked by civilian casualties, senseless destruction, and deepening despair.

The events depicted here, which occurred during a period of relative calm, point to the limits of cultural diplomacy—the exchange of ideas and information, a small but vital component of US foreign policy. The University of Iowa's International Writing Program, which I direct, has from its founding in 1967 played a role in American cultural diplomacy efforts, working with the State Department to bring writers from around the world for residencies and arrange tours of American writers to places of strategic interest. We often host Israelis and Palestinians at the same time; and while they always disagree about politics they tend to find common ground in their preferences for cuisine, literature, music, and weather; for more unites them than divides them. This first principle of cultural diplomacy was sorely tested during our visit to Ramallah—an emblem, if you will, of our continuing failure to find a just solution to this seemingly intractable conflict.

The Luncheon

Palestine, May 2007

The restaurant had set an elegant table for twenty guests, in a separate room on its second floor, with American and Palestinian flags propped crosswise in a centerpiece of flowers. Our luncheon in Ramallah with alumni of the International Writing Program (IWP) was to be a reunion, and I looked forward to seeing old friends—poets, novelists, and filmmakers, whose haunting portraits of life in the Occupied Territories offered insight into the repercussions of what Palestinians call al-Nakba, the Catastrophe, the 1948 UN declaration of Israeli statehood, which formalized the expulsion of hundreds of thousands of Arabs from their homeland and inaugurated a new phase in what many view as the endless conflict in the Middle East.

I was particularly eager to see Ghassan Zaqtan. Born in Beit Jala, a Christian town near Bethlehem, he came of age during the civil war in Beirut, editing a literary journal for the Palestinian Liberation Army (PLO), and by the time we met, in August 2001, he had published several volumes of poetry and a novel. He also directed documentary films and the House of Poetry in Ramallah, which an Israeli tank leveled soon after he arrived in Iowa City—the third attack in a year on the cultural center, which the Israelis called a terrorist institution. The editorial offices, library, archives—everything was destroyed. Ghassan shrugged it off, as if to suggest that he had seen it all, as perhaps he had, having fought against Maronite militias and Israeli forces in Beirut, fled with the PLO to Tunisia, and survived two intifadas and several marriages. He brought to our discussions a level-headed perspective, balancing the animus that some of his fellow writers harbored toward the United States in the weeks after 9/11, as the nation prepared for war in Afghanistan, and he seemed to revel in the absurdities visited upon him. During the IWP travels around the country, for example, he was the only writer whose one-way plane tickets did not attract the attention of airport security personnel. Unaccountably, this former PLO fighter was never taken aside for separate screening.

No doubt he saw the absurdity in the fact that we could not meet. For after the Palestinian parliamentary elections, in which Hamas, a militant Islamist group listed as a terrorist organization by Israel, the US, and the European Union, had swept to a surprising victory, the Bush administration instituted a no-contact policy with the Palestinian Authority—an edict that covered all public employees, including Ghassan, who had just accepted a position with the Ministry of Culture. As it happened, his new wife, who directed an NGO, had contracted with the US Consulate in Jerusalem to organize our meeting with IWP alumni, and while she was quite upset that Ghassan could not join us—it was her birthday, after all—she continued making preparations until the eve of our journey to Ramallah, when she abruptly ordered the writers to boycott the lunch. (Ironically, one month later, after Hamas took control of the Gaza Strip, its militias routing the forces of Fatah, the mainstay of the PLO, the Bush administration reversed its no-contact policy with Fatah, hoping to strengthen its hold on the West Bank.)

The next morning, during a class at Bir Zeit University, where a blind English professor and her students listened politely to our discussion of writing and literature, I held out hope that friendship would trump politics. But after the session, when I walked out into the blinding sunlight, my heart sank. The white walls of the engineering building were plastered with posters announcing the agenda of the Hamas-led Islamic Bloc, which had just won the student council elections. Their message was unambiguous: *We have a solid plan to kidnap Zionist soldiers, and our elite Mujahideen are ready to act.* And: *One of our women in prison was attacked by three Zionists.* And: *We have captured a group plotting to kill our children.* Groups of students studied the texts, nodding in agreement. How to compete with *that*? I wondered. On the drive past the compound in which Yasser Arafat had lived under Israeli siege for two years until his death, in 2005, I resigned myself to not seeing my friends. And in the restaurant we stood around the table, in an uncomfortable silence, until it became clear that I should ask the maitre d' to seat us in the main part of the restaurant, without the centerpiece.

Presently we were joined by the blind professor and a Sorbonne-educated translator. When the waiter brought food to the table, the professor asked the translator to teach her the secret of making stuffed grape leaves. The translator folded a piece of pita bread into the blind woman's hands, then cupped them in her own, explaining how to measure the filling for each leaf. The professor applauded her vivid description, and said that she should host a cooking show on TV—an idea that the translator found preposterous. She had given up her professorship because of the army checkpoint near the entrance to the university—she lived in daily fear of being arrested and deported to the Gaza Strip, the residence listed on her identity card, which made no mention of her marriage. Indeed it had taken her eight years of pleading with the Israeli authorities to add her children's names to her identity card—which simply meant that if she was deported she could take them with her. She looked at me.

"The Israelis are very generous," she said, deadpan.

She told me that she had met her husband in Canada, and in the first flush of hope after the signing of the Oslo Peace Accords they returned to Palestine, settling in the West Bank—a better place to find jobs and start a family, they thought, than in her native Gaza. But then her mother took sick, her father had to hire a taxi from Gaza to visit her in the hospital in Jerusalem, and no one was with her when she died. It took a full day to retrieve her body—and this was as nothing compared to what happened when her father died. He never met his grandchildren, and she could not attend his funeral, the second intifada having closed everything down. It was a wonder that she had convinced the authorities to add her children's names to her identification card. They still refused to recognize her marriage.

"Very generous," she repeated.

Our conversation turned to the security wall built to protect Jewish settlements on the West Bank—hundreds of kilometers of concrete barriers snaking through Palestinian land, dividing families and farms. Palestinians viewed the wall as another land grab, in violation of the Geneva Convention prohibiting an occupying power from settling land under its control. Israelis argued that it prevented suicide bombings. Both were true. At this table everyone had a story to tell: how a woman accustomed to crossing the street several times a day to check on her elderly mother now had to drive for forty-five minutes to a checkpoint, where she might wait for an hour or more, depending on the mood of the guard, before learning whether she could even continue her journey; how a muralist was turning his portion of the wall into a rural scene, all trees and fields, until an army patrol ordered him to paint it over; when he argued that the Israeli side of the wall was decorated in a similar fashion, the soldiers aimed their guns at him; and so on.

It's a time of walls, someone said, noting that American contractors were erecting walls around Sunni parts of Baghdad, accelerating the division of a city marked by its rich mixture of people into separate confessions. Another mentioned the administration's plan to build a wall along the Mexican border to prevent illegal immigration. And on the drive back to Jerusalem Tony Eprile, a South African-born novelist, said that the wall reminded him of his childhood experience of apartheid. I mentioned the ire that President Jimmy Carter's best-selling book, *Palestine Peace Not Apartheid*, had provoked in some political circles. The title alone was enough for several critics to accuse him of anti-Semitism.

"Looks like apartheid to me," said Tony.

For some the wall offered contrasting visions of Israel—a law-abiding democracy protecting its citizens or an imperial power encroaching on occupied lands, in defiance of international law. Israel or Greater Israel? The grievous divide between Arabs and Jews brought to mind a day in Tel Aviv, when from the esplanade I saw dozens of kayakers paddling around a jetty, racing to shore, where a beach party was in full swing, and then, beyond the next jetty, a circle of women in *burqas*, holding hands in the waves. The two peoples were inextricably linked, as they had always been. The wall kept out suicide bombers, a terror tactic brought by the PLO upon its return to Ramallah, and protected the settlers, who routinely took the law into their own hands. Put it another way: the wall faced in both directions, as in the old joke. A woman tells the rabbi that her marriage is failing because her husband is mean. You're right, says the rabbi, and sends her home. The next day the husband tells the rabbi that his marriage is failing because his wife is mean. You're right, says the rabbi, and sends him home. The beadle cannot believe his ears. How can both be right? he asks. You're right! says the rabbi.

Our Palestinian driver sped down the road built for the settlements, which along with Israeli military bases occupy more than half of the West Bank; the walls surrounding them were topped with barbed wire. There were no other cars on the road.

"Paid for with your tax dollars," he joked.

MARIANA AITCHES

As a professor of Native Studies and nationalism in the US, I've long been aware of the tendency to assign unequal value to human lives.

You Cannot Write a Poem on October 25, 2014

You cannot write a poem about the dead today.
Like elements of chemistry, they all
get marked with varied signs, specific weights.
Some of the gone have names you'll never find,
the names of those who do not register
in history. Stories have lifespans too:
like Watergate or Bay of Pigs, Pilgrims
and 1492, Normandy,
Lincoln and Gettysburg or 9/11.
What about 1890 and Wounded Knee?
Even Jerusalem, and Edward Said?
It might be easy to write some lines about
Jewish boys Hamas captured and killed.
Everyone knows who plays the villain
and who the hero. But you'll never find enough
good words to make enough good people care
for a fourteen-year-old in Palestine—
American boy, brother, son, and cousin,
never father, never husband, murdered
by soldiers in Gaza in morning light.
No, you cannot write a poem every day.

Why I Had to Write *The Wall*

WILLIAM SUTCLIFFE

In February 2009, the Royal Court theatre in London staged "Seven Jewish Children: A Play for Gaza." It is a ten-minute play, written as an immediate response to the 2008–9 Israeli assault on Gaza, by the British playwright, Caryl Churchill, who is a patron of the Palestine Solidarity Campaign.

The play, the text of which is freely available online, is powerful, all the more so for the unique rapidity of its response to current events. It met with high praise in some quarters, opprobrium in others. One of the most vicious attacks on the play came from the novelist Howard Jacobson. In the *Independent* newspaper, he wrote that Churchill had "repeat[ed] in another form the medieval blood-libel of Jews rejoicing in the murder of little children . . . This is the old stuff. Jew-hating pure and simple . . . you don't have to be an anti-Semite to criticise Israel. It just so happens that you are."

Although Churchill launched a cogent rebuttal of Jacobson's accusation of racism, the exchange left me, as a British Jewish writer, deeply uncomfortable. Churchill is a prominent and skillful enough writer to defend herself, but others aren't. And even she must have been stung and affronted by Jacobson's personal assault. The Board of Deputies of British Jews also attacked the play, and a letter condemning it in the *Daily Telegraph* was signed by fifty-nine Jewish public figures.

In this climate, with false accusations of anti-Semitism being used to attempt to intimidate critics of Israel into silence, it struck me that it was time for Jewish writers who felt the criticism of Israel was legitimate to stand up. The allegation of racism is a powerful slur. If people cannot tell the truth about the West Bank and Gaza because they are afraid of facing this accusation, our culture has strayed into dangerous territory. The most powerful way to diffuse this line of attack is for Jews to stand alongside the gentiles who are unjustly vilified by this slur.

Ever since the start of the construction of Israel's wall in the West Bank in 2002, my mind had begun to circle around it as the possible subject for a book. This wall struck me as something unique and specific to a particular time and place, but also as an interesting metaphor for the world as it is now—for the ever more stark divide between the haves and the have-nots, for the extent to which the first world is happy to exploit the third world while denying this exploitation. Every day we wear clothes and tap into phones assembled by people whose living conditions are unimaginably horrific. We live in intimate proximity to these people, yet they are physically and psychologically absent from our consciousness. Over the last decade, this dichotomy has been rendered in concrete and steel across the West Bank.

I wanted the novel to be about a person crossing from one side to the other, someone who discovers a richer truth when they see what is actually beyond the wall. This person had to be a teenager: young enough to believe what his parents have told him, old enough to think for himself when the evidence doesn't match what he has been taught, at the stage of life when we are most likely to challenge our parents' ideology. But for several years, I had no idea what to do with this notion.

The separation barrier is chiefly an obstacle to the freedom of movement of Palestinians. It is also an obstacle to the freedom of thought of Israelis. By preventing contact, it stops Israelis, particularly young Israelis, from understanding or even contemplating the lives of those on the other side. It is a psychological and a physical wall.

This sparked in my mind an interesting parallel with a common trope in children's fiction. Again and again we read stories of a protagonist stuck in dull, mundane reality who finds a portal to a world of fantasy and wonder. The children of Israeli settlers, as I see it, are raised in an ideological and geographical fantasy land. The story of a settler child crossing to the other side of the wall would invert this trope. It would be a narrative of a child raised within a fantasy discovering a portal to reality—an old formula turned upside-down.

This was my starting point. I composed a first draft, set in a semi-real version of the West Bank. Following an email to the organizers, I was then offered a place on the Palestine Literary Festival, which allowed me to witness the reality of the occupation first hand, visiting East Jerusalem, Bethlehem, Ramallah, Hebron, Jenin and Nablus. One of the most viscerally traumatic events on the trip was the crossing, on foot, through the wall at the Qalandia checkpoint. The dehumanizing, intimidating brutality of the procedures involved in making the once-simple journey from Arab Ramallah to Arab East Jerusalem hit me hard. It is one thing to know something intellectually, but quite another to feel it. No amount of foreknowledge prepared me for the emotional impact of comprehending what it is to be under military occupation. Whoever you are in Palestine, an Israeli teenager with a uniform and a gun is all-powerful. I had read book after book about this dehumanizing powerlessness, but only with my feet on that soil, face to face with Israeli soldiers, did I begin to understand it.

I must emphasize that word, "begin", because I was on a short visit, soon to return to my comfortable home. I can claim only the slightest inkling of what it must be like to live under those conditions every day of your life. And no West Bank resident under the age of 47 has ever experienced anything else.

I cannot launch into any "poor me" narrative of how upsetting I found this visit, given the microscopic nature of my suffering compared to that of the Palestinians, but nonetheless, on my return, I found myself unable to continue with the book. A stew of anger, confusion and revulsion prevented me from even looking at my first draft. I knew I couldn't piggyback on the suffering of others in pursuit of a mere novel, yet I couldn't ignore what I had seen, either. I couldn't walk away and forget the book-in-progress, go back to my earlier life and write about something else, about the world around me: placid, materially comfortable, politically disengaged middle class London.

I was stuck. I couldn't write about it, nor could I ignore it.

After a few months, an idea emerged. The dark heart of the occupation is Hebron. The dark heart of Hebron is the semi-abandoned road that was once its commercial hub. Here, IDF soldiers patrol a street of shuttered and abandoned Palestinian-owned shops, most of which now have crowing Stars of David graffitied on the abandoned storefronts. This is familiar imagery to any historically aware Jew, but to see this graffito reanimated to mean "Jews In," instead of "Jews Out," is truly sickening.

On this street, settler cars occasionally zoom past. One grinning boy waved a victory salute at us out of his window. You can almost smell the violence. The feeling hangs in the air of a residue of panicked flight, of lives abandoned at the point of a gun. I have never felt more uncomfortable, nor breathed an atmosphere so poisonously repugnant.

This street bore no relation to anything I had witnessed before. Yet it was also familiar. Familiar from the world of dystopian fiction. Most of us in the west have never personally seen a gun fired in anger, yet we have all seen it countless times on TV and film. Finding myself in a place of genuine violence for the first time—a feeling I sensed throughout the West Bank, not just in Hebron—I wrestled constantly with this disorienting sense of unreality. I was in an all too real place, yet the only imaginative points of contact I could make were with fictional worlds.

My breakthrough came when I reread *Animal Farm*. I wanted to see how Orwell had written a single text that works as a dual narrative: a barnyard fable for children, an allegory of Stalinism for adults. The duality is, of course, richer than that. All readers except the very youngest probably carry with them both meanings in parallel.

Inspired afresh by *Animal Farm*, I went back to my early draft of *The Wall*. I realized that I couldn't dabble with this subject, using it as a platform for a vague setting that was and also wasn't the West Bank. I could, however, take inspiration from Orwell, and be at once specific and general. I saw that if I researched further, I could make the setting of the book entirely accurate to the West Bank, with only small modifications, but if I used fictional place names, a novel set here, with a teenage protagonist, would come across (particularly to younger readers) as a fantasy dystopia, of the kind familiar to any reader of YA fiction. I could write a dual narrative.

Most books have to choose whether they want to be real or fantastical. Yet having seen the occupation with my own eyes, I understood that I could write with a verisimilitude verging on reportage, and would end up with a text that would read almost like a fantasy. This dichotomy struck me as not just an interesting literary exercise, but also as a way of engaging readers who wouldn't normally touch a book on the subject of Palestine.

To achieve this, I knew I would have to make another research trip, to the other side of the separation barrier. It took me a while to find a way to do this, but one Israeli tour company made it possible. Green Olive Tours, run by Fred Schlomka, is one of the only Israeli tour companies that take tourists beyond the green line into the West Bank, to see the occupation, visit Palestinians, and gain a non-Zionist perspective on the region. Fred also has a few contacts among settlers, and (usually for journalists or diplomats), he sometimes arranges bespoke tours to stay with settler families. He set one of these up for me.

For very different reasons, this trip was just as unsettling as the previous one. On this side of the barrier, the feeling of unreality was even deeper. Strangest of all was that the wall itself, which I had come up against repeatedly on the other side, eight meters of looming impenetrable concrete dominating whole towns with its presence, from this side was all but invisible. I discovered that the wall was designed not just to keep Palestinians out, but to render their exclusion and expulsion as imperceptible as possible for the Israeli settlers.

On the Palestinian side, it was impossible to forget for a moment that you were in a zone of military occupation. Here, often deep into the West Bank, on the settler road network, in settlements themselves, it was hard to see a single sign of it. This enormous barrier, I realized, was like a two-way mirror. It was an immovable mass—$2.6 billion worth of civil engineering—yet through the layout of roads, houses and checkpoints it was from one side entirely porous and almost invisible.

When I explicitly asked to be taken to the best view I could get of the wall from a settler road (one would never need to ask to see it from the other side—you can't miss it), it took me a while to parse what I was seeing. The same slab of concrete that I had witnessed surrounding Bethlehem could barely be seen from the settler road that ran right alongside it. Looking closely, I saw a bank of soil which had been used to halve the apparent height of the wall. Above this, the visible upper half of the wall had been given a decorative, textured pink cladding. This wall was one object, with two faces—one monstrous, one apparently benign.

When I asked one of the settlers how he felt about bringing up his children so close to the wall, he replied, "Oh, we have walls like that along the freeways in New

Jersey, and we call them sound barriers." Anyone who has seen the wall from the other side will recognize this statement as jaw-droppingly foolish, yet having seen what he has seen, I can understand that it is almost as if this response was written into the design blueprint. Has there ever been any other civil engineering project on this scale designed to invite psychological denial of its very existence from the people who benefit from it? Can there be any other object on the planet so solid and imposing (the barrier is currently 525 kilometers long), so utterly there, yet at the same time seemingly not there when viewed from one side. There is a malevolent Alice in Wonderland quality to this almost fantastical fusing of reality and unreality—of brute militarism somehow rendering itself invisible behind a gossamer mask.

The wall screams of aggressive omnipotence from one face. From the other, it says, "don't see me", and, obediently, the non-seers don't see.

The suburban banality of the settlements themselves adds to this feeling of unreality. Standing on one of these hilltops, only by looking at a map, recalling my time on the Palestinian road network, could I be reminded of the violence and injustice all around me. For all I could see with my own eyes, I could have been in Orange County.

Even among settlers, the gun-toting crazies are a minority. These seemingly normal families living seemingly suburban lives in seemingly dull towns almost indistinguishable from any other satellite of Tel Aviv were mostly not, on a personal level, loathsome people. Yet they are doing no less damage than those overtly racist settlers who are blatant about their belief that Palestinians should just go elsewhere and leave a Greater Israel, as far as the Jordan River, to the Israelis. Again, it was a case of one monster with two faces. An honest brutality facing one way, a disguise of benign obliviousness facing the other.

I returned from this trip just as disturbed, yet this time enthused to return to my manuscript. I now had much more detail on the look and feel of the settlements, and of the network of roads and checkpoints they use, which is utterly different from the Palestinian geography over which this layout is arranged. On this trip, I had gone within the space of ten minutes from a California-like children's playground to an off-grid Bedouin village of un-mortared rock shacks with corrugated iron roofing. This felt like being sucked through a portal from the Los Angeles hills to rural Afghanistan—like falling down a rabbit-hole to another universe.

No two-dimensional map can illustrate this place. You have two worlds, overlapping but rarely intersecting—two places in one place—a far-fetched sci-fi concept rendered real. The adult/YA style of the book I'd envisioned seemed to fit better than I had expected with the bizarre nature of the settler world; childrens' literature is more comfortable with this ordinary/extraordinary dichotomy, less skeptical about flipping from one world to another within a paragraph. I felt more confident than ever that my goal for the book, to aim for a sense of place that felt simultaneously real and unreal, was a sound one.

I named the fictional town in which the novel takes place Amarias, an obvious anagram of Samaria. This seemed apt for several reasons. Those who oppose the occupation refer to the land between the green line and the Jordan River as the West Bank or the Occupied Territories. Those who support it refer to the land as Judea and Samaria. They use the word Samaria because a short-lived Jewish kingdom of this name existed in the northern half of the West Bank in the ninth and eighth centuries BC. In other words, go back as far as the Vikings, go back in time the same distance again, add a few more centuries, and you find a Jewish kingdom that lasted a fraction as long as the Moorish rule of Spain. This is the basis of the settler belief that Jews should rule this piece of land today. The word "tenuous" doesn't even come close.

Despite that, the claim is taken seriously in some quarters. It is no coincidence that Ariel Sharon named his son Omri, a name little used in the Jewish tradition until the second half of the twentieth century. Omri was the Jewish king of Samaria. Sharon's choice of his son's name is a perfect example of the double game played by politicians of the Israeli right. However much you pay lip service to the notion of peace and a two state solution, if you name your son Omri, you are giving an unambiguous signal to your Israeli audience that you hold the occupation of the West Bank as a deep-seated ideology on which you will never give ground. It is a message that has the added benefit of being absolutely clear to those who want to hear it, and indecipherable to those who don't.

The word Samaria has a different connotation in the New Testament. Every Western schoolchild knows the story of the good Samaritan, a tale of a Jew travelling from Jerusalem to Jericho—in other words, crossing the West Bank—who after a robbery receives no help from a priest or a Levite, but is instead helped by a Samaritan, a group who were at this point perceived as enemies to the Jews. A modern concomitant of this story is at the heart of my book, which tells of a Jewish boy who receives unexpected help from a Palestinian girl, though my novel never uses the word "Jewish" or "Palestinian", nor does it name the two languages spoken by the protagonists. The only place name we hear is Amarias. The text aims to find its own space as a kind of fabular reportage.

Those who are not experts on the Middle East are often encouraged to ignore the subject of Israel/Palestine by being led to believe that it is impossibly complex, and that every opinion has a valid counter-opinion. This is untrue. Many of the facts are extremely simple. The moral case against the occupation can be understood by anyone, adult or teenager. By simply shining a light on the occupation, on the separation barrier, on the disparity between the life chances of a settler child and a Palestinian child living within half a mile of one another, one is exposing an egregious moral wrong.

When it comes to the West Bank, the question of "taking sides" comes down to the simple matter of seeing the truth or ignoring it. The overwhelming majority of the western media opt for the latter. Any writer who finds a way to tell the truth on a subject such as this, where truth is in short supply, is doing useful work.

No novel will make a material difference to the politics, or to the lives of those living under occupation, but the simple fact of having taken sides, of having made a minuscule contribution to a cause in which I believe, makes this feel very different to my previous novels; and this must be why, after twenty years of living as a professional writer, *The Wall* is the book of which I am proudest.

Excerpt from *The Wall*

By the time Liev arrives home, I've washed and changed, and I'm curled up on the sofa in a nest of cushions, watching a cartoon. It's about a dog who keeps on trying to leave his house to get the bone he's left outside, but whenever he does he's smacked in the face with a plank by another, bigger dog, who hides in wait for him. The smaller dog never gives up, and keeps on looking for new routes to his bone, but every time he gets close, the bigger dog appears with his plank and whacks him over the head. It's quite funny.

Liev does what he usually does when he walks in. He goes to the kitchen. Mum is there, cooking, and I can tell by the tense gabble of her voice that she's telling Liev what I've done—or what she thinks I've done—and is asking him to tell me off. From the suck and slap of the fridge door, I can hear that Liev is snacking as she talks.

I feel him appear in the doorway, but don't look up.

'Your mother tells me you did something stupid today,' he says.

I shrug, contemplating my options. I could ignore him, putting off the conflict, but that would just make him angrier. I could be sarcastic, calling Mum 'your wife' to match his 'your mother', which might be briefly satisfying, but would ultimately make everything worse. It's never worth getting Liev angry. Most conversations I have with him, I'm thinking ahead like a chess player, figuring out my best moves to give away as little ground as possible without pushing him into one of his rages.

I glance up and see that though he's facing toward me, his neck is turned, and his eyes are on the cartoon. This is a good sign. If he was in the mood for an argument he'd have switched the TV off before speaking, to get my attention. He would have positioned himself in front of me, with his hot breath on my face. Having other people's attention is a big thing for Liev. Few things make him crosser than the idea that you might not be listening to him.

The way he's standing and his weary tone of voice give the impression he's ticking me off only to satisfy my mother. She clearly hasn't succeeded in communicating the level of her panic. Everything looks calm now. No one is missing; no one has been harmed. It seems as if he just doesn't believe anything bad really happened. He's going through the disciplinary motions as a domestic chore. I just have to play along.

'I lost a ball in the building site. It wasn't even me that kicked it there.'

'You gave your mother a terrible fright.'

'I know. I said sorry.'

'Well that's good,' he says. 'But if you ever . . .' his voice tails away, distracted. The small dog is climbing up the chimney, but the big one has seen what he's doing through the window, and is hiding behind a chimney pot with his plank. The small dog's head appears. He looks around and smiles, thinking the coast is clear. He jumps out and is all ready to leap down from the roof, when the big dog stands up with his plank and swings it like a baseball bat. WHACK! With the sound of a long, descending whistle, the small dog flies into the far distance while the bigger dog runs around the four corners of the roof like he's scored a home run, acknowledging the cheers of an imaginary crowd. Liev gives a tiny, comma-sized smile, and turns back to me. 'If you . . . ever . . . you know, lose something in there again, you have to promise me you won't go in.'

'OK,' I say.

That seems to be it. Easy. If he knew what I'd really done . . . where I'd been . . . He's already on his way out when curiosity gets the better of me. 'Why?' I say.

He stops and turns, his face now blank and puzzled, as if he's already forgotten what we're talking about. 'What?' he says.

'What's in there that's so forbidden?'

'Nothing. It's just private property.'

'Whose is it?'

'Well . . . it's private, but I suppose it belongs to all of us.'

'So it's public?'

'It's . . . disputed.'

'By who?'

'The people who used to live there.'

'Who used to live there?'

'No one.'

'No one? So who's disputing what?'

'You know what I mean, smart guy,' he says, with a sneer. 'They abandon their houses then they act like it's our fault.'

'I saw it. I was in there,' I say. 'I saw the house.'

He stares at me, not blinking, a cold, level gaze.

'Have you seen it, too?' I ask.

He shrugs. 'They're bad people. They build without permits. They don't listen to the government, they don't listen to the army, they only understand violence.'

'I just . . . it was weird. The house. It's smashed up, but everything is still there, as if they didn't even pack—as if something just fell out of the sky in the middle of an ordinary day and crushed the place. It felt spooky.'

'You don't have to worry. Nothing fell out of the sky. It can't happen to us.'

He's now looming over me, and above his beard I can see his face is flushed, with tiny deltas of purple veins lit up around the rim of his nostrils. I shrug and turn back to the TV. The big dog is now hammering the smaller dog into the ground like a fence post.

American Witness

ADAM STUMACHER

I sat in a chair in an East Jerusalem café, and wept. Outside, the streets bustled with life, the fearless chatter of hawkers and tourists and businessmen and students. Inside, under the steady electric lights overhead, with a plate of sweets in front of me, piled high with baklava and kunafa and halva, technicolor pistachios drenched in rosewater, I reached out and took my first bite, and it happened: I started crying and couldn't stop.

Ten hours earlier, I had woken up in Askar Refugee Camp, outside the West Bank city of Nablus. Ten hours, a long and dusty bus ride through twelve checkpoints, head bobbing and body rocking with the potholes, as we wove between ditches and boulders, nodding off against the window as outside an old man pulled a donkey cart piled high with melons past a boy with a machine gun. After each checkpoint, the roads grew smoother and smoother until we were passing the highrises and Redbox DVD rental machines of West Jerusalem and then entering the frenzy of Damascus Gate, where we disembarked and stumbled through the too-bright colors and too-loud clatter to a rundown guesthouse. After a shower so long, so hot it couldn't possibly have been real, here I was.

This was the end of my summer as a human shield in Palestine. Nights, I slept in the spare room of an apartment occupied by the family of a suicide bomber, on the understanding that the Israeli army would be less likely to demolish their home if somebody with a navy blue passport happened to be around. Days, I rode with ambulances through checkpoints toward isolated villages, on the understanding that the soldiers—a bunch of scared kids with AK-47s—would be more likely to let the doctors through if somebody with a navy blue passport happened to be sitting in the front seat. I am not a physician or a soldier or an engineer or a carpenter, and I don't even speak Arabic, so pretty much the only way I could make myself useful was to brandish that passport in one hand, to clutch a pen in the other. I was there as a witness, an American witness.

Back in June, my girlfriend and I had bought the cheapest plane tickets we could find to Amman, landing in the middle of the night and negotiating the fare with an enormous mustachioed driver, who drove us through the desert at night to the

King Hussein bridge, which we crossed just after dawn. I was lugging a backpack crammed with notebooks and antibiotics, a folded paper with a list of scribbled names and phone numbers tucked into my boot. I felt as if I was in a movie, as if after all those years of waiting for the casting call, my feature was finally starting.

"Why are you here?" asked the border guard, a beautiful woman with curly hair.

"I'm Jewish," I said, and she nodded, satisfied. She even smiled.

Then she turned toward my girlfriend, looking over her US passport. "Is that an Arab name?" she asked.

"She's with me," I said, and the guard paused for a moment before waving us through, her grin gone. Behind us, at the head of the line for Palestinians, a woman in hijab was crying, whimpering something incomprehensible, and a soldier was shaking his head. A long line behind her snaked around the corner, out of sight.

I crossed the Jordan River valley, went through East Jerusalem and from there to Bethlehem, where the International Solidarity Movement (ISM) held its trainings, filled with a sense of outrage, a sense of responsibility. ISM was a loosely coordinated group of international activists—idealistic young French couples, flinty Scottish anarchists, hard nosed Japanese paramedics, and naïve American college kids. During two days of training, they taught us how to approach soldiers at checkpoints, passports held high, how to respect local customs but act and dress conspicuously foreign enough not to get shot. The Israeli army doesn't want international observation or media attention, we were told, so just make your presence known. Wear a fluorescent jacket until they get close enough to see your passport. At the end of the training, we broke up into groups, some going toward Ramallah, others to Jenin. My girlfriend and I chose Nablus—the city her father had fled as a boy, the city she had never seen. After making our way through checkpoint after checkpoint, after walking down the cratered street and that first tank passed by, so loud I thought the ground itself was opening up and I reflexively threw my body against the side of a mountain until it passed, after settling in with our host family in the refugee camp, after the real work began, my righteous indignation was gone and all I felt was numb and helpless.

This was the summer of 2002, during the second intifada, and when we arrived, Nablus had been under twenty-four-hour military curfew for over seventy consecutive days. Shops were not allowed to open, children not allowed to attend school, people not allowed outside their homes to get food and basic supplies. The few remaining clinics and medical facilities were barely functional, since ambulances were usually detained or turned back at military checkpoints. Tanks and jeeps piled through the streets at all hours, arresting and occasionally opening fire on anything that moved—stray bits of trash, stray dogs, stray children. The bulldozers dug up streets and piled debris into roadblocks, sometimes breaking open sewage lines and contaminating the water supply. Every direction you turned, all you saw was the twisted wreckage of bombed-out buildings and vehicles, surrounded by billowing piles of garbage.

I realized pretty quickly that no, this wasn't my movie; I was an extra in a story much bigger than me. What exactly was my role? Some days it was to escort an old woman through military checkpoints so she didn't have to wait in the desert sun for hours. Other days to stand near a gathering of children flying kites as distant tanks opened fire into the sky. When a young boy could not get to his chicken coop because a tank was parked beside it, my role was to walk with him past the soldiers while he gathered eggs for his family. When soldiers set up impromptu checkpoints in the middle of the street and began detaining civilians, my role was to smile and wave as I approached in my fluorescent jacket, which was always enough for the soldiers to release everybody and drive away, kicking up clouds of sand. In short, I did nothing special, but my mere presence seemed to work some sort of magic.

Still, that sense of futility never went away. I wasn't *doing* anything but walking around and watching a tragedy unfold. Every waking minute of every day, I never knew what to do with my hands. Sometimes I stood uselessly on the front steps of the local elementary school—which we'd turned into an improvised medical clinic—watching old women and mothers with newborns stand in line for hours to meet the first doctor they'd seen in months. Sometimes I sat drinking thick Turkish coffee as old men told stories in a language I couldn't understand, though later a fellow volunteer translated: they were talking about risking gunshots to cross the settler road and tend to their family's olive grove. My hands were clumsy around those little coffee cups, but at least I knew how to grip a pen, to write it all down. And at least there were those days I got to help tear down roadblocks—crude piles of rock obstructing villages from the city—and I was grateful to hold a shovel, pick up a stone, toss it aside. Still, even those days, the Palestinians beside me worked harder and faster, drank less water. I knew the reason I was there was because my navy blue passport kept the soldiers, whose tanks were parked nearby, from firing. Maybe it was the weight of that passport, or maybe it was sheer adrenaline, the way constant danger forces coldness into your veins, but that whole summer I didn't cry.

Not in the bombed out center of Nablus or in the refugee camps or further outside the city, in the village of Saalem, where we came upon an outbreak of Hepatitis A that had killed hundreds of kids, which an old man said over coffee was caused by tanks breaking a water main on their way into town, and the vaccine still hadn't made it across the green line. Not when we walked across the settler road to the town of Beit Fureek, where there was a water shortage so severe local farmers had stopped watering their livestock. According to the mayor, there was a spring within city limits that could have met the needs of the entire local population of 16,000, but its output was diverted to a nearby hilltop settlement. Rumor had it that up in the settlement they had green lawns and a swimming pool.

It was all too overwhelming, the forces at play too huge, so what could I do? I could take notes, writing down how the mayor's eight-year-old daughter served us one cup of coffee after another, her face serious. I wrote how, when I tried to goof around and make her laugh, she didn't have a single reaction, how her father turned to me and said, in English, "she doesn't smile." What I didn't write was how I seemed to have lost my ability to smile, too. How that whole summer, I lost my ability to feel.

Ask me why I chose to spend a summer as a human shield in Palestine and I have many answers, all of them partly true. I could describe a photograph I once saw, a destroyed house marked with the Star of David. How much it hurt me as a Jew to see the symbol of my faith used to mark the site of a massacre. But in fact I'm not even sure it was my faith. I've always been a pretty lousy Jew—the kind that can tell you where to find the best pork dumplings in Oakland but not where to find the closest synagogue. I could also say how as an American I felt a sense of responsibility for the Apache helicopters purchased with my tax dollars, and that's part of it too. But I also know that my tax dollars had paid for plenty of atrocities elsewhere in the world, and I chose to come *here*.

There are other answers, other partial truths. For example, I might tell you how I was the son of a musician who runs a peace organization in the New Hampshire hills, so I'd grown up listening to trios of a Palestinian violinist, a Syrian cellist, an Israeli pianist. I could say how I had just started dating a girl who happened to be Palestinian—how she was as bad of a Muslim as I was of a Jew, how when she suggested the trip, I wondered if it was some sort of test. I could explain how I'd been chasing adventure for years, spending my summers riding the chicken buses and climbing glaciers, addicted to the rush when everything is new and strange, when you might as well have stepped off that airplane and landed on Mars. All of which is to say that, when she made the suggestion, I said, sure, why not? We'd only been dating a few weeks, and who knew what the future might hold? But then a few weeks became a few months, and summer was coming up fast, and before I knew it we were researching flights. I began to wonder if the adventure I'd been chasing had finally arrived.

I'm no stoic. I've never been mistaken for a cowboy, never had a stiff upper lip, never been a dude who hangs out with other dudes, punching each other in the chest or spitting or doing whatever it is that dudes do. As a child, when I hit the wrong note on the piano, I burst into tears. I still get misty-eyed during the lamest Hollywood flicks, the ones where you know the ending twenty minutes in;

I can't say why, but I get choked up near the finale just as the romantic lead wades through water to a boat or maybe a young girl is lying in bed dying of cancer or somebody makes a tearful speech on the witness stand as the camera pans to the face of the jurors and the violins swell. It's embarrassing, but I find myself wiping away tears. Even when I know I'm being manipulated, not even all that skillfully, at least I *feel* something.

But that summer in the Nablus, I was nothing but a pair of eyes and a pair of hands. I observed minute details and wrote them all down. I listed numbers: how many days since the last medical visit to this town? How many tanks in the street today? How many mortar fires did we hear? How long since my last shower? How many cups of coffee did I consume, and how many figs, how many pieces of bread? I wrote how, as I walked through little villages, people would call out to me in French, then German, then English. And I wrote about my fellow human shields, the grizzled old-timer from Newcastle with the shaved head and the incomprehensible accent, and the Japanese woman who looked maybe twelve years old but had published three books, and the Dutch guy with the ponytail who had survived a full year in the West Bank thanks to moonshine and bathtub gin. I observed it all, wrote it all down, understood next to nothing.

And I never, never cried. Not even that last night in Askar camp, the night before I was going to cross back over to Jerusalem, catch the flight back home. Abu Saeed, the father of the family where I had been staying, asked me to sit, drink one more coffee.

"Sometimes I hear the tanks outside," he said, "And I wonder if they will be stopping here, for us. But you have to go."

I tried to explain I had my own life to get back to; I had a teaching job, an apartment lease, responsibilities. And as I gave my excuses it hit me: I had never been more than a tourist here. This was only my summer, but it was his life.

When I quieted down, Abu Saeed pulled out a photograph of his dead son, the suicide bomber. He placed it in my lap.

"Okay," he said. "You go. But I want you to look at this first. This was my boy."

The kid was thirteen, maybe fourteen years old, with wild curly hair and a smart-ass grin. He could have been one of my students. Still, even at that moment, all I felt was a deep, deep fatigue. And Abu Saeed must have seen it in my face: I was already gone.

"Okay then," he said. "Here, you eat." His daughter brought in a tray of figs. "I'm sorry this is all I can offer you. Later, after the war, you will come back and I will give you a feast."

"It's delicious," I said. And it was true; those figs seemed to be the sweetest thing I'd ever tasted. As I ate, Abu Saeed pulled out the deed for his family farm.

"When you go," he said. "I want you to do something for me. Please tell them I have this paper. And tell them about my boy. Tell them what he did isn't what

I want. I don't want to kill Israelis. I just want my granddaughter to go to school. Please," he said. "Just tell the story."

"I will," I said, closing my eyes. That moment, all I could think was that I needed to go home.

But I had to make it through one more night in their apartment, and whatever I felt or didn't feel wasn't what mattered. I was a tourist, and the whole arrangement was temporary. It was a privilege to even wonder why I had this numb sensation inside. No, what mattered was my blue passport, my fluorescent jacket, my eyes, and my mostly useless hands—all of which I was taking away the moment I left.

On my way out of the West Bank, my notebook pages were full, but I hadn't read a word. That summer I was too overwhelmed, too busy copying down new stories to go back over old ones. But on that ten-hour bus ride through those twelve checkpoints back to Damascus Gate, I flipped through the pages, and for the first time, I read.

My eyes rested on a page about an elderly man, a resident of the Old City in Nablus, who earlier that summer went onto his rooftop for a breath of fresh air during the night. He was shot by army snipers from a nearby building. His family didn't notice he was missing until the next morning, when his daughter went onto the roof garden with a basket of laundry and came across his blood-encrusted body.

On the next page, I read about the municipal garbage collector, who had a permit to be on the street despite curfew but still was shot in the back of the head by passing soldiers. I read how Nablus normally hires approximately four hundred drivers to deal with garbage collection and other city repairs, but under the twenty-four-hour curfew, the Israeli army only issued fifteen drivers the permits allowing them to be outside, leaving most of these tasks incomplete. How after the killing of one of these remaining drivers, the majority of the others did not show up for work the next day, leaving garbage piling in the streets.

Next was the story of the Abu Saufa family in West Nablus. For over a month, their multi-story home was occupied by Israeli soldiers. Their house previously had twenty-four residents, but the soldiers determined it provided a useful vantage point over the city, so all but six residents were kicked out. The remaining six were forced into a single room in the basement, and barbed wire was layered over the one window. That entire month, nobody was allowed to leave the room. The only way the family survived was by whatever food and water that international aid organizations were able to negotiate with the soldiers to deliver. One of the women was pregnant, and stress and lack of proper medical care led to a miscarriage. Meanwhile, upstairs, the soldiers threw parties in the family's home and played loud music throughout the night, parking up to seven jeeps and APC's at a time in the front yard. And when they left the house, they broke all the family's furniture and dishes, and then proceeded to defecate on their rugs.

I read and read until I had to close my eyes, leaning against the window, absorbing the softer and softer shocks of the potholes as the road grew smoother and we approached the final checkpoint before my escape.

Which brings me back to the café, back to that first bite of halva. I can't exactly say why that was the moment when all the emotion I'd been suppressing all summer came out. But part of it has to be the way I ate and ate throughout my time in the West Bank. The thing that I have a hard time explaining—one of the many things I have a hard time explaining, since my return—is that, as I made my way between bombed-out villages in the middle of a war zone, I was so well fed I actually put on a few pounds. Families who barely had enough to feed themselves always managed to put out a spread. The fuul, the hummus, the bread, the fresh figs. Always with the apologies for not having more, the apologies for not having meat, the apologies for not having something sweet. And I sat there, grateful and humbled, listening to their stories, and counting down the days to my departure.

Maybe that's why, when I sat down in that East Jerusalem café, I couldn't take a single bite. Maybe it was the guilt, since I could leave to a place where finding meat, finding something sweet at the end of a meal, would never be a problem. Whatever the reason, that sweetness stuck in the back of my throat, and even now I can't seem to wash the aftertaste away.

Because once those emotions arrived, they stayed, and from that moment on I felt it all, felt it too much. When I got back home, I couldn't talk about my summer as a human shield, couldn't even taste coffee or smell cardamom without tearing up. A few months after my return, when I read about a young American named Rachel Corrie, a fellow ISM volunteer who was killed trying to block an Israeli army bulldozer, I broke down crying on the subway. Her death told me what I should have known all along: there was no magic to a navy blue passport. I had just been lucky.

So I pulled out those notebooks and wrote like hell, setting down story after story after story after story, but for a long time everything I wrote about Palestine was shrill and unreadable. Later, after my girlfriend and I married and then divorced, after heated arguments about Israeli policy with members of my own family, I kept struggling to get that summer down on paper, but it never came out right; I was too angry, too emotional, too close to see the things clearly. That wave of emotion that convulsed through me as I swallowed that first taste of halva, cradled my head in my hands, and finally let myself grieve—it was keeping me from fulfilling the promise I made to Abu Saeed that last night in Askar camp, when I said I would tell the story.

As a human shield I learned the lesson of patience, since so much of my time in the West Bank I was just sitting and waiting, trying to balance those little coffee cups in my clumsy American hands. After my return, I needed that lesson, as I had to wait years before I could tell the story. Finally, after countless failed attempts, I managed to write about the experience through fiction. It was a struggle, but I kept at it, and sometimes I managed to capture that calm I felt as the tank passed by close in the street. It helped to remember that it wasn't my movie, that I was just an extra, a witness. It helped to remember that being a witness might not be the same thing as being useless after all.

Still, even now, on this first attempt at writing the truth of that summer, not as fiction but as I lived it, I have to hold on tight to the lesson of patience. Just sit and wait, I remind myself. It's the least you can do. Because you are lucky enough to have choices. You had the choice to make your way to some plastic chair in some café where you can sit and bawl until snot runs down your face and the waitress asks if you're okay. You chose to visit the site of an atrocity, and then you chose to leave. And with those choices comes an enormous responsibility: the responsibility to speak.

Three Variations on Fado Themes

MARILYN HACKER

These three fado poems are imbued with *saudade*, that untranslatable word implying longing, desire and loss of something which, in some uncertain future, might be regained, a poetics of displacement that I could not avoid associating with (for example) some of Mahmoud Darwish's lyrics set to music and sung by Marcel Khalifé or the Joubran Brothers. That's my explanation for having transplanted two of these poems to another landscape, and made of David Mourão-Ferreira's young woman on her rooftop balcony in Alfama someone whose name is also a "dawn" in another language.

Beitunia is a large town with about twenty thousand inhabitants, about four kilometers southwest of Ramallah, whose main livelihood was the cultivation of the adjacent olive groves, grapevines and wheat fields. Seventeen thousand dunams (over four thousand acres) of its agricultural lands were effectively confiscated by the erection of the Israeli Separation (or Apartheid) Wall in 2004. In the past Beitunia had lost about one thousand dunams to a military outpost, two thousand dunams to the settlement of Givat Zeev, and another three thousand dunams to "Israeli only" bypass roads on which Palestinians are not allowed to drive. On March 30, 2004, a group of one hundred fifty citizens of Beitunia, joined by twenty international and Israeli peace activists, held a nonviolent demonstration called "Palestinian Land Day." This report is by two members of the International Solidarity Movement:

The protesters walked up a hill toward the soldiers . . . A peaceful sit-in ensued with demonstrators chanting songs and waving Palestinian flags. After 30 minutes the organizers decided to walk back to the village. An Israeli military jeep began to follow; several Israeli activists stood in front of it, but the jeep continued to drive forward . . . One Israeli activist was pushed upon the hood of the jeep as it sped down and up the hill. As he got off the jeep, the demonstrators attempted to verbally engage the Israeli soldiers . . . As the demonstrators retreated, roughly a dozen soldiers charged after them aiming their weapons and firing dozens of rounds (of rubber-coated bullets). When the protesters dispersed to the next hill on the edge of town, the soldiers fired tear gas canisters from their weapons and continued shooting up the hill. Six peo-

ple were injured by rubber-coated steel bullets, including one international medical volunteer with the Union of Palestinian Medical Relief Committees.

—and the wall construction continued.

David Mourão-Ferreira's fado poem "Libertacão" is not, of course, a ghazal, as I transformed it in my "imitation," but it shares with the ghazal a disjunction among its short quatrain stanzas, encircling and implying rather than narrating fragments of a story, further informed by the title.

Amalia Rodriguez, when she sang many or most of these lyrics, was not a young woman, nor am I, and I allowed that particular *saudade* to inform my version of "Barco nero."

Tahrîr

Through the skein of years, I had nothing to fear from this place.
How final and brief it would be to disappear from this place.

The tangle of driftwood and Coke cans and kelp in the sand
made me think of the muddle that drove us (my dear) from this place.

An orchard, a vineyard, a stable, a river. A wall.
The impassible distance today once seemed simple and near from this place.

There was the word *refuge,* there was the word *refugee*
who, confused and disrupted, began to appear from this place.

The silence that lasted for decades, for months or for hours
will sooner or later be broken. You'll hear from this place.

There is a wall, and the words that we write on the wall.
Libertação! Can you make out *Tahrîr* from this place?

From your bedroom window with the sun coming up
I could see dusty jitneys crawl toward the frontier from this place.

My name's rhyme with yours and the things that are done in our names
in whatever language no longer sound terribly clear from this place.

Sahar al-Beiṭounia

She lives in Beitounia
And her name is Sahar
Her name is the hour
Between sunrise and morning.

Her bougainvillea
Overlooks Beitounia
Where a mango-bright bedspread
Hangs over the railing
Lit by first light
That reflects from a wall.

Not the wall of a house
Or her family's orchard.
She can see the graffiti
Ich bin ein Berliner

Marwân had orchards
Al-zaytûn wa-l-'inab
Olive trees, grapevines,
Where they went out to work
Between sunrise and morning.

She is *bint Marwân*
(and also *bint Su'âd*).
She is *ukht Târiq, ,*
Ukht Mahmûd, ukht Asmâ.

When jeeps and bulldozers
Converged on Beitounia
A hundred and twenty
All walked out at midday

Were chased back with teargas
And rubberized bullets.

Seventeen thousand dunams
Of orchards and wheatfields
With a wall thrust between them
And the doors of Beitounia.

Her name is Sahar
At dawn in Beitounia
Where the first light reflects
On the wall of a prison.

Ismuhâ Sahar
Bayn al-fajr wa-l-subh
—her name is Sahar,
between sunrise and morning.

Fado: Black Boat

If you were there when I woke
With my barbed wire, with my scars
You would avert your green gaze
I would feel the chill of regret

Though you said something else
In sunlight, over wine.

I saw a cross on a tall rock
And a black boat danced on light
Someone waved, was it you,
A brown arm between white sails.

Old women know
That more go away
Than will ever return
Than the morning has scars.

In the wind as it blows
Wet sand against the panes
On the water that sings
In the fire as it dies
In blue sheets warmed by
Someone sleeping alone
On an empty park bench
When they lock up the square
You are still there

Brown arm green gaze black boat blown sand barbed wire.

TED CONOVER

In 2005 I traveled to Israel and the West Bank for *The Atlantic*. I was working on a book about roads and their power to change places, and the roads in the West Bank were fascinating. Some were just for Israeli settlers. Others connected Palestinian towns and villages. All of them were (as they are today) subject to control by the Israeli Defense Forces, which monitored passage on them by means of two kinds of checkpoints—large and semi-permanent ("terminal" checkpoints) and small and impromptu ("flying" checkpoints), set up by soldiers with a couple of vehicles and a set of collapsible steel "dragon's teeth" laid across the road to keep cars from driving around them.

I began my visit by moving in with a company of Israeli paratroopers on their base north of Ramallah. Among their activities was setting up flying checkpoints, sometimes in hopes of catching people they were looking for. After a couple of weeks I then left the paratroopers and Omer, their captain, and traveled in the company of Palestinians, through many of the same checkpoints I had previously visited with soldiers.

Excerpt from *The Routes of Man*

One day Omer drove me up the hill overlooking the Hawara checkpoint, past an Israeli-only road leading to Bracha, a Jewish settlement of 400 to 450 people (checkpoint soldiers have barracks there, too), and, a little higher up, through an ancient town of Samaritans, who are now Israeli citizens. The hill, which is called Mt. Gerizim, is mentioned in the Bible; Abraham, having just received the promise from God "I will make of thee a great nation," had brought his tribe to set up camp in the oak grove between Gerizim and Mt. Ebal, a hill to the north. Out of that camp grew the biblical city of Shechem, which today is Nablus, home to 300,000 Palestinians. It's an affront to many of them—and illustrative of the problems facing this region—that Israeli road signs refer to their city not as Nablus but as Shechem.

My mental image of Nablus, based on the descriptions of soldiers I talked to, was of a large, foul-smelling slum. So I was surprised to see gleaming white buildings, many of them tall and invitingly perched on either side of a valley. At least from a distance, Nablus was beautiful. But to Omer the view was less glorious. He pointed out one landmark after another where bad things had happened to him and his company. As we made our descent, he pointed out a building that the soldiers called the Disco: it was a Palestinian party hall that the paratroopers had taken over during the tensions of 2002 in order to provide the settlers with additional protection. One night, as the soldiers slept, two Palestinian militants attacked, killing a sergeant and a lieutenant before they themselves were killed. Losing those two soldiers seemed to be Omer's most painful experience, and yet I could see that some part of him really wanted me to know what had happened in Nablus. It had been his idea to come here. Weeks later, when I met up again with Omer and told him I had gone back to Nablus alone, he seemed amazed—and also a bit envious.

Israeli civilians are forbidden by military order to enter Palestinian towns; indeed, it would be dangerous for most of them to do so. But I'd been told it wouldn't necessarily be dangerous for me, as a non-Israeli and a non-Jew. It felt very strange to cross sides, but I was spending a few days on one side and then a few days on the other. I wanted to understand the checkpoints around Nablus from a Palestinian point of view. One way to do this, I thought, would be in the company of a Palestinian commuter, and I found one in the person of Abdul-Latif M. Khaled.

255

Abdul-Latif, a hydrologist, is a tall, well-dressed man in his late thirties who was educated in Holland. He lives not in Nablus but in Jayyus, a village about twenty miles to the west, a literal stone's throw from Israel. His daily commute had once been an easy thirty minutes, he told me. Now between home and office loomed two permanent checkpoints and as many as five flying checkpoints, and the trip often took more than two hours each way. I met Abdul-Latif in his office in Nablus and attended his presentation at a nearby hotel to officials from more than two dozen local villages on the subject of water conservation. At day's end, we boarded a shared "service taxi"—an aging yellow Mercedes wagon typical of the semi-public transportation available in the West Bank—for the journey to his house in Jayyus.

As the two of us settled into the taxi, he chatted with the other passengers about the evening checkpoint situation, trying to assess what lay ahead. It was the Palestinian version of a radio traffic report. There was no alternate route, but at least he would know what to expect.

After passing through a flying checkpoint inside Nablus, we disembarked from the taxi at Beit Iba, a dusty neighborhood on the city's northwestern edge, and walked to a terminal-style checkpoint similar to the ones at Qalandia and Hawara. With roughly 250 people massed in front of us, Abdul-Latif predicted that it would take us about half an hour to get through, assuming all went well. When I sighed, he told me just to be glad we weren't there on a Thursday afternoon, when the students at nearby An-Najah National University headed home for the weekend. Their numbers, he said, usually swelled the queue to several hundred.

After fifteen or twenty minutes the tides and currents of the crowd separated us, and I found myself pushed up against a man in a checked shirt—or, rather, pushed up against his satellite dish. Apparently he planned to hand-carry the waist-high dish through the queue. As absurd as this seemed at first, it soon occurred to me that he probably had no other choice, and so I did what I could to help. Others did too. Before long the crowd had deposited me at the turnstile just ahead of him.

As I waited in a short line to reach the soldier who would examine my papers, I heard a clanking and saw that the satellite dish was stuck in the turnstile. Undeterred, the man in the checked shirt managed to dislodge the dish and started sliding it through a set of vertical bars next to the turnstile. When the job was almost finished, I reached over to help steady the satellite dish against the bars on my side.

Big mistake. The soldier in whose queue I was waiting stood up and shouted at me, demanding that I come directly to the front. His English wasn't good, but he made it clear that I had broken the rules and that he was not happy about it. I was very apologetic; it was my first time through this checkpoint, I said, and I hadn't realized I was doing anything wrong. When he took my passport and Israeli press pass, I thought I was going to be okay. But he pointed to the back of the sea of humanity in which I had recently been adrift and declared, "End of line!" Startled by this punishment, I tried to stall, promising it wouldn't happen again. Abdul-Latif, who was in front of the next soldier over, began to argue on my behalf. For his troubles he was sent away to the holding pen, a small area of hard benches behind a clump of bushes, which was filled with eight or nine other men who, for whatever reason, had run afoul of the authorities. Still I dug in my heels. "End of line!" screamed the soldier.

As I started to turn back, a silent alarm seemed to go off among the soldiers: something had gone wrong toward the back of the line. My tormentor and five other soldiers picked up their M4s and ran outside the shed, quickly disappearing into the crowd. The checkpoint was now officially closed.

Twenty minutes later the soldiers returned and slowly resumed their duties. No explanation was offered, and the crowd was so big that I couldn't see what had caused the ruckus. The soldiers were uniformly young and dull-eyed, their burnout showing through and through. I approached my soldier again, and he began to reexamine my passport with an air of studied indifference. Abdul-Latif could see me from the pen and started shouting at the soldiers; they ignored him.

The soldier called over his commander, who asked me questions for fifteen minutes or so before deciding to let me pass. Abdul-Latif, however, had to stay. I walked past the soldiers and took up a position at the far end of the terminal to wait for him. The indignity of the regimen was hard to watch, but somehow it was especially unsettling to see a person of Abdul-Latif's stature treated disrespectfully: it was like a slam on Palestinian social structure. Several times he pointed at me; I feared that for championing my cause, he might get himself beaten up.

But after about twenty minutes the soldiers decided to let him go. Abdul-Latif was red in the face when he told me that his detention would have continued had he not been able to point at me and tell the soldiers about the bad publicity they were creating for themselves. When I blamed myself for his problems, he brushed it off. Before they would release him, he said, he had been forced to say "I am namrood." He asked if I knew what that meant, and I said it sounded like "nimrod"—"idiot"? "troublemaker"? Yes, he said, though in Arabic it was more like "naughty."

In the parking area beyond the checkpoint we ran into the mayor of Jayyus, who offered us a ride in his pickup truck. As we climbed in, Abdul-Latif said, "Sometimes they keep you in that pen until past closing time, until all the taxis have left." He pointed to a clump of bushes next to the lot. "Once I had to sleep there, next to those."

There was only one more checkpoint to navigate on the way home, but the relatively clear road didn't improve Abdul-Latif's mood. We came to an intersection where, he said, the week before soldiers at a flying checkpoint had collected everyone's IDs, kept them for more than an hour, and then dropped them in a pile on the road. This prompted a mad scramble that had only amused the soldiers. Without an ID no Palestinian over the age of fifteen can go anywhere.

Excerpt from *The Routes of Man*   257

AMMIEL ALCALAY

The first text included here is a verbatim transcription of a 1988 hearing that I was covering for Amnesty International, in which Faisal Husseini, director of an institution in Jerusalem called The Arab Studies Society, was arrested and detained for having prisoner art displayed at an exhibit in his institution. The work of art in question was a wooden letter opener in the shape of Palestine, at a time when it was illegal to display the colors of the Palestinian flag. At issue, as well, was whether the letter opener was carved out in the shape of pre-1948 historical Palestine or according to the 1967 borders, following the occupation of new territories by Israeli forces.

The poem was written in New York City twenty-six years later, in August 2014. I began writing it in the subway on my way to a demonstration about the attack on Gaza, and finished it that evening, after having been inspired by the ingenious slogan chanting of one of my graduate students, Conor Tomás Reed. I began sending it to friends all over the world. Very quickly it was passed around, translated into Arabic by Anton Shammas, into Turkish by Ulku Tekten, and published in *Warscapes* by Bhakti Shringarpure. Responses flooded in. The first defense against propaganda always lies with the image-makers—writers, poets, journalists, photographers, painters, filmmakers, actors—whose roles must include resisting lies and finding their natural peers in places of urgency.

The Trial: A Real Farce (1988)

The defendant, Faisal Husseini, was led into the courtroom by three guards; his feet were chained. Besides the officials in attendance, Faisal Husseini's family, a member of the Arab Studies Society, and the lawyer Henry Schwartzschild from the American Civil Liberties Union were also present. The primary purpose of the hearing was for the court to hear the defense's witness, Dr. Mahdi Abdul-Hadi (President of PASSIA; Palestinian Academic Society for the Study of International Affairs), and a fellow at the Harvard Center for International Affairs, regarding the prosecution's evidence. The hearing lasted approximately three hours and concentrated on three pieces of evidence: the letter opener and two drawings done on cloth.

The following is a sampling of the kind of exchanges that took place:

Prosecution: What difference would it make, in your opinion, whether we were dealing here with work done by professionals or amateurs?
Witness: First of all, to anyone familiar with Arab culture, the style of the work before us is clearly that of amateurs; by emphasizing this, my point is that the people doing this reflect the values of a popular culture, not a well educated or an academic artistic culture. The work expresses the culture of the street, the local school, the family, the mosque or the church.
Prosecution: You said the colors used were not particularly "artistic."
Witness: Yes, the colors are vague, unclear.
Prosecution: Do you have any background in the arts?
Witness: Although my expertise is in history, I certainly do have enough under-standing of the arts to say whether a work is connected to a particular tradition or not.
Prosecution: Could you tell us, in your opinion, what the significance of the vagueness of these colors is?
Witness: As I said, the people who painted these pictures are expressing things from a popular level, things that cannot come from an organized entity like a party, a club, an organization . . .
Prosecution: Is the PLO one of those organizations you refer to? Are these works not connected to that organization?

Witness: No, these works are not connected.

Prosecution: You've said that these colors [used in the flags depicted in the works] have been connected to the Palestinian National Movement since 1917?

Witness: Yes, since 1917. These colors were endorsed for a flag after the Arab revolt of 1916. The Palestinians participated in that revolt but shared the flag that was used by Sharif Ibn Ali in 1916.

Prosecution: Does this flag resemble the flag of any present Arab country?

Witness: Yes, the Jordanian flag, from 1921 until the present. On the Jordanian flag, however, there is a little white star which does not appear on this flag.

Prosecution: Besides this, is there another country that has such a flag?

Witness: From 1947 until the present, the Ba'ath Socialist Party of Syria has adopted this same flag.

Prosecution: We spoke of states, does Syria use this flag?

Witness: The Syrians use the colors of this flag in a different sequence. I have to add also that the Hashemite emblem uses the same sequence of colors but has no star.

Prosecution: I ask again: does the Hashemite Kingdom use this flag?

Witness: The seal, the symbol [Faisal Husseini points to the Israeli emblem hanging above the judge's desk] of the Hashemite kingdom has this same Arab flag, which, I would like to reiterate, was adopted in 1917, except for the star. The flag does have a star, but the symbol does not. My emphasis here is on the Arab factor, evident in all the countries whose flags have the same colors but are used in different sequences and arrays. This is so because the original source for all these flags is the flag used officially since 1916, adopted by the Palestinians in 1917! These flags have been used at all kinds of inter and pan-Arab meetings and the form we see here is precisely the same one. So this flag is nothing new, it does not come out of nowhere nor was it invented recently: it has a long history dating back from 1917.

Prosecution: So, besides Jordan there is no other country in which the array of colors appears in the sequence of this one?

Witness: Yes, Iraq. From 1921 to 1958. On that Iraqi flag there were two stars since Iraq was the second Arab state to gain independence, after Syria.

Prosecution: [Displays copy of the Iraqi flag] So this is how the Iraqi flag looks?

Witness: Yes.

Prosecution: So you would say that today only Jordan uses such a similar flag?

Witness: Yes, but I would have to add, as I said earlier, that the Ba'ath Party uses the same flag.

Prosecution: Yes, but today, who else uses this flag?

Witness: The Palestinian Arab people, as they have been since 1917; this has not changed since then.

Prosecution: Do you mean the PLO?

Witness: Not necessarily.

Prosecution: What do you mean?

Judge: Here I would like a very clear answer.

Witness: Not necessarily because when a Palestinian Arab individual, a family or an institution raises this flag it does not mean that they are raising a PLO flag.

Prosecution: If the PLO raises a flag, do they raise this flag or another one?

Witness: The PLO presently raises the flag of the Palestinian people and not the other way around.

[A discussion on the exhibits followed, in minute detail. The judge finally intervened.]

Judge: We're playing with words here and going in circles—let's just see a flag.

Prosecution: I can be of some help here. Now, here is a flag made by amateurs [unfurls flag with red triangle on the left, three stripes in the sequence green, white and black]. Is this the flag used today by the PLO?

Witness: The colors used on this flag are the same colors as those used by the PLO. The correctness, the better likeness is gotten here by the higher professionalism of the work.

Prosecution: Couldn't you just say that this form, the red triangle, the three stripes and so on—is this the flag raised by the organization? IS THIS THE FLAG RAISED BY THE ORGANIZATION? I want a clear answer.

Witness: This is the flag of the Palestinian people that the PLO also raises.

[Further discussion on the amateur/professional issue follows; the judge intervenes].

Judge: I think we're going in circles. I think his answer is clear, that the flag could be used by the PLO but does not necessarily have to be.

[Prosecutor presses on about the likeness of the flags in the exhibits].

Witness: Yes, there is a likeness but not an absolute identity.

Prosecution: Could it be the flag of another organization?

Witness: Yes, as I said, the Ba'ath Party, for instance.

Prosecution: Is this more like the Ba'ath flag or this flag I showed you?

Judge: We all have eyes, we can come to our own conclusions.

[Drawings on cloth are exhibited before the court, witness is asked to describe them.]

Witness: There is a woman with a Palestinian shirt carrying her daughter and there is a sequence of colors from the Arab flag, very vague and unclear, with also a Palestinian head covering and there are some shackles raising a torch.

Prosecution: The essence, I think, you've not pointed out. Isn't this the Land of Israel, Palestine?

Witness: The drawing is not really clear as to whether or not it's a depiction of the historical land of Palestine but someone looking at this could certainly give it more than one interpretation.

Prosecution: Do you see here Palestine, the Land of Israel?

Witness: Yes, in a very inexact manner.

Prosecution: Are the colors the same here?

Witness: Yes, there are colors, not artistically accurate, but yes, they do resemble the other colors.

Prosecution: But here there is not a message of peace, but rather a violent message, a Kalashnikov being clasped.

Witness: The average Palestinian does not have sufficient military knowledge to know whether or not this is a depiction of a Kalashnikov.

Prosecution: But do you know who drew this? If I told you that it was drawn by a Palestinian prisoner, would that change your opinion?

[Defense objects].

Defense: We all know that the show centered around "The Day of the Palestinian Prisoner" but there were many other displays there as well which haven't been discussed; books and pamphlets from the non-violence center, for instance.

Prosecution: Here is another piece, with a flag.

Witness: The style of the flag is quite incomplete and doesn't really resemble that of any organization.

Prosecution: We all know this is an inexact drawing but does this triangle here resemble that triangle.

Witness: No, not really.

Prosecution: Doesn't this flag resemble the Land of Israel?

[Extended discussion over resemblance of color and shapes follows]

Prosecution: Are you an expert in history or in art?

Witness: I am an expert in history but I do have enough understanding of art to differentiate a bad rendering from a genuine one.

Prosecution: Do we not see a PLO flag here?

Witness: No.

Prosecution: Do we not see the Land of Israel?

Witness: There is some likeness to the coast of Palestine here but very inexact. Yes, one could say that this is a likeness of historical Palestine albeit a very inaccurate one. Nor would I say that this here is a Palestinian flag but that the colors used here resemble those of the flag.

Judge: What is the significance of the words: "You have nothing to lose but your chains and your tent, Revolt!" [inscribed on one of the exhibits].

Prosecution: [Interjecting to the witness] So you didn't translate the first word ["revolt," coming as the last word in the translation and not the first word as in the Arabic original]. Meaning: make revolution, be violent! Arise and fight, meaning that if you do that you will have nothing to lose but the refugee camps [here there is a play on words in the original Arabic between tents and refugee camps].

Defense: First of all, this is inexact. This is a copy of a Western slogan that has been introduced into all kinds of Arab movements and resembles, both in history and usage, the slogan "Workers of the World Unite." The adoption of a slogan already fitting to the tone or mood of a people's movement doesn't mean that the movement itself either has to fit or be the originator of the ideology from which the slogan was adopted. What this means, in essence, is that not everybody who would draft or repeat this quotation is necessarily committed to the source or the ideology from which it was originally extracted but is simply copying or repeating a phrase with no deep knowledge of its context; nor does it mean that they will necessarily or are about to follow it through. To say "Workers of the World Unite" is not any indication of the truth of that statement at the time it is being said.

Prosecution: [examining letter opener] These colors at the top of this Palestine-shaped object—does this not suggest, along with the slogan, the need to fight in order to return to the land from the camps?

Witness: Again, I want to emphasize that these colors are those of the Palestinian Arab people. The saying written along the side there is taken from a standard Western slogan except the only word added here is TENT. No, the three things, the slogan, the map and the colors put together do not mean that you are calling for a revolt. The phrase, in fact, "you have nothing to lose," is also a phrase long used by Arab nationalists beginning from 1915 still during Turkish rule, through the Mandate and in the Jordanian period in open organizations and meetings. What we see here is simply a COPY and repetition of very common phrases. When people copy this it does not mean they are part of a secret organization. DOES NOT MEAN THEY ARE PART OF A SECRET ORGANIZATION.

Prosecution: In the context of "The Day of the Prisoner," with this combination and this map, that is, a map of the land prior to '67, before the occupation, don't you think that this then takes on a completely different significance: that of a full return to the land taken by force by the Jews?

Witness: As someone who has some sense of history, the first thing I would notice is that the Palestinian people are the first Arab people, historically, to demand independence from the Turks; in Syria there was also such a movement, involving both Arabs and Jews . . .

Prosecution: I am speaking of the Land of Israel, not the Turks, but of the Jews in the Land of Israel. Now, the same artist who painted this, would it be too far-fetched to think that he might have had, in his mind, the Palestinian return to his territory?

Witness: I still don't understand the question.

Defense: Wait a second [reaches for the letter opener], I don't see this at all like that. Where's the Dead Sea? Look, right here . . .

Prosecution: Right, well then, this does include, this is after '67.

Defense: I haven't intervened so far and I usually don't like to do that but I think that the questions should concentrate on the exhibits at hand because we've gotten pretty far from the point here.

Prosecution: I say that this represents the State of Israel with the territories, do you agree?

Witness: It is an inexact likeness of historical Palestine in the Mandate period.

Prosecution: Even though you're a historian, I want you then to speak about 1986 to the present . . .

Judge: Just a second, you know that a historian can also deal with the present . . .

Witness: In terms of what?

Prosecution: Do you agree that it is the Land of Israel with the territories?

Witness: I've already said that for me this represents an inexact likeness of historical Palestine, that is what I see TODAY [points]. I cannot really say with much certainty that this is that or that—

Prosecution: I am not arguing ideologically here; wouldn't it be clear to practically anyone that this is the Land of Israel with the territories?

Witness: I am not a geographical expert, I can speak of historical knowledge, in terms of what I see.

Judge: So let's talk about the present then.

Witness: In terms of what?

Judge: The prosecutor is not asking for political positions but geographical questions. The question was simple. Do you see this piece of wood as a likeness of the territories that would include the State of Israel and the territories under military control?

Witness: Yes, roughly.

Prosecution: Is it not true that one or even the central idea of the PLO is to return to the whole Land of Israel?

Defense: I have to object. We are talking about these exhibits here and whether or not they have any connection to the PLO [discussion on procedure follows].

Witness: There are a number of trends within the PLO that differ from each other. The PLO itself as a political infrastructure does not support this policy, there is a faction or trend within that does. In general, though, you would have to say that as a policy the PLO does not. The PLO as a whole accepts the 1947 partition principle. Arafat signed a document with McCloskey in Lebanon accepting all UN resolutions, starting with the '47 partition. In 1974, the Palestine National Council accepted the two-state partition concept. This exhibit, for instance, would under no circumstances either represent or express the full range of the PLO spectrum, nor does this particular piece really demonstrate allegiance to any particular movement or ideology.

Defense: I would object again here; there is actually no proof that this piece was created by a prisoner [reads label]. In fact, from this, it is obvious that it comes from some kind of student organization, from the Faculty of the Humanities, 1981.

Prosecution: But it was done for "Prisoner's Day."

Judge: Let's be clear here—how do you know that?

Prosecution: Alright, are you familiar with the Palestinian National Charter? [defense objects on the grounds of irrelevancy and asks which charter is referred to].

[After a long discussion on versions of the Palestinian National Charter, a search for a legal volume containing the charter, the witness pointing out that the charter, written in 1964 is "not a sacred text but a political document" transformed over time, the "question of Jerusalem," whether the PLO recognized partition, and which borders are under discussion, 1947, or 1967, and, indeed, whether the PLO of 1964 is the same as the PLO of 1988, the hearing was postponed for a future date.]

Letter to the Americans 2014

You know as well as I do that a people under occupation will
be unhappy, that parents will fear for the lives of their precious
children, especially when there is NOWHERE TO HIDE.

You know as well as I do that a husband's memory of his wife forced to
deliver their child at a checkpoint will not be a happy one. You know as
well as I do that the form of her unborn child beaten to death in the womb

will never leave a mother's mind. And you know as well as I do that a girl will
have cause to wonder at the loss of her grandfather, made to wait on his
way to the hospital, and she'll have cause to cry at the bullet lodged

in her brother's head—You know as well as I do that watching
someone who stole the land you used to till water their garden
while you hope some rain might collect to parch your weary throat

might cause bitterness—You know as well as I do that a family,
a village, a city, and a people punished for the act of an individual
might not react well to the idea of "two sides." You know as well

as I do that Hamurabi's Code was a great legal precedent and that
the translation of an eye for an eye and a tooth for a tooth means
ONE PUNISHMENT FOR ONE CRIME—no thing more and

no thing less. You know as well as I do that aerial bombardment
and white phosphorous and naval blockade and tanks and snipers
and barbed wire and walls and house demolitions and land

confiscation and the uprooting of olive trees and torture without
trial and collective punishment and withholding water and
access to the sea and even the sky itself are no match for rocket

propelled grenades and all the nails ever put into every homemade

bomb ever made even though metal still pierces every skin—You
know as well as I do that justice dwells in the soul as in the soil

and though you can't ever know what you'd do if you were in
someone else's shoes, maybe you *would* have the strength to carry
your elders on your back, the courage to stay at the operating table

or drive an ambulance after your children were killed, the nerve
to face the daily grief compounded by loss after loss until all
you have left is the unutterable scream you possess in the

heave of your breast and the depth of your chest. But you also
know as well as I do that the size of the prison increases the
capacity to resist, and the extent of the suffering makes fear

just another feeling among many because the most
occupied are also the most free since there are no
illusions left but the vision of freedom and how to

realize it. You know all this but you know
too, just as I do, that enough is enough
and those below will continue to rise up.

August 1–3, 2014

DREAM/CHILDREN

FANNY HOWE

On a newscast about two years ago, I saw a still photo of a laughing boy, his sister weeping (live) under a tree, and a bomb blasting a hole in the roof above her. The story was brief, but loaded. The bond between children and old people during a war is the most symbolic of the empty value of violence. In this case, a young boy was annihilated under the watch of his sister and grandmother. The poem is simply a projection of the story as I witnessed it on a news report. Nothing much in the annals of the Palestinian struggle.

This I Heard

She rarely comes out from among
the persimmon trees

where the old
who are quiet hold her hand.

She can't forget her little brother
before the bomb dropped

on the roof after she gave him
permission to climb up.

In Dreams

CLAIRE MESSUD

We've been talking at our house about how odd it is when you can't do things in dreams. In dreams, you'd think, you should be able to do whatever you want.

My husband recently dreamed that our family was staying in an open-plan hostel in Oslo, Norway. He was worried about his snoring, which, honestly, is loud: worried for some reason—it was a dream—that his snoring might prompt people to attack us in the night, to murder us—not just him and me, but the children, too. In the dream, he was worried enough to feel we must leave the hostel and go to a hotel, even though we hadn't any money. He found a computer and looked up hotels on the Internet: the only room available, at the Continental, was a "Classic Room with Flowers," at $1200 a night. We didn't have the money but he did have a credit card and he was ready to book the room, even eager; but he couldn't. For all he tried, he couldn't make the computer mouse move onto the icon that said "Book Now." He desperately wanted the room—it might save our lives—but he couldn't get it.

Over breakfast, we marveled at this inexplicable incapacity—what, we wondered, had stayed his hand?

The same night, our son dreamed that the Germans were about to drop a nuclear bomb on Cambridge, Massachusetts (he'd watched a World War Two film the day before). He and his sister had been separated from us, their parents, and were searching everywhere through the town, jostled, breathless in the frantic mêlée of panicked people, all of whom were terrified at the impending disaster. In the dream, it's true, he was able at last to find us, so that then we were all four together, the family safe and intact in our togetherness—but it was only a brief consolation. He wasn't able to stop the bomb, which fell as anticipated. Then, he said, everything turned to liquid, and it was all over.

These are the surprising darknesses from which we wakened into the glistening snow-lit January dawn. The kettle on, the sandwiches made and wrapped in wax paper, the ordinary day launched, a day in which our little lives, delicious in their routine insignificance, are comprised of the satisfactions of work, of laundry, dog-walking, soccer practice, perhaps a supermarket run. There are inconveniences, to be sure (ice on the roads; queues at the gas station; inevitably someone's rudeness or ill-temper), but our fundamental incapacity to control our lives, our inability to choose our fates, our likely failures, our certain deaths—these incontrovertible truths will remain largely hidden from us as long as we're awake. This beautiful state of illusion is our freedom. It takes our dreams to remind us how precarious, how provisional our banal, beloved lives are, what a fantasy our secure autonomy actually is.

◆ ◆ ◆

Years ago, When my sister and her husband had their first child, my husband and I, along with my parents and their dog, joined them in Paris for the birth. My sister and her husband lived in Russia then, and wanted their daughter to be born in France, as her mother had been—in the same hospital, as it happened, where my mother had had my sister, attended by a doctor who'd been there when my sister was born.

My parents, like us, flew in from the States. We all piled into a little flat in an ugly modern tower block along the Seine. The rooms were mean, the walls wafer thin, the corridors lingeringly scented by other people's cooking. The elevators, temperamental, functioned only sometimes. My parents' Jack Russell clicked restlessly around the cheap parquet, sniffing, bristling, barking when strangers passed the door. My husband and I, the least relevant people there, slept on the lumpy living room sofa-bed, wakening to the vast fifteenth floor view, the lowering sky and the beautiful forlorn expanse of Paris in winter, wadded in its thick and sodden grey.

A week after mother and baby returned from the hospital, my sister and I stood in her "bedroom"—Paris spread out behind us from a slightly different angle, still so profoundly grey—trying to master the breast pump, in order that we might slip out for an hour, the two of us, without the baby. My sister, goose-pimpled in the chill, was naked from the waist up, her usually small breasts pendulous, veined and swinging; the tiny baby lay mercifully asleep in a quilted basket on the bed. We puzzled over the medieval contraption of rubber tubing and plastic, the attachment of the little bottle, the screwing and plugging and pumping of it. We laughed until tears ran down our cheeks, until our knees buckled, until the expanse of Paris out the window behind us grew wavery and surreal; I pressed the flange to her bosom; she tried to pump; the suction caused her pain but no milk came; we adjusted; began again; readjusted; began again, drunk on our laughter. In the middle of it, the baby awoke and began to cry. Her reedy, persistent wails provoked the Jack Russell to growl and then to bark—he was just doing his job—and my sister and I were reduced to hysterics, still laughing, laughing, until I realized she was crying also, laughing and crying both, because this insane and fruitless cacophony was reality, was now her real life.

Several weeks later, back in the States, in our then tidily childless life, I turned to my husband and said, out of the blue, truly struggling to comprehend it, "Can you believe they've still got that baby?" Try as we might, we couldn't begin to grasp what it must be like.

• • •

More than a decade later, in another time and place, I felt a similar confusion. This was in May, 2009, in the penultimate stretch of an extraordinary week in Palestine under the auspices of PalFest, a literary festival organized by Ahdaf Soueif and sponsored by the British Council, as I loitered with my fellow travelers—writers and publishers from various Anglophone countries—in the dusk on the Israeli side of the Bethlehem checkpoint, waiting for the bus to return us to our hotel in East Jerusalem. The bloody sun was setting behind a monolithic stretch of Israeli settlements. The wire-caged runs for the checkpoint queues were all but empty at nightfall, looking like some strange, brutalist artwork.

We'd just returned from a long day in Hebron, perhaps the most bitterly contested and scarred city in the West Bank. In the morning, we'd met with students at the Islamic university there, and had held creative writing workshops. I was teaching with the publisher Carmen Callil, in a classroom with only small windows, high up, so that when we were seated we couldn't see out. Nobody turned on a light. The overriding impression was of darkness.

Carmen had asked our group of students—young men and women, the former voluble and irascible, the latter distinctly fewer, veiled and mute—what stories or elements of their culture they felt it would be most important to pass on to their children. Young man after young man expressed a variation upon one theme: the children needed to understand the Occupation, the violence and oppression of the Israeli soldiers; they needed to know guns and grenades; they needed to learn to fight with whatever means they had. They needed to understand that the struggle against Israel was the most important thing in their lives.

This was very different from our earlier visit to Bir Zeit University in Ramallah, where the students—many of them gregarious young women, many of them unveiled, all of them more apparently prosperous, with more prospects—held out hope. Those students had spoken of wanting to edit newspapers or run radio stations or lead organizations, of the need to foster new businesses and women's autonomy in Palestinian society. But Ramallah is a thriving and cosmopolitan city under Palestinian control. The students in Hebron—where the Israeli military holds sway—were confronted by a different, darker reality altogether.

Eventually, Carmen asked if there were really no other stories to pass on to new generations—only this one? A first young woman finally spoke up: "We have songs," she said. "I would want the children to know our songs." And another:

"We have special recipes, food that is part of our culture. And we have customs and folk stories. We would want to pass on these things." And a third, "I'd want to tell them what it was like for me growing up—not just the Occupation, but about my family, and my friends." After a brief silence, the young men spoke up again, resumed the tales of war.

After the university, we were taken by a guide to the Ibrahimi Mosque—site of the massacre in 1994, in which an American-born right-wing Israeli attacked unarmed Muslim worshippers at prayer, killing twenty men and wounding one hundred and twenty five—and to the old city of Hebron, where tensions between the Palestinians and the Israeli settlers run unbearably high. The only other visitors were a busload of Muslim Indonesians on pilgrimage: the mosque is one of Islam's holiest sites. Below the mosque, a quaint little strip of tourist shops opened for our benefit, offering local pottery and textiles, a few postcards, bottles of water. We were their only customers; when we moved on, they told us, they would shut for the day.

Across the baking dirt road, a large settler café and gift shop with plate glass windows and diner-style tables enjoyed modest custom. A couple of their clients, burly, bearded, in polo shirts and jeans, wandered by with machine guns strapped casually around their chests, one of them accompanied by a large German shepherd. The café was equipped with large megaphones on its roof that blared pop music into the plaza at top volume. The Palestinian shopkeepers explained that this aural assault, from early in the morning until late at night, aimed to harass the Muslim worshippers, to show disrespect for the holiness of the mosque. One shopkeeper confided that the settlers had offered him $1 million USD for his shop: "I will never sell," he said. "We will never leave."

In addition to the roaming armed settlers, the little row of shops was attended at one end by the military, a camouflage-draped checkpoint around which a cluster of Israeli soldiers shuffled impatiently, anxiously, their guns at the ready. They didn't like us taking pictures of the street; or of the café; or, above all, of them; and harangued some of our number on this account. Inevitably, we had to pass their security to proceed to the old town.

The open dusty stretch where the shopkeepers closed their ears, and their shops, to the din of the settlers' café proved an Elysium next to the main market street not far away. As they'd always done, the Palestinians kept their stalls along this narrow, damp and faintly fetid stretch of cobblestone, where children frolicked among the wares and in the dark doorways. Like anywhere in the Middle East, there were olives and spices, breads, oils, keffiyehs and djellabas, plastic shoes, brassieres and metal coffee pots for sale.

But now the settlers lived in annexed apartments above them along the route. They had a tendency vindictively to pelt the Palestinians with garbage. To deal with the problem and to protect the Palestinians, the Israeli military had stretched netting over the length of the street, to emphatically claustrophobic effect: it was now as if the people on the ground moved like animals in a cage, contained the way my friends in college kept their pet snake, to be monitored from above. The netting was distended and soiled in places by the detritus—plastic, paper, rotting food—tossed from on high. Accustomed, the children and their parents didn't appear to notice; only the tourists looked up, aghast.

Our guide eventually deposited us at a Visitors' Center where we were shown a film about the struggles between the settlers and the Palestinians, including footage of settler children hurling insults and rocks at Palestinian children whose path to school—the only school in their district—lay across territory claimed by the Settlers. I've since read about further violence these Palestinian schoolchildren must endure—beatings, vandalism, even having their hair set on fire by settler kids their own age, under the eyes of the Israeli military.[2]

In the course of our afternoon, we gleaned only the slightest glimpse of what it might be like—only a flicker of the constant haranguing, the barrage of hostility, the incipient violence in the air. Both sides are angry, enraged, even; but only one side has the power. Only the settlers and the soldiers carry weapons. Approximately thirty-seven thousand Palestinians live in the old city of Hebron, alongside six to eight hundred Jews, the latter protected by approximately two thousand Israeli soldiers.

As we stood at last on the Israeli side of the Bethlehem checkpoint, eager to get back to the hotel for dinner and a shower, we all felt profound relief—like an actual weight lifted—to be away from Hebron. We were grateful even for the brief bus ride from Hebron to Bethlehem—thirteen crucial miles—for any distance we could put between ourselves and that unrelieved and palpable distress. As we waited in the dusk, I turned to my fellows: "Can you believe all the people we met are still there, still in Hebron?"

We couldn't really imagine it. How long would the shopkeepers wait for another busload of visitors, their doors padlocked? Did the café blare music even now? What might happen in the darkness? How long until a gun was fired? What might be the fate of a frustrated Palestinian child, a boy of twelve, say, or a girl of nine, who spoke rudely to a soldier, or worse, who threw a rock?

If, before I had a child, I couldn't imagine what it must be like to be a parent, how much less could I imagine what it must be like to be born in Hebron, to grow up under a net, in the sights of a gun, harassed each day by noise and insults, pelted with rocks and garbage when walking to school or to the market, with minimal job prospects, no hope for the future, and no obvious way out. The physical dread I felt in Hebron I have experienced nowhere else: like a held

2 Lena Odgaard, "For Palestinian kids in Hebron, Little Joy on Back-to-School Day," Al-Monitor, September 9, 2012. http://www.al-monitor.com/pulse/originals/2012/al-monitor/grim-back-to-school-day-for-hebr.html#

breath, it didn't seem possibly sustainable. How hard, then, was it to believe, sitting over coffee at the King David Hotel in East Jerusalem a couple of days later, that everyone in Hebron was *still there*, in that same unbreathable air? Had we not dreamed them? How could we not hope that we had? How much harder still to believe, a month later, back in Boston; and still now, after years . . .

This vision of utter powerlessness and doom, this thick aura of impending violence, this utter inability to act for oneself or for others—this reality for thousands of Palestinians—I know it, in my life of inordinate privilege, chiefly when asleep: in nightmares from which I have every expectation of awakening. Ironically, it's in dreams that we confront the hardest truths—it's there that we encounter insurmountable adversity, true hopelessness—even though in dreams, you'd think, you should be able to do whatever you want. In waking, lulled by contentment or the anticipation of it, we avert our eyes from what we cannot bear to know. The children of Hebron have no such luxury.

Till My End and Till Its End

by *Mahmoud Darwish*

(Translated from Arabic by Marilyn Hacker)

Are you tired of walking
My son, are you tired?
—Yes, Papa
Your night stretches out on the road
And my heart spills on the earth of your night.
—You've always been agile as a cat!
Climb on my shoulders
And we'll take a shortcut through
The last forest of terebinth and oak
Galilee is to the north of us
And Lebanon behind us
And all the sky is ours from Damascus
To the beautiful walls of Acre
—And after that?
—We'll go home
Do you know the way, my son?
Yes, Papa
East of the carob tree on the main road
There is a little path hemmed in by cactuses
At first, then it goes to the well
Getting wider and wider, then it leads
To the grapevines of Uncle Jamil
Who sells tobacco and sweets,
Then it loses itself on the threshing floor before
It picks itself up, comes in and sits down in our house
Like a parakeet.
—Do you know our home, my son?
I know it as well as I know the path
Jasmin grows around the iron gate
There are footprints of light on the stone steps
Behind the house a sunflower stares into the distance

And domestic bees prepare Grandfather's breakfast
On a wicker platter.
In the courtyard, there is a well, a willow and a horse
And one of these tomorrows our pages will be leafed through behind the wall . . .

Papa, are you tired?
I see drops of sweat in your eyes.
—Yes, my son, I'm tired . . . Will you carry me?
—Just the way you carried me, Papa
And I'll carry that tenderness
Until
My beginning and its beginning
And I'll follow this road until
My end . . . And until its end

Under the Table

CLARENCE YOUNG

I only remember the name of one of my friends from when I was eight years old: Vincent, a boy that the adults around me urged me to fight with the words "deal with him." Violence solidifies useless memories.

State-level violence? That creates fossils. Bones, hearts and minds of stone that believe killing people is okay because of words like these: retaliation; defense; sovereignty. We call those "policies," and we use them to justify killing. Policy is as foolish as a group of adults encouraging a child toward a pointless fight. I'm sure they thought they were toughening me up, just as those who send others to kill create excuses for behaving as though damnation is always for others.

I don't know what I can possibly write that will change a single mind in the Israeli government. Benjamin Netanyahu has dug into the role of embattled righteousness, a hole which governing bodies tend to peer out of only at night, and only at what they want to see. We won't pretend Israel hasn't planned to hem Palestine into the tightest, most volatile circumstance they possibly can, because they have. You cannot be an occupying force demanding and expecting quiescence even as further encroachments are made. You cannot create unyielding barriers and expect the ghetto to garden. Israel has created an untenable situation. We also won't pretend that, being a superpower compared to Palestine, Israel has not and does not have the capability to end what might as well be known as the world's Forever War. Israel has the resources to capitulate.

When I was growing up we heard all about the PLO. This generation gets "Hamas." Groups that see violence as a means. What would they do if, at some point, someone on both sides of Gaza decided to be the adults who saw no value in fighting, someone on both sides who stepped out of the industry of war—and make no mistake, no large country that has been at war for generations is doing so without a large profit component, and the United States has plenty of bullets to sell—and realized there is actually no reason their children need to be found buried under tables, under rubble, during the bright light of day when television cameras are at their most active and anguish, pure and vibrant in high definition suffering, races across social media to fuel our days' ire. Today, Netanyahu bathes in what he sees as righteous blood.

Yet violence is never given life without it demanding life in return. The death of the body for one, the death of the spirit for the other. We don't need to kill to be heard. We don't need to kill to live. It is my hope that a thousand voices will speak better than I have. It is my hope that my voice will join others that will form a nation that will say to Israel: "Enough!" We speak blithely today of radical this and radical that. I want to imagine radical peace.

The only reason to find a child under a table is because that child was using it for shade from the bright sun. Using it to sit and read. Or perhaps to dream.

MARY JANE NEALON

I wrote this piece as a response to the negativity I experienced when I finally took a position publicly against Israel's actions in Gaza in the summer of 2014. People I considered friends told me to educate myself, and that statement silenced me for weeks. I kept telling myself the tipping point came with the deaths of so many children. I realized then I did know what I was talking about; I knew what a child's death looked like up close, and I knew what it meant to hold a child in my arms against anxiety and fatigue. I am allowing myself to take this stand—the execution of innocent children trumps all other argument.

This I Know

In the summer of 2014, I finally said it: *Goddammit. Israel. Stop it.* Just like that, only once, which in the darkness of such slaughter was nothing and I knew it. Everything else went on as before. When I left for work each morning I adjusted the sign notifying the police and firemen that if a fire should start while I was at work there were two dogs in my home. I feared losing everything, my home and my dogs, even in this town where neighbors communally clear snow off the street and fix each other's lawn mowers. Yet every morning I woke to news of children dying in the small piece of land called Gaza, news that made a gulley in the day, a dark, shadowy split. On the day I called out to Israel on Facebook to *stop it*, it was not so quiet. People I knew for thirty years turned their backs on me. There was derision. Someone said *educate yourself* before they cut me off. I am almost sixty years old old but I doubted that morning that I knew anything at all.

◆ ◆ ◆

In 1991 I was working as a research nurse for a Phase I trial of liposomal amphotericin. *Amphoterrible* is what the young patients called the medicine because of the high fevers and extreme rigors they experienced when the yellow bag dripped its liquid into their central line catheters. In the bright white rooms they did all sorts of things to prepare: wrapped themselves in thin hospital blankets, wore socks, listened to meditation. It was hard to believe, that these young boys and girls with leukemia were surviving their cancer, in remissions that were sturdy but dying instead from fungal infections, and so this was why they would have to take *amphoterrible*. Despite their willingness to withstand this treatment, it was often not enough to save them from fungal infections like aspergillosis. But what if, a scientist had asked, what if we encapsulated the medicine in fat cells that would change the way it passed through the kidneys? Could we then maybe give ten times the dose?

The first woman I gave the medicine to died. Right there as I was watching it go in. And she was going to die anyway, right? That's why her husband signed the consent form. She died shaking and spiking a fever over 104. As she shook and spasmed, I pushed Demerol into her vein but by then her heart, oversized from Adriamycin, found it was impossible to spasm and pump and her husband leaned toward her, toward me and asked if she was going to be okay. When he said that, I was calling the code so others would run into the room to try and save her and even if she couldn't be saved I wouldn't be alone with her, with him. While I was doing that I was remembering how, two months earlier, a friend was riding her bike in Central Park when a handsome man pulled alongside her on his bike and said *how are you doing?* And she said, *oh . . . okay,* and then the man pulled a gun, pointed it at her and said, *you are never okay.*

◆　◆　◆

I stopped paying for television after the attacks on the World Trade Center because I couldn't bear to keep seeing the replay of what I had watched from my bedroom window. The sick glee of all the twenty-four-hour newscasters at finally having enough news to fill the entire day. The self-righteous, newly appointed *experts* in languages and history and weapons. Everyone seemed to know so much about everything. In the streets on that day, when the burned and stunned survivors were coming off the ferryboats in New Jersey, people who had never said, even once, any politically incorrect thing, said things like *it is our blind support of Israel that has led us here.* The fact that we uttered those words filled us with shame. Even minutes after people said it, they denied saying it. We felt their historic trauma, the crime of the holocaust, of families with seventy-five or a hundred members reduced to one single survivor who had gone on to make another wide and accomplished family of children and grandchildren who were told about all their massacred ancestors. Wasn't anything they did after that sanctioned? This was the broad sweep of forgiveness we always offered our friends in Israel, no matter what. After September 11th no one said *educate yourself.* The comments were given no weight. They were wiped off the lips of those who said it even as the sounds were still coming out, the guilt of the thought that we should reconsider our friendship with Israel was so strong.

◆　◆　◆

The anti-fungal study didn't get pulled just because one person died. But I had to fill out a Serious Adverse Event Report. The doctor I worked with encouraged me to recruit the next person, to scrutinize culture reports looking for just the right candidate. Someone who was on the old formula but who hadn't responded, someone whose kidneys were holding up to the drug. *I just don't want to do a kid,* I said. *Don't worry, nobody on pediatrics is going to want this.*

◆　◆　◆

Kin Moy was ten years old. His doctor called me first thing Monday morning. *Hey, you can enroll kids on the liposomal ampho study, right?* Shit. *Yes.* Shit. Kin's parents spoke a rare Chinese dialect. There were Cantonese interpreters, and Mandarin and Fukinese interpreters, but no one could communicate with them. Kin had to interpret the doctor's words. I wonder if he conveyed the sense of fear and doom in the room from all of us. He was matter of fact, and his parents gazed down at his small frame in the bed and nodded and signed the paper. I took the order to the pharmacy and waited for the bag of thick medicine while the pediatric nurses gave Kin Benadryl and Demerol and Tylenol to try and prevent the fevers and rigors.

Shake and bake, the kid in the next bed said, *get ready to shake and bake, Kin!*

I had to get a special blood pressure cuff for his thin upper arm. He had three action figures on his bedside table: the Hulk, Spiderman, and one I didn't know with dark purple plastic clothes and a lightning rod across its chest. He held the Hulk in his left hand when the fever first took hold. But his body withstood the rigors valiantly. The muscles tightened and collapsed as he rode the fever. His heart kept a fast but steady beat. Then he had a bright and ferocious period of sweating and then, when I'd changed his pillowcase and rubbed my hand over his bald and perfect head, he slept.

◆　◆　◆

On the eleventh day Kin was on my study, and I went down to give him his dose. *He's been moved to 506,* the charge nurse said. *He's crashing, we're trying to reach his father.* Kin's father delivered vegetables to small markets, he could be anywhere on the island of Manhattan. *His mother is in there.* 506 was a private room, when the doctors think a kid is going to die they always move them into a private room to allow the parents privacy and to protect the families who still believe they have a chance to make it.

I realized I had begun to look forward to seeing Kin each day, his determination. The day before, the doctor tried to tell his mother that the fungal pneumonia seemed to be resisting even this new magical medicine we'd been so hopeful about, and that he probably couldn't get chemo again and that the white cells in his body, which should be 10,000, were 650,000 and that's what the pain in his legs was about, and look, even these little balls under his skin, these are white cells. But that we'd give him good pain medicine so he wouldn't suffer. Even after Kin interpreted that for his mother and father, and the doctor's eyes watered at their puzzled looks, and they followed the doctor into the hall, where of course no one could explain or help them, even then Kin asked me to hand him his notebook. *What are you going to do, honey?* I asked. *My homework,* he said, *I don't want to be behind when I go back to school.*

      ◆   ◆   ◆

Eman Mohammed is a Palestinian photographer. I friended her on Facebook after all my friends of thirty years had blocked me for taking a stand against Israel. *The numbers make no sense,* I said. *Nothing excuses the death of so many children.* One person, before she wrote me off completely, argued, *they are being used as human shields. Blame Hamas.* I thought about all the TV shows I used to watch as a child: *Mannix, One Adam 12, Kojak.* Everyone knew that bank robbers escaped by taking a hostage, usually a woman in a shift dress and spiked heels. By pulling a damsel from her work station and exiting the bank with her held in a chokehold, a gun to her left temple. Because no one kills the hostage, not intentionally. She works as a shield *because* she is innocent. No one shoots an innocent. Eman posts photographs of parents holding the clothes of their dead sons and daughters. Tiny lace dresses, a sweater knitted with zigzags. Emptiness makes its way into every aspect of my house all summer long: a space in the breadbox where muffins were, holes in the yard the dogs dig to fill with half-eaten bones, the dead squirrels' right eye socket taken by a magpie. The sweater of the Palestinian boy, four years old, in Eman's photo, that I print and fold and carry in my pocket.

      ◆   ◆   ◆

When I entered room 506, I noticed the NY Mets baseball cap hanging from the IV pole next to Kin Moy's bed. He was drowsy from morphine that dripped now from his bag; he smiled at me and put his hand out. His mother was frowning and sitting in the corner. She shrugged her shoulders. What was happening to her boy? I went over and touched her back. She shook her head. And then, Kin made a gasp. He was sleeping but his chest and his breath were asynchronistic causing him to labor for breath. His mother ran to him, started screaming and shouting something in Chinese, and his body, light as milk weed, stirred. *No,* I said, *no.* I rubbed my own hands up and down his limbs which were all bones and bumps of white cell clusters, *Kin,* I whispered, making my voice melodic, *Kin, it will be beautiful, Kin, you will be as light as air, Kin. Look, Kin, there's your father at the market, and look, Kin, your little brother, in his history class, he's paying attention, Kin, see him?* His mother watched and then she nodded and caressed his other leg and said something that was filled with tenderness and she and I together, in our languages, moved him into the next world as easily as a cloud moves in the sky under a summer wind.

      ◆   ◆   ◆

Someone I really admire, a journalist, posts thoughtful things on Facebook about the conflict in Gaza. I "like" his posts but I am hesitant to engage. One morning, someone posts under one of his statements, *they should evacuate (sic) the children.* I think about all the stories of Jews in WWII hiding their children. I remember my friend's photos from Vietnam of children leaving Saigon on a Pan Am jet. And yes, I know about repercussions and lost identities and all of the reasons not to do that but I spontaneously post: *I never thought of that, yes, why haven't we done that?* I feel a moment of hope that something can be done, the death toll among the children now so close to five hundred. But the journalist I admire says, *they don't want to leave their country,* and dismisses us both by name. He has lived in Gaza for three months and has more credibility than I. I am disappointed in myself. At my fear of public embarrassment. Still I ask him, *but then how can the children be saved?* I ask, though I know I am annoying him with my naiveté. *They can't.* His post is the final one in the string.

◆　◆　◆

Flying to Montana in the summer of Gaza I think of those words, *they can't.* And once again I allow myself to feel Kin's hot bumpy legs under my hands and his mother's hands alongside mine. We couldn't save him, but we honored him, we escorted him from this world with the reverence he deserved. As I hurtle through the skies over Montana at five hundred miles an hour, I see the empty sweater of the four-year-old Palestinian boy. Each one that went unsaved left an empty space. Below us, land where an ocean once was, land that no one owns, covered with snow that is almost all melted this summer, feeding its whiteness into rivers.

Gaza

HAYAN CHARARA

Stay with me, my boy
says every night before falling
asleep. He makes it easy
for me to be sentimental.
I love that he loves a toy
elephant he named
Elefante and a girl
named Amelia who loves
that he loves running
after her. I love that he believes
the sun, like grass
and distant trains
and fish in the ocean sleep
when he sleeps. I love
that he does not know
the half of it. And tonight,
I can't help myself—
I love most of all
that there will be no sirens
waking him, no warnings
to flee the house, no roof
falling upon him, which
mothers and fathers
are cheering.

•　•　•

From an interview with Randa Jarrar, author of the novel *Map of Home* and editor at *The Normal School*, October 15, 2014. Reprinted with the permission of the author.

RJ: "Gaza" has a surprising turn—it mentions the phenomenon from this past summer when Israelis would watch bombs drop in Gaza from mountaintops and cheer. How did you find the space and energy to create a poem out of that, especially so soon after the event itself?

HC: I've had years to think about it, actually. Nearly every incursion by Israel into Gaza, or elsewhere—like Lebanon—comes with stories like this one. As far back as the 80s and 90s, I remember seeing images of Israelis—men, women, and even children—writing messages on missiles, which they took to be cute or funny, like "From Israel, with love." These are missiles that kill people, crushing them to death, exploding their bodies, scattering them into bits and pieces. So why didn't I write about this until now? I have children now—two boys, a two-year-old and a three-year-old. With this latest invasion of Gaza, I had a very basic reaction. As a parent, I imagined my own children in the shoes of these other children. The thought kills me. But I was more devastated by the realization that this perspective, that of a mother or father, could be so comprised, so corrupted, that mothers and fathers were dancing and singing over the deaths of other people's children—boys and girls like their own boys and girls.

Something in you is dead when you celebrate the death of children. My writing a poem was a pushing back against that kind of destruction—of human life, yes, but also the destruction of what makes a person humane and human.

Palestine

CRISTINA GARCÍA

The killing is personal

    boys captured blown up

         muzzled

history's reluctant footnotes

No war ever began

without aggressors

swearing victimhood

first

Silence is too exorbitant

Our children, our children's children

    will talk

slow rivers of words

Violence isn't confidence

      they'll say

terror isn't mastery

Each boy had a name

I've been reading a great deal about World War II in the last two years, especially regarding Third Reich policies at home and on the Eastern front. This is for a novel I'm working on. It strikes me how the same arguments are used by perpetrators again and again to justify the unjustifiable. Even their language barely changes. In the end, it's always the children who suffer most. We need to remember their names.

Ice Cream in Gaza

KAFAH BACHARI

Red wool, and falsely brightened, since

we need the help.

    A child because

    the chambers of the heart will hold so

little.

    —Still Life, Linda Gregerson

There was once.

A little girl named Lala lived with her mother in a place named Gaza, and all who knew her loved her, most of all her Uncle Hashem, who gave her a red coat and called her Little Red Riding Hood, after a story he'd read once, many years before, in America. In that story the girl was foolish and was devoured by a terrible wolf, but Uncle Hashem knew Lala was clever and would never betray herself to a wolf. Also their lives were not fairy tales—tempting as it was to imagine a clever woodsman bestowing, before the bitter end, the end to their sufferings—and it was more likely that Lala would be killed by fire flying out from the darkness of night than an anthropomorphized wolf, an otherwise peaceful creature made ugly by man's imagination. He told her the story as a cautionary tale, saying, "I know your actions will demonstrate the strength of your mind, not the foolishness of your heart." He believed he was imparting a special kind of wisdom to her, hopeful that she'd be able to pass it on some day, in some fashion, to the next generation. Maybe.

Lala wore the red coat with pride and was admired by the other little girls and could be seen, a great vibrant redness against the dull brown sand of the refugee camp, from kilometers away in many directions, but not too many kilometers lest one be touched by the blue of the sea or the barbed wire of an old armistice line. In this way, Lala and the little red coat became inseparable from one another and one couldn't imagine Lala without also imagining the little red coat.

Uncle Hashem did not live near the camp like Lala. It was a matter of pride. When he returned from America, he took his wife and their newborn out of the house Lala and her mother and father lived in, and moved into an old seaside villa. He was an American educated doctor and his home would have a view of the sea. A view of the sea was a view of all that Gaza wasn't, even if the view was from the top of a crumbling building that had survived, inexplicably, the last war no one had heard of and which even he was beginning to forget, as a man might forget the circumstances of his birth or the fact of his impending death. Never mind, it was a luxury to live in such a mindset, and he wouldn't give this up, not even for Gaza. On the first floor he had a medical practice where he would see patients complaining from any number of illness that were all really something else. For example, extreme boredom presenting itself as a terminal and most definitely fatal chest pains by one hysterical Umm Hamdi Hamoodi, or an utter lack of interest in mathematics masquerading as a developmental delay in a boy of fourteen named Hamdi Hamoodi, or depression cloaked as a stubborn insistence on revisiting certain events of the past and asking why over and over again by one Ms. Jamilah Hussein, widow of Mr. Hussein Hussein, who perished heroically in a firefight in the last war no one had heard of and which Jamilah could not forget. In all their charts he wrote, "Diagnosis: Gaza. Patient suffers from Gaza." Once Uncle Hashem wrote Umm Hamdi a prescription which read, "Leave Gaza, get a life" and she laughed, a great big sound coming from the cavernous mouth of the forty-seventh most anxious woman in Gaza.

"Dr. Juda. This is my homeland. It's yours too."

"Learn to swim Umm Hamdi. There is a sea here at your disposal. Please, it will do your heart some good and my time can be spent watching LBC in peace."

"I'd be better off learning how to dig, Doctor."

At that very moment the TV screened flashed with the start of a game show. All of the game shows on LBC featured beautiful women, as did all of the other shows on the LBC, the news, for example, and the dramas, and the comedies. Watching LBC gave one the distinct impression that all the women in Lebanon were voluptuous brunettes with silken skin so white it glowed and perfect little noses and great moons for breasts and voices a surgeon's knife never touched. Uncle Hashem could fall asleep listening to them, or thinking of them, or wondering if an army of them might charm the world into mundane quietude.

"I'll see you next week." Umm Hamdi walked out slowly, as if there was no better place to be in the world but inside the office of an irritable middle-aged man who may have been diagnosed with any number of illness associated with a diet just less than the 2,279 calorie intake recommended by the World Health Organization and a broken heart. The lights flickered on and off and on again but the TV screen remained dark and the LBC girls were gone, for now, at least.

"Damn power."

Uncle Hashem suffered his patients all morning and again, after lunch, all afternoon, until Lala appeared at his door and said, "Mama says it is dinner time." And he took off his white doctor's coat and put on a light jacket and walked through the narrow streets with Lala's and imagined he was her father, and his own daughter wasn't dead, and that she was his daughter, and her own father wasn't dead and that they were on an early evening stroll as banal and unremarkable as a cypress tree.

"Uncle Hashem, why did you come back from America?"

"This is my home. I was only in America to study. I had to come back." What he meant to say was he'd already had a child and the child was waiting and the mother couldn't leave, and after all, this was home like a millstone around his neck, and he missed the bread his wife made and his mother's coffee on Friday mornings. He should have stayed on in that small town in Georgia, where he was mistaken for black, when he was mistaken for anything, and it was better to be black in America than an Arab man with a dead wife and a dead child in the pene-exclave of Gaza, but that wasn't something he wanted to tell Lala. He was home and apart from himself, he was alive and as good as dead. But he didn't say any of these things. They were all disjoined and confused in his head. Sometimes he didn't believe himself. Why had he come back? Why had he left? Why did he exist at all and as a Gazan, which seemed a particularly difficult burden to bear once one had borne exile—even a very temporary one. Don't leave Gaza is what he should have said to Lala, I shouldn't have left myself. It is better to know only Gaza or if you leave, to hold the fading memory in your heart like a stone, rather than come back.

"Hamid of Ramallah says if he could go to America and study like you did he would never come back here. He says Gaza is a bad place and that no one who has brains enough to leave, should stay, let alone come back. Is that true?"

"Look," he wanted to tell Lala, "There isn't a truth more noble than the fact of our existence. Even the Israelites who dared to leave two centuries ago came back singing their birthright songs. No one who leaves can stay away and no one who returns can forget where they have been. Lala, we are the Israelites who stayed behind. We stayed with this land too long. We became Christians. We became Muslims. We became fools over and again. We died so that we could live in the next world with those who had died before. That is the truth as I know it. The dust and the sea and the old armistice line like three wise men hunting the brightest star that someone turned off long ago. A dream you can feel but can't remember. A divine message in analog when all that we can hear now is digital. Land of milk and honey and horseshit. Land of Dr. Hashem Juda's despair. Land of songs and solitude, madness and repentance." He might has well have added, "There was once, in an anemic strip of land along a very blue sea, a man who prayed for dust and two thousand years later, a long blink in the eye of the God of Bonbons, dust rained and bloomed and shimmied like slow motion angels down upon the villages of Gaza and buried those who stayed and those who loved the dust returned to claim what they took to be promised to them alone."

But he didn't because she was a child, and she was new in the world, and it was already too much for her—for any child—to be born with the burden of a disappeared nation, let alone hear the affected musings of a man who'd lost everything and nothing over and over again. In time, she would learn about the terrible dilemma of citizenship to a land no one recognizes, and what it meant or didn't mean to belong to a place trapped in the gap between oblivion and annihilation, and of the desires of a free people to be free.

Instead, he squeezed her hand and said, in a fatherly way, "He is correct and incorrect, Lala. Gaza is our home and so we are drawn here, no matter how far away we travel. And while it may be inhospitable to our dreams at times and make us terribly sick, we can not deny that it is a part of us, and that it shapes us, and that we are damned to long for it, and some of us, damned to return."

He stopped walking and turned to look Lala in the eyes, "Do you understand, Lala?"

Her eyes filled him with a strange mixture of hope and sadness. "Suffer but weep not," he wanted to say now.

"Uncle, do you think the grocery store will have ice cream bars today?"

On certain Thursday afternoons it was possible that the small grocery store on the far side of the camp would have a special and limited collection of ice cream bars smuggled into Gaza by Hamid of Ramallah. Hamid of Ramallah could get ice cream bars, Dove brand soap, Camel Light cigarettes, generic ibuprofen, lentils, tomato paste, soccer balls, tampons, condoms, and keyboard pianos. If someone wanted chocolate, say to give to someone they liked, sometimes Hamid of Ramallah could bring a Dairy Milk chocolate bar hidden in the leg of his pants the next time he crossed Eretz. But his specialty was ice cream bars and no one knew how he managed to keep them cold but he did and he was the most beloved smuggler of goods among children and adults alike, even though he was from Ramallah and a refugee, as opposed to a native of Gaza, which is different. A native wasn't displaced the way a refugee was displaced. A native was imposed upon, forced to share, given over to giving into the open maw of the need of the refugee. Such was the burden of the natives of Gaza, including Uncle Hashem and his lot.

The grocery shop owner was a native, of course, and Hamid of Ramallah was his friend, even if he was also a refugee. And so it was no surprise to find both of them inside the shop on Thursday afternoon and for both of them to smile when they saw Uncle Hashem and a red coat with his little Lala inside.

"Peace be upon you," they each said in turn and shook hands and kissed each other's cheeks.

"Lala dear, I have a package of pink bubblegum just for you!" said the shop owner.

"I was hoping for an ice cream bar today. Hamid of Ramallah, did you bring any?"

Hamid of Ramallah looked at Uncle Hashem, then sighed and turned to look woefully at the shop owner, who shrugged.

"My dearest, I was not able to bring ice cream on this trip but I promise to try the next time I come."

"But you said next week last week, Hamid of Ramallah."

"Lala, don't be rude. It isn't easy to bring such things. Why don't you try the gum?" Uncle Hashem squeezed her hand gently.

"Thank you for the gum." Lala said and placed it in the pocket of her little red coat.

"Gentlemen, I trust you and your families are well?"

"Thank God. We are well in our house. But Hamid of Ramallah is in trouble; tell him, brother."

Hamid of Ramallah hesitated. "No, it isn't the time, not now."

"Lala, wait for me outside dear."

"No Uncle, I want to hear what is wrong with Hamid of Ramallah."

"Yes, but some business is only between a man and his doctor, Lala."

"Then why does he get to stay?" said Lala and pointed to the shop owner.

"Come on then Lala, I'll wait outside with you." The shop owner took her hand and they walked out and stood in the street.

"Hamid, tell me. What is it?"

"Umm Hamdi's daughter is pregnant."

"Does your mother know?"

"No, of course not. Umm Hamdi doesn't know either."

"No one has told you this yet, so I will, you are an idiot." Uncle Hashem slapped Hamid of Ramallah on the back of his head.

"I don't know what to do. She'll be ruined if anyone finds out. She's meant to go to university in Egypt next year. This will ruin it for her."

"How far along?"

"Not far."

"There is a medicine you can obtain that will help her avoid this embarrassment. It is available in Jerusalem or Tel Aviv."

"My next trip is in three weeks."

"That is too much time wasted. Go sooner, if you can, while this is a problem that can be fixed."

"Brother, these things are out of my hands. The borders are closed."

"You might have considered that before you got yourself and a nice girl in trouble."

When they left the shop Lala asked her Uncle what was the problem with Hamid of Ramallah but Uncle Hashem was silent.

In the small house at the far other side of the camp Lala helped her mother, Tamara, turn a pot filled with thin chicken and rice upside down onto a silver tray.

"Voila," Tamara said and smiled at Uncle Hashem.

"Tamara, this looks wonderful as usual. You are a magician of culinary magnificence. You are, dare I say, the best cook in Gaza."

"You, brother, are the best liar in Gaza."

The evening passed in this way as it always did; polite conversation, dishes washed and dried, coffee, and maybe after Lala went to bed, Tamara would have a cigarette with Uncle Hashem and they would speak in voices so low Lala couldn't hear, but sometimes she could discern the soft crying of her mother and the warm voice of her Uncle saying it would be alright, all suffering has an end.

Occasionally, the lights went out or the curfew began early and Uncle Hashem would sleep on the couch in the living room. Lala liked those nights the best because she didn't worry about Uncle Hashem all alone by the seaside in his office. On such nights Lala slept deeply, without dreaming of ice cream or wondering what heaven was like and whether Aunt Sara, her father and Tala kept each other company while they waited for Tamara, and Uncle Hashem and Lala. On such nights it was silence and velvet darkness; the kind that didn't come screaming so very alive.

"You could sleep here every night," Lala said as Uncle Hashem tucked her in.

"Good night Lala."

Uncle Hashem didn't need to worry about waking up in time to open his office the next morning when he stayed with Tamara and Lala. Lala was always dressed and beside him before dawn.

"Uncle, I'll walk with you to your office. Mama says I can if I promise to come back right away without any stops."

In the early morning sunshine the streets were still quiet, still recovering from the deep silence of night, slowly emerging but still endowed with a fine coating of honey colored dust. A million little motes captive in the long tendrils of sunshine. The shop windows, the street sweepers, the carts pulled by donkeys from an era before, the era they lived in perpetually, were all still faint suggestions of themselves. Uncle Hashem gritted his teeth.

There was once.

Mornings with coffee in a prosaic student apartment. In his student days in that small town in Georgia—where everything shined clean and new, even if it was old, and everything smelled of soap and hopefulness, because the world was very so completely open—one didn't need a view of the sea to feel a moment of escape from endless dust, one didn't feel continually submerged and emerging from some invulnerable menace. One was simply of the world, nature didn't have a second meaning; trees grew because they could, boys and girls laughed without complications, and if there was a window you could open it. And it didn't have to end until someone said, "tell me again how to say your name?"

"Lala, I had a very dear friend in Georgia and he was a Palestinian like us, but he'd been born in America, and couldn't ever come back here."

"How was he a Palestinian like us if he wasn't born here?"

"His parents were born here but then left."

"They didn't come back?"

"No."

"And so he also couldn't come back? Because they didn't?"

"His friends and everything he'd ever known was in America, even if he constantly spoke of being Palestinian. If he came here, if he could, he would miss America the way we would miss Gaza."

"I bet he has all the ice cream he wants whenever he wants."

"For you, everything is measured in ice cream."

After they arrived at the office, Uncle Hashem watched as the image of Lala's red coat got dimmer and dimmer until his eyes couldn't discern her anymore. When he opened his office there was barely a moment before his patients began to arrive, his patients who oppressed him with their millions of unnamable anxieties all morning and all afternoon and into the evening and beyond, for weeks, until one singular explosion stopped all their whining and half the sky collapsed upon them. Don't believe what scientists say about the nature of time. Time stopped long enough after the explosion for Uncle Hashem to say, "wait."

There was once.

He emerged thinking only of Tamara and Lala alone across the city and made his way toward them even as the buildings shook and smoke billowed up like so many dancing jinns all around him. Every so often he was confused by the thought that perhaps this was a dream from which he wouldn't wake up and that he was at college again, making friends with Palestinians who'd never seen Palestine, eating ice cream in an ice cream shop with a gaggle of young people who couldn't decide between a movie or dancing, or that maybe he'd had too much to drink and at any moment he'd be woken up by an alarm or maybe he was dead, finally, and somehow that was the most comforting of all of his thoughts; to go to sleep and to die in a dream and to find perhaps the better life you prayed for, the better life you deserved but for the skin you were born into, the better life served up without strings attached like so much water in a land of thirst. But then the buildings stilled for a moment long enough for Uncle Hashem to continue his way toward the small house on the far other side of the dust filled camp, to find the last two people to whom he belonged.

In every war the land is remade and reshaped to suit the desires of the conquerors. There was once. A house built on the edge of what became a refugee camp. A girl who might have been Little Red Riding Hood in a fairy tale about the darkness of the woods and the evil lurking there. Once there was and now there wasn't. The building where Tamara and Lala lived was gone, a faint column of smoke remained there as a reminder perhaps or it too was confused and lingering like Uncle Hashem. Here is the place where the table was set for dinner and there was the windowsill where we sat and spoke of what had passed. That was where I took your hand and said, "don't cry Tamara," and lied through my crooked teeth, "you will see him again," because the truth didn't matter to me as much as your comfort and I couldn't think of how else to mend your broken heart but to lie about an afterlife where your dead husband would be waiting. And there was the narrow bed where Lala, your only living child, was tucked in and told to dream of pretty things, so that she wouldn't wake up screaming, a scream like a woman's scream, not a child's scream. A scream that lived into the morning and the afternoon and the evening because what else was there here, but a million orphans screaming and waiting for the day they could sleep and dream of nothing. The house was gone. Tamara and Lala were gone. If anything remained it was the suggestion of a red coat, somewhere among the rubble.

"Uncle Hashem, why are you kneeling in the sand like that?" Lala said. She must have been standing behind him for some time with her mother, regarding Uncle Hashem on his knees with handfuls of sand, crying out.

"You were gone."

"No," Tamara said. There was nothing to betray fear or even relief in her voice. Her voice was her voice.

"She went to the grocery store after school and when I found her she was eating ice cream with Hamid of Ramallah." And then after a breath she touched Lala's hair and said, "Thanks to her the house didn't collapse on top of us. We are still alive. Still here."

Whether Tamara had uttered a statement of fact or a question regarding the nature of existence Uncle Hashem didn't know at that moment. Years later, beneath a hasty pile of twisted metal and concrete, he would say the same thing to no one in particular and an inch of sky.

"Hamid of Ramallah brought me strawberry vanilla crunch and vanilla chocolate swirl. And he said his problem was fixed but he still wouldn't tell me what it was, but I think he left Gaza and realized he missed Gaza and so he came back, not just to bring ice cream and cigarettes and gum, but because he wanted to, because his heart wanted to be here."

"Lala, where is your coat?" Uncle Hashem asked.

There was once. Once, there wasn't.

A Heart in the Sea

NATHALIE HANDAL

GAZA
Once in a tiny strip
dark holes swallowed hearts
and one child told another
withdraw your breath
whenever the night wind
is no longer a land of dreams

THE GAZANS
I died before I lived
I lived once in a grave
Now I'm told it's not big enough
to hold all of my deaths

TINY FEET
A mother looks at another—
a sea of small bodies
burnt or decapitated
around them—
and asks,
how do we mourn this?

THE CHILD ANTHEM
The children are not dead
They are shadows in every tank
They are echoes in every soldier
The children are not dead
They are in every house
in the eyes of every father
every mother
in the soul of a people

They are in every location
in the heart—
the children at the beach
in the houses
on the streets
by their brothers and sisters
are everywhere now
The children are not dead
They will move in the world
without being stopped
They will move
They will move us all

HAIFA BLUES

I've known you most of my life
but my voice couldn't reach you

and here we are together again,
neither of us moving

your breath on my back,
the sun darkening the room we sleep in

the blue wrapping us together
as if it's our last chance together

perhaps the human noise we make
will save us

perhaps time is against us
and there is too much to feel

perhaps I don't have enough
of the Arabic language to say—

With you, I never see an end

I would like to believe this love
doesn't lessen our chance

to be this city together

after all—

the key to the sea is in the heart

but I don't think we realized
love is no slight thing

TALHAMIYEH*
I heard
I'm an Armenian
who believes that stars
are the pieces of lightning
history left to space,
I heard
I have Roman blood
and my brother is Turkish
and Greek,
I heard
my heart is
by the Mosque of Omar
by the Nativity
beside a talisman
and an old man
without teeth or keys,
I heard
my poems turned into stones
with Aramaic letters,
I heard
that here
invaders push natives aside
natives hand their names to trees
and trees rehearse the verses
freedom left,
I heard
I was a house
made of Mediterranean light
except I only heard this in Springtime
and Spring might not exist here anymore—
they took all of our trees—
perhaps Jesus can explain what happened
or perhaps all I need to remember

is that
I heard—but this I know—
I'm an Arab,
the seven quarters
of the old city
has left me seven keys
so I can always enter.

* Talhamiyeh means "Bethlehemite" in Arabic.

IN AKKA
I arrived to your old port
without poems or echoes
without a record—
But I record
sixty-seven years of ruined autumns
and every summer you grow
further outside of time,
I record
we built these ruins
these stones houses
the gardens of each home,
I record
Um Ahmad
they want to demolish her house
but our phantoms will never leave
the ruins will disturb them,
I record
the storefronts are emptier
the *shababs* are left with little to do
besides the drugs they are given
the crime they are forced to resort to
so you can call them dangerous
but their grandfathers will return inside them,
I record
Not for Sale—
We will not move or surrender
perhaps no one cares what we say
but the sea the sea the sea
has memorized us,
I record

I haven't seen your
children grow up
I wasn't given that choice,
I grew up in the confines
of other places,
none can be compared
but I've missed you
and didn't know how much,
forgive me,
I record
we are together
even if we don't know it
and this city is a city
beyond our uncertain freedom
and those who betray us
those who try to free us
those who pity us
those who love us
those who guilt us
tell them
look at the moonlight
against the sepia stones,
no army can destroy
that kind of love,
I record
I see you in 2014
and I'll see you
every day in every dream,
Akka,
I apologize for not writing sooner
apologize for not singing
the songs the sea composed for us
and the eternity it rehearsed for us
and even if cemeteries multiply
remember that, like Jerusalem,
even if this city is broken
a survivor will stand
in every one of us
everywhere in exile,
and be the city.

HERE
The Old Port of Jaffa
is here
the sunlight poised
on our memories
here
the old stone houses
with our tiles tiles tiles
evidence of homes buried
in different names
here
the years we never defined
here
the echoes we collected
in each other
here
the shivering breeze
against our skin
the dark paradise
under our eyes
here
but you were not here
and I was not here
they say
but we were here
we are here
we are here

QUDS
Every street is still
a stone white sky,
I pay respect
to those who aren't
allowed to enter
as I enter Al Aqsa,
as I pray
I look at the spiral colors
in God's ceiling,
think of all I love
who I love
and

his voice breaking
his Arabic aching
wounds me.

HEARTSONG
Only they saw the waves
Only they saw the wind
as the houses collapsed
Only they dreamt of dreams
There were no birds
There were no trees
No hands to cover their eyes
No rain to record their footsteps
Only they saw their photos fading
into the walls
Only they saw their stories
hidden in the sounds of strangers
Only they
they stayed to tell us
they were never gone
they lay in their shadows
guarding their origin
their heart in every note
of every song
they stayed to tell us
there will always be
a heart in the sea
with our names

July, 2014.

THE UN/MAKING
OF HISTORY

Three Questions

ALAN SHAPIRO

Was there a there
there—some last
Pangaea
of the newly human
thinned to a suffering
few—drought-driven
starved, or hunted
eastward out
of the birth valley
that the first half-
song, half-cry—more
cadence of a cry
than cry—kept
freshly present to them
in its being gone?

And could it be
the more they sang it,
the more it was
the song itself
of being driven out
that drew them on,
that made them think
it could be theirs
again, if nowhere else
than in the singing
of its loss?

And is it now—
if ever—even audible—
somewhere inside

the iron echo
chamber of the outraged
logic still driving us
to drive the others
out because they—
before they—
some ghost inflection
of the single air
we might have sung
once for a last
time as we faltered
forward salt stung
nearly blinded
under massive sky
across an isthmus
through the loudening
boom and hiss
we almost couldn't
lift our voices
high enough against
to hear each other sing?

Trajan's Column

Among the crammed together tiny figures on a lower panel
of the frieze of figures coiling up the hundred foot high marble column

like a flowering vine of butchery and triumph there's one figure
among the vanquished who, half naked, in profile slumps

against a wall—his face expressing nothing even while
he holds his arms out in hopeless supplication to the victor

towering over him with sword in mid-swing at its peak:
the killer's face too just as blank, mechanical, as if

it hardly had to do with him, whatever force it was
or law whose necessities he served, that played itself out

through this moment before it moved on to the next and the next
in a tumultuous unreadable sleepwalk through the hacking and

being hacked spiraling up and away from us beyond what we can see.
The height of the column is the height of the great hill

the emperor razed to the ground, or his slaves did, shovelful by shovelful,
to build the tower to memorialize the glory, which the emperor himself was

really nothing but the humble servant of. Under the brick arch
of the concrete entranceway to the downtown factory where I worked

one summer there was this drunk, a woman, whose face, buried
in a mess of scarves, I never saw, whose body I had to step across

to get into the building, holding my breath against the almost solid
force field of stink around her, as if it were

my punishment for being not the one stepped over but
the one, head turned away, who got to do the stepping.

And I did it, and got used to it, in no time really,
I admit it, my face blank, unreadable, and hard

as the concrete entranceway I entered by,
so that it came to seem simply the nature of the place,

an aspect of the job itself, the shrieking riveters and pressers I became
so good at running I could half doze as I stood there

hour after hour, day in day out, feeding them
the many different kinds of leather they obediently

would then shit out as many different kinds of belts
that women all over the city and the state would wear

while the belts were still in style, then donate to the poor when not.
Maybe, who knows, the drunk wore one of the belts we made.

But I didn't think about that then. Coming and going,
every moment of the day I didn't think of anything

till the summer ended and I returned to school,
as was expected, then went beyond school, as expected too.

And not once did I ever think about that time and place, that woman;
not once till now, till my writing this about the lower panel

of a machine-like slaughtering that's only one of thousands
twisting up serenely to the very top of the column where

a statue of the good emperor used to stand, and now
a statue of St. Peter does, looking down triumphantly

on all that famous rubble at his feet.
The factory was shut down long ago.

And in its place colossal towers made entirely of glass rise up
so high that all you see now overhead are the rippling images

of buildings inside buildings like a line of columns carved
from giant waves caught at the very moment they're about to break.

Wailing at the Wall

ROBERT SHETTERLY

You have what you desire: the new Rome, the Sparta of
Technology and the ideology of madness. —Mahmoud Darwish

In April of 2014 I was part of Lily Yeh's small Barefoot Artist team (www.barefoot-artists.org), recruited to paint murals in each of three places—the Balata Refugee Camp, in the Old City of Nablus, and in Al-Aqaba, a small Palestinian agricultural village in the Jordan Valley that has been resisting demolition by Israel for forty years. This was my first trip to Palestine and although I had read extensively about the Occupation, the illegal settlements, the apartheid, the checkpoints, collective punishment, and the Separation Wall, I was ill prepared to actually see and feel—to witness—the extent of them.

Even though these various means of ethnic cleansing are parts of the same supremacist project, it's the Wall that haunted me. I'm not referring to The Western Wall, commonly called the Wailing Wall, in Jerusalem. More about that wall later. I'm talking about the other Wall, the barrier that Israel has built to separate itself from the Palestinian people while enabling itself to appropriate resources from Palestinian land. Here are some reflections from my attempts to comprehend it. At times the Wall felt as big and incomprehensible as the cosmos, rolling away beyond words, like a giant gray snake over the arid and rocky land. It seems a fact that is also its own myth. I think we assume that facts are most amenable to explanation, but the fact of this Wall challenges words. Here are some approaches.

I

We are told that for Zionists this is the Promised Land. A promised land is a garden, a private garden, for the cultivation of one's unique character. We've all seen gardens whose perimeter is demarcated with tin edging, a miniature wall, that separates the rich garden topsoil from the weeds. The Wall is a mammoth, concrete version of that metal edge. The Palestinians of the West Bank are the weeds.

II

Walls built to separate one country from another, rich from poor, powerful from weak, ideology from ideology, represent failures of both dialogue and humanity. They are anachronisms, medieval. In the US one of our most replayed triumphal moments is Ronald Reagan's crowing, "Mr. Gorbachev, tear down that wall!" That triumph is framed both in Cold War victory and moral imperative. Walls are abhorrent. And yet, the US government continues to build an enormous wall on the Mexican border, and supports the building of Israel's Wall. (An Israeli company, Elbit Systems, won a $145 million contract from the US Department of Homeland Security to put guard towers on the US-Mexican border fence. As Elbit says, their technology is proven.) If Israel's Wall were simply a result of paranoia and fear, if it strictly followed the Green Line, the border between the Israel and the West Bank, it would elicit one kind of response. But because this Wall is used as a weapon of occupation, apartheid, land and resource appropriation, ethnic cleansing and economic strangulation, it requires a different response. If Zionism and its dogmatic belief that all land in Palestine is by God's decree Israel's were a worldview shared by all religions, there would be no problem. But championing the right of Jews to celebrate their own religion and, at the same time, accepting their right to take another people's land by religious fiat are two very different things. The crime and tragedy of the Holocaust and the sympathy it rightly provokes justify neither imperialism nor fundamentalism. Rather, they cry out for their opposite. The Wall's ominous guard towers function the same way they do in maximum-security prisons. They imply surveillance with impunity, humiliation as daily ration, omniscience not by your god, but by your enemy's.

Are Palestinians meant to accept these walls, to believe that they deserve them, to perceive them as normal? There's a term for such acceptance—internalized racism, adopting your oppressor's assessment of you as correct. All oppressors aim to achieve this.

III

It's probably safe to assume that smiling, cheerful instructors teach kids in Israel's elementary schools about the value of fairness. Of course, this value hardly needs to be urged on young kids, who are acutely aware of fairness, of who's taking more than his share, whose greediness for time or food or art supplies is compromising what's available for others. At what point do those same teachers inculcate a distinction between others—like themselves—and "others"—unlike themselves in their students? Some people deserve fairness and some people don't. Anywhere there is systemic inequality, the value of fairness is taught and then qualified. This qualification is our ticket to a moral abyss.

IV

A Wall implies its negative. It implies what it hides and what it makes impossible.

Therefore the Wall implies a future; it implies a horizon; it implies expectation and dreams; it implies a journey; it implies possibility, hope, surprise, wonder and development because it denies them all.

The implacable fact of the Wall commands you to abandon any ideas about fair access to a shared future and personal dreams. The Wall denotes that its builders have both the right and the power to erase the notion of horizon from your experience and that of your children, replacing it with concrete power, concrete finality, the closure of expectation, prison, and death. The Wall says, our God instructs us to remove your horizon, and that you, the un-chosen, are squatters on our Promise.

V

It's ironic that the color of the Wall is gray. There is nothing gray about it. It speaks in black and white, in absolutes, about good and evil, yes and no, clean and unclean, free and not free. It turns justice into a one-way conversation. The Wall appears to crouch on the land in monolithic silence, but it's garrulous, prattling on, justifying its presence. It says, beat your head on me and learn who you are in relation to me. It says, I am God's commandment made concrete. It says, because your history ends right here, mine flourishes.

VI

Outside the little town of Bil'in we participated in a demonstration against the Wall. It was hot, the sun intense, the dry land rolling and rocky with sparse vegetation, a few olive trees. The environment felt, well, Biblical. Just visible over the top of the Wall were the red tiled roofs of an illegal Israeli settlement. As the small group of protesters—men and women, Palestinian and Israeli, local and international—approached the Wall, the confrontation seemed to mix historical eras. The Israeli soldiers clustered on the medieval ramparts were decked out in the black paraphernalia of high tech storm troopers, as anonymous as futuristic robots. The demonstrators, in t-shirts and jeans, bright bandanas and a few gas masks, looked like a wandering tribe from the 1960s. They chanted and shouted at the soldiers. Some young boys wrapped in black and white Palestinian keffiyeh scarves, the symbol of resistance, used slings to fling stones. The soldiers shot blue-gray tear gas that blew down along the Wall away from us. I noticed then that the ground was littered with spent teargas canisters. Some were hung up like netted birds in the rolls of barbed wire. I picked one up—hard black rubber, the shape and size of a pear, or maybe a heart. Made in Pennsylvania. Not surprising to see there were Americans on both sides of this issue, some profiting from it. I sat under an olive tree and held the black heart in my left hand while I drew a picture of it in my sketchbook.

VII

We met Amer Amin, a young Palestinian graphic artist, in a coffee shop in Bethlehem, where he was exhibiting a selection of his political posters. One poster was dominated by a picture of the Wall with a thin strip of blue sky above, the perspective of a person standing close to it. In that strip of blue sky Amer had written a line from a song by the great Lebanese singer Fairouz: "You see how big the sea is! That's how much I love you." The irony is that Palestinians in the West Bank, exiled from their homes near the sea after the 1948 Nakba, may never see the sea again. Just as the Wall denies them the experience of salt water, it also denies them the experience necessary to understand this metaphor of love. As I read this quote, I imagined another spoken by an Israeli, "You will never see how big the sea is! That's how much I _____ you." What word would fit?

VIII

Think of the Wall in relation to art and imagination, how a massive creative undertaking can inspire awe. The artist Christo's 1976 art installation, "Running Fence," was twenty-six miles of eighteen-foot-high white nylon, bellying in the wind and making what many people thought was a beautiful statement, a flowing white line on the golden contours of California hills. Others objected to its transitory existence because it blocked the free movement of animals. It was taken down after 14 days. Art can be controversial. Or, think that the Great Wall of China, built for security concerns now irrelevant, is considered one of the wonders of the world. Its architectural achievement, like the Great Pyramids, raises it to the level of art. *This* Wall, a relentlessly ugly, relentlessly cruel solution to a relentlessly unjust condition will never be considered as art. Perhaps, though, as a monument to anti-art. This Wall is, unlike China's, aggressive. It is appetite. It is a refusal to talk, to consider your enemy as human. It is a four-hundred-mile-long diatribe of justification for supremacy. The Israelis refer to the settlements, the military bases in the West Bank, the private roads, the checkpoints as facts on the ground. The more facts on the ground, the more clarity of control and domination, ownership. The more such facts, the more proof of no going back. The greatest of these physical facts is the Wall. It is the crescendo of factual immorality.

IX

As this Wall dehumanizes the Palestinians, it ultimately questions the humanity of the author more than the victim. The Wall reduces Israelis to this one colossal concrete fact of national hatred. It says the Israelis do, in fact, believe in a one-state solution: the state will be theirs, the Palestinians will be gone. For the Palestinians it is a barrier, for the Israelis it's a shield from behind which they can launch incursion after incursion until the West Bank is all theirs.

X

What the Wall cannot do: It cannot suppress the vivacity of the people, their love of life, their friendliness, their pride, their outrage at injustice, their thoughtful means of creative resistance. The Wall was meant to kill Palestinian spirit. It seems, rather, to have concentrated it. Rather than teach Palestinians a lesson in inferiority, it teaches a much sadder lesson about those compelled to build it.

XI

The holiest Jewish site in Jerusalem is The Western Wall, the remaining section of the Temple Mount destroyed by the Romans in 70 BCE. A prayer uttered in this sacred place is thought most likely to reach the ear of God. It is often referred to as the Wailing Wall because of the nature of the prayers—loud lamentations over the destruction of the temple and the centuries of discrimination, pogroms and the Holocaust. It seems to me, though, that the lamentations ought to be concentrated now at the other Wall, the one that does not symbolize the theft of Jewish sacredness, but rather, epitomizes its forfeiture.

XII

Many Israeli citizens are distressed about the separation Wall, the settlements, and apartheid. Just as there were many Americans opposed to slavery. In both cases the numbers were small at first but inevitably grew. I have read numerous times—hard to believe in such a small country—that a large proportion of Israelis don't even know about the extent of the wall and the harm it does. I want to envision a day when Israel and Palestine jointly establish the RPPA, the Reconciliation Peace Project Administration, which will employ equal numbers of Palestinians and Israelis to disassemble the Wall and reassemble the pieces into houses, schools, and bridges of understanding. The solution must be one state because a state of mutual and integrated respect is the only state that makes survival possible. That term, "one state," for many Israelis suggests a state where the majority would in time be Palestinian. What would happen then to Israel's right to exist? Yet it's clear that the current solution for them *is* one state—a state from which the Palestinians have been largely removed. What does that solution say about the right of Israel to exist? A kind of survival, of existence, may be possible without respect, without justice, but it's an existence in which everyone's humanity is slowly extinguished.

XIII

The ingredients used to mix the concrete of the Wall have been equal parts historical trauma, fear, violence, racism, fundamentalism, supremacy, profit and greed. It's a potent mix. Those are the aspects of persuasion employed by all of history's sad lineage of despots and demagogues. It sets up, clenches, as hard as steel and as cold as stone, as intransigent as hatred. The Wall imprisons Palestinians; it proclaims Israel's right to exist as a failed state. The Wall forbids wisdom. It promotes surveillance, but blinds its makers to the consequences of their acts. It exists in a world where the words freedom, redemption, forgiveness, compassion have ceased to exist, where we are defined by our righteous anger. Who wants to live there?

Letter to Palestine (with Armenian proverbs)

NANCY KRICORIAN

In a foreign place, the exile has no face.

You wake up in the morning and forget where you are. The smell of coffee from the kitchen. The sound of slippers across the linoleum floor. It could be any country.

When you look in the mirror you see the eyes of your grandfather. He expects something from you, but he won't tell you what.

Better to go into captivity with the whole village than to go to a wedding alone.

The fabric was torn. With scraps you have made a tent, you have fashioned a kite, you have sewn a dress, you have wrapped yourself in a flag.

They have separated you with gun, grenade, barbed wire, wall, prison, passport. They have underestimated your will.

The hungry dream of bread, the thirsty of water.

Passing from one village to the next, without obstacle, without document, without your heart thumping up near your throat.

Turning the key in the lock, you enter through a door you have never passed through before except in your grandmother's stories and in your dreams.

NOTE ON THE POEM:

Many years ago when I was a student in Paris, I was required to take a French for Foreign Students course before the start of the term. The class was a veritable United Nations, with representatives from Argentina, Poland, Greece, Germany, Iraq, and Iran, among other countries. I was the only American, and when the teacher taught us French slang, she laughed uproariously at my Boston accent. One day our teacher asked us to pair up for an oral presentation. I was assigned the one Palestinian, a handsome guy with a beard. We went for a coffee to prepare our assignment, and he told me: "I'm glad we're doing this together. We will talk about our people, the Palestinians and the Armenians, and their histories of dispossession and struggle." I looked at him blankly. I was a young American, who knew little about my own people's tragic experiences in 1915, and far less about the travails of the Palestinian people. This poem is an homage to the extraordinary grace with which that young man, whose name has sadly escaped me after all these years, met my terrible ignorance.

AHDAF SOUEIF

I wrote this article in May 2010. I was in Jerusalem with the third edition of Pal-Fest, the Palestine Festival of Literature. We had not yet learned to avoid the anniversary of the establishment of the State of Israel; the 15th of May. So that year, in Silwan for the first time, we saw Israelis celebrate "independence" and Palestinians commemorate the "Nakba," the loss of their land—even as more land and houses were being taken.

This was the first time I had witnessed the actual process of dispossession: the state setting in place the necessary legal and administrative framework then watching from the sidelines as the settler corporations come forward to make use of it, the state ready and waiting to provide the muscle to enforce the law and the ceremony to legitimize the takeover.

Every year since then we have witnessed the growth and development of the City of David project; the guided tours, the movie screens, the sound and light show, and every year what has become more obvious is the integration of this project within the Israeli vision for the future of Jerusalem. This article describes the beginnings.

Last Stop to Jerusalem

If you walk out of Jerusalem Old City through its southeastern gate and onto the perimeter road encircling it, you'll most likely see several large coaches with elderly Western tourists climbing out of them. You'll see them stand at the low wall at the edge of the road and peer down into the lush valley with its pretty houses that nudge and lean against each other. The tourists may notice the woman marking exercise books on her sunny terrace, they may smile to see the bright-haired four-year-old riding her tricycle round the yard. Some of them will think of a favoured grandchild back in Kansas or Ottawa.

Now, if this were a scene in Italy, in Spain or Turkey, we might have left it there: the tourists come, stare, spend some money and go. But here their effect is devastating—and most of them don't even know it.

For the town that nestles here, in this valley on the southern flank of Jerusalem, is Silwan, home to some fifty-five thousand Palestinians, annexed by Israel, along with Jerusalem in 1967, and currently one of the hottest spots in the contest between the rights of the Palestinian townspeople and the plans that Israel has for the area. Plans put into effect through suites of administrative measures, clandestine coalitions, and progressive-sounding projects. None of which could work without the funding that floods into Israel from the West.

What do the tourists know of this? These gentle, grey-haired folk have come here, on their Jewish National Fund coaches, to visit the archaeological dig for "Ir David," the City of David, claimed to lie below the Wadi Helweh neighbourhood in Silwan and to justify the shafts, and the tunnelling going on in the belly of the hill and the foundations of the homes of the people who live here.

Maryam, the teacher marking exercise books on the terrace, puts them aside: "*This road, from Jerusalem all the way down the valley was a main road. People did good business here, if you had an ice-cream shop, a café, a barber, food shops, souvenirs. Then Elad came, the City of David Organization.*"

Silwan, and particularly the beautiful Wadi Helweh (the Valley of Sweet [Water]), has always welcomed strangers. Traditionally, it's been the last resting spot for travellers approaching Jerusalem from the south and a favourite recreation area for Jerusalem's residents. People came here for picnics, and in summer the cool caves of Ein Silwan Spring were a favoured playing space for children. Even now people ask if I'm visiting Silwan for a *shammet hawa*, a breath of air, though there's hardly air to breathe with the dust and the noise Elad is generating.

"Elad" is an acronym in Hebrew meaning "To the City of David." Dedicated to "strengthening Israel's current and historic connection to Jerusalem," it was founded in 1986 by David Be'eri, who "inspired by the longing of the Jewish people to return to Zion" left his elite army unit to set it up. On its Board were three members of the Settler leadership, the Yesha Council.

Elad set up a two-pronged strategy: to strengthen Israel's "connection to Jerusalem" they started to dig—under Silwan and into the land mass under the al-Aqsa Mosque—or the biblical City of David and to create the Ir David tourist site. To help "the Jewish people to return to Zion" Be'eri started in 1991 (well supported by Ariel Sharon as Minister of Housing Construction) to acquire Palestinian property. His target was principally two Silwan neighbourhoods: Wadi Helweh and al-Bustan (the Garden).

The Abbasi home, with its nine apartments and two warehouses, was Be'eri's first target. Be'eri's wife, Michal, has said *"Abbasi was the guard of the spring . . . so Davida'leh took a tour guide card and put in his picture, and for a long time he would take bogus tourists on a tour . . . and slowly he befriended Abbasi . . . and of course it was all staged."*[2] In 1987 Elad pressured the Custodian of Absentee Property to declare the Abbasi house Absentee Property and in October 1991 Be'eri led a semi-military Settler invasion of the house with the intruders singing and dancing and waving the Israeli flag on the roof at daybreak. The Abbasi family went to court and the Jerusalem District Judge found "no factual or legal basis" for the takeover, indeed found it characterized by "an extreme lack of good faith." Still, the property continues to be caught up in legal proceedings and Elad people continue to live in it—and to acquire Palestinian property.

To date, Elad have gained control of a quarter of the Wadi Helweh neighbourhood through three main instruments—all part of the weave of the Israeli administration of the affairs of the Palestinians under its control.

The first is the Absentee Property Law: someone, usually a Palestinian collaborator, will sign a deposition stating that X was absent from the property she owned on a designated date in May/June 1948. This allows the Ministry of Finance (through the Custodian of Absentee Property) to register the property as Absentee-owned. Registration is not public and the owner—even if she lives in the property—does not know it has happened. There are no legal measures to stop the expropriation and there is no entitlement to compensation. She can go to court and seek to cancel the registration if she can prove that she was not absent on the relevant dates in 1948. This law applies only to non-Jews.

---

[2] (Silwan Report, n.16)

The second is expropriation of property by the state for public use, and then transfer of the property to private right-wing settler organizations.

And then there's confiscation or demolition of a home because of illegal construction. But since 1967, Israel has very rarely granted permits to build, and so a growing Palestinian family who builds a needed extension to their house, on their own land, will find themselves criminalized. AQ built a children's room onto his house in Wadi Helweh, *"one storey, on my own land and within the building percentage allowed by the law. I've applied for a permit but the municipality delays considering the application. If they give me a permit it will cost around $50,000. At the same time every year they give me a fine. We've paid till now seven fines totalling $10,000. And there's the 'arnunah' (the property tax.) Once we couldn't meet the installment and they came and took away the TV, the receiver and the DVD player. Later we paid the installment but we never got the equipment back. The salaries of the whole government of Israel,"* he says, *"comes out of the fines of the Arabs."*

What is happening in Silwan is not unique; it's part and parcel of what's happening across Israel and the Occupied Palestinian Territories. Only the specific tactics are different. Before I came to Silwan I had been travelling in the West Bank for a week, noting how every Palestinian community has its appointed settlement, its stalking "other." There is hardly anywhere you can look up and not see a settlement lowering at you: bristling with barbed wire and flags and antennae and cameras and floodlights and—although you can't see them—arms. Bir Zeit has Psagot, Bethlehem has Har Homa, Beit Jala has Gilo. Hebron is special having Kiryat Arba on its outskirts and four settlements in its heart. And Jerusalem is extra special with the massive Ma'ale Adumim gripping it from the East and now the settlements in Sheikh Jarrah and the Old City in the centre and Silwan to its south.

Elad's settling of property in Silwan is the familiar Israeli tactic of creating facts on the ground. The Ir David project is creating facts in people's minds. Most scholars agree that to this day no evidence of the presence of Kings David or Solomon at the site has been found. But our group of elderly North American tourists are spellbound by the stories they are hearing from Elad's guides, stories which are conjecture, projection, myth and sometimes downright falsification: *"I found a Byzantine water pit,"* archaeologist Professor Ronny Reich says, *"they (Elad) said it was Jeremiah's pit. I told them that was nonsense."* But for a long time the guides would tell the tourists that this was the hole Jeremiah was thrown into. Close to half a million visitors come here each year and are treated to the Elad version of history. Professor Binyamin Ze'ev Kedar, chair of the Israel Antiquities Authority Council, in a 2008 letter, writes: *"The Israel Antiquities Authority is aware that Elad, an organization with a declared ideological agenda, presents the history of the City of David in a biased manner."*

Given David Be'eri's background, it is natural that Elad should have a particular interest in the military. In fact Elad funds tours (and lunches) for soldiers. Army organizers say that Elad will not talk about Christian or Muslim history in the area but only present to the soldiers the Second Temple period. A National Service Guide, speaking in 2005, said *"I guide mainly soldiers so it is important for me to emphasize that we have to be here. On one of the tours I said that it was a village of terrorists and murderers until we settled here, and then an Arab neighbour started yelling at me . . ."*

None of this activity would have been possible without the support of the Israeli State. An Israeli activist tells me: "If you ask the Israeli government what is happening in Silwan, they say it's not a government matter; these are private people buying and moving in legally. But now [the east Jerusalem settlement of] Nof Zion is being built. The Zoning laws only permit building there on 37.5 percent of a piece of land. But Nof Zion has permission to build on 125 percent of the land! And inside Ras el-Amoud, above Silwan, they are building five-storey apartment blocks for Settlers. But they refuse to allow Palestinian families to build a third floor on their own house. A Settler organization buys a police station from the government. A bus line in Ma'ale Zeitim is diverted to serve a settlement. In Silwan the City of David Organization is managing the City of David National Park for the Israeli State. It is telling the archaeologists where to dig and what to look for. So one has to ask the question with regard to the City of David Organization and the State of Israel: who is the tail and who is the dog. Or maybe we can just say that they find their interests coinciding."

In the critically important Ir Ameem study "Shady Dealings in Silwan," Meron Rappaport reaches the same conclusion: "Elad, which is officially a private organization, serves as a direct executive arm of the government of Israel, and enjoys comprehensive and deep backing by the Israeli administration."[2] More chillingly, Doron Spillman, Elad Director of Development said in January 2008: "This is a government project . . . we are almost a branch of the government of Israel, but without getting buried under government bureaucracy."

The main government project right now is for Jerusalem. And in Silwan and Jerusalem, on Jerusalem Day, you can see it clearly.

Silwan is on alert. The Settler, security, police and army vehicles racing up and down the roads are quietly monitored by neighbourhood watch people. In the café at the bottom of the valley three young men wipe tables and set out chairs and stock the fridge while keeping an eye on the young blond man with a gun and a green polo shirt who patrols in front of them.

"These are private security for the settlers. They don't go anywhere without them. They cost around fifty million shekel a year. And they're paid for by the government. Out of taxes."

---

[2] Ir Ameem, "Shady Dealings in Silwan," Appendix 3.

"And the security are protected by the police, and the army's always round the corner. Just think what it's costing."

Yesterday at the annual Jerusalem Day celebration, Prime Minister Binyamin Netanyahu declared: "Jerusalem is our city and we never compromised on that, not after the destruction of the First Holy Temple, nor after the destruction of the Second . . . There is no other nation that feels this deeply about a city."

Now we stand above al-Bustan, its eighty-eight houses threatened with demolition to construct an "archaeological garden in the spirit of the Second Temple."

M: *So they distribute bits of paper that say that since King David used to go for walks here it's wrong that our houses should be here and it must just be a park. You notice that for them he is King David but for us he is el-Nabi Daoud; David the Prophet. So who holds him in higher esteem?*
N: *Plus there's no evidence he ever walked here—*
M: *And what if he did? It was empty. He didn't send fifteen hundred people into the wilderness so he could go for a stroll—You know, there's one thing we've held against our parents, our grandparents: that they left their land. They thought they'd be back in a couple of weeks. We don't have the excuse of ignorance. We are not leaving. And my children will not wash the dishes in their national park.*

What is happening in Silwan is not isolated; it is part of the ongoing Israeli process of establishing Jewish settlements on Palestinian lands occupied in 1967. But in Silwan the conflation between Settler right-wing ideology, government policy, big money, real estate interests and bad taste produces its unique blend of kitsch and nightmare.

Under cover of excavation massive infrastructure work is done in Wadi Helweh in preparation for the construction of a 115,000 square meter commercial centre, without a town planning scheme and without permits. Five residents file a petition. They are detained by police. The work stops when it comes up against the foundations of Palestinian homes.

"*The streets cave in. You see that darker stretch of tarmac? We had to patch up the road. And the school, the UNRWA school: the floor of the classroom collapsed under the girls. Fourteen girls fell two meters into the tunnel they'd dug below the school. And we had to hush it up because they would have said the school was unsafe and closed it down.*"

Darkness settles.

The Israeli police and military barricade the road into Silwan. A couple of hundred meters away, in the heart of the Old City, thousands of Settler kids jump up and down and beat their drums and chant that Jerusalem is theirs. The Palestinian residents of Silwan feed their kids and hush them. They visit each other, chat, watch the news. They keep an eye on the road into their town and what it might at any moment admit. In the café at the bottom of the hill the young men are courteous but not chatty. The food they serve is good. On their TV screen Alan Curbishley talks about the match that's about to start: the final of the Europa Cup. The young men keep an eye on the screen, the other on their town.

On the rocky ledge jutting out from the hill above the café—and hidden from it's view—is the stage set up by Elad. We walk round to where we can see its "Lion of Zion" banners and its blue lights bathing the charred hillside. We hear the amplified voices celebrating Anita Tucker, Rabbi Yoel Schwartz and General Aharon Davidi, three Israelis each being awarded the $50,000 "Lion of Zion" Moskowitz Award for deeds that "deal with the challenges facing Israel in the fields of education, research, settlement, culture, security and more".

This celebration, described by Richard Silverstein of Tikkun Olam as *"an attempt to add luster and prestige to the notion of killing Arabs and stealing their land"* is conducted with the full support of the Israeli State. The event is protected by the police and the army, and features such speakers as Minister Moshe Yaalon and Brigadier General Avigdor Kahalani.

From the al-Aqsa Mosque further above comes first the call for evening prayer, then, for good measure, Surat al-Rahman (the Chapter of the Merciful): *which then of your Lord's signs do you deny?* The lights in the Palestinian houses dot the hillside and the trees around the small café where I sit are also strung with fairy lights. In a layby twenty meters away an Israeli army personnel carrier stands poised, its blue lights flashing.

Ir Ameem expresses *"grave suspicion that Silwan is but the cornerstone of a policy that extends far beyond the City of David both geographically and politically."* One could perhaps prophesy that making life unlivable for Palestine's Palestinians is the prelude to transforming Palestine itself.

The place itself will be changed. It will be impossible to look out at the landscape and think of continuity, or eternity. In place of the old, mellow stone, of the interdependent structures, softened and polished by time, there will be the jagged and the new and the fake. In place of trodden paths along the valleys, the children playing freely in Christ's spring, there will be the chair-lifts and viewing points and fast food outlets and always, always the iron gates and the security checks and the ticket kiosks and the merchandising. In place of the thousands of stories laid down over the ages above, below, around each other, there will be one story—and it won't, actually, be the Jewish story, because the Jewish story in Jerusalem is indivisible from the Byzantine, the Arab, the Muslim, the Christian. It will be a fake. Like the fake mezuzahs the settlers carve into the Arab houses when they take them over, the fake "Jerusalem Stone" with which they clad concrete structures. Soon, in Jerusalem, if the world does not wake up, there will be but one duet: the gun and the cash register. You can already see the future in the Jewish Quarter in the Temple Shop with its projected Third Temple printed onto tea towels and doilies. But this future cannot happen without the tax-free donations from the kindly folk, the tourists and the patrons from the west.

I find some hope in this: "Silwan" translates as "heart's ease" or "solace"—from the Arabic root s-l-a: to find comfort after sorrow. The town is named after its spring, Ein Silwan: it was here that through love and compassion, the gift of sight was restored to the blind.

Note: I am much indebted to the Palestinian activists and residents of Silwan and Jerusalem Old City, to E and Y from the Israeli Committee against Home Demolitions and to Advocate Seidenbam's excellent Ir Ameem (City of Nations) and its publications.

The Concrete of Bint Jbeil

MICHAEL COLLIER

Pulverized is another way of thinking of travail
which is why dust rising midday from the streets
is white and burns your eyes and nose. Great machines
have done this to the mortar, block, and stone,
while smaller forces shovel rubble and rebuild.

Not far from here, south, in green valleys,
the realm of the better guarded has dust the color
of raw almonds, the kind its citizens eat happily
and call dessert or victory, but not with ease,
for dust drifts in scrolling clouds across their borders

obscuring what it will, and almonds unripe in their pods
aren't anything like dust. They lie in mounds near piles
of layered grape leaves, bristling with a sheen
of pale-green light so delicate you think the hand
that offers them is God's? But the hand is dark and swollen,

just like the one that bundles chamomile in tight bouquets,
whose small bright flowers are not the yellow of forgiveness
but the yellow that casts its shadow on the woman
who sells almonds, leaves, and flowers—the one
who makes an invitation with her hands,

a gesture with her covered head and sits for hours
on the ancient paving stones of Jerusalem, inside
Damascus Gate not far from Bint Jbeil or Dearborn,
in Lebanon and Michigan, where like everywhere, water
and cement mix with sand and gravel to make concrete.

In May 2007, I was a part of a contingent of writers organized by Askold Melnyczuk and Munir Akash that traveled to Lebanon and Syria to visit Palestinian refugee camps in order to meet writers and artists. A family conflict made it impossible for me to be with the group for the entire time, so I traveled to Beirut several days ahead of the others and then to Syria in order to see Damascus on my own, which I otherwise would have missed. Returning to Lebanon, I spent two days in the South visiting the father and brother of a Lebanese friend. My friend's brother, Bilal, managed a café in Beirut's Hamra district. His father, Mohammad, lived in Deir Kifa, a small village forty-five miles directly south of Beirut and less than twenty miles from the Lebanese border with Israel. He had worked in Saudi Arabia for many years and after he had retired, he moved back to Deir Kifa, his ancestral home, where he built a large house on top of a hill. From the top of the hill, you could see the Mediterranean, although at a distance of several miles, it was hard to distinguish sea from sky.

Bilal had reported for the Pacifica radio network during the 2006 Lebanon War. He had also assisted foreign journalists, many of whom stayed in Tyre, acting as a translator and taking them closer to the fighting, although they didn't have to go far to find it. Later in the afternoon, after we had left his father, who was involved with getting a generator repaired, we drove to Tyre, only seven miles away. Bilal made sure to point out an apartment building whose upper floors were still vacant and charred from an Israeli rocket. The building had been suspected of housing a Hezbollah communications center. One of the tallest structures in Tyre, it over looked, the magnificent Al-Bass hippodrome. The beach resort where the journalists stayed was within sight.

On the way to Tyre, we planned the next day's drive through the South, down to Lebanon's border with Israel, less than twenty miles away. En route, we would stop at Qana, where the Wedding at Cana purportedly happened, but where more recently, in 1996 and 2006, two massacres of civilians occurred, the result of Israeli bombs and rockets. In addition to Qana, Bilal wanted to go through the area around Yatar, where Hezbollah had shot down an Israeli military helicopter, a feat that had become a rallying cry not just for Hezbollah but also for all of Lebanon. After that, Bilal suggested we finish our tour in Bint Jbeil. Something akin to a town meeting was going to be taking place to discuss plans for the town's rebuilding. Architects, engineers, local officials, citizens, and other interested parties, including acquaintances of his who were urban planners and designers were going to attend. Their hope was that Bint Jbeil might become a model for how destroyed towns and villages in the South could be restored in a manner that would create more livable towns and foster closer communities.

"The Concrete of Bint Jbeil" is a response not only to the particular destruction I saw in Bint Jbeil but to all of the generic devastation that repeated itself in the towns and villages, less than nine months before. The dust of the war had settled, so to speak, but all else was still "smithereened apart," to borrow a phrase from Hart Crane. The poem itself didn't get written until three years later, when I had the opportunity to visit Palestine and Israel with my oldest son. We stayed in East Jerusalem, not far from Damascus Gate, and it was there, when I saw a woman inside the gate selling, among other things, almonds and bouquets of chamomile, that the poem took shape.

Diary of an Israeli Summer/2011

KAZIM ALI

I entered the country not mine and everywhere was mistaken for Jewish. Even in the West Bank people would not believe I was Muslim until I began reciting. Not until I went to Haifa did I learn why: in 1948 nearly all of India's thirty thousand Jews came to Israel and so it seems reasonable that an Indian person might be thought of as Jewish.

Meanwhile in Jerusalem, at the gates leading into Al-Aqsa—"the Far Place"—my documents for entry are the syllables in my mouth, settling deep in my throat into the guttural sounds you can only make with years of practice.

What was once the Green Line is now a major artery, with art galleries, shopping plazas, and luxury apartments lining it.

Young Israelis are erecting tent cities. First I think it is part of a solidarity movement with displaced Arab families who are evicted from their houses but it turns out that it is people who are protesting economic difficulty in Israel and the lack of opportunity for the young. They are calling their movement "Israeli Summer" riffing off of the "Arab Spring" which happened earlier in the year. There seems to be no irony in the naming and when I ask someone if she thinks that the bad economy is due to the fact that so much money goes to financing the Occupation, she looks at me in complete confusion.

A city in quarters but more than that refracted in all directions and backward and forward in time at once.

* * *

Today we went first to Al-Aqsa, called by Israeli Jews the Temple Mount. As we climbed the creaky wooden causeway we could see through the slats, Jewish worshippers who had come to the small fragment of the Western Wall. And there, just ahead of us on the causeway, the other side of the whole equation—twenty or thirty body-length riot-shields, stacked with easy reach for quick use.

On the Mount itself, the enormous Dome of the Rock and a mosque, built and destroyed many times. Around the mosque in the great tree-lined park, many small groups of men reciting the Quran. As with many Muslim mosques, it is not the building but the space itself that is important. In this case, the rock under the mosque. When you go inside there is a little stairwell under the rock you can climb into to pray.

Where one can and can't pray is fraught here with all kinds of meaning. When a group of Jewish men came up onto the plaza the Muslim men began reciting loudly at the top of their lungs, a sonic resistance but a resistance nonetheless. One of the Arab men called the Jewish people "settlers."

Though I had always thought of settlers as people out in the territories building their kibbutzim, it isn't so. There are settlers inside Palestinian cities like Hebron and there are even settlers buying up or confiscating Palestinian buildings and apartments inside the Muslim Quarter of the old city and in East Jerusalem. You know them by the enormous Israeli flags hanging from the roof and by the barbed wire wrapping the houses, surveillance cameras and other security measures. We saw Ariel Sharon's house from the outside seating area of the café in the Muslim Quarter where we ate lunch.

Unlike the Jews who are not supposed to go inside the Dome of the Rock or the Al-Aqsa mosque, I went straight up to the Western Wall. I put my hands on it and made a prayer of peace. But what is "peace?" There can be no peace without justice. I thought about writing a note explaining this and wedging it into the wall, but felt I should leave the spaces in the rock for others.

We drove out to East Jerusalem and there found another wall—the huge concrete barrier constructed around the territories is inside Palestinian land. It separates neighborhood from neighborhood, and chokes off the livelihood of countless Palestinians, preventing them from reaching their jobs, squelches the growth of their economy and isolates them from Jerusalem, still the largest Palestinian city, with a population of more than 300,000 Arabs.

Nothing is simple in this place. How does one travel from one wall, representing the lost hopes of a scattered people, to another—which not only metaphorically represents but physically actualizes the lost hopes of another scattered people?

As we speed down the highway between Jerusalem and Tel Aviv one can peek into the pine forests—forests brought here and planted with intent—and see the stone foundations of old villages.

I try to remember all the jagged facts I have learned: Lands turned over to the new state by the Greek Church in 1948 have ninety-nine year leases; 750,000 Arabs were displaced in the initial war and those inside the borders lived under military law until 1966; During the 1987 Intifada, Rabin instructed the police to "break their bones."

Afterward, control of Palestinian cities in the West Bank reverted to full Palestinian control while the surrounding areas were given to Palestinian civil control only. Much of the land of the West Bank remains under full Israeli control.

And who controls my body, I wonder to myself, in the bus, hot and dehydrated from the high desert climate of the West Bank, and exhausted by the barrage of information.

And who are you when you don't know where you are in space?

◆　◆　◆

We drive down to Sderot, an Israeli town formerly on the outskirts of Gaza City, but now separated from the city by the Wall. We meet with Nomika Zion, one of the founders of Sderot, where hundreds of rockets have landed, launched from Gaza.

"Our immune systems are in crisis," she tells us, deciding to tell of the wounds of the individual person, her psyche, rather than a social abstract. "Sometimes there were ten to sixty rockets a day for months at a time."

At the gateway to Sderot a sculptor has welded together a menorah created from the fallen rockets.

"So many people left," she says, "about a fifth of the population. Those of us who stayed would sleep in our clothes and all together in one room. We sacrificed our family life, our intimate and sexual relations. Across the street my neighbor lives. She has two children. One day during an attack she ran with her one daughter to the crisis room knowing that the other was playing out side but that she dare not risk going outside to get her."

She goes on to tell us of the relationships between people from Sderot and Gaza City: "Before the wall, we went back and forth a lot. There are many Moroccan immigrants in Sderot and most of the merchants in our market were from Gaza."

Gaza, fertile strip of land producing strawberries, other fruit, and beautiful flowers for export all over the world.

"We worked there, we went to the beach there, we would go on the weekends for shops and restaurants." Her voice breaks, her eyes fill with tears. "These were our friends," she whispers.

"We know that there must be people on the other side of that wall who feel the same way, who miss us, their neighbors and friends. And when all the farms and orchards were destroyed to make the 'buffer zone' for the Wall there were even more rockets fired."

"We are addicted to war," she says. "'Peace' is a curse word in Israel. We are damaged inside. We are in spiritual crisis."

There's a moment after she says this when we ourselves, her listeners, seem to internalize the crisis. Someone drops her water bottle. Another's sunglasses slip from his head and clatter to the ground.

"During the war," she says, "people made a festival out of it. They took chairs up to the hill to watch the bombing—like *fireworks*."

"I am not a lonely voice," she claims then, wiping her tears and straightening her shoulders. "I am a common one which has been silenced. After the war people came back here. We have been getting back to our daily lives. But not the people in Gaza."

She stops. She points out the window. "Two miles from this room is the largest open-air prison in the world."

◆ ◆ ◆

We drive from her in silence to a kibbutz in the hills on the way to Jerusalem. It is one of the last that still follows socialist principles of collective economy; most of the other two-hundred-plus have privatized, some of them producing military technology or medical equipment.

One of the founders of the kibbutz, Arieh Zimmerman, an older man with a soft and gentle voice, a steel-grey beard shot through with white, speaks with us. He tells us of his growing alarm at the militarism present at all levels of his society. He began to do research on the people who previously lived where their kibbutz was founded. He learned it was bought from under the feet of the people who lived here whose homes were evacuated and the people taken to Gaza.

He began to work as a volunteer driving people from Gaza into Israel for medical treatments. "I came here from Europe because of the Holocaust and because of the kibbutz. I didn't know anything about the Palestinians who lived here and I didn't think about Israel as a nation."

So what happened to all the myths of a homeland? Either in the United States or here? Who comes from wild places? And what do they find when they arrive?

"Soon enough those of us who talk of peace or reconciliation or reparation will be ostracized. Or we'll be tried as treasonous," he surmises sadly. "And meanwhile your Congress gives Netanyahu standing ovations."

Tomorrow we will go through the Qalandia Checkpoint to Ramallah.

◆ ◆ ◆

We cross through the Qalandia Checkpoint by bus. This morning we are to meet students from Bir Zeit University outside Ramallah. At the checkpoint we are made to disembark and walk through. There are holding areas surrounded by chain link. I feel like an animal in a pen, or a human in a cell.

One of our number, a quiet woman, is taken apart into another room for questioning. We cannot determine why she is being profiled out of all of us. Later, on the bus, she tells us that they made her take out her camera and erase all the pictures she had taken.

Once we are at the university we hear from the students that there are checkpoints inside the West Bank too. They turn twenty minute journeys into three-hour-long excursions. Often the roads to the university from Ramallah are closed. Several times this has happened during final examinations.

No students from Gaza are allowed to come here and the checkpoints make it very difficult for students from East Jerusalem, Bethlehem or Hebron, though those places are all very close.

The university salaries have not been paid in two months. Taxes are paid into Israel and then disbursed to Palestinian National Authority. But often this money is frozen.

◆ ◆ ◆

The population of Palestine is divided into four parts, none of whom can meet: Palestinians in Gaza, Palestinians in the West Bank, Palestinians who are citizens of Israel and the refugees who live internationally and who are not permitted to come back. And even the Palestinians in the West Bank have a hard time getting to each other because of the checkpoints.

Palestinian musicians and artists are jailed or denied their traveling permits to go to Israel or travel internationally but in 2005 Israel launched a campaign to send Israeli artists and cultural figures around the world. They sign contracts not to talk about politics.

The Israelis are trying to "normalize" the Occupation and the Palestinians are doing everything they can to not let that happen.

And now the Knesset has criminalized even talking about boycotts or referring to the Israeli War of Independence by its Palestinian name, the "Nakba" meaning "catastrophe."

"Though," cracks one of the young women we talk to, "they don't need a law to arrest us."

◆ ◆ ◆

In order to qualify for student housing in Israeli universities you must have served in the Israeli army. A privilege/responsibility reserved denied Palestinian Arabs.

During the Second Intifada Nablus, another ancient city, founded by Greeks—its name is an Arabicization of "Neapolis" or "the new city"—was bombarded nightly. Its historic soap factories, the main source of industry—some dating back to the 1400s—were leveled. Many of the youth who were young children in that time are suffering from PTSD. We meet a group that is doing art therapy with students and youth with PTSD from the air raids. Drawing, comic books, puppet theater.

Everywhere I see signs of people who are trying to hold on to their humanity.

◆ ◆ ◆

In the morning we drive north out of the territories. We climb down from the bus and walk through the pens again. The concrete barricades are stamped with a logo in English of the USAID. The checkpoints have been built with international aid money.

We visited two unrecognized villages, one in the mountains, and the other just next to the shopping district of Karmiel. These shantytowns were erected by people who were not on their ancestral land when the census was taken after 1948, but they were still inside the Green Line. They have no homes and so build these shantytowns on the sites of their old destroyed villages.

Periodically the army comes to evict them and destroy the dwellings. If they are lucky, they return when the army leaves and begin again. If they are unlucky they come back to find a development in progress.

Afterward we went to al-Birweh, the home village of Mahmoud Darwish. There's nothing left but brambles. Walking through you can sometimes see the stone foundations, the remnant of a wall. If you squint you find the pattern of streets still exists.

On the slopes of a hill overlooking the village are the remains of an ancient church. On the other side of it is what used to be the cemetery of al-Birweh. On the crown of the hill is a large roofed enclosure for keeping cows. The cows must be driven through the cemetery; everywhere there is manure and bones.

Among the broken headstones and cracked cenotaphs I gather what bones I can. I do not know if they are human or animal. I cover them with stones and read a *sura* or two.

Later we are taken to a house for dinner. The people tell us that the only way to survive is be happy in the moment. One man sings a beautiful mournful folk song and then we go out under the stars and they teach us how to dance *dabka*. We link arms and match their steps.

◆ ◆ ◆

Bil'in: a village of eighteen hundred people, land of four thousand acres; 60 percent of this land was confiscated by Israel to build the security wall. Nearly one thousand olive trees were uprooted from this land and transferred back to the villagers but they are not apportioned enough water by the Israeli authorities to water the trees, some of them more than a thousand years old, back into the ground. So they die.

Sometimes the Israelis take the olive trees and transport them back into Israel for use as centerpieces of traffic roundabouts or to put in plazas in the cities.

We are staying at one of the Burnat brothers' house. There are five of them.

One of them is Eyad, who leads the Popular Committee Against the Wall, another is Emad who is making a film called *5 Broken Cameras*. His video cameras are habitually broken in the weekly demonstrations that take place, hence the title of his film.

In the kitchen next to the phone there is a photograph of Al-Aqsa. Next to it is a poster, which reads, "Goodbye Bassem, you were a friend."

Demonstrations happen weekly. The soldiers shoot tear gas canisters from twenty feet away into the crowd. They are not supposed to shoot from this close, neither are they supposed to shoot the canisters at people but during one of the protests one tear gas canister shot into Bassem's rib cage.

9/4/2007: the Israeli Supreme Court rules that the wall must be moved back five hundred meters.

6/1/2011: The Occupation Forces comply with the Supreme Court ruling. That same month a canister of high-grade tear gas is shot at the feet of Bassem's sister. She inhales the gas and sickens from it, dies that same day at the hospital.

Her picture hangs next to his.

The black canisters of gas litter the countryside. The children run and collect them to use as toys. The women use them to build borders for their gardens.

◆　◆　◆

We sit around the table and listen to the stories of the villagers:

"They wake up in the night when we sleep."

"During the protests they sometimes set the olive trees on fire."

"They spray sewage at us to make us disperse."

A young boy, ten years old, says, "When the army came to take my dad at night I started screaming."

"The Green Line is six kilometers from here, if they want a wall they should build it on the Green Line. The wall is on our land now."

"By international law the wall and the settlements are both illegal. They have no right to be here and no right to uproot the trees that are five hundred or a thousand years old and take them to Israel to put in their shopping malls and traffic circles."

The Palestinians build temporary shelters daring the Israelis to destroy them. It reminds me of the Jewish holiday where one constructs a temporary shelter, a sukkah, outside their stable homes in order to remember the wandering after Egypt.

The village of Bil'in was closed down every Friday from 8am–8pm, temporarily ruled a closed military zone, in an effort to stop the protests.

The military still come at night but they do not arrest the older seventeen- and eighteen-year-old boys like they used to, instead they take the young brothers ten to twelve and interrogate them about their brothers' and their fathers' activities.

◆　◆　◆

Bassem Abu Ramah (who used to carry an olive branch and wave it at the soldiers during protests, who was sports director of the local football club, whose nickname was "Fil," Arabic for "elephant," on account of his towering and broad stature, who used to fly a rainbow kite in the sky during demonstrations, who was trying to protect an older Israeli demonstrator when he was hit, Bassem, him, that one, brother, son), 1977–2009.

◆　◆　◆

Darwish I am in your country, unlettered, unfettered.

I walked in the ruined cemetery and built houses out of bone and every stone I could find.

Here from the rooftop of Bil'in you can see the lights of Tel Aviv and beyond it: the sea.

A cool breeze blows the heat off the day.

The men sit in a quiet circle, smoking. We hear the women's laughter downstairs, a clattering of glasses.

Not that much farther than that: the sea.

Bassil is a schoolteacher. He used to live in Jerusalem but the wall separated him from his family. Now he travels up and down the territories to work with communities affected by the wall.

What goes through such a wall? Light. Wind.

The army here reels off a thousand words for "no."

We invent our stories. Even our imagination is occupied.

The occupation is not just by settler and soldier: they are the least of it. It is the other things that poison our minutes and days. The most dangerous is when they occupy your soul.

"There are stories," one man says, "that are so horrible that we don't even talk about them to each other. Otherwise we would become discouraged."

"Which stories?" I want to know.

All the men get pensive. Finally one of Eyad's other brothers mumbles, "What happens to us in the jail."

Sumud is the Arabic word for "steadfastness" though in Israel I heard it translated as "stubborn."

◆　◆　◆

From this rooftop terrace with its exposed rebar and crumbling concrete walls, its jury-rigged satellite antenna and ubiquitous black water tanks and fraying copper wires, you can barely make out the skyscrapers of Tel Aviv.

Huddled over the meal of noodles and chicken or couscous-stuffed squash, they confess their fervent desire to see the Mediterranean again.

Qamar, the lady of the house, who had prepared our meal, hasn't been there since she was a teenager. She will be thirty-three next year and one of her friends, knowing she can't apply for the permit until she is forty, jokes, "You can go next year."

Everyone laughs at the particularly Palestinian humor of the joke and for a moment we feel good. As they quiet down again, Qamar gets introspective. "Seven more years," she says quietly, ladling me another stuffed squash.

Men have to wait even longer.

Qamar, whose name means moon, shows us some of her embroidery that she is selling. In an economy where people cannot work (since many refuse to take the jobs in the settlements) people make ends meet however they can.

The separation wall has choked out export business such as the flowers from Gaza and the soap from Nablus and the oil from Tubas. It cuts off 10 percent of the West Bank territory. The three largest settlements are on top of the main aquifers. The water is tapped there and piped back to Israel before redistribution between the settlements and the villages.

While the olive trees whither and died, the settlements receive enough for swimming pools, fountains and in one case, a water park.

As evening grows long, Emad shows us some footage of his film.

We watch with our own eyes Bassem's death. He was wearing a bright yellow Brazil football jersey. He is shouting at the soldiers. He is struck, he stumbles and falls down a small slope. He does not move again. The others rush to his side screaming, "Fil! Fil! Get up!"

He does not get up.

Advised Ben Gurion: "The old will die and the young will forget."

We stay up on the terrace with the men, talking late into the night.

Inspired by a Poem from the First Intifada

ALICE ROTHCHILD

My trees in Israel,
Were rooted in the ashes of Treblinka,
Watered by the tears of refugees.
Each quarter in that blue and white box,
Rolled back another grain of sand in the Negev,
Greening the Galilee,
With orchards and olive groves,
Every Bar Mitzvah boy, a seedling waving in the Mediterranean sun,
Two hundred forty million strong, gracing the dream of Zion.

But now I shudder,
For my dreams are soaked in blood and bombs.

The poison and rot of every bulldozer,
Ripping out the ancient olive groves of Jayyous and Nablus,
Wrenching from the terraced land a thousand cumulative years of bounty,
While scarved women yell, weep, and gather the crop shaken loose,
And angry young men taste the bitterness of loss and despair,
Hearts straying to revenge on cataclysmic bus rides to Jerusalem,
While kippah'd, bearded settlers shake their angry fists and guns.

A trail of tears soaks the Naqab.
Uprooted Bedouins on their own long march to nowhere,
As water hungry Eucalyptus saplings,
Invade the grieving sands.

And the fierce and broken mothers of Rafah, Khan Younis, Beit Hanoun,
Keen in the rubble,
As stark branches of shattered concrete,

Arch toward the sky like fractured trees,
And filthy water, poisoned bomb soaked earth, and broken bones,
Pulses across the landscape and into the sea.

The trees of Israel
Have gone to battle,
Claiming the Jerusalem Hills and the Martyr's Forest,
Where saber cactus refuse to die.
Clear cut for the bypass roads to the settlements of Adam, Ariel, Beit Haggai,
Betar Illit, Elon Moreh, Givat Ze'ev, Ma'ale Adumim, Ma'on, Neve Yaakov, Tekoa,
Yitzhar, Zufin . . .
Like ugly gashes on an old and ravaged face.
While the gnarled and twisted olive trunks,
Lose their place in the glorious sun,
And the sparkling springs of a hundred Nabi Saleh's
Are seized like prisoners of war.
Where concrete walls, eight, ten meters high,
Embrace Qalqilya, Tulkarem, Habla,
Islands of villages caught in its brutal grip,
Obscuring the sunset and its warmth.

As they sang in South Africa:
Senzeni na?
What have we done?

This poem has been gestating and evolving for years. I was inspired by the First
Intifada, which was an attempt to "shake off" the Israeli occupation and was, for
many of us, our first glimpse into Palestinian reality. I felt a need to start where I
had first begun, with Israel as a post holocaust redemptive project where planting
trees, claiming the land, was essential to Jewish identity and security, and then
to move beyond that construct to a recognition of the trauma and dispossession
for Palestinians. The Jewish National Fund Forests were planted to cover over
destroyed Palestinian villages; the trees were used to create an alternative reality
and, along with the massive uprooting of Palestinian olive groves represents, for
me, the war not only over the land and water but also over the historical narrative. As the years have gone by, I added the growing number of Jewish settlements, the separation wall (both massive illegal land grabs) and the displacement
of the Bedouins, rounded up into development towns, their lands planted over
with The Ambassador Forest. Then there are the recurrent attacks on Gaza that
not only have resulted in a massive amount of civilian deaths and destruction

of infrastructure, but also the desecrating and polluting of both the land and the sea with the weapons of war and the untreated sewage that now flows due to the destruction of the treatment plants. The saber cactus and the mention of Nabi Saleh speak to Palestinian resilience and resistance. The parallels with South Africa have become more apparent to me with the boycott movement and the obvious apartheid conditions in the occupied territories.

The Extravagance of Grief

TOM SLEIGH

In thinking over what I learned about the lives of the Palestinians I talked to during a trip I took to Lebanon and Syria a year after the 2006 war between Lebanon and Israel, and then again in 2009, I want to focus on feeling: not so much my feelings—but on the feelings that the people I talked to seemed to be experiencing as they told their stories. The two dominant emotions that came through as the refugees talked about how they'd been forced out of their homes during the 1948 Nakba—the forced removal of Palestinians from their homes by the newly established state of Israel—were grief and grievance. Of course, as soon as you use the phrase "forced removal," or the term "Nakba," you are entering a vast and contentious web of claims and counter-claims: Nakba in Arabic means "catastrophe." The Israelis call the same war "The War of Independence." Atrocities were committed on both sides: and so the terms of argument are far more vexed and complex than most versions of, say, Stalin's state terror.

In one case, an old man told the story of watching how, as a small boy, Israeli soldiers murdered his mother, father, and brothers. The old man, tightly controlled, told the story with a muted intensity: he looked calm at first, but under that were grief and anger—and not a stupid or unreflective anger, but articulate, historical as well as personal. And yet, as I listened, I confess that it was easier to take in his grief than his grievance.

At times, in fact, I found it hard to listen to that sharpness in the voice, full of blame and anger, that was directed at the Jews, the West, the United States, and the other Arab countries. But the more I listened, and the more I've reflected on my reaction since I've been back in New York, the more convinced I am that grief and grievance cannot be separated. And that one of the main reasons why there is no real "peace process" and why Western and Jewish and Palestinian and Arab policy makers keep making the situation ever more desperate is their absolute insistence on keeping grief and grievance separate from one another, as if the emotional immediacy of grief would verify the justice of the grievance, or the grievance would be weakened by having to feel the other person's grief. In a sense, what I'm talking about is the difference in feeling between a political conviction and what you might call a political emotion—political emotions are contradictory, they require a fresh response to every new provocation. Nor do they easily resolve into settled opinions, or fit neatly inside some prefab ideology. They partake of political convictions, but only as that conviction is put to the test in our daily lives.

But to make grief and grievance more complex terms, I'd like to put them in apposition, and perhaps opposition, with two other terms, poetry and politics. Robert Frost has two little sayings that, in fact, amount to one saying, in which all four of these terms play off each other. In these formulations, Frost means poetry as the kind that's written by self-conscious poets, but I want to expand the definition of poetry to something more basic: and what I mean by poetry is the ability to communicate to others, to impress upon them, whether through words, gestures, force of personality, whether literate or illiterate, the full lived value of your own experience.

But here is how Frost puts grief, grievance, politics, and poetry in relation: "Politics is an extravagance, an extravagance about grievances. And poetry is an extravagance about grief." You can sense in Frost a kind of skepticism about grievance, as if grievance as a source for poetry were too partial of an emotion, too self-limiting, in fact too self-interested to reliably express the full range of a person's experience. And in our time, we all know that self-interest is the core of politics, particularly the kind of self-interest that is often pitched against the community's interest. And while I share Frost's suspicion, in the hard conditions in the Palestinian camps that I visited, Sabra, Shatila, and Haret Hreik, there's something a little luxurious about being able to decouple politics and grievance from poetry and grief. And so I want to give you two examples of how politics and grievance and poetry and grief are all on a seamless continuum, and that without the politics and grievance you can't have the full expression of poetry, at least in the definition that I've proposed.

One of the places I visited during my 2007 trip was the Golan Heights. I spent part of the day in a ruined Syrian town, Quneitra, absolutely destroyed in the 1973 Yom Kippur War between the Syrians and Israelis. Before the Israeli army withdrew after the 1973 ceasefire, the Israelis evacuated the thirty-seven thousand Arabs living there and destroyed the town, stripping buildings of windows, doors, anything that could be carted off: these were sold to Israeli contractors, and then bulldozers and tractors moved in and knocked down most of the stripped buildings, now mangled slabs of concrete and rebar. All that was left of the human presence in the village were herds of cows pasturing on what was once somebody's yard or garden. There was birdsong everywhere, made all the louder by the absence of any human voice or the rattle or clank or roar of a machine. A garden full of roses run wild might once have been a passionate gardener's delight and pride. As a ruin, it was almost picturesque; as a place of suffering, it held an air of melancholy and menace.

The village was kept as a shrine/memorial by the Syrian government, which of course used it for propaganda purposes as well. (Since 2014 of the Syrian Civil War, control of most of the region has fallen into the hands of the anti-Assad Islamic State.) The hospital, which is only an empty shell of long cinderblock corridors, was pocked all over by what looked like twenty-millimeter shell holes. At the axis of the hospital, you could look down the hallways at the empty concrete window frames and see the green countryside stretching away to neat lines of olive trees planted on the slopes of the Golan Heights. Swallows swooped in and out of the building, and the floor in some of the rooms was deep in powdered concrete.

In a church—the same church where Christ is said to have stopped on a trip to Galilee—there was graffiti written in Arabic on the walls: "Let fever make Sharon sweat." From the empty frames of the windows you could see Syrian checkpoints, white-washed buildings where some teenagers were kidding around with the soldier on duty, and in front of the church, I could see slabs of gray, weathered concrete from the ruined houses cantilevered at crazy angles.

The impression this made—a ghost-town in ruins, scenically pastoral, but a monument to still current suffering—put politics, grief and grievance into such complex relation that what I've called "poetry" would have been slighted if you'd settled for the Syrian or Israeli governments' official versions of what happened. The ruins themselves couldn't be turned into mere fodder for self-justifying rhetoric. And the way that Quneitra became a subtly different emblem from what the Syrian or Israeli governments intended it to be was made even clearer by a visit we then made to a Palestinian refugee camp in the Golan Heights, which of course is much more than a plateau—in fact, it's some of the most fertile land in the region. And so Syria keeps demanding its return.

We were looking for someone to talk to, and went into a carpenter's shop. People began to gather, and soon we were talking with a man in his sixties, who took us into his home, served us coffee and soft drinks that looked like wine, and talked to us for about two hours. His house was modest, but comfortable, unlike the homes in Lebanon, which are truly miserable and really deserve the word "camps." In his living room, we sat on cushions on the concrete floor. A ceiling fan hung down, the floor was carpeted in warehouse brown carpet, there was a large wooden dresser displaying family pictures and teacups and plates neatly stacked, plastic flowers in a wall sconce, and even a modest chandelier hung down from the high ceiling. He told us he was a retired teacher who had basically been an exile since he was three years old. He went to preparatory school in the village he ended up in after his family was expelled, then went to Damascus for high school, and then spent thirty-eight years in Saudi Arabia as a teacher.

He told us his views about the Lebanese Palestinian camp near Tripoli where Al-Fatah, an Islamic militia, had taken refuge, but now refused to surrender. He said dialogue was the one way to resolve the conflict, but that a political vacuum develops when you resort to indiscriminate shelling, as the Lebanese Army would eventually do, destroying the camp in the process. But he also said that there would never be peace until the European Jews returned to their original home-lands.

As he talked about his past, at one point he asked if we'd like to see the deed to his family's holdings in Golan. And when he said that the deed was covered in the blood of his brother, whom the Israeli soldiers had killed back in 1948, I thought he was making a metaphor, since he'd just said that living as a refugee in a tent when he was a child was like "living in a spider web in the heart of a well." And that the life of an exile was a life "in desert places that resembled the life of a slave." So when he said that watching his mother being killed, his four brothers being killed by the attacking Israelis was like a "lake of blood, and that the deed was stained with blood," I assumed his reference to the deed was a metaphor. But then he asked us again if we'd like to see the deed, and he called his nephew on his cell phone, and the nephew came with the deeds to his family's property. (I learned later that many Palestinians have the keys to their old homes.) And yes, the deed was literally stained with blood, three long brown, faded stains that had bled across the legalese. He said the deed was found when his uncle and cousin came over to the house after the soldiers dynamited it, which he also said he wit-nessed . . . as well as seeing one of his brothers, still a baby, sucking at his dead mother's breast.

As we drove out of the village, we saw a slogan written on the Syrian side of the UN zone: "Peace Is Our Target; The Peace Which Retrieves Our Occupied Syrian Golan." When you see how grief is ignored for the primacy of grievance in coupling a word like "Peace" with a word like "Target," it becomes clear how the official diplomatic language tries to split off grief from grievance, even though grief and grievance, politics and poetry, are everywhere in tension with one another in what Quneitra as the background to the old man's story came to mean. Sure, you can credit a man's grief—that's the easy thing, but what do you say to his grievance? How do you ignore the ruined concrete and rebar and the brutal, systematic intention that created it?

But my confusion about the old man's use of the word "deeds" has about it a kind of poetic richness which makes grief and grievance inseparable, part of a seamless continuum between private experience and history, between the desire to see your enemies' return to their homelands so that you can return to yours: and though nobody, probably not even the old man, really believes that such a solution is remotely possible, it expresses a collective wish that both grief and grievance be redressed.

And what happens if both grief and grievance are denied? If there was such a place as a universally recognized Palestinian homeland, then Mahmoud Darwish might well qualify as the Palestinian national poet. The UN vote in 2012 to grant the State of Palestine "non-member observer status" of course means that there is an official state—or does it? In emotional terms, being a "non-member observer" is as much a term of exclusion as inclusion. It lacks the foundational, historical, blood-warm confirmation of a word like "homeland." The old man said, "The blood of my brother is on these deeds. This proves that this land is for us, and not for them. Our only hope is that America will wake up." Note that he used "America," and not the more official designation, "the United States," to make his point. Americans have the luxury of assuming a homeland, while his last words to me as we parted were: "We will resist the Jews by word, sword, until the last drop of blood."

So between his feeling for the deeds and his feeling for his brother's murder, between his geopolitical understanding and his personal grief and grievance, lies the contradictory territory explored in many of Darwish's poems. Having endured the Nakba, as well as the personal Nakba that Darwish suffered as a refugee, his poem "Murdered and Unknown" takes up the ambiguities and ironies of grief and grievance that lie behind calling yourself "a victim":

> *Murdered, and unknown. No forgetfulness gathers them*
> *and no remembrance scatters them . . . they're forgotten in*
> *winter's grass gone brown along the highway between*
> *two long tales about heroism and suffering.*
> *"I am the victim." "No. I alone am*
> *the victim . . ."*

The voices seem to be competing for the right not only to be the victim, but the sole victim. It makes King Lear's claim, "I am a man more sinned against than sinning," seem like a reasonable position, as opposed to mere self-justification. It's as if Darwish were both satirizing and memorializing the collective wound. Or, as a Hezbollah official said to me about the Israelis, quoting an Arabic proverb, "He hit me and then he cried." Of course, it didn't seem to occur to this official that this same logic might also apply to Hezbollah. But Darwish's poem is much darker than mutually blind opponents insisting on their own victimhood. The grass in Darwish's poem—unlike Walt Whitman's vision of grass as a cosmic principle of connection between all created things—possesses the neutrality of something dead, but without any elegiac potential. In other words, grief and grievance are irrelevancies. The poem relies on no tragic gestures, no discourse about "witness."

And besides, most of the people I met—the old Palestinian man, the guides at Quneitra—were just trying to get on with their day to day lives: if a rhetoric of victimhood was part of that, it was also a coping mechanism, a way of maintaining hope in what can seem like a hopeless situation. But it must be said that their relatives indeed had been murdered—and were, for all the world cared, virtually unknown. No one would much notice if the survivors thought of themselves as victims or not—if they thought of them at all.

And now that the province of Quneitra, at least as of October 2014, is mainly in the hands of the Islamic State, it becomes even more difficult to say who is the victim and who the victimizer: the Assad regime, IS, the US, the IDF, the UN peacekeepers from Fiji and the Philippines—everyone would seem to be the victim of everyone else, everyone's grievance takes precedence over everyone else's grief.

In the following poem, which comes out of my visit to the town of Qana in southern Lebanon, where most of the fighting occurred in the 2006 war, and where twenty-eight members of an extended Lebanese family were killed by a US-made, Israeli Defense Force missile, I take my lead from Darwish's refusal to resolve his poem either in favor of grief or grievance. Perhaps in an age like ours, the once useful term, "poetry of witness," needs to be reconsidered. Amidst the blizzard of tweets and hashtags, so many different viewpoints can be broadcast over digital media that the notion that one person can stand in front of history and tell us how to feel about it—who the victim, who the victimizer; which grief is legitimate, which grievance is not—seems like nostalgia. And so the accurate expression of mixed emotion has become for me the core of the poetry I most care about. In one of the most riddling and difficult paradoxes about the competing claims of art, W. B. Yeats once wrote that the purpose, as well as the challenge of art, was to hold reality and justice in a single thought. And given the difficulty of knowing what either of those terms really means in any given situation, I suppose what I'm really aiming for is a comprehensive music of clashing tones, rather than the clanging and banging of what Seamus Heaney once called "the anvil brains of some who hate me."

A Wedding at Cana, Lebanon, 2007

He said, "It is terrible what happens."
      And "So, Mr. Tom,
do not forget me"—an old-fashioned ring, pop tunes,
salsa! salsa! the techno-version of Beethoven's
Fifth, Fairouz singing how love has arrived,
that's what he heard after they dropped the bombs,
his ambulance crawling through smoke while cellphones
going off here here here kept ringing—
how the rubble-buried bodies' still living
relatives kept calling to see who survived.

And when he dug through concrete scree scorched black
      still smoking
from the explosion, squadrons of jets droning overhead,
houses blown to rebar, he saw cellphones'
display lights flashing from incoming calls
and when he flipped the covers, saw phone camera pics,
pics of kids, wives, dads, single, grouped, some wearing
silly party hats, scenes of hilarity
compacted on the screen: it was "not good"
he said, to have to take the phone out of the body

part pocket: *Hello—no, no, he's here,*
      right here, but not—
and then he'd have to explain . . . and so he stopped
answering. A soft-spoken young man
studying engineering, only moonlighting
as an ambulance driver, he stood at
the crossroads where Jesus turned water
into wine and where, rising out of rubble, floating down
the cratered street, bride and bridegroom came walking
in the heat and as they came the wedding guests held up

cell cameras clicking when the couple climbed, waving,
      into TRUST TAXI
blazoned on the car's rear windscreen. The muezzin's
nasal wail began to blare all over town, and the pair
drove off to ululating shouts and cries, firecrackers
kicking up dust in the square. The show over, we
got back into our car, our tires crunching
over rubble. As I sat there rubbernecking
at a burned-out tank, he shrugged: "All this—how embarrassing."
And "I hope this is the story you are after."

STEVE WILLEY

In August 2013 I visited Palestine for the second time. I worked with the Lajee Center and at the Palestine Writing Center in Bir Zeit to run a series of poetry workshops for children living in Aida and Jalazone refugee camps. I participated in a poetry reading in Ramallah, spoke to Palestinian refugees and friends about their experience of occupation and imprisonment, and was a participant-witness to street protests and the mechanisms of their suppression: tear gas, rubber-cased metal bullets, arrest and military incursion. This trip was made possible by the Artists' International Development Award, a British Council and Arts Council England fund. A year later I was the Summer Resident at The University of Arizona Poetry Center. With images of Operation Protective Edge reaching me via the US media I revisited the materials I gathered a year previous. 'Living In: In Sufficiency', was one of the results. What follows is a selection from that poem, part of a longer, ongoing sequence called *Living In*.

Living In: In Sufficiency

1.
What do I want
        you to feel, the absurdity
of that question,
        wanted you to go, go
in immediacy, to Hebron's lilac
        doors in the star plash—
to go as what, and for what,
        the poem has removed itself,
effaced its thought, your need for it,
        stand and turn, look toward rain,
saw only iron latticed rain,
        where ideas are wrought in metal
where we are not is Hebron
        clouds descend in squares—

2.
Jerusalem's outskirt taxi bruise of roads at night, the driver fearful turns
        to warn against walking up past Mount of Olive's white tomb promises
won't drive to the high hotel his politics: day watches
        all mute details have their day to think in,
small January skirmishes, Prisoner of Love,
        looking at them now in full and careful earnestness
stone thrown land to listen in

3.
No ideas but in Palestine, every poem-space yells go, go to Palestine & in sufficiency live in

4.
        Dawud's cousin leant
back, took one wistful glance at the ceiling,
        said: *in Somalia guns are like bread*

remember this exchange—
      five days later, interviewed Dawud
about his six years,
      spent in Israeli jails,
cigarette loosely hung inside fingers and lips like stars,
      in Israeli jails cigarettes were rationed,
you get four cigarettes a day
      but a lighter only twice a day,
that was once the way
      it was no longer the system used
cigarettes are now bought, he said,
      but during interrogations it was common to be given
four cigarettes in the morning but not to receive a lighter
      at any point during the day
but what we use to fix this problem, he said,
      and prompted by the unmistakable
catch of the flint on the wheel of his lighter
      as it ignited the gas we notice the complex
defiance of his timing, of the lighting of his cigarette
      cinders of sound caught on the recording
I am using to recall these exact words:
      we make, he said, we use the paper, of the, the bathroom paper,
            and, and we take a long one, for two or three meters,
      and we roll it in a special way, like we, do like, you know,
            like the thing you roll it, for the bomb, yeah, a fuse, I say,
      yeah we use it like this, he says, this is a special way,
      and not a lot of prisoners can do it, we roll it, and after that we burn it,
      from the cigarette, and it will stay, you have a fire for a few days, but when, if
      they catch,
      if they catch this thing, they will, they will not give you cigarettes for two or
      three days
      but we always like, create and discover many things to make our lives easier,
can you think of another thing you created in the jail,
      I ask, almost without pause he responds: *we create chess players from bread*

5.
Still to stay and to speak to the fact of the staying, to the choice,
      to the dying sustain that echoes that sound of the note that is staying,
bread, her head, that falls as a stone in her hands is that staying,
      memory of sand and the flag, that flicks in the black and the white
in the red and the green in the day of the barb that is staying

rooms full of poets that listen and stay is what's staying
the need of the walls and the floors,
    and the logic of glass the flesh
that has structured the sound of this staying
    and to stay and to speak to that sound as the feeling of loss that is staying,
you can't feel, you can't feel, anything,
    just your mind working, and all sections of your body
like, you are a dead, a dead man, with a working mind,
    and the fuse on the floor that stays the light is what's staying this sentence
that binds to my mind as the lilac on doors of his staying

6.
    Alternate, inside sounds, 'Palestinian', 'Somali', make
in my mouth, recall likeness, Dawud's cousin sought,
    between Somali guns, and the ubiquity of Palestinian bread,
how toilet paper becomes a fuse, and bread a game of chess,
    on the land flung torso of itself, what sure thing can you find
beyond the ballad exchange, to see the pieces move in advance,
    to advance their metal guns, with bleeding gums
of yeast, to measure occupation's counterpoint
    a force that that screws on value, how the dwindled fuse of that paper
turns: preservation, dignity, cunning, nation, in all this imprisoned, overdubbed time

7.
For what you mistake for the length of my breath is the slow persistent clench of
a fist

8.
    I am in the car with you, friend, of terrorist-stars,
Dawud is to my right, and it is 10 pm in occupied Palestine,
    this friend was with me in prison, I met this man in prison too,
then pointing to the man in the front, *this man was the head of Fatah in prison,*
    a good person to learn from then, I coolly say,
yes, he says, catching the reference to what he had said the previous day,
    he had received his *true education* in the prison,
I, telling you, what Dawud had told me, while he was chained, to the *honor chair,*
    a mirror had been left in the room, it had been known for the mirror
to be used as a punch line to a joke,
    if and when the prisoner falls asleep, the mirror is moved closer to their face,
so when you wake you get a *bad surprise, so simple, but very hard on the prisoner,*
    jaw-wired, I laugh, without sound, in Palestine: mouth of clogged bread

9.

I am in Qalandia says one, I am of Qalandia another says,
    from a concealed pocket they pull
copies of some old document, old leaves, decaying,
    with your still one half-good eye you try to read,
on it a flock of black-headed gulls, ochre over serif cliffs glare
    I am the Balfour Declaration says one: I am in Qalandia another says

10.

This life has this quality of glimmered absence, even lies shine out the truth in them

11.

Registers of violence shift, escalations give no sound
    relation the letters need more,
absence filled by past burdens of proof
    that any property was not absentee fell upon its owner,
displacement the present mass of this absence
    violence sculpts its owned reality, offcuts observed turn memory,
no speaking on behalf of, cliffs,
    blood currents build up far off, climb up surface speed off,
solutions foreign to its constituents: mirrors to all that we are

12.

We are throwing stones on the street,
    if manufacture: ground,
Saleh, my friend, throwing the stones,
    if researched: copper, lead, or steel,
we were in the street throwing stones, it was a game,
    if taper, primer, propellant: division of labor,
not here, round there, round the corner,
    if before flight: mould,
I saw the soldier here, there, here in the tower,
    if there is assembly: firm seating,
we, Saleh was on the street, throwing stones,
    if there is length: there is crimping,
soldier had a sniper, I saw the sniper,
    if there is moisture: failure of sealing,
I could tell cause it was, it was long,
    if there is feed: primer is flush,
I told Saleh, don't throw stones, the soldier has a sniper,

if there is flight: correct charging,
Saleh did not listen, he did not listen,
if quality control: correct sequence,
he came round this, this corner, to throw the stone,
if alteration: check barometric pressure,
I heard some soft thing thud,
if slight deviation: adjust for humidity,
I did not hear, I did not hear no thing,
if vibration: see wind on the casing,
Saleh is, was on the ground,
if mushroom expansion: possible cavity,
I did not go up to him, I saw his head,
if expansion in cavity: multiple pathing,
if pathing unrecorded then this is the difference between:
the blood on the stone,
and the blood that he saw on the stone
in the incoercible perfumed streets that I am
difference between: I saw the blood on the stone,
for it is not here for you to see it,
and I saw the blood on the stone,
because you were not here to see it,
the blood that I saw on the stone,
and the blood that was there on the stone
when I lie to you I was as a flex of steel cloud
the difference between: the blood that was there on the stone,
and the blood he said he saw on the stone
because you were not here to see the blood
he said he saw on the stone,
or the blood that was there on the stone,
and the blood he said he saw on the stone
and the blood that was there on the stone,
is not here for you to see it,
before crimson trauma I claim this my liars right

13.
The arch of the tear gas is the glee on their faces, a dance in the scream of the
street

14.
In the end, in the end, it was an honor for me to be
one of the prisoners, from the Palestinian prisoners

and it was an honor for me to be
      the first prisoner, from Aida Camp, in this intifada,
it was an honor to sit in the interrogation chair: it is an honor chair.

Unreferenced Sources: Section 11: 'Absentee Property Regulations' issued by Israeli government, December 1948. Charles D. Smith, Palestine and the Arab-Israeli Conflict (Boston, New York: University of Arizona, 2007), p. 230. Section 12: recollected (but unrecorded) account of a young Palestinian's story about his friend Saleh, who was shot by an Israeli sniper. Section 14: taken from a transcription of an interview with Dawud conducted by the author (Aida Refugee Camp, August 2013).

PHILIP METRES

As long as I can remember, I have been writing against the forces of violence and war, and all the dislocations, traumas, and pain that trail in their wake. In the past ten years, I have been teaching a course called "Israeli and Palestinian Literatures." Influenced by postcolonial theory and peace studies, I am interested in the ways in which poetry and literature might offer a staging ground for peace building, by imagining others and embodying subjectivities in counterpoint—giving each a space to breathe on the page, and say their piece.

This intellectual and emotional work found its way in my first book of poems, *To See the Earth* (Cleveland State 2008) in "The Familiar Pictures of Dis" and "Installation/Occupation." *A Concordance of Leaves* (Diode 2013) is a poetic sequence of my sister's wedding that I witnessed in a small village in Palestine. Presently, I'm working on a book of poems on Israel/Palestine called *Shrapnel Maps*. We need poetry that can span the distances through the act of imagination that our bodies and minds are able to travel already, physically and virtually. Given that our contact with other peoples and cultures has very real consequences that sometimes feel very distant, we need arts that suture that space.

In terms of my own poetic practice, I have a lover's quarrel with documentary and lyric modes; as I write, I am trying to answer how much I will let the violence and oppression speak their truth, and how much I (and language) will push back against the "pressure of reality" (Wallace Stevens) and remind myself of the reasons we live, and love, and write in the first place. Witness without love is like death without life. I am aware that my own desire to see this conflict not as an intractable or eternal measure of our hatreds may impede my writing, and may risk the dishonesty of partial seeing. But I know of no other way to proceed, in my half-blindness. I want to see if writing, in its own language and seeing, might participate in the larger project of peace building—and what that might look like.

To echo Herodotus, I write to "prevent these deeds from drifting into oblivion"—striving first to chronicle what has happened—not only Operation Protective Edge, but the ongoing Nakba. But as importantly, I wish to articulate and map the contours and fleeting images of a more just, peaceful, sutured, sustainable world. Naomi Shihab Nye articulated this vision of belatedness and hope in her poem "Jerusalem": "it's late but everything comes next."

The Familiar Pictures of Dis

1.

                                        -truction: crushed cars ditches
of roads broken pavement dis-

     }

mantled stone walls   loose cables & clouds
of dust & dirt   an envelope   returning

     }

to sender: no one by that name   still   ill
living & so the dead letter returns

     }

every night the neighbors hiding in houses heard
sounds of smashing   they could not see

     }

what the soldiers hurled through
the windows of the Ministry of Culture

     }

after all something needs to be broken   to cor-   ore
respond   an objective cor

     }

-relative   & sorrow is a house no one
would visit   unless it visits upon one

2.
past midnight   the sound of barking:
a soldier had attached a speaker to a tape

      }

playing a recording of barking dogs   the village
dogs joined   a neighborhood chorus of de-

      }

fense   we will not sleep together   gather
stones   to live in the basin of some ancient

      }

ocean: the stones rise & break   ache
the surface of the earth   this is the holy

      }

riddled with the stones: in the Ministry   tree
they took everything or took stones

      }

to everything: computers cameras photocopiers
chimeras scanners hard   disks smashed or scat

      }

tered   there is a sentence   stamped out
the broadcast antenna broken   a sentence

3.

written over our bodies   each of us

owns a few letters this unread sentence   tense

        }

without the bodies proximate   we refuse   fuse

& in the department for encouragement

        }

of children's art   the soldiers soiled the walls   all

with gouache & all the children's paintings

        }

smeared with urine & shit   they did their business

on the floors in the flowerpots in drawers in handbags

        }

in water bottles they did their business in photocopiers   ears

in sayings scrawled on walls   refuse & return   turn

        }

to sender   someone had forgotten his dog tags

you can read his name in the papers

        }

but not his whole name   & the sentence remains

unread   the address illegible   return to sender

Installation/Occupation (after Vera Tamari)

1.
there was a time you couldn't paint red white
green or black   could be a flag   imagine

you couldn't paint poppies or watermelon
now you can paint all you want   & yet this state

of uncertainty   will the doors hold out
can you leave your house can you walk around

this occupation   when the tanks come
crack down   drive the sidewalks for fun   for weeks

all these smashed cars lining the city streets
my friend's red Beetle   flipped over   its legs in the air

so in a field   we paved a road to nowhere   & placed
the crushed   in a column   as if in a rush hour

line of traffic   we had an opening   at our piece
a huge party on our road   & then walked home

2.
before dawn a column of Merkavas
came back   my house was opposite the field

& I could see the tanks pull up   & yield
two heads emerged from turrets   trying to read

the scene   then went back inside the hatch
& ran over the exhibit   over & over

again backwards and forwards   then shelled it
& for good measure christened it with piss

I caught it all on video   this metamorphosis
of the piece   there's the story of Duchamp

once the workmen installing his exhibit
dropped a crate of paintings   the floor

shattering the glass   Duchamp ran over
thrilled   now he said   now it is complete

Excerpt from *A Concordance of Leaves*

قرو

(

consider the olive: it gnarls as it grows
into itself / a veritable thicket / it throws

(

up obstacles to the light to reach
the light / a crooked path in the air

(

while beneath our sight it wrestles the rock
wrests water from whatever trickles

(

beneath / it doesn't worry it looks like hell
refuses to straighten for anyone

(

each spring offers itself meat to be eaten
first brambles / then olives

قرو

)

scarved sisters are radiant with wide
mouths & waves & teeth & singing

)

& though there is the great unhappiness
framed in silent unsmiling faces

)

hammered on insides of houses
watching over all preparations

)

night is lifting the women
are drumming the tabla their voices inviting

)

a heart to break itself & open
a space another could nest inside

قرو

)

because there is a word for love in this tongue
that entwines two people as one

)

& there is a word for love in this tongue
that nests in the chambers of the heart

)

& a word for love in this tongue that wanders
the earth, for love in this tongue in which you lose

)

yourself in this tongue & a word that carries
sorrow within its vowels & a word for love

)

that exudes from your pores & a word
for love that shares its name with falling

قرو

)

If to Bethlehem we must pass through Wadi Nar

)

If your license plates are painted blue & black

)

If your permit permits no passage across bypass highways

)

If from a distance the road carves alephs or alifs

)

If no man's land is where men live who have no land

)

If you lower your sunshield & block the hilltop settlement

)

If Wadi Nar is the Valley of Fire

)

If we must travel beneath the level of our eventual grave

)

If we arrive & they ask *how are you,* we are to say *thank God*

ورق

)

& though the border guards will advise us
this is a dangerous time to visit

)

& though we had to lie & say we were tourists
& not guests at our sister's wedding

)

to spare ourselves the special interrogation
on the borders of fear / in Ben Gurion

)

& emerge blinking into the light of a modern Oz
beyond the wall / blooming with English lawns

)

the dancers in their purple spangled parachute
pants will turn wheels in the dust until the dust

قرو

)

is a violet fire & though the checkpoints hunker
in bunkers & Uzis with Uzis will raise them

)

at our unwitting arrival & cause us to lower
cameras & eyes & though hawkers hawk songbirds

)

at Qalandia Checkpoint where garbage bags tumble
free as emptied skulls in No-Man's-Land

)

& the lines of the people are mute with waiting
the *ataaba* singers will arrive in the village

)

& name-check our families *marhaba Metres
marhaba /marhaba Abbadi marhaba*

قرو

)

& though some seaside café will split into
thousands of shards of glassy dreams

)

& these people will have had nothing to do
with it, & the bulldozers will doze their roads

)

so that every road ends in a wall
every car will pick a path through olive groves

)

& though we won't see the sea the wind
will haul it & the whole village will arrive

)

at the village, until the village will be
a living map of itself, actual size

قرو

)

& though there is a boy whose cheek
is a scar & no father, his eyes like broken eggs

)

the children will flock to every flat roof
to watch the village become the village

)

& see the wedding from enough distance
it looks like a story that could be entered

)

& see the men pin paper money to the suit
of the groom, until he's feathered with future

)

& though everyone will eat, & eat again,
some miracle of loaves & lambs

قدرو

)

& though the bride's arms and legs will itch
with arabesques & scripts of henna

)

a second skin won't be scratched away
& though her mother will be angry

)

the women & children will wait
until all the men have been served

)

& even the bride plays a role she only
learns on hennaed heels

)

& though tradition is an invisible
author only the old hands hear

قرو

)

& though the sun will be too bright for the bride
to see much farther than her own eyes

)

& though the bullet in the groom will begin
to hatch in his side, & the stitches in his skull

)

will singe another verse in the book of dreams,
& though the bride's questions will beak their shell

)

years from now, now, now let there be dancing
in circles, let the village become flung arms

)

bringing bodies to bodies & let heads nod
& eyes widen, which we translate as meaning:

قرو

Accept this . . .	*tfaddul*
Congratulations	*mabrouk*
How much?	*adaish hadah?*
I don't understand	*ana mish fahim*
Tomorrow	*bukra*

Apricots	*mish-mish*
Tomorrow, when the apricots ripen	*bukra fil mish-mish*
Tomorrow never comes	*bukra fil mish-mish*
Ready?	*y'allah?*
Let's go	*y'allah*

قرو

)

you my sister you my brother
outside the walls / in the wind

)

if Aristophanes was right
& we walk the world

)

in search of, a split-
infinitive of *to love*, if two

)

outside the walls / in the wind
should find in each other more

)

than mirror, then we should sing
outside the walls / in the wind

)

you my sister you my brother
that tree & stone may answer

)

outside the walls / in the wind
& let *our eccho ring*:

Coda

like strapping a small bomb
to your third finger / that ring

)

about which we could not
speak upon our arrival

)

& departure from the country
of memory where we left you

)

sister / among the fragile
projectiles inside the book

)

whose pages the wind rifles
searching for a certain passage
(Toura, Palestine)

Nightwalk for Rachel Corrie

1.
The salmon talked me into it.
A hole, a pipe in the bulkhead

of East Bay Marina—every year
the salmon swim into that hole,

trying to get back home. Salmon
have to make it all the way up

Plum Street in that hole. That hole
is Moxlie Creek. Once you know

salmon swim down there, you can't
forget. You imagine moony eyes

as you walk home in slutty boots.
It's hard to be vacuous—

salmon in the back of your mind
nosing toward light, Watershed Park.

2.
To place herself / between the home
& bulldozer. The dozer turned

to face her / neon & bullhorn
twenty meters / mound of earth

building in front of its mouth.
To shout her / unheard words.

To climb this growing / mound of earth
& place her head & shoulders

above the blade, before his eyes.
To stand & face what she would face—

another man who could not hear.
Above the rising mound to slip

from sight / into the yawn
—until only her body was gone.

DINA OMAR

I come from a small village of farmers tucked away in the hills between Jericho and Jerusalem, but I've lived most of my life in America's inner cities, affiliated with academic institutions where my primary goal is to read books and discuss their meaning. I am constantly moving between worlds of extreme scarcity and worlds of abundance, and poetry helps me navigate the unequal distribution of protections and resources.

Poetry is what I write in liminal spaces between reading Kafka's short stories and Malinowski's ethnographies. My poems are written through the sorrow and outrage ensued by personal loss, between watching Operation Cast Lead—the unfolding massacre of more than fourteen hundred people in Gaza—and protesting in Oakland, California after Oscar Grant was tackled to the ground and shot in the back at close range by BART police. Poetry is my attempt to honor and defend who and what I love.

What Does One Wear for War?

Mornings are for contemplation
sun light beams through the curtains like an industrial crane forcing me
to rise like a cat stretching in slow motion,
I press out the gunk at the corner of my eyelids.
I've become to be more interested in gathering metal scraps,
shards of glass, and incomplete sentences for reflection
bushels of jasmine and triticum seem so passé.

Lather my body with olive oil soap
not for cleanliness
because I've come to love the layer of dust
amassing my skin, it offers comfort against comfort.
And the scent of Nablus lasts like armor.
It is not that I want to rub out the metallic images of diluted blood on concrete
but contemplating where to bury dead relatives requires
a clean body and an intimacy with dirt.

It is that I want to remember
my Sito Sada.
I wear her thob
as I lie next to a Gazelle
on the beach of Deir al Balah.

I take off Sito Sada's thob
and cover the Gaza sunset with it

u7ibeck
hata i'll ta3ib
hata i'll ta3ib

This night I go to sleep
a tired virgin
and wake up with the morning light
a man-of-war.

Excerpt from "Cartographies of Disappearing: Meditation on where to bury 'our' dead"

IV.

TRANSPORTING BODIES
. . . We just left! We were holding his hand whispering prayers in his ear, looking crossly at that stupid plastic pink pitcher found in every hospital—the one that laughs at you—reminding you of the monotonous experience you are having, reminding you that there are mass produced experiences just like yours and everyone of them have a plastic pink pitcher.

My mom, his wife Dounia, my aunt Zanib, my cousin Maher, his friend Tom, my mom's sisters, were still physically with Ihab in San Diego, California, on the fifth floor of Scripps Memorial Hospital. My sisters and I were away, my aunts were in Michigan, Ihab's kids were with friends in Las Vegas, Nevada. My father was in Palestine, more specifically in *Ramoun*, more specifically in the ground next to his father and diagonal from his mother. They lie in the cemetery less than a kilometer behind the house my father grew up in, right next door to the house my mom grew up in. This is the only place that ever really belonged to us.

I was in New Haven when I received the news:

> *Shiddi 7alik ya' Dina . . .*
> *Allah yerhamoo, wa' yodkhall fuseek il'Jennah ya'rub . . .*
> *Allah khalee uladou wa' ya3teekoom il'sa7a wa' salaama*

And then.

> *Where should we bury him?*

It is between a Friday and a Saturday and we have to make a decision. I can't seem to get through to anyone back home; Friday is the holy day for Muslims and Saturday is the *Sabbath* for Jews and no one is picking up the goddamn phone!

As I started making my way to JFK I did not know if I should catch the next flight to Tel Aviv, Michigan, or California. The last time I tried to go back home I was denied entry, how am I supposed to get my dead brother into the country?

I must have left twenty messages on various voicemails between The Palestinian Ministry of Planning and International Cooperation and the Israeli Ministry of Foreign Affairs.

My father also died in California and we were able to bury him back home in Palestine, I was only twelve then, but the process was less invasive. We had relatives with *wasta* (connections) and my uncles Imran and Tayseer took care of things there because they were my father's friends. But uncles are now dead too, and we have not been so good at keeping up with the ones who are not. And all the men in our life have gone away. So my cousin takes on the man "responsibilities."

I was already back in San Diego when I finally got through to the Palestinian authorities. The person on the other end of the phone explained that if we wanted to bury Ihab back home that the process has changed a great deal since I was twelve. We would have to hire a private Israeli company and they would have to apply for a permit through the Israeli Ministry of Foreign Affairs, and upon approval we would have to figure out how to transport the body from the Tel Aviv airport to *Ramoun*. Also, recent Israeli regulations now require impounding for cargo packaging, and when human remains are shipped, which requires that the body be opened and the organs inspected. The border authorities are also given access to the open body for *security*.

As I relay this information to my sister-in-law we look at one another and know that between the two of us we can't. We just can't. And she says that we should not wait any longer.

> *Karam't il-me'it, il-diffin*
> *(the dignity of the dead is to be buried)*

I am haunted that we lowed my brother's body into the earth in West Covina, California. Knott's Berry Farm is two exits away and there is a Target up the street from the cemetery . . .

VI.

. . . Stay still body, one thought at a time.

Shaking and consumed with where to bury this semicolon, this comma verses this long dash, in my notebook, this brother of mine who is made of the same stuff, the same grammar, who took me to Padres games, was sharp as a knife, who pulled my hair, and hugged his baby sister like he meant it. Where do I bury him in this notebook? In this life? How do I punctuate the beginning and end of my brother's life the way I do a sentence?

◆ ◆ ◆

Now I am typing what I wrote in my notebook into this Microsoft Word document. The bright computer screen and the letters on the keyboard blur together. Again, I am back in graduate school where I fight like hell from retreating deep into the greatest silences of myself.

And I know that to be free from it all, that Nietzsche is onto something. We must destroy the meaning of all things that we do not possess within ourselves. Where's the hammer? Give it to me so I can destroy the history of violent displacement I have inherited, and raze whatever pain I felt as a result of loss. If I wish to say, "Yes to life even in its strangest and most painful episodes," I must purge the idea that there is a homeland where our graves must lie. To be "liberated from terror and pity," to escape the haunting reminders of a fractured life, I must break the monuments built in my mind in the image of a land that we call ours, and laugh at how it has denied us entry.

Because the weight of generations of burial traditions is too heavy to carry in this world . . .

And this is where I *get over* all this philosophizing about the self versus god and ask for mercy.

I think about the thousands of Syrians who have lived their entire lives in Damascus, Homs, Hama, and Aleppo. I imagine that they probably buried family members and loved ones in the same cemetery for generations. Routine and a sense of place gives one comfort. How does one cope with the fact that their loved one is amongst the hundreds of corpses stacked up in Syria's overflowing morgues?

I ask for mercy.

I think about Ghassan Kanafani's novel *Men Under the Sun*. After the driver discovers the three refugee men dead in the water tank, he leaves their corpses on the side of the road and drives away as fast as he can so that at least he would be able to make it to Kuwait safely.

Sometimes sentimentality is paralysis; it's what we do to survive.

I ask for mercy.

I think about the fact that I took most of my undergraduate classes in Krober Hall at UC Berkeley—built over Ohlone sacred burial grounds.

I ask for mercy.

I think about the hundreds of dead children wrapped in white sheets and piled up and nowhere to store them in Gaza. There is no room. No room in the morgues, so restaurant vegetable freezers and ice cream trucks have been transformed into corpse refrigerators. And I wonder how they buried the nephew of my sister's husband and if anyone had a chance to recall the legacy of his short life before moving on to dealing with the new dead.

I ask for mercy.

I think about all the men I've ever loved in life, the fact that their bodies have disappeared. They are no longer visible in my life. They have been swallowed by the ground or taken away by gigantic orange and turquoise birds in my nightmares. Thinking about their absence is the sound of a goat before its throat is sliced for sacrifice. We forget about what screams sound like when chewing the meat.

I ask for mercy.

There are roads, and alleyways, and trains we take away from the carnage but they never lead to a place where we can see beyond the mountains of dead bodies in our memory. We walk through doors into fancy buildings despite the sacred sites over which they were built.

I ask my Israeli friend to bring me back a piece of earth with her when she returns to America from our homeland Palestine. I compress that piece of earth into the pile of dirt on top of my brother's grave.

I ask for mercy.

WHAT WE DO

XHENET ALIU

"Empathy" seemed to me like 2014's literary buzzword, between the studies on how reading fiction can expand our senses of it, accolades for Leslie Jamison's *Empathy Exams*, and the *Boston Review*'s article "Against Empathy." But it was a particularly rough year for those among us who exercise it. In addition to the many domestic acts of violence and injustice we witnessed in 2014, the 2014 attack on Gaza triggered in me—and in others, based on news articles and the social media response—a terrible sense of sorrow and confusion and, I speculate, powerlessness. To express it like the child that I sometimes felt like, I was very sad and very angry, and I had absolutely no idea what to do about any of it. In general I'm extremely uncomfortable on social media, and frankly skeptical of its ability to change minds or even provoke in any way other than in the seventh-grade sense. I wanted to explore some of the reasons for and possible outcomes of the silence with which I, and maybe others like me, respond to extreme acts of humanitarian dysfunction, especially when they seem almost abstract, as in the case of Gaza to most Americans.

Not Nice

A lot of people think I'm nice. I'm not nice. I stay at home most of the time just so I don't have to act nice. I don't want to apologize to the bartender for interrupting the text-fight he's having with his girlfriend to order a drink, and I don't want to smile in a neighborly way at the rednecks down the street who release their hounds to crap in my front yard. I stopped using Facebook because I don't want to deal with people like the fully insured academic acquaintance who "tested" last year's dysfunctional healthcare marketplace website and assured idiots like me who actually need health insurance that hey, he checked, the website's working just fine. I don't like you if you were the one who posted, in response to the *New York Times'* question about what your children ate for breakfast that morning, this horseshit: "Currant buckwheat bread toast (from the French Poilane bakery), assorted fruits (grapes, blueberries, strawberries and pear), a 1/2 tablespoon of 'crackers,' aka biodynamic unsweetened cornflakes (special treat), and a small glass of milk." I probably don't like the Baby Bjorns you're feeding that stuff to, either, but to be fair, your biodynamic offspring never stood a chance.

I'm not nice. I'm sometimes quiet, which people confuse for nice. That's my problem.

But I feel quiet rage every goddamned day. I felt it the other night for this frat boy I stood next to at the grocery store who was telling his buddy, *Dude, she was a five, I told her she was a nine, I was being nice, she kicked me the fuck out.* I looked him dead in his dead little eyes and hated him and didn't say a word, which probably made me seem nice and maybe bumped me up to a six in his uncurious little Sigma Chi-branded head.

I felt it for AnthonyStark, a troll arrogant enough to liken himself to a third-rate superhero when he makes comments such as, "Mike Brown was unarmed because he tried and FAILED to steal the cop's gun. Had he been successful, we'd been treated to business-as-usual, black on white murder."

And: "Yup, we know what causes poverty: fighting, abusing drugs, partying and getting pregnant."

And: "ISIS and Al-Qaida boastful goal is to convert the world to Islam, or exterminate those who resist. While not a religion, it is the enforcing arm of a religion."

I felt rage that AnthonyStark, a man who has not yet learned to use possessives, never mind studied the Quran or, for that matter, the Bible I'm positive he'd claim to live by, made me feel anything. My partner suggests that the solution to that is to stop reading the comments sections of shitty newspapers, but I haven't, so I must simply want to feel this way. I must get off on it or something.

Yeah, I must like rage. It must make me feel conscious and noble. It must make staying at home feel absolutely appropriate.

As if I know the first thing about rage.

Because here's the thing: if you took the healthcare guy, the biodynamic family, every member of Sigma Chi, AnthonyStark and every single other troll with an anonymous profile on *USA Today*, stuck them all in the house of the people with the fiberful free-range mutts down the street, and handed me a detonator that would bring them all down with the push of a button, I would think you were insane for even suggesting that those people should be killed. Even if you added in Donald Rumsfeld, Vince Vaughn, and every person who has brought or wished me personal harm, including the man who held a gun to my head and the man who told me I deserved it, I would be appalled if you expected me to want them dead.

Because really, I don't know the first thing about rage.

What do I know about the conditions that would drive someone to take another person's life, never mind a stranger's life, never mind life on a mass scale? What I feel in response to the photos of dead Palestinian babies and the men who don't have time to cry as they flee with the bodies of their sons and daughters—it feels like a fire in my belly, it feels like enough to make me want to quit everything altogether, but surely that feeling can't be rage, because isn't rage the thing that leads to the things captured in those very pictures that I can barely stand to look at? Isn't rage a crop that's reaped after years of oppression, violence, enforced poverty, legislated dehumanizing, things that it's almost impossible for a girl from Connecticut—even the offspring of people who fled hunger and dictatorships, even one born in the projects of a city that routinely ranks at the bottom of the *Places Rated Almanac*—to even begin to understand? Living in a housing project in Connecticut meant having a home in motherfucking Connecticut. Eating government cheese meant eating motherfucking life-sustaining food. So if I claim to have enough perspective to understand my own privilege, to understand that what I'm entitled to is not rage, what is it really that I feel when I look at those photos on the *New York Times*, paid for with a subscription that I buy with money I earn, the currency that's left over after paying for food and rent and subsidized health insurance?

My conclusion is that it's not important what I feel, so I'm quiet. I'm nice and quiet. I don't have a horse in this race.

Because this Israel-Palestine thing is about faith, right? A faith I don't share with either side. I don't get it. I can't. I'm Muslim by inheritance, but the only thing people who hate me for my Muslim name can do to me is annoy me. Maybe

I'll never get the pre-check stamp on my airline tickets. Maybe someone won't respond to my requests for more information about an apartment rental they've advertised, or want to sell me a bicycle even if they've re-posted their Craiglist ad after I've written to them about it several times. If I use the email address I've set up under the name Jenny, I can preclude even that. I show up as Jenny with my light skin and speak in my neutral American accent and I've got a shot at that apartment, and that bike is as good as mine. I get to feel superior when I refuse them anyway, because I don't want to line the pockets of a racist.

See, I don't have a horse in this race.

I'm not even religious. I knew I wasn't when my Muslim father's friends told me I was damned for eating that hot dog I ordered at Friendly's, and I knew I wasn't when my Catholic mother was cut off from the church for having children out of wedlock with a guy like my father. I used to celebrate Passover with my Jewish best friend while wearing my aunt's letter jacket from Holy Cross High School. I still know every word to "Hava Nagila" from singing it in Special Chorus, which I was appointed to by virtue of my general compliance in the classroom and not my singing voice. I summon God's name only to damn things. I have relatives who are born-again Christian and relatives who wear the veil. This fluidity in the American identity, these are the things that lead to an existential crisis, right? I have an MFA, I know how fertile a place that is. That's the place where Richard Yates novels come from. He was a Connecticut person too, wasn't he?

I get it, unless the existential crisis is literally a crisis in existence, as in living, as in not being shelled while walking a beach, or living in an apartment or a hospital or a school that has the misfortune of being located next to a house where Hamas allegedly placed a soldier or weapons. Yates novels don't come from that place. Rage comes from that place. Terror, grief, the kind of self-preservation that can be accomplished only through the destruction of those intent on striking you first.

I don't know that place, so I stay angry, with whatever version of anger I think I'm entitled to. The quiet version I feel at home, or sometimes in grocery stores.

It's hard to stay quiet sometimes. Those pictures. Tell me those babies deserved it for being born in an apartment next to the one Hamas decided to maybe plant a weapon in. Tell me that you're allowed to defend your life by sacrificing 2,100 others, most of whom are no kind of soldier, and I'll summon God's name to damn yours. I'll add you to that house down the block with Rumsfeld and Vaughn, and probably I'll move out of the neighborhood, pelting the door with rotten eggs on the way out of town.

But I still wouldn't detonate, even though I know, I know, *I know* you're wrong, so what do I know about rage?

Maybe I don't know you're wrong. Maybe I only feel that you're wrong. Because the other pictures, the ones that show the other side grieving? The ones that show

Israeli rage? That rage looks real to me, too. The Israeli people in the news photos don't look triumphant to me, even though clearly they've won: depending on which organization provides the number, between one thousand and fifteen hundred Palestinian civilians killed in the summer 2014 war to Israel's five. Five. On paper, to me, the sheer numbers add up to wholesale slaughter. To me, the justification for the slaughter doesn't at all stir my soul: *We have the right to defend ourselves.* Sure, but against civilians and babies who can't perpetrate the harm they very well may wish upon you? Is someone hating you enough of a reason to kill them? And if killing them makes them hate you even more, does that mean you get to kill even more of them in retaliation? Why not keep things professional? Why not send your trained soldiers on ground missions to seek out the enemy trained soldiers, even kill them if you have to? I understand that this is war. The soldiers understand that they've signed up for this.

Unless they didn't. Unless they're conscripts. Unless they're soldiers willing to die for a righteous cause but not this one. Unless the soldier is your son or brother, in which case the numbers in the *New York Times* and politics and faith don't mean a whole goddamned much. Tell the mother of any of the five Israeli civilians killed that she won. Tell the mother of any of the sixty-something dead Israeli soldiers that she did.

War is political, right, so maybe this isn't about faith after all. This war is about oppression and human rights and the right to self-determination. What do I know? I know only rhetoric: freedom, security, evildoers, our way of life. Our way. *Ours.* It's crazy how you can put a "y" in front of that word and it's a completely different thing—*yours. Yours* is different enough that we can rationalize its destruction at our hands.

See how flimsy my arguments are? They're wordplay. It's not even good semantics. I know nothing. I believe things, and what's that saying about opinions and assholes? And what's that other thing about if you can't say something nice, don't say anything at all?

My brother fought in a war I didn't believe in. He'd talked about being a soldier his whole life, and the fact that he enlisted and was sent off to a war that I couldn't defend had no bearing on how I felt upon learning he was dead. I can only imagine that my response would not have been different if he had died defending a cause that I myself would die for, because I realized at that time that grief doesn't have a context. There's just alive and dead and the whys don't matter, even if you never stop asking them. That my brother died by his own gun shortly after being diagnosed with PTSD—his biochemistry debilitatingly altered after mere *months* of living in a warzone, of being asked to take lives, knowing that many people were willing, even desperate, to take his—doesn't make me feel better or worse. He's dead either way.

Months of living in a warzone did that to him. I wonder what a lifetime of that would make one capable of.

That's one of my problems. I'm too reductive. My brother would certainly tell me that, over Thanksgiving dinner, were the topic of the Israeli-Palestine war to come up, which it almost certainly wouldn't. The rest of the family wouldn't follow. To them, the words Gaza Strip are like the stock prices: they show up almost daily in the paper and have nothing to do with their lives. My brother, though, would school me on intifada, state-sponsored terrorism, and the manipulation of casualty data, and on the other side, of land appropriation, occupation, and attacks on civilian infrastructure. He'd remind me of failed peace treaties and two-state solutions and the violations of international humanitarian law by both sides. He was a Poli Sci major and a captain in the Army, and I am a bleeding heart who wants to talk about feelings. He'd offer to listen to my proposed solution to a conflict which thousands of scholars, politicians, and religious leaders have yet to resolve.

And I'd be quiet, because I wouldn't know what to say. And I'd feel angry, because I hate not knowing, or, even worse, being wrong. It makes me feel that burning rage-like feeling that can't be rage. I'm probably even wrong about what I think my brother would say, which also makes me angry. It's more than just politics that he understood better than me; it was also suffering. He was the one who witnessed it up close, not me. He was the one who engaged. He was the one who ultimately succumbed.

I'm still here, with the nerve to get upset by innocuous Facebook comments about the health insurance exchange.

Yet I can't help but believe, even when I try to reason my way out of it, that our ability to understand suffering is innate, not learned. They say babies are born with a fear of falling, which to me suggests that it's part of our humanness to imagine pain. Even if I'm wrong, you don't have to imagine it. This pain is explicit. Look at the picture of that child on the sand, his limbs at angles you've only before seen on the arms of a clock in the early afternoon, at a few minutes past the hour. Don't imagine, just look.

That one of a man consoling another after the funeral for ten children killed at a park in a refugee camp, dried blood still on the sitting man's shirt who knows how many days later.

Then look at that other picture of an adolescent on a bike in a UN school in Gaza, surrounded by younger kids, maybe siblings or cousins, and two adults with something resembling smiles on their faces. A snapshot of normal, as it's become to them. That's the one that breaks my heart most, I think. That's the feeling I think I too often confuse with rage.

Maybe that's the slippery part about rage: it wears disguises. It looks sometimes like anguish, sometimes like hunger. It sometimes wears the veil, sometimes an IDF uniform. Sometimes it looks like your brother, or some asshole kid who's been too loved by his parents and therefore too insulated from hardship to know any better. It sometimes looks like the righteous indignation of a lefty self-anointed working-class hero with a fridge full of bougie ingredients she can't bear for other people to talk about. It's sometimes mistaken for worthless, and often bastardized, and, like nuclear power, it's incredibly powerful and efficient and useful but never entirely clean. Sometimes it looks right, and it sometimes looks wrong. It has a reputation for being loud and wild but it just as often takes the form of silence. Silence, in turn, has a reputation for politeness, for docility, for niceness, when we all must know by now how it can abet in destroying the humanity we polite people are so afraid to offend.

I'm not nice. And now, at least for a few thousand words, I'm not silent. I'm not sure what I'm saying, other than sloppy, contradictory things, things that can be seen and called out for their wrongness. Tell me I'm wrong, then. Let me get angry about it. Don't let me be nice.

Gaza Traces

KIM JENSEN

We have been asked where we stand as writers and artists in relation to the systematic human rights violations against the Palestinian people. In order to approach this question, I want to draw closer to this mesmerizing image of three children on a beach in the Gaza strip that was widely shared on social media during the Israeli assault this past summer. Studying the photograph and the story of its origins may shed light on what it means to bear witness to a human catastrophe.

During the military siege on Gaza in the summer of 2014, many international journalists were staying at al-Deira Hotel, overlooking the Mediterranean. Reporters and cameramen often watched the children of fishermen playing on the beach in front of the hotel, and sometimes went down to play with them.

At 4 pm on July 16, a day of heavy bombardments, the Israeli navy targeted a ramshackle hut where fishermen stored their nets. No Palestinian resistance fighters were present, as numerous eyewitnesses testified, but a group of children

was playing nearby. After the first explosion, the survivors ran for safety. A few seconds later, the Israelis let loose a second attack directly aiming at the fleeing children. Four of them—Ismael Muhammad Bakr, Zakaria Ahed Bakr, Ahed Atif Bakr, and Muhammad Ramiz Bakr—were killed. Journalists who witnessed and filmed the incident later reported that it was abundantly clear, even from a distance, that the running figures on the beach were unarmed children.

This haunting photograph was captured and tweeted by the Irish rugby player and Palestine solidarity activist Trevor Hogan. On the evening of the beach massacre, he was sitting in his living room in Dublin watching the news coverage, and happened to notice a fleeting image of running children. Rewinding and fast-forwarding—Trevor finally managed to isolate the frame. He snapped an iPhone picture and posted it online, creating one of the most indelible images from Israel's summer offensive.

I choose to reflect on this image and not the images of the aftermath: the children's bent, dismembered bodies in the sand. The disturbing pictures of their corpses—the unthinkable outcome of modern warfare—are revolting and obscene. To demand an extended gaze upon them is a different project, equally legitimate. It is important for people, especially those of us whose governments perpetrate such war crimes, to see and to know exactly what bombs, mortar shells, and missiles do to living bodies—and to confront our own complicity.

But I want to return to the spirit in which Trevor Hogan created this image. Overwhelmed by feelings of horror, disgust, and helplessness, he worked with a clear intention: to create something that would "allow people who don't wish to view a graphic image of war crimes to connect with the gravity of what had happened while highlighting the split second in time before their lives were taken." His objective was to move people to action.

How to read this photograph without context? At first glance and to the uninitiated, it might read simply as a blurry snapshot of some appealing children in the distance. Upon further study, we might think of it as a representation of childhood itself, wistful, hazy in detail—a frozen moment of transient, ephemeral innocence. Even if we knew of the tragedy surrounding the children, we might believe that this was the boys' last moments of play on the beach.

But this is not an image of joy; it's an image of terror. These children weren't playing; they were fleeing for their lives.

They have now become traces on our screens, traces left behind from the persistent carnage inflicted on the people of Palestine. Like raindrops streaking a windowpane, the image lifts this moment into permanence. It resurrects other stories. In a cascade of associations, it reawakens the memory of Huda Ghaliya who watched her family slaughtered before her eyes on a beach in Beit Lahia. It resuscitates twelve-year old Muhammad al-Durra dying in his father's arms during the Second Intifada, and the powerful requiem that Mahmoud Darwish wrote to him:

"Muhammad/is a poor angel, trapped at close range/by a cold-blooded hunter/in the eye of a camera that captures each movement/of a child becoming one with this shadow."

For me the photograph also conjures the sad, luminous spirit that inhabits the writings of American poet and novelist Fanny Howe who has spoken of her work as an attempt to "describe a preserved radiance—and to show that there is an invisible 'elseness' to everything." She writes: "You go on because of it, but it's the thing you can't quite see."

This image from Gaza, something of the magic and sorrow in it, provides a visual corollary of that preserved radiance and that "elseness" that Fanny Howe describes. The enigmatic combination of beauty and grief. The glow of the yellow sand, a kind of halo for the fleeing children.

The fact that we have this image at all is a matter of chance and craft. It was chance that Western journalists were on hand to film to the casual, deliberate slaughter of innocent Palestinian civilians that has been ongoing for over sixty years. It was also chance that this committed activist happened to be watching the news and realized he had seen something important.

Chance is at play in the symbolic elements of the composition. The children's clothing—the green, red, and white shirts when combined with the looming shadow on the foreground form the colors of the Palestinian flag—lifting this fleeting moment to the level of mythos and national iconography. Fate is already printed here, maktoob, written, as if martyrdom was already stamped on this moment.

The children's faces are darkened, anonymous—like most of the nameless victims of war and violence. Their facelessness makes them all the more universal. In their impersonal presence they become emblematic of all children—we recognize that these could be any children, could be our children, your children, our neighbor's children.

They hover in shadow in that tenuous space just before they become bodies. The photograph neither memorializes them as the boys that they were with their individual personalities and traits nor does it reduce them to inanimate flesh.

These are some of the elements of chance, but craft is also at work.

Trevor intentionally captured the perfectly matching strides of the children, apprehended midflight like sea birds, the joy of innocence, the tenuous connection to the earth at that instant. The graininess of the photograph is part of its quiet splendor. The children's vertical figures are the only rupture in a study of horizontal lines. They disrupt and animate the composition. Bewildering, fragmented, and anachronistic—the forms come to us as if through a filter of sadness. It has the quality of a prayer or a sacred text in that it has the potent ability to reach the deepest recesses of human trauma.

This low-quality, third-hand image that I now call "Gaza Traces" is, in its way, a work of art. It has elements of fiction—the artifice of the frozen moment, which is an impossible, imaginary figment. The artifice manages to save these children, protecting them for eternity from inevitable violence.

Despite the preserved nature of the image, we do see fate arriving. The children are already silhouettes, thin limbed, almost disappearing. The composition already suggests their vulnerability. The shadow before them and the indifference of the ocean behind them seem to want to swallow them.

Once we read "Gaza Traces" this way, and we make the decision to face the gravity of the situation, we are also faced with an inevitable question: Do we have the right to extract a private meaning from the unthinkable grief of others?

As a poet and writer, I find Herbert Marcuse's defense of the revolutionary nature of art helpful in answering this question. Marcuse argues that by virtue of its aesthetic transformation, authentic art estranges the viewer from oppressive social conditions, and indicts the established reality. "Art," he says, "alienates individuals from their functional existence and performance in society—it is committed to an emancipation of sensibility, imagination and reason . . ." Authentic art does not exploit pain, it helps us to see and feel our way through it and past it.

A critic may argue that this moment of aesthetic transformation cannot help these children in a besieged place that has become nothing more and nothing less than the first concentration camp of the twenty-first century. This is correct. It does not.

But it does help those who are still living to come to greater awareness of the despotism that is around us and in us. As the veils of false consciousness are torn asunder, like bodies rendered, the true nature of social reality is exposed and we have no ethical choice but to strengthen our resolve to be more committed, more receptive, more compassionate, and more engaged.

Despair is chronic; no one can say that this is the world they would have chosen. But art does puncture holes in this pervasive despair and renders things visible that were previously invisible. Art shows us where to look and what to see. We need to see these children. Before and after. We cannot turn away from the Palestinian people and their need to be free from violence, dispossession, and cultural erasure.

It is nearly impossible to know what our "responsibilities" are as artists when we face this kind of ongoing human catastrophe. I would say there is no special responsibility that artists have above and beyond the responsibility that all humans have. The thing that distinguishes artists is that we have made it a regular and formal practice to observe, think, frame, reframe, to try to create work that will do justice to our moment. These activities put us in proximity to ethical questions as a matter of course.

But let's be reminded that the fishermen's children were filmed almost by accident and preserved in the public sphere by a young activist who does not identify himself as an artist, but who took the time to see and to act. This shows us the potential each of us has—to activate our senses and to take a stand on matters of universal concern. There is nothing elite, nor sanctified, nor otherworldly about making art.

Nothing we can do will bring back the children who were killed on the beach on July 16, 2014, or the thousands who lost their lives last summer. Nothing will bring back the limbs of the limbless, or repair the skin of those who were permanently disfigured, or close the wounds of those who were left psychologically and emotionally scarred. The personal and collective loss is unfathomable.

The words we write here, the poems we share, the images we capture will not undo the pain and injustice, and we would be naive to think they do. Yet they may help us find solace in community and rediscover joy in a shared liberational vision. These works can give us the strength to keep going—to reach out in solidarity to a people in struggle.

Muhammad

by *Mahmoud Darwish*

(Translated from Arabic by Zahi Khamis and Kim Jensen)

Muhammad
nestles in his father's embrace, a bird
afraid of the blazing sky: Protect me father
from flying away. My wing
is too weak for this wind . . . and the light is black.
Muhammad
wants to go home
without a bicycle . . . or a new shirt.
He wants to return to his school desk
and grammar books. Take me home,
father, so I can do my homework
and live out my life, little by little
by the seashore, under palm trees
and nothing further than this.
Muhammad
faces an army, without a stone or the shrapnel
of stars. He doesn't notice the wall
where he might have written:
"My freedom will not die."
He has no freedom to defend yet
no horizon for Picasso's dove.
He is still being born
into a name that carries the curse of that name.
How many times will he give birth to himself
a boy without a homeland . . . without a chance at childhood?
Where will he dream, if a dream came to him
when the earth is a wound . . . and a temple?
Muhammad
sees his death approaching, but remembers
a panther he saw on TV.
The powerful cat had cornered a nursing fawn,

but smelled the milk and shied away
—as if milk could tame a devouring beast.
I'll be saved then—says the boy
and he weeps: My life is over there
hidden in my mother's cupboard. I will survive
and I will testify.
Muhammad
is a poor angel, trapped at close range
by a cold-blooded hunter
in the eye of a camera that captures each movement
of a child becoming one with his shadow.
His face, like the morning light, clear.
His heart, like an apple, clear.
His ten fingers, like candles, clear.
And the dew on his trousers, clear.
His hunter could have reconsidered the case
and said: I'll leave him until he can spell
Palestine correctly . . .
I'll leave it to my conscience for now
and kill him later when he rebels!
Muhammad
is a little Jesus sleeping
and dreaming inside an icon
made of copper and an olive branch
and the spirit of a people renewed.
Muhammad,
blood far beyond what the prophets have needed.
Ascend then,
O Muhammad
to the furthest bough in the highest heaven!

Informed Compassion

SUSAN MUADDI DARRAJ

I wrote the essay below on the morning of July 17, 2014, in an attempt to articulate my horror at the events of the previous day: the murder of four little boys on the beach of Gaza, who'd been playing soccer in the sand in the moments before their killing.

Perhaps because of the fact that I teach African American literature, I kept thinking of the four little girls killed by a KKK bombing at the 16th Street Baptist Church in Birmingham, an event that I discuss at length with my class during the unit I teach on literature of the Civil Rights Movement. We focus on the idea that some events shock people out of their complacency about political events, some events cannot be ignored, some events move even the most reluctant citizens to speak. Usually, and unfortunately, those events involve the brutal treatment of children.

But not, apparently, Palestinian children.

I had spent the days before July 16 glued to my laptop, searching news sites, in numbness as the corpses piled up, but also feeling cold at the inability of many to simply say, "The murder of children is wrong. The murder of children cannot be allowed to continue." The silence was especially apparent on social media, where the bravest people would venture only so far as "The killing on both sides has to stop."

And yet, I know that many of my colleagues and friends feel that the killing of children is abominable, because that same summer, Michael Brown was gunned down in Ferguson, Missouri, and people exploded in frustration.

Where are these voices when Palestinian children are killed?

July 16 changed my perspective. "Feel-good compassion" is not enough. Compassion must be informed, and it must be brave.

On July 16, 2014, I was sitting in the library of Bryn Mawr College in Philadelphia, reading and writing while waiting for my three children, who were attending a summer camp there. The previous week, I had told my children how this beautiful college was one of the first to offer serious programs of study for American women.

"Why couldn't girls go to school?" my six-year-old son asked.

"It was a different time, but things changed," I told him. "They're a lot better now."

I tried to make the connection to faith. We'd been attending, as a family, a Quaker meeting back home in Baltimore, and I shared with my kids that Bryn Mawr College was founded by a Quaker. Last week in First Day School, they'd learned about Lucretia Mott and had even made little candles as they talked about her vision and ideas.

Fairness. Justice. And especially—compassion. All the things my husband and I try to emphasize to our kids. The world is better when we all show compassion.

On July 16, I sent them off to their classes with their teachers, sat in the library and started writing. A few hours later, I took a Facebook break and saw my newsfeed filled with the latest headline out of Gaza.

Four boys, aged 9–11, all cousins, playing soccer on the beach. The beach is supposed to be a safe area. There aren't many nice places in Gaza for kids to play and enjoy the summer sun, but the beach was supposed to be safe.

On July 16, it wasn't.

A shell hits an area close to the boys. It kills one. The other three begin running toward the Al-Deira Hotel, where journalists, who frequently stay there, yell uselessly at the gunner, "They're only children!"

The gunner is unseen, but he can see. And seconds later, another shell explodes right behind these boys. It kills them, disfiguring their bodies in ways that most people hesitate to share on social media and others refuse to look at.

And yet people had the nerve to ask, "Are these photos real? So many aren't." Such a comment was made when Anthony Bourdain, in his own expression of compassion, tweeted a photo of one of the boys, lying dead in the sand, his legs twisted horribly around his body.

People won't look at these pictures. I know some of my friends have been annoyed with how frequently I have posted about this latest atrocity in Gaza.

The murder of children disquiets everyone. People want to demonstrate compassion, but they also want news that makes them feel good. People respond when you post a picture of Jews and Arabs breaking their fast together. It's an evening news headline, to round out the update on the "exchange" of fire between Israel and some nation called Hamas.

Say that you are praying "for both sides" and they will affirm. Say that you feel for "Israeli and Palestinian children alike" and they will agree.

I'm no longer interested in this kind of verbal pat-on-the-back.

I've been asked to speak at an event to raise awareness and to do some peace building.

I refused.

Because here's what I'm not able, this time, to do: I am not able to be the representative Palestinian, to sit beside a representative Israeli, and to talk about compassion in a general way.

I don't want to hear nice things, about how "we all just need to get along," and how the Jews and Arabs are really so much alike.

"We're cousins, for God's sake. Our cultures are so similar." They will nod.

"Both sides need to just stop the killing." Yes, they will murmur.

And someone will inevitably say, "Salaam and shalom are really derived from the same Semitic root word for peace."

I don't care anymore about this "feel good" approach.

Here's what I am interested in saying: Israel's government is trying to eliminate the Palestinian people, its infrastructure, its history and its culture.

That's what colonialism means—to take over someone's land, exploit his resources, and then erase any memory of his presence on it.

And while you erase him, you tell yourself that he deserves it.

So, no, thank you. I'm not going to be speaking as part of a panel that is more concerned with representing "both sides" than with sharing factual information. Because if I leave that safe platform, and if I talk about the unequal death rates, and the stifling blockade of Gaza, and the occupation that has lasted six decades, people feel queasy.

They don't want to get "too political."

I'm interested in saying that no child deserves to die: Palestinian. Israeli. Syrian. Iraqi. No child anywhere. Nothing political about that.

I want to say: I've been telling my children that the world has changed. Things are so much better now.

And yet that's not true.

Here's what is true, what horrifies me most: Someone saw these little boys running, running for their lives. Someone saw Ahed Atef Bakr, Zakaria Ahed Bakr, Mohamed Ramez Bakr, and Ismael Mohamed Bakr abandon the soccer ball and run. And this culture of hate—this product of years of occupation and colonialism—allowed that person to press the trigger anyway, to blow them out of the sand, out of their clothes, out of their skin. Pretty words and feel-good gestures will not bandage that villainy.

To Be In Solidarity With Palestine

SARAH SCHULMAN

Solidarity with Palestine is an aspiration that, for me, is constantly being interrogated, rearranged, deepened, upended. It is a path filled with error, hubris, longing, and above all the obligation to strive toward the goal of being Self-Critical, "Big Picture" and Effective. There is no clear definition out there waiting to be applied. Many people use the word, but few agree on its meaning, which remains elusive until we take it on. We do know one thing: Palestinians are asking internationals to participate in Boycott, Divestment, Sanctions (BDS). But exactly how to carry that out, and what to do in addition to BDS, is something to be discovered on a daily basis. After all, no one knows what gesture, moment, turn or event will produce an end to the Occupation.

Each investigation into the meaning of "Solidarity" opens up a new range of questions. One Palestinian leader living in exile told me, "Solidarity means decolonizing your mind." An Israeli dissident and draft resister described it as "a grey zone." Another Palestinian leader, who lives in Palestine, said, "Solidarity, for me, has the same high standard as friendship."

But what is friendship?

THE RESPONSIBILITY TO INTERVENE

When we see another person being brutalized, scapegoated, blamed for things they have not caused, punished unjustly, shunned, falsely accused, subjected to unjust state intervention, displaced, incarcerated, or murdered, and that person is asking us to help, I believe that we each have a responsibility to intervene. Even if we don't "know" the person, even if we don't "like" the person, Justice is, by definition, not a popularity contest.

We especially have a responsibility to intervene if we are implicated: if our community, our nation, our clique, religion or race are the aggressors. If we know the names of the people who are driving the aggressors, are providing false justification for the cruelty, or are trying to impose a code of silence about the cruelty. If we have their email addresses, then we have a special responsibility to intervene.

The problem arises exactly at this moment, when the people taking unjust action are the people we know, live with, are related to or are people we are dependent on for approval or access or recognition. When the people acting unjustly are our "friends."

So, Solidarity with someone who is being brutalized by people we know, identify with or fear, by definition implies a loss. But the fact remains that the "loss" of the approval of family members, or of arts funding, or of having parties to go to, will never equal the loss of the 2,200 people who were murdered by aerial bombing in Gaza in the summer of 2014. The bother of having to practice the politics of repetition required to raise consciousness about Palestine, the annoyance of being yelled at or slandered by supporters of the Israeli state, even the fear of threats and accusations, censorship or loss of employment, will never equal living in a refugee camp, being denied a passport, having your water stolen, and being subjected to violence by Israeli police and soldiers.

Real friendship is dialogic, not obedient. Real friendship means asking questions, looking at the order of events, challenging assumptions. We are morally obligated to question our governments, families, communities and friends who are participating (passively or actively) in the shunning or degradation of others, including the subjugation of Palestine. Unfortunately, people who justify bullying, group aggression and shunning or silencing equate silent submission with friendship. So, being in solidarity with Palestine means upholding an ethic of interactive, communicative engagement as a definition of friendship. And that can be a dramatic change in the way one lives.

THE RESPONSIBILITY TO LISTEN AND ALSO TO HEAR

Palestinians are shunned. That means that they are not allowed into the conversation about their experience, reality, condition and future. As an American, I have to work hard to hear Palestine. I have to look for alternative media like the Electronic Intifada, Mondoweiss. I have to use social media intelligently, follow Twitter from Gaza, for example. I have to attend public talks, I have to read books that are not reviewed in the *New York Times*. I have to both listen and hear, which are two distinctly different actions. From the very late date (shamefully 2009) when I began to put my attention fully toward hearing Palestine, the intake of information has forced a constant re-evaluation of myself, my past, the history of my religion and my family. It has also forced me to pay attention to my new opponents, supporters of the current Israeli state, and to notice the depth of commitment in their refusal to rethink. I see a deep connection between authoritarian bullying and refusing to hear other people's experiences. To internalize and accept the pathology of this insistence on stasis in others, makes us understand in our own lives how truly corrupt it is to refuse to examine group bullying, even though it is falsely represented as "loyalty."

But the most challenging, of course, to my own supremacy ideology, is to listen to individual Palestinian people who I now know and work with/for/beside.

For example, when I first began my involvement, I conceptualized of Solidarity as "support," so I primarily put my efforts into the already ongoing attempt to create platforms for Palestinians to be heard in the United States. My first action was to organize a US tour for leaders of the Palestinian queer movement. After that, I co-organized the first LGBT delegation to Palestine. After that, I kept asking the people I was working with "What do you want us to do?" Finally, one leader just said to me "It is not my responsibility to think up your strategy." As I recorded in my book *Israel/Palestine and The Queer International* (Duke University Press, 2012), I met in Ramallah with Omar Barghouti, one of the best know Palestinian leaders of the Boycott, Divestment, Sanctions movement. At one point I asked him "What can I do?" and he answered wisely, "You will think of something."

As PACBI (Palestine Academic and Cultural Boycott of Israel) said in their call for internationals to practice Boycott, Divestment and Sanctions (BDS):

> During years of intensive work with partners in several countries to promote the cultural boycott of Israel, which is supported by an overwhelming majority of Palestinian artists, writers, filmmakers and cultural institutions . . . PACBI has thoroughly scrutinized many cultural projects and events, assessing the applicability of the boycott criteria to them and, accordingly, has issued open letters, statements or advisory opinions on them. The three most important conclusions reached in this respect were: (a) **many of these events and projects fall into an uncertain, grey area that is challenging to appraise,** (b) it is important to emphasize that the boycott must target not only the complicit institutions but also the inherent and organic links between them which reproduce the machinery of colonial subjugation and apartheid, and (c) **strategically, not every boycottable project must be met with an active boycott campaign, as activists need to invest their energies in the highest priority campaigns in any given time**.

It can be a bumpy road. But the request by PACBI that international supporters of Boycott, Divestment, Sanctions practice, as PACBI often puts it, "common sense," is enlightening, nuanced, and a bold investment in the responsibility of individuals to be informed, to reckon with what Palestinians are expressing and requesting and to make intelligent, compassionate and most importantly informed decisions about how to best support their desire for autonomy and recognition.

So, Solidarity with Palestine does not mean "doing what you are told" but rather requires individuals to be conceptual, conscientious, and interpretive which can only be productive if there is some deep listening involved. Sometimes this backfires. For example, I worked with the Armenian-American pro-Palestinian writer and activist Nancy Kricorian for a number of years to realize a Palestinian Writers panel at the PEN-American annual conference. For years PEN had resisted this idea and imposed unacceptable obstacles like having Israelis or American Jews on the panel. Also, every "country" participating had to contribute $10,000. And since Palestine is not a "country" with a functional cultural budget, we had to raise this money independently. We did this in cooperation with Arte East and private donors. Finally, we were successful and PEN invited three Palestinian writers: Randa Jarrar, Adania Shibli and Najwan Darwish. This was to be the first time that a Palestinian-only panel of writers would be featured as an organic part of a high profile, mainstream publishing event in New York City. We were ecstatic. Then we heard from PACBI. They found the PEN conference to be "boycottable" because, like many of the countries participating in the event, Israel had also paid the "fee" required for their writers to sit on other panels, and therefore PEN listed Israel as a "sponsor." I was upset because I felt that PACBI did not comprehend the significance of the event. But, it really didn't matter what I thought, the principles were more important than any specific event. Many people argue for the exceptionalism of their own actions. It's arrogant. The Palestinian writers, of course, could decide whatever they wanted to decide, but for Nancy and I who were in "Solidarity" we could not ignore PACBI. So, we were highly motivated to find a solution. Only when Judith Butler negotiated behind the scenes with PEN to organizationally re-conceptualize the mandatory national donations to a separate category and away from the label "sponsors" did PACBI change their finding to "No Position," not endorsement and not opposition. The panel went on, and was a meaningful, significant success, allowing literary New Yorkers to hear Palestinian intellectuals without mitigation or obstruction. It required communication, negotiation and problem solving. In other words, it required an authentic relationship: neither obeying nor ignoring, but listening and communicating.

THE RESPONSIBILITY TO BE EFFECTIVE

Have you ever been the object of injustice, and asked for help? If so, perhaps you experienced someone else come along, who—in terms of your experience—is privileged and protected. They say they will help and then they make one gesture. They may send an email, or have one difficult conversation. Then, when their own supremacy self-concept fails to transform an embedded situation, the person throws up their hands and drops the effort. "It's too complicated." Or "It will just take time" or other banalities get thrown at you, as the dilettante moves on to another arena where they will instead be obeyed. "I tried!" they insist and then go back to their comfortable bubble where they can tell anyone who asks "I did that one thing." Well, the point of Solidarity is to be effective. It is not to cover your ass.

But how do we be effective when the odds are so great? One necessity is to *build campaigns*, not just do isolated actions, or singular gestures. PACBI has been very clear that not every BDS campaign can win. Not every divestment vote will be successful, but that each effort is a step in raising consciousness, building support and informing the public. So, actually trying to help someone who is being treated badly means being in for the long haul, and organizing that haul so that there is—at least—a chance of success in the long term.

How do we build campaigns? First look at the range of things Palestinians are asking for and select one realm in which you think you can be effective. For example, lets say you choose to be active in the Israeli or Settlement product boycott.

First step is to set a goal that is winnable, doable and reasonable.

This means that a campaign to make every store drop every Israeli or Settlement product, when you have four people in your town working on this thing, is not a good goal. Instead, learn from the SodaStream campaign. They picked one item. They picketed stores, they went after Scarlett Johansson when she became SodaStream's celebrity endorser. And they continue to have successes in getting institutions and retail venues to drop the product.

A similar campaign was organized around Sabra Hummus (obnoxious name). For example, the Wesleyan College cafeteria was persuaded to drop Sabra Hummus from their food service.

Certainly an organized campaign aimed at, let's say, Whole Foods, with pickets outside the branch stores, would be able to convince customers to boycott one specific product, especially because so many other brands are already in the display cases. Little "Boycott" stickers could surreptitiously be applied to Sabra packages on the shelves, and daily leafleting at peek shopping hours could inform both customers and corporate managers. As we learn from Cesar Chavez's grape and lettuce boycotts, getting a major chain to drop the product is a very significant victory. And movements need victories. Especially emblematic ones.

I once had the experience of marching in a parade carrying a sign that said "End Gay Tourism to Israel." Now, Pinkwashing is a subject close to my heart. And exploiting the hard won gains of the Israeli LGBT movement to make claims of racial or religious supremacy (Israeli "tolerance") as justifications for the Occupation must be opposed. And carrying signs that call attention to *an ongoing campaign* make sense. But if there is no specific goal, no organized strategy, and no action planned to propel that strategy, for me to carry that sign was simply ineffective. It was hypocritical. I was acting as if I was part of a campaign, but actually there was nothing organized beyond the sign itself. I was wasting my commitment, posing and being lazy. Asking for too much, or having vague goals, and not backing them up with actions is bad organizing and does not fulfill the promise of being in Solidarity.

THE RESPONSIBILITY TO BE MORALLY CONSISTENT

Everyday I see people post on Facebook and Twitter (I am too old to function on Tumblr) expressions of solidarity with someone. People post or report statements in favor of peace, against injustice and for negotiation and change. Yet many of these people are complete hypocrites. They won't endure the most minimal personal discomfort to actually realize the values they publically claim to hold. Especially if it's close to home. Fortunately change, in America, has never depended on majority action, it has always been driven by a *critical mass* of focused, brilliant individuals who take responsibility for moving the society forward.

When someone publically identifies themself as being in Solidarity with Palestine they are asking a lot of other people. They are asking Israelis, Palestinians, Americans, Canadians and everyone whose government funds Israel to change their self-concept. We are asking for enormous changes to be enacted by other people. We are asking people to think differently, act differently and live differently. So, in order to truly be *in Solidarity* we also have to be willing to do the same. People in Solidarity with Palestine must be people committed to change, negotiation, deep listening, peace making, reconciliation and repair. If we are not, then we are hypocrites, and if we are hypocrites then we are useless to Palestine. People in Solidarity with Palestine cannot shun, cannot hide behind technology, cannot participate in group bullying, cannot be complicit with misuses of the state. People in Solidarity with Palestine need to sit down and listen when there is a conflict, ask themselves and each other hard questions, look at the order of events to determine what is at the base of conflicts. If we are asking others to change the world, we cannot be the people who enact the formations of injustice. People who shun cannot create positive change on earth. In conclusion, if we, in Solidarity, are not effective, do not listen, cannot sit down and negotiate to solve our own conflicts, i.e. if we don't have the Big Picture, then we are actually not in Solidarity with Palestine, or anyone else. And we will not be able to realize the changes that we publicly claim to seek.

Finally, what are we asking for in return? It can't be much. Palestinians, are, after all, people. They can be petty, mean, arbitrary, cold, punitive and snobby like anyone else. And I have certainly experienced negative behavior personally, from individual Palestinians that has been hurtful and unnecessary. But, so what? Being in Solidarity with someone requires identifying with them to the degree that we can take in the dimensions of their experience with empathy, compassion and fierce active engagement. It requires loving someone to transcend all the layers oppressing them. But they are not required to love me back. No one should have to be grateful when someone else does the right thing. When it's two ways, it helps, but when it's not, that's the way it goes. Solidarity, after all, cannot be an ego-boost. It's not about elevating yourself. It is finally, about ending the Occupation. And that, ultimately, is what we want.

Postscript

STEVE WILLEY

I've been meaning to write
To you again
Need to spell out a few things
I regret these letters
Their false starts
Cut out my tongue
It starts
I'm sorry I wrote you
This letter
I deplore its forged nostalgia
Its staged retreat
Its black logic
Its entire lack of yelping dogs
Last year when the roofs
Were knocked in Gaza
Inside the letter
Moved hands of mowed up grass
Tonight my prisoner kissed
The ground of their cell
Tonight in Aida Camp
That glowing stone
Its starlings and its shrikes
In the presence of friends
In their bodies
In their seams of loving scars
You have two minutes to leave your life
Get out of your house
So I give you tonight
And every single other night
To say: Free Palestine
Against the occupying army

Against their petty checkpoints
Their poems of racist laws
Say Free Palestine
Against their wall
That field of profit
Their webs of ordered silk
Their humiliations, prisons
Their slow control of faucet's
Poisoned water
As in 70% of your body
And then with what remains
Of your flesh say
Free Palestine
Against the tourist, the thief
In a hail of stones
In a certain hail of peace
In endurance
In boycott
In Oslo
Say, Free Palestine
And these are your only words
Free Palestine
At Arizona's border
Inside David Cameron's hemlock lung
In Balfour's bleeding ear
In the ventricular halls of England's colonial heart
Say Free Palestine
It ends in music
Yes, it ends in frozen coins of blissful glass
Say Free Palestine
It starts in your mouth
It ends in the streets
Say Free Free Palestine
Say its been good writing to you
Say it clear as hell
And then say it again
Free Free Palestine
Go on I know these words are in you.

APPENDIX 1

The Russell Tribunal on Palestine: Extraordinary Session on Gaza: Summary of Findings

FRANK BARAT

When the International Organizing Committee of the Russell Tribunal on Palestine was dismantled in December 2013, few would have imagined that less than a year after, another session of the tribunal would take place.

Yet this is what is at stake for anyone working for justice in Palestine; you have to be on your toes, ready to act at any given moment. The impunity that Israel enjoys worldwide and the complicity of third parties—including states, corporations and institutions—in its violations of the law, enable that state to attack Palestine at will. Whenever and wherever it wants.

Our extraordinary session on Gaza, in September 2014, focused on the latest assault by the Israeli army, known as "Operation Protective Edge," a name designed to evoke the scepter of justified defense. The witnesses and experts who testified in front of the tribunal gave us a much broader and scarier picture of the situation on the ground, a bleak overview of a sick society, a warmongering government and a complicit media apparatus. Nurit Peled, one of the people that called for the tribunal, wrote a book entitled *Palestine in Israeli School Books* (Tauris Academic Studies, 2012), which explained and demonstrated how biased and distorted the history of the "conflict" was. What was even more startling was to understand the way, from the words to the colors to the script used in the books, that the Palestinians, or the Arabs as they are called in Israel, are portrayed as animals and dangerous terrorists. From a very early age, Israeli Jews learn that their neighbors, who are historically the indigenous people of this land, are not to be trusted and need to be avoided and fought against.

This brainwashing, from the moment of birth, creates the kind of warped society that one of our witnesses, Israeli journalist David Sheen, showed us during his presentation. A society so closed, so paranoid, so utterly convinced that its very existence is at stake, that it is ready to condone and support the most barbaric actions by its army and its government. Seven hundred tons of munitions were dropped on Gaza in fifty-one days. You have to go back to Laos and Cambodia in the seventies (and swap Israel with the USA) to find examples of such ferocity in the carpet-bombing of an imprisoned population. Still, despite the facts, despite the images and the reports, 95 percent of Israeli Jews backed the war. They in fact did much more as they pushed their government to go further with their carnage. Genocidal calls were heard in the Knesset, on social and mainstream media, from religious leaders and from army commanders.

Despite all this, despite the blatant war crimes committed by the Israeli army, what did western states do? Most of them did indeed phone Benjamin Netanyahu very quickly after "Operation Protective Edge" was launched. Did they ask him to stop? Did they ask him to act with restraint? Proportionally? (You would think that it was the least they could do, when one of the most powerful armies in the world, an occupying power for more than fifty years, attempts to obliterate an occupied and defenseless population.) No. They actually did the opposite. "We're fully behind you Prime Minister. Do what you can to defend your people," is what was repeated day after day by the "leaders" of the Western world.

The Palestinians, asking for justice and redress, have very few allies. The peoples of the world are with them, as showed in the huge outpouring of support in the streets of hundred of cities worldwide during the Israeli aggression. They have themselves, of course, their spirit of sumud (steadfastness) and resistance. But the actual institutional means for justice are often blocked for them and very far from their reach, hence the need for a popular tribunal, lead by the people, for the people. Here is an excerpt from our report.

THE RUSSELL TRIBUNAL ON PALESTINE
EXTRAORDINARY SESSION ON GAZA: SUMMARY OF fiNDINGS
BRUSSELS, SEPTEMBER 25, 2014

Members of the Jury: Ahdaf Soueif (novelist and cultural critic), Ken Loach (film and TV director), Vandana Shiva (activist and author), Ronald Kasrils (writer and activist), Paul Laverty (lawyer and scriptwriter), John Dugard (professor of law), Roger Waters (songwriter, guitarist, vocalist), Christiane Hessel (activist and writer), Radhia Nasraoui (lawyer), Miguel Angel Estrella (pianist), Richard Falk (professor of law), and Michael Manfield (lawyer).

May this tribunal prevent the crime of silence.
                                        Bertrand Russell, London, November 13, 1966

The Russell Tribunal on Palestine (RToP) is an international citizen-based Tribunal of conscience, created in response to the demands of civil society (nongovernmental organizations, unions, charities, faith-based organizations) to educate public opinion and exert pressure on decision-makers. The RToP is imbued with the same spirit and espouses the same rigorous rules as those inherited from the Tribunal on Vietnam (1966–1967), established by the eminent scholar and philosopher Bertrand Russell. The Tribunal operates as a court of the people, with public international law (including international human rights law, international humanitarian law, and international criminal law), constituting the frame of reference.

The occupation, blockade and siege imposed on the territory of Gaza amount to a regime of collective punishment, but the most recent conflict in July and August 2014 represents a clear intensification of the campaign to terrorise the civilian population. Not only was "Operation Protective Edge" the third major military assault on Gaza in six years, but it was marked by a significant escalation in the scale, severity, and duration of the attack. It was Israel's heaviest assault on the Gaza Strip since the beginning of its occupation of the Palestinian territories in 1967.

Over the course of fifty days, approximately 700 tons of ordinances were deployed by the Israeli military forces through sustained aerial bombardment and ground offensive, a total of two tons of ordinance per square kilometre of the Gaza Strip. These actions resulted in: the deaths of 2,188 Palestinians, at least 1,658 of whom were civilians; 11,231 civilians injured; damage to 18,000 housing units (13 percent of all available housing stock in Gaza was completely or partially destroyed); the internal displacement of 110,000 civilians; the complete destruction of eight medical facilities and damage to many others, such that seventeen out of thirty-two hospitals were damaged and six closed down as a result; massive destruction of water facilities leaving 450,000 civilians unable to access municipal water supplies; the destruction of Gaza's only power plant facility rendering the entire Gaza Strip without electricity for approximately twenty hours per day, thereby having a profound impact on water treatment, food supply and the capacity of medical facilities to treat the wounded and displaced; numerous attacks on and destruction of UN sponsored and controlled infrastructure, including three UNRWA schools which were being used as temporary centres of refuge; the total destruction of some 128 business and approximately US$550 million worth of damage caused to agricultural land and livestock; attacks on cultural and religious property; and finally, leaving approximately 373,000 children in need of direct and specialised psychosocial support.

Given this pattern of violence and the likelihood of its continuation, the members of the Tribunal were conscious of the need to give a voice to the people of Gaza and to express the overwhelming need for urgent action. The Russell Tribunal on Palestine hopes to act as a voice of conscience and to contribute some measure of accountability for these appalling and inhumane acts.

The Tribunal was reconvened in an urgent special session in the wake of the July assault, to examine the nature of potential international crimes committed by Israel. During the course of this session the RToP heard eyewitness accounts and expert opinion on a range of issues of direct relevance to the events in Gaza in the summer of 2014. Following the hearings and the deliberations of the jury on September 24, 2014, the findings are summarized as follows.

I. THE USE OF FORCE
Under international law, people living under foreign occupation are entitled to resist that occupation. An aggressor cannot claim self-defense against resistance to its aggression. The occupying power, Israel, took actions that were not a response to an armed attack by the military forces of another state, rather, Israel's actions were those of an occupying power using force to maintain its occupation and to suppress resistance. The ongoing occupation of Palestinian territories and the permanent blockade of Gaza are themselves acts of aggression as defined by the UN General Assembly in Resolution 3314 (1974) (Art. 3, a and c). Operation Protective Edge was part of the enforcement of the occupation and ongoing siege of the Gaza Strip. This siege amounts to collective punishment in violation of Article 33 of the Fourth Geneva Convention.

II. WAR CRIMES
Israeli forces violated two cardinal principles of international humanitarian law—the need to distinguish clearly between civilian targets and military targets; and the need for the use of military violence to be proportionate to the aims of the operation. It has done so through the scale of its bombardment of Gaza and its shelling of civilian areas, including hospitals, schools and mosques. Further, terrorized civilians in Gaza were denied the right to seek protection and assistance as refugees from war, in breach of the right to leave one's country pursuant to article 13 (2) of the UN Declaration on Human Rights.

War crimes committed by Israeli forces include (but are not limited to) the crimes of:

willful killing (including executions by ground troops and killings of civilians by snipers from Palestinian homes occupied by Israeli forces inside Gaza);

extensive destruction of property, not justified by military necessity (including essential services of power, water, and sewage disposal);

intentionally directing attacks against the civilian population and civilians objects (including the aerial bombardment of densely populated civilian areas);

intentionally directing **attacks against buildings dedicated to religion or education** (including targeting UN schools operating as places of refuge for civilians);

intentionally directing **attacks against hospitals, medical units and personnel** (including shelling of hospitals, and the targeting of visibly marked medical units and ambulance workers);

utilizing the presence of a civilian or protected person to render certain points, areas or military forces immune from military operations (i.e. the use of Palestinian civilians as human shields);

employing **weapons, projectiles, and methods of warfare intended to cause superfluous injury or unnecessary suffering or which are inherently indiscriminate** (including flechette shells, DIME weapons, thermobaric munitions—'carpet' bombs—and munitions containing depleted uranium);

the use of violence to **spread terror among the civilian population** in violation of the laws and customs of war (including the employment of a 'knock on the roof' policy whereby small bombs are dropped on Palestinian homes as a warning signal in advance of larger bombardments to follow).

III. CRIMES AGAINST HUMANITY

The Contextual Elements of Crimes Against Humanity

To reach the threshold of a crime against humanity, there must be a widespread or systematic attack against a civilian population, and the acts of the perpetrator must form part of that attack and be committed with knowledge of the wider context of the attack. Article 7 of the Statute of the International Criminal Court lists several specific crimes against humanity: murder; extermination; enslavement; deportation or forcible transfer of population; imprisonment or other severe deprivation of physical liberty; torture; rape and sexual violence; persecution; enforced disappearance; apartheid; and other inhumane acts. While the Tribunal is confident that findings could be reached under each of these respective headings, given the specific focus of this extraordinary session and the resources available, the RToP limits itself to findings with respect to: (i) murder; (ii) extermination; and (iii) persecution.

The sheer scale of civilian deaths, injuries, and the destruction of civilian housing provide a clear indication that a *prima facie* case can be established that Operation Protective Edge was overwhelmingly directed at the civilian population of Gaza.

The testimony received and the data compiled by the various offices of the UN provide a compelling evidence for establishing a strong *prima facie* case that the attack against the civilian population of Gaza was widespread *and* systematic. The Tribunal draws attention to three policy directives of the Israeli military—namely, the Dahiya Doctrine (the deliberate use of disproportionate force to collectively punish the civilian population for the acts of resistance groups or political leaders), the Hannibal Directive (the destruction of an entire area for the purpose of preventing the capture of Israeli soldiers), and the Red Line policy (which involves the creation of a 'kill zone' beyond an arbitrary and invisible 'red line' around houses occupied by Israeli forces). Each of these policies flagrantly disregard protections afforded to civilians and civilian property under international humanitarian law, and fundamentally involves indiscriminate violence against the civilian population of Gaza. As such, their implementation amounts to a *prima facie* case of a specific policy institutionalized by the Government of Israel to target civilian areas with disregard for civilian life.

The Tribunal finds a compelling case to be made that the contextual elements of crimes against humanity, as outlined above, are satisfied for the purposes of Article 7 of the Statute of the International Criminal Court; specifically with respect to the selected crimes of (i) murder; (ii) extermination; and (iii) persecution.

I. Murder

The RToP has heard testimony relating to a number of individual incidents, such as the deliberate execution of Salem Khalil Shammaly for crossing an imaginary red line while searching for family members in Shuja'iyya and the deeply disturbing circumstances of the killing of sixty-four-year-old Mohammed Tawfiq Qudeh in his own home. The RToP finds that their deaths are *prima facie* examples of the crime against humanity of murder, in addition to the war crime of wilful killing.

II. Extermination

Under the Statute of the International Criminal Court, the crime of extermination includes mass killings *and* the intentional infliction of conditions of life (depriving access to food, water or medical treatment) calculated to bring about the destruction of a population. There is, therefore, a degree of common ground between the crime against humanity by extermination and the crime of genocide.

The deliberate targeting of medical infrastructure contributed substantially to the loss of civilian life. Additional deliberate attacks on civilian infrastructure also contributed to the increase in the death toll. Additionally, the denial of a humanitarian corridor, the sealing of the Erez and Rafah crossings and the targeting of UNRWA infrastructure contributed to the infliction of conditions of life calculated to bring about the destruction of the population of Gaza.

III. Persecution

The crime against humanity of persecution is the intentional and severe deprivation of fundamental human rights against members of a group or collectivity. The group must be targeted for a discriminatory purpose, such as on political, racial, national, ethnic, cultural, gender or religious grounds. This element of discriminatory intent makes the crime of persecution somewhat similar to the crime of genocide. The RToP determines that persecutory acts may be considered under the following three categories of conduct:

- Discriminatory acts causing physical or mental harm;
- Discriminatory infringements on freedom;
- Offences against property for discriminatory purposes.

The Tribunal finds that the actions and policies of the Government of Israel and the Israeli military are inherently discriminatory against the Palestinian people, specifically, in this instance, the people of Gaza, on the basis of, *inter alia*, political affiliation, nationality, ethnicity, religion, culture, and gender. The Tribunal finds that additional crimes and violations of fundamental human rights have been and continue to be committed on discriminatory grounds against the Palestinian people and the population of Gaza. The Tribunal notes the following non-exhaustive list of violations: murder; torture (e.g. case of sixteen-year-old Ahmad Abu Raida, who was abducted by the Israeli military, whipped with a wire and threatened with sexual assault while under interrogation, and forced to act as a human shield for the Israelis); sexual violence (e.g. Khalil Al-Najjar, the imam in Khuza'a who was forced to strip in public); physical violence not constituting torture; cruel and inhumane treatment or subjection to inhumane conditions; constant humiliation and degradation; terrorising the civilian population (e.g. forcing Gazan citizens into their homes and then subjecting them to bombardment); unlawful arrest and detention; imprisonment or confinement; restrictions on freedom of movement; and the confiscation or destruction of private dwellings, businesses, religious buildings, cultural or symbolic buildings or means of subsistence.

IV. GENOCIDE

The international crime of genocide relates to any of the following acts committed with intent to destroy, in whole or in part, a national, ethnic, racial, or religious group, as such:

a. Killing members of the group;
b. Causing serious bodily or mental harm to members of the group;
c. Deliberately inflicting on the group conditions of life calculated to bring about its physical destruction in whole or in part;
d. Imposing measures intended to prevent births within the group;
e. Forcibly transferring children of the group to another group.

Direct and public incitement to genocide is also an international crime, irrespective of whether anyone acts as a result of the incitement.

Palestinians constitute a national group under the definition of genocide. Israeli military activities considered under the subject war crimes and crimes against humanity meet the acts set forth in sub-paragraphs (a) to (c) above.

The crime of genocide is closely related to crimes against humanity. Where persecution as a crime against humanity aims to protect specific groups from discrimination, the criminalisation of genocide aims to protect such groups (national, racial, ethnic, religious) from elimination. The sometimes fine distinction between the two crimes, characterised by the 'intent to destroy,' was clarified by the judges at the Yugoslavia Tribunal: 'When persecution escalates to the extreme form of wilful and deliberate acts designed to destroy a group or part of a group, it can be held that such persecution amounts to genocide.'

Israel's policies and practices in Palestine have for decades aimed at ensuring that Palestinians submit to Israeli domination, beginning with the displacement and dispossession of Palestinians since the establishment of the state of Israel in 1948, and continuing with the settlement of the West Bank. Additionally, the imposition of a regime of apartheid and segregation, the siege of Gaza and the prolonged collective punishment of its people, repeated military operations, and systemic violations of Palestinian human rights have ensured that Palestinians forfeit their right to self-determination and continue to attempt to flee their country.

Throughout Israel's occupation, policies appear to be aimed at the control and subjugation of the Palestinian people. Recent years have seen an upsurge in vigilante style 'price tag' attacks on Palestinian people, homes, and religious sites in the West Bank and Israel, and racist threats against Palestinians, across all forms of media and public discourse in Israel. The scale and intensity of Operation Protective Edge indicates an unprecedented escalation of violence against the Palestinian people. For these reasons, the RToP is compelled to now, for the first time, give serious examination to Israeli policy in light of the prohibition of genocide in international law.

The Tribunal heard evidence demonstrating an upswing in racist rhetoric and incitement during the summer of 2014. Such incitement manifested across many levels of Israeli society, on both social and traditional media, from football fans, police officers, media commentators, religious leaders, legislators, and government ministers. This can be understood in varying degrees as incitement to racism, hatred, and violence. The evidence shows that the speech and language used in the summer of 2014 did, on occasion, reach the threshold where it can only be understood as constituting direct and public incitement to genocide.

Some of this incitement, in a manner similar to genocidal situations elsewhere, is characterised not only by explicit calls for violence against the target group, but in the employment of sexualised (rape), gendered, and dehumanising memes, motifs, and prejudices. The RToP heard evidence of multiple examples of such incitement, one notable instance being Israeli legislator Ayelet Shaked's widely reported publication in July 2014 defining 'the entire Palestinian people [as] the enemy', arguing for the destruction of 'its elderly and its women, its cities and its villages, its property and its infrastructure', and stating that the 'mothers of terrorists' should be destroyed, 'as should the physical homes in which they raised the snakes.'

The RToP notes that the legal definition of genocide demands proof of a specific intent on the part of the perpetrator not simply to target people belonging to a protected group, but to target them with the intention of destroying the group. It would be for a criminal court to determine whether such specific intent is present, and to prosecute the perpetrators. The RToP notes that alternative, broader understandings of genocide beyond that defined for the purposes of individual criminal responsibility be applied to the situation in Gaza. The cumulative effect of the long-standing regime of collective punishment in Gaza inflict conditions of life calculated to bring about the incremental destruction of the Palestinians as a group in Gaza, and exacerbated by the scale of the violence in the Operation Protective Edge, the continuation of the siege of Gaza and the denial of the capacity to rebuild. The Tribunal emphasises the potential for a regime of persecution, such as that demonstrated in section III above, to become genocidal in effect. In light of the clear escalation in the physical and rhetorical violence deployed in respect of Gaza in the summer of 2014, the RToP emphasises the obligation of all state parties to the 1948 Genocide Convention 'to take such action under the Charter of the United Nations as they consider appropriate for the prevention and suppression of acts of genocide.'

The evidence demonstrates that the state of Israel is failing to respect its obligations to prevent and to punish the crime of direct and public incitement to genocide, and the Tribunal echoes the warning issued by the Special Advisers of the UN Secretary-General on the Prevention of Genocide, and on the Responsibility to Protect, in July 2014, in response to Israel's actions in Palestine: 'We are equally disturbed by the flagrant use of hate speech in the social media, particularly against the Palestinian population.' The Special Advisers noted that individual Israelis had disseminated messages that could be dehumanizing to the Palestinians and had called for the killing of members of this group.

Previous sessions of the RToP established that the Israeli state is implement-ing an apartheid system based on the dominance of Israeli Jews over Palestinians. Beyond the atrocities documented above, we add the increase in aggravated rac-ist hate speech. We recognize that in a situation where patterns of crimes against humanity are perpetrated with impunity, and where direct and public incitement to genocide is manifest throughout society, individuals or the state may choose to exploit these conditions in order to perpetrate the crime of genocide. Alert to the increase in anti-Palestinian speech, which constitutes the international crime of direct and public incitement to genocide, and the failure of the Israeli state to fulfil its obligations to prevent and punish incitement to genocide, the RToP is compelled to place the international community on notice as to the risk of the crime of genocide being perpetrated. The jury has listened to alarming evidence over the course of this extraordinary session; we have a genuine fear that in an environment of impunity and an absence of sanction for serious and repeated criminality, the lessons from Rwanda and other mass atrocities may go unheeded.

V. CONSEQUENCES & ACTION

In view of the above findings, the Russell Tribunal on Palestine calls upon global civil society:

- To fully support, develop, and expand the Boycott, Divestment and Sanctions movement;
- To support activism aimed at denying Israeli firms and organizations sup-porting or profiting from the occupation access to international markets;
- To show solidarity with activists taking action to shut down firms aiding and abetting the commission of crimes against Palestinians such as Elbit Systems in the UK;
- To actively lobby and pressure governments to take immediate action to ensure they are not contributing to Israeli crimes and to ensure they are act-ing in line with the edicts and principles of international law.

Link to complete report: http://www.russelltribunalonpalestine.com/en/wp-con-tent/uploads/2014/09/Summary-of-Findings.pdf

APPENDIX 2

Against the Wall: Letter to David

MARLENE DUMAS

Dear David,

I've been trying to write to you about 'the why' of my paintings. Write it clearly so that it is not only my sentimental story, but something that is similar to a public statement, but the more I try, the more I get tangled up in places I don't want to go.

Is it because the rhetoric of South African apartheid feeds my distrust of definitions and at the same time my longing for them. The naming of things and people. The spirit of the Law against the letter of the Law. The artist as some stuttering Moses having heard the commanding voice from the bramble bush. Here I go back to the Bible for my metaphors again. The first book in my life, teaching me that love and fear go hand in hand. Everything that is important enough to move me stirs these simultaneous emotions.

I often open books at random to see if there's a message for me. Still do. Now too.

I read the Bible, therefore I paint *Against the Wall.*
I read therefore I paint?
It's been said that the Protestants read the Bible and
the Catholics look at the pictures.

At this stage of my life, I paint the pictures and then I read the books.
The images come first, then the thoughts.
I 'fall' from the one wall to the other,
from one type of arms into another.
First out of context and then into context.
From belief into disbelief.
But the more I understand, the less I can speak.

Thinking about religion, I always saw Christianity as a Jewish sect.

Only in recent years I heard that some Christians blamed the Jews for killing Christ. Always understood that the Romans killed him (crucifixion didn't exist in Jewish Law, nor executions on Fridays). Never understood why it was important who killed him, as he was supposed to die for everyone's sins, and also didn't stay dead but was resurrected.

Dead or alive you have to go through the Bible to get to Palestine.

◆ ◆ ◆

Rabbi Menachem Froman
     Interviewed in *Newsweek*, April 16, 2001

Jerusalem is the easiest problem to tackle. Material issues such as water and land are much more difficult . . . You cannot ask either side to give in, since both sides feel that Jerusalem belongs to God and therefore cannot be given away. So I say: give Jerusalem to God.

The temple mount has no oil, no gold and no water. It contains the deepest emotions of Christians, Jews and Muslims. It contains the holy faith. The religions committee that I propose will be responsible for removing the Temple Mount from the politicians' jurisdiction. It is forbidden to enter a holy site with arms. Let us take arms out of all holy areas.

White South Africa used the Bible more than all of the time. Everybody used it to justify anything. Love your neighbors but pray that you do not have to touch them. They can work among you but not live among you, because deep down they are so different from you that they could not have the same political rights.

Never trust them.

You want peace.

They want war.

They were violent, not because you took their land and started to introduce more and more discriminating and oppressing laws, but because that was their nature, not yours.

They did not need freedom.

They were ungrateful.

Maybe my true subject matter is: self-deception.

Shlomo Sand
Author of *The Invention of the Jewish People*, 2008
Interviewed in *de Volkskrant*, November 13, 2009

The state Israel exists, and the Israeli nation, but not the Jewish nation. The demand of premier Netanyahu that the world and especially the Arabic world must recognize Israel as a Jewish state is wrong. The world must recognize the Israeli nation and the Palestinian nation, because they now exist in reality. Israel must become a land of it's citizens and not of an imaginary people.

Desmond Tutu
Transcribed from an interview on *Democracy Now!*, 2008
For me, coming from South Africa and going—I mean, and looking at the check-points and the arrogance of those young soldiers, probably scared, maybe covering up their apprehension, there is no way in which I couldn't say—of course, that is the truth. It reminds me—it reminds me of the kind of experiences that we underwent.

. . . and now you have that extraordinary structure that—the wall. And I do not, myself, believe that it has improved security, breaking up families, breaking up—I mean, people who used to be able to walk from their homes to school, children, now have to take a detour that last several—I mean, it's—when you humiliate a people to the extent that they are being—when you do that, you are not contributing to your own security.

Nelson Mandela
On 31 January 1985 the state president of South Africa, P.W. Botha offered Mandela his freedom on condition that he "unconditionally rejected violence as a political weapon." His daughter, Zindzi, read his reply to a mass meeting in Jabulani Stadium, Soweto. He did not accept and was only released, unconditionally, in 1990. A few lines from his answer: *Only free men can negotiate. Prisoners cannot enter into contracts . . . I cannot and will not give any undertaking at a time when I and you, the people, are not free.*

Maybe this is enough about 'the why' of my paintings.

◆　◆　◆

The works on the wall. How are these paintings different from my previous works and how are they still the same? Always was interested in how things that look the same can be very different and vice versa. In a sense they are my first landscape paintings, or should I say 'territory paintings.' That is why they are so big.

For once it is not zoomed-in vertical frontal heads and naked figures that take the main stage, but a man-made architectural structure in a more perspectival narrative space.

It leads us not into a holy land, but rather to a barren no-mans land.

Never liked architecture. Never thought I would bother to ever paint concrete slabs! Never wanted to or could draw mechanical straight lines. As a person, but also as the type of painter I am, I was often very unhappy working on them.

It seems I have taken my own sentence—a painting needs a wall to object to, literally.

But David, just one more thing I want to mention: which painting started all the others.

It is the one called *The Wall*. I saw this rather tranquil image in a Dutch newspaper and at first glance I assumed that it was the Wailing Wall.

Until I read the caption.

In Bethlehem at the concrete security wall that separates Israel from the Palestinian territories, Orthodox Jews are preparing to go and pray at the grave of Rachel. She was the favorite wife of Jacob and her grave is one of the most important Jewish holy sites (It didn't mention that it was also so for the Muslims and the Christians).

This site is also especially visited by women who cannot have children.

◆ ◆ ◆

It is late at night, I should just stop writing now. But one last thing.

I want to end with poetry rather than what is known as politics.

Words by the Palestinian writer Mahmoud Darwish (1942–2008) that said: *The first teacher who taught me was a Jew. The first love affair in my life was a Jewish girl. The first judge who sent me to prison was a Jewish woman. So from the beginning, I did not see Jews as devils or angels but as human beings.*

I don't decide to represent anything except myself. But that self is full of collective memory.

Marlene
February 25, 2010
Amsterdam

Previously published in exhibition catalogue *Against the Wall*, 2010, page 49–55

Contributors

Corban Addison is the author of two international bestselling novels, *A Walk Across the Sun* and *The Garden of Burning Sand*, which together have been published in over 20 countries. His forthcoming novel, *The Tears of Dark Water*, will be released in the fall of 2015. In addition to being a writer, Addison is a litigation attorney and a supporter of human rights and social justice causes around the world. He holds degrees in law and engineering, and lives with his family in Virginia.

Mariana Aitches taught American and Native Studies for 35 years. She has tried to emulate great teachers like Edward Said in making students conscious of and responsible for peace and justice. She is the author of two collections of poetry and is currently working on a history of the San Antonio government housing project where she grew up.

Kazim Ali's books include four volumes of poetry, *The Far Mosque, The Fortieth Day, Bright Felon* and *Sky Ward;* three novels, *Quinn's Passage, The Disappearance of Seth* and *Wind Instrument;* and three collections of essays, *Orange Alert: Essays on Poetry, Art and the Architecture of Silence, Fasting for Ramadan* and *Resident Alien: On Border-crossing and the Undocumented Divine.* He has translated work by Faiz Ahmed Faiz, Sohrab Sepehri, Ananda Devi and Marguerite Duras. He is the editor of collections on the work of Jean Valentine and Agha Shahid Ali. He is on the faculty of Oberlin College.

Xhenet Aliu's fiction and essays have appeared in journals such as *Glimmer Train, Hobart, The Barcelona Review, Necessary Fiction, American Short Fiction,* and elsewhere, and she has received multiple scholarships, grants, and fellowships from the Bread Loaf Writers' Conference, The Elizabeth George Foundation, and the Djerassi Resident Artists Program, among others. Her debut fiction collection, *Domesticated Wild Things and Other Stories,* won the Prairie Schooner Book Prize in Fiction and was released in September 2013. A native of Waterbury, Connecticut, she currently lives in Athens, Georgia, after recent stints in New York City, North Carolina, Montana, and Utah.

Ammiel Alcalay is a poet, novelist, translator, and critic who teaches at Queens College and The Graduate Center, CUNY. His books include *After Jews and Arabs, Memories of Our Future, Islanders*, and *neither wit nor gold: from then*. His translations include *Sarajevo Blues* and *Nine Alexandrias* by Bosnian poet Semezdin Mehmedinovi. A 10th anniversary edition of *from the warring factions*, and new essays, *a little history*, was published in 2013. He is the General Editor of *Lost & Found: The CUNY Poetics Document Initiative*, a series of student and guest edited archival texts emerging from the New American Poetry.

Sinan Antoon is a poet, novelist and translator. His translation of Mahmoud Darwish's last prose book *In the Presence of Absence* (Archipelago Books, 2011) won the 2012 American Literary Translators' Award. His translation of his second novel, *The Corpse Washer*, won the 2014 Saif Ghobash Banipal Prize for Literary Translation. He is an associate professor at New York University.

Ibtisam Azem is a Palestinian writer and journalist. She was born in Taybat al-Muthallath, Palestine, in 1974 and studied at the Hebrew University of Jerusalem and later at Freiburg where she completed an MA in Islamic Studies and German and English Literature. She is the New York correspondent for *al-Araby al-Jadeed* and is co-editor and editor of the Arabic page of *Jadaliyya*. She has published essays, short stories, and two novels; *Sariq al-Nawm* (The Sleep Thief) (Beirut, al-Jamal, 2011) and *Sifr al-Ikhtifaa (The Book of Disappearance)* (Beirut, al-Jamal, 2014.)

Kafah Bachari is a short story writer, poet, and aspiring novelist. She lives in Houston Texas, with her two young sons and teaches business law at the University of Houston Law Center. Currently she is at work on her first novel, *Azadistan*.

Frank Barat is a human rights activists and author. He was the coordinator of the Russell Tribunal on Palestine and is now the president of the Palestine Legal Action Network. His books include: Gaza in Crisis (2010), Corporate complicity in Israel's occupation (2011) and On Palestine (2012). He can be contacted @frankbarat22 on twitter.

Matt Bell is the author of the novel *In the House Upon the Dirt Between the Lake and the Woods*, a finalist for the Young Lions Fiction Award. His next novel, *Scrapper,* will be published in Fall 2015.

Reginald Dwayne Betts is a writer and poet. His collection, *Shahid Reads His Own Palm*, won the Beatrice Hawley Award. His memoir, *A Question of Freedom: A Memoir of Learning, Survival, and Coming of Age in Prison*, received a 2010 NAACP

Image Award. He has won a Soros Justice Fellowship, a Radcliffe Fellowship and a Ruth Lily Fellowship. He is the national spokesperson for the Campaign for Youth Justice, and was appointed to the Coordinating Council of the Office of Juvenile Justice and Delinquency Prevention by President Barack Obama. He studies law Yale. His latest collection is *Bastards of the Reagan Era.*

Chana Bloch's *Swimming in the Rain: New and Selected Poems, 1980–2015* includes selections from her four earlier collections, *The Secrets of the Tribe, The Past Keeps Changing, Mrs. Dumpty,* and *Blood Honey,* as well as new work. Bloch is co-translator of the biblical *Song of Songs* and of Israeli poets Yehuda Amichai and Dahlia Ravikovitch. She has won two Pushcart Prizes, two NEA fellowships, the Felix Pollak Prize in Poetry, the Di Castagnola Award of the Poetry Society of America, and the PEN Award for Poetry in Translation. Bloch is Professor Emerita of English at Mills College.

Nate Brown is the web editor of *American Short Fiction* and has received fellowships from the Wisconsin Institute for Creative Writing, the Vermont Studio Center, the KHN Center for the Arts, the Ucross Foundation, and multiple work-study scholarships to the Bread Loaf Writers' Conference. His fiction has appeared in the *Iowa Review, Mississippi Review, Five Chapters,* the *Carolina Quarterly,* and elsewhere. He lives in Baltimore, Maryland, where he coordinates the PEN/Faulkner Foundation's Writers in Schools program in Baltimore City Public Schools.

Hayan Charara was born in Detroit, Michigan, in 1972, the son of Lebanese immigrants. His first book of poems, *The Alchemist's Diary,* was published in 2001, followed by *The Sadness of Others* in 2006. His most recent book is *Something Sinister,* forthcoming in 2016. He edited *Inclined to Speak* (2008), an anthology of contemporary Arab American poetry, and his children's book, *The Three Lucys* (2015), won the New Voices Award Honor. He lives in Texas.

Teju Cole is a novelist, art historian, photographer, and Distinguished Writer in Residence at Bard College. He was born in the US in 1975 to Nigerian parents, and raised in Nigeria. He is the author of a novella, *Every Day is for the Thief,* a national bestseller and *New York Times* Editors' Pick; and a novel, *Open City,* which won the PEN/Hemingway Award, the Rosenthal Award, the Internationaler Literaturpreis, and was shortlisted for the National Book Critics Circle Award. He is Photography Critic for the New York Times Magazine, and is currently working on a book about Lagos.

Michael Collier's books of poetry include *An Individual History (2012) and The Ledge* (2000), which was a finalist for the National Book Critics Circle Award, a translation of *Medea* (2006) and a collection of essays, *Make Us Wave Back* (2007). He edited the anthologies *The Wesleyan Tradition: Four Decades of American Poetry* (1993) and *The New American Poets: A Bread Loaf Anthology* (2000). His honors include fellowships from the Guggenheim Foundation and the NEA, the Alice Fay di Castagnola Award, and an Academy Award in Literature. He served as Poet laureate of Maryland from 2001–2004, and is the director of the Bread Loaf Writers' Conference. He teaches at the University of Maryland.

Ted Conover is the author of *The Routes of Man: Travels in the Paved World* (Vintage, 2011), and other books including *Rolling Nowhere, Coyotes,* and *Newjack: Guarding Sing Sing. Newjack* won the National Book Critics Circle Award and was finalist for the Pulitzer Prize. He teaches at New York University's Arthur L. Carter Journalism Institute.

Ramola D is the author of *Temporary Lives* (2009) winner of the AWP Grace Paley Award in Short Fiction, 2008, and *Invisible Season* (1998), co-winner of the 1998 Washington Writers' Publishing House Poetry award. She is a recipient of a 2005 NEA Poetry Fellowship, and her work has appeared in *Greensboro Review, Prairie Schooner, Agni, Northwest Review, The Writer's Chronicle, Best American Poetry 1994, Best American Fantasy 2007, Enhanced Gravity: More Fiction by Washington DC Women Writers* (2006), and *All About Skin: Short Fiction by Women of Color* (2014).

Marlene Dumas is an internationally renowned painter recognised for her contribution to the development of painting and for her visual critiques of racial, sexual and social issues through her work. She has succeeded in lending pictorial form to the fragility of existence, to feelings of fear and anxiety but also of commitment love and hope. Her work has been shown in retrospectives in Japan, South Africa and the US. Her last retrospective, 'The Image as Burden,' began in Amsterdam (2014) and travelled to Londen and Basel. A new edition of her publication, *Sweet Nothings: Notes and Texts* was published in 2014.

Duranya Freeman has worked as a journalist for Sri Lanka's The Nation, and is a staff writer for two of Colorado College's student publications, the Cipher and the Catalyst. She is a 2015 recepient of a South Asian Journalists Association award for her writing on post-war rehabilitation and reconciliation in Sri Lanka. She is a freshman at Colorado College with a passion for studying public health and global conflict.

Tess Gallagher is the author of nine volumes of poetry including *Dear Ghosts, Amplitude,* and *Midnight Lantern: New and Selected Poems* (2011). Her fiction includes *The Man from Kenvara: Selected Stories*. She also authored *Soul Barnacles: Ten More Years with Ray*, and *A Concert of Tenses: Essays on Poetry*. She spearheaded the publication of Raymond Carver's *Beginners* as a single volume. She companioned the production of the film "Birdman," directed by Alejandro Gonzales Inarritu, which uses the work of Raymond Carver. She divides her time between Lough Arrow in Co. Sligo in the West of Ireland and Port Angeles, Washington.

Cristina García is the author of six novels, two anthologies, works for young readers, and a collection of poetry. Her latest book, *King of Cuba*, is a darkly comic portrait of Fidel Castro. García's work has been nominated for a National Book Award and translated into fourteen languages. She's taught at universities nationwide and recently moved to the Bay Area.

Suzanne Gardinier is the author of five books, most recently *Iridium & Selected Poems 1986–2009*. In 2003 she served on a panel at the American Studies Association annual meeting on "American Jews, Israel, and the Palestinian Question," with Carolyn Karcher, Amy Lang, & Irena Klepfisz. She has trained teachers from Teachers College and from Bank Street College of Education in the teaching of writing and in discussing race in the classroom; since 1994 she's taught writing at Sarah Lawrence College, where she now serves as resident director of the Sarah Lawrence Program in Cuba. She lives in Manhattan and Havana.

David Gorin's poetry and prose have appeared in *A Public Space, The Believer, Best American Experimental Writing*, and elsewhere. He is the recipient of a MacDowell Colony Fellowship, a Dorot Fellowship in Israel, and an MFA from the Iowa Writers' Workshop. He works as a poetry blogger for the *Boston Review* and as a doctoral student in English Literature at Yale University, where he teaches poetry writing and curates the *WAVEMACHINE* reading series.

Marilyn Hacker is the author of thirteen books of poems, including *A Stranger's Mirror* (Norton, 2015) *Names* (Norton, 2010), and *Desesperanto* (Norton, 2003) ,an essay collection, *Unauthorized Voices* (Michigan, 2010), and thirteen collections of translations from the French. *DiaspoRenga*, a collaborative sequence written with Deema Shehabi, was published by Holland Park Press in 2014. She has received two Lambda Literary Awards, the PEN award for poetry in translation, the PEN Voelcker Award and the international Argana Prize for Poetry from the Beit as-Sh'ir/House of Poetry in Morocco. She lives in Paris.

Nathalie Handal's recent books include *The Republics*, which Patricia Smith lauds as "one of the most inventive books by one of today's most diverse writers;" the bestselling *The Invisible Star*, which explores the city of Bethlehem and the lives of its exiles worldwide; *Poet in Andalucia*; and *Love and Strange Horses*, winner of the Gold Medal Independent Publisher Book Award, which *The New York Times* says is "a book that trembles with belonging (and longing)." Her most recent plays have been produced at The John F. Kennedy Center for the Performing Arts, the Bush Theatre and Westminster Abbey in London.

Jane Hirshfield's most recent, eighth poetry collection is *The Beauty*, published along with *Ten Windows: How Great Poems Transform the World*, both Knopf, 2015. A chancellor of the Academy of American Poets, her honors include The California Book Award, the Poetry Center Book Award, fellowships from the Guggenheim and Rockefeller foundations and NEA, and finalist selection for the National Book Critics Circle Award. Her work appears in *The New Yorker*, *The Atlantic*, *Poetry*, *TLS*, *Harper's*, *The Paris Review*, and eight editions of *The Best American Poetry*.

Fanny Howe has written numerous books of fiction, essays and poetry and has won the Ruth Lilly Lifetime Achievement Award. Her most recent collection of poetry *Second Childhood*, a Finalist for the National Book Award 2014, was published by Graywolf Press.

Leslie Jamison is the author of *The Empathy Exams*, a New York Times bestselling essay collection, and a novel, *The Gin Closet*, a finalist for the Los Angeles Times First Fiction Award. Her work has appeared in *Harper's*, *Oxford American*, *A Public Space*, *Boston Review*, *Virginia Quarterly Review*, *The Believer*, and the *New York Times*, where she is a regular columnist for the Sunday Book Review. She was raised in Los Angeles and currently lives in Brooklyn.

Kim Jensen is a Baltimore-based writer, poet, and political activist whose books include, *The Woman I Left Behind*, *Bread Alone*, and *The Only Thing that Matters*. Her fiction, poems, and essays have appeared in many journals and anthologies. Active in the peace and justice movement for many years, especially the struggle for Palestinian liberation, Kim is associate professor of English at the Community College of Baltimore County. She is married to the Palestinian painter and educator Zahi Khamis, and was visiting with family in Palestine during the latest assault on Gaza in the summer of 2014.

Lawrence Joseph is the author of five books of poetry, most recently *Codes, Precepts, Biases, and Taboos: Poems 1973–1993* (Farrar, Straus and Giroux). He is also the author of two books of prose, *Lawyerland* (FSG) and *The Game Changed: Essays and Other Prose* (University of Michigan Press, Poets on Poetry Series). He holds degrees from the University of Michigan, the University of Cambridge, and the University of Michigan Law School. His work has been widely anthologized, and translated into several languages. He is Tinnelly Professor of Law at St. John's University School of Law, in New York City.

Nancy Kricorian is a New York City-based writer and activist. Her most recent novel, *All The Light There Was*, is set in the Armenian community of Paris during World War II. Her honors include a New York Foundation for the Arts Fellowship, The Anahid Literary Award, a Gold Medal of the Writers Union of Armenia, and the Daniel Varoujan Prize of the New England Poetry Club. In 2010 she traveled throughout the West Bank as part of the Palestine Festival of Literature. Kricorian has been on the staff of CODEPINK Women for Peace since 2003.

Rickey Laurentiis is the author of *Boy with Thorn* (University of Pittsburg Press, 2015), selected by Terrance Hayes for the 2014 Cave Canem Poetry Prize. He is the recipient of many honors, including a Ruth Lilly Fellowship from the Poetry Foundation, as well as fellowships from the Atlantic Center for the Creative Arts, the Civitella Ranieri Foundation in Italy and the National Endowment for the Arts. His poems appear widely, including *Poetry* magazine, *The New Republic*, *The New York Times*, *Kenyon Review* and *Boston Review*. Born in New Orleans, Louisiana, he currently resides in Brooklyn, New York.

Kiese Laymon is a black southern writer, born and raised in Jackson, Mississippi. Laymon attended Millsaps College and Jackson State University before graduating from Oberlin College. He earned an MFA from Indiana University and is currently an Associate Professor of English at Vassar College. Laymon is the author of the novel, *Long Division* and a collection of essays, *How to Slowly Kill Yourself and Others in America*. He has two books forthcoming from Scribner.

Farid Matuk is the author of *This Is a Nice Neighborhood* (2010) and *My Daughter La Chola* (2013). His work has recently be recognized with an &Now Award for Innovative Writing and the Headlands Center for the Arts Alumni New Works Award. Matuk serves on the editorial team at *Fence* and as contributing editor for *The Volta*. He is an Assistant Professor of English and Creative Writing at the University of Arizona and lives in Tucson with the poet Susan Briante and their daughter.

Colum McCann is the author of six novels and three collections of stories, including *Thirteen Ways of Looking* (2014). His honors include the 2009 National Book Award for *Let the Great World Spin*, the International Dublin Impac Prize in 2011, a Chevalier des Arts et Lettres from the French government, election to the Irish arts academy, the 2010 Best Foreign Novel Award in China, and an

Oscar nomination. His work has been published in over 35 languages. He lives in New York with his wife, Allison, and their three children. He teaches at the MFA program in Hunter College.

Christopher Merrill's books include the poetry collection *Watch Fire*, several edited volumes of translations, and the non-fiction book, *Things of the Hidden God: Journey to the Holy Mountain*. His latest book, *The Tree of the Doves: Ceremony, Expedition, War*, chronicles travels in Malaysia, China and Mongolia, and the Middle East. His work has been translated into over thirty languages. His honors include a Chevalier from the French government in the Order of Arts and Letters. He directs the International Writing Program at the University of Iowa, and serves on the U.S. National Commission for UNESCO, and the National Council on the Humanities.

Askold Melnyczuk's first novel, *What Is Told*, was a *New York Times Notable Book;* his second, *The Ambassador of the Dead*, was selected as one of the *Best Books of the Year* by the *Los Angeles Times;* the most recent, *The House of Widows*, was chosen by the American Libraries Association's *Booklist* as an Editor's Choice. Founding editor of *Agni* and Arrowsmith Press, he's taught at Harvard and Boston University and currently teaches at the University of Massachusetts Boston and in the Bennington Graduate Writing Seminars.

Claire Messud is the author of four novels and a book of novellas. Her novel *The Emperor's Children*, an international bestseller, was chosen as one of the New York Times' top ten books of 2006. Her most recent novel, *The Woman Upstairs*, was long-listed for Canada's Giller Prize, the IMPAC Award and France's Prix Fémina. A frequent contributor to the *New York Review of Books* and the *New York Times*, she teaches in the MFA program at Hunter College, CUNY, and lives with her family in Cambridge, MA.

Philip Metres is the author of a number of books and chapbooks, including *Sand Opera* (2015), *A Concordance of Leaves* (2013), *abu ghraib arias* (2011), *To See the Earth* (2008), and *Behind the Lines: War Resistance Poetry on the American Homefront since 1941* (2007). His work has garnered two NEA fellowships, the Watson Fellowship, five Ohio Arts Council Grants, the Beatrice Hawley Award, two Arab American Book Awards, the Creative Workforce Fellowship, the Cleveland Arts Prize and the PEN/Heim Translation Fund grant. He is professor of English at John Carroll University in Cleveland. http://www.philipmetres.com

Tomás Q. Morín's poetry collection *A Larger Country* was the winner of the APR/Honickman Prize. He is co-editor with Mari L'Esperance of the anthology,

Coming Close: Forty Essays on Philip Levine, as well as the translator of Pablo Neruda's *The Heights of Macchu Picchu*.

Peter Mountford's novel *A Young Man's Guide to Late Capitalism* won the 2012 Washington State Book Award in fiction, and his second novel The Dismal Science, released in 2014 by Tin House Books, was a NYT editor's choice. His work has appeared in Boston Review, The Atlantic, Granta, The Sun, ZYZZYVA, the Southern Review, the New York Times Magazine, and elsewhere. He is currently the events curator at Hugo House, Seattle's writing center, and he is on faculty at Sierra Nevada College's MFA program.

Susan Muaddi Darraj is the author of the short story collection, *The Inheritance of Exile* (2007), a collection of short-stories about the Palestinian American community. Her second collection, *A Curious Land: Stories from Home*, received the 2014 AWP Grace Paley Award and will be published in 2016. Her work appears in several anthologies, including *Dinarzad's Children: An Anthology of Contemporary Arab American Fiction* and *Colonize This!: Young Women of Color on Today's Feminism*. She is a recipient of a grant from the Maryland State Arts Council. She teaches at the Johns Hopkins University Advanced Academic Program in Creative Writing.

Mary Jane Nealon, RN, MFA is the author of two collections of poetry: *Rogue Apostle* and *Immaculate Fuel*, both from Four Way Books in New York. Her memoir, *Beautiful Unbroken*, won the 2010 Bakeless Prize for Nonfiction and was published by Graywolf Press in 2011. She is the Director of Innovation at Partnership Health Center in Missoula, Montana.

Dina Mohammed Omar is a writer and graduate student in medical anthropology at Yale University. She is a founding member of National Students for Justice in Palestine and served on the National Executive Board for the Palestine Youth Movement (2010–2011). She teaches English and creative writing in high schools, universities, and prisons and is committed to building community through the collective writing process. Her writing is published in the *Believer Magazine, The Berkeley Poetry Review, Mizna,* and *Yellow Medicine Review.* She is from Ramoun, Palestine.

Alicia Ostriker is a poet and critic, author of *Feminist Revision and the Bible* (1992), *The Nakedness of the Fathers: Biblical Visions and Revisions (1994)* and *For the Love of God: the Bible as an Open Book* (2007). Her most recent books of poetry are *The Book of Seventy* (2009), *The Book of Life: Selected jewish Poems 1979–2011) (2012),* and *The Old Woman, the Tulip, and the Dog* (2014). She is a Chancellor of the Academy of american Poets.

Ed Pavlic's next books are *Let's Let That Are Not Yet: Inferno* (National Poetry Series, Fence Books, 2015) and *'Who Can Afford to Improvise?': James Baldwin and Black Music, the Lyric and the Listeners* (Fordham University Press, 2015). Recent works are *Visiting Hours at the Color Line* (National Poetry Series, Milkweed Editions, 2013), *But Here Are Small Clear Refractions* (Achebe Center, 2009, *Kwani?* Trust, 2013) and *Winners Have Yet to be Announced: A Song for Donny Hathaway* (U Georgia P, 2008). He teaches at the University of Georgia.

Roger Reeves poems have appeared or are forthcoming in *Best American Poetry, Poetry, Ploughshares, American Poetry Review, Boston Review,* and *Tin House,* among others. Reeves was awarded a 2015 Whiting Award, a 2014–2015 Hodder Fellowship from Princeton University, a 2013 Pushcart Prize, a 2013 National Endowment for the Arts Literature Fellowship and a 2008 Ruth Lilly Fellowship. *King Me,* (2013) his first book of poems, won the 2014 Larry Levis Reading Prize and the PEN Oakland/Josephine Miles Literary Award. He is an assistant professor of poetry at the University of Illinois at Chicago.

Alice Rothchild retired from her professorship at Harvard Medical School in November 2013 and is now a Corresponding Member of the Faculty of the medical school. She co-founded and co-chairs American Jews for a Just Peace Boston, co-organizes the AJJP Health and Human Rights Project, and is on the coordinating committee of Jewish Voice for Peace Boston. She is the author of *Broken Promises, Broken Dreams: Stories of Jewish and Palestinian Trauma and Resilience* (2007). In 2013 she released a documentary film, "Voices Across the Divide."

George Saunders is the author of eight books, including *Tenth of December,* which was a finalist for the National Book Award, and won the inaugural Folio Prize in 2013 (for the best work of fiction in English) and the Story Prize (best short story collection). He has received MacArthur and Guggenheim Fellowships, the PEN/Malamud Prize for excellence in the short story, and was recently elected to the American Academy of Arts and Sciences. In 2013, he was named one of the world's 100 most influential people by *Time* magazine. He teaches in the Creative Writing Program at Syracuse University.

Jason Schneiderman is the author of three books of poems: *Primary Source* (2016, Red Hen Press, winner of the Benjamin Saltman Award), *Striking Surface* (2010, Ashland Poetry Press, winner of the Richard Snyder Prize) and *Sublimation Point* (2004, Four Way Books). He is Associate Editor of *Painted Bride Quarterly* and Poetry Editor of *Bellevue Literary Review.* He is an Assistant Professor of English at the Borough of Manhattan Community College and lives in Brooklyn.

Sarah Schulman is the author of 17 books including Israel/Palestine and the Queer International (Duke, 2012) and the novel The Cosmopolitans (Feminist Press, 2016). Her awards include a Guggenheim in Playwrighting and a Fulbright in Judaic Studies. Sarah is on the advisory board of Jewish Voice for Peace, and is faculty advisor to Students for Justice in Palestine at the CUNY College of Staten Island where she is Distinguished Professor of the Humanities.

Alan Shapiro is author of 12 books of poetry (most recently Reel to Reel and Night of the Republic, a finalist for both the National Book Award and The Griffin Prize), 4 books of prose (including Broadway Baby, a novel from Algonquin Books). Winner of he Kingsley Tufts Award, LA Times Book Prize, an award in literature from The American Academy of Arts and Letters, 2 NEAs, a Guggenheim and a Lila Wallace Reader's Digest Award, he is also a member of the American Academy of Arts and Sciences.

Robert Shetterly is a Maine-based artist. He obtained his undergraduate training in English Literature at Harvard, and taught in southern West Virginia before relocating to Maine. In 2002 he gave up his career as a surrealist painter and illustrator to begin the *Americans Who Tell the Truth* project, an on-going series of portraits—now over 200—of Americans from the past & present who have struggled for social, economic, racial and environmental justice. The portraits, which travel to schools, colleges, museums, and libraries all over the country, are meant to provide people wih role models of citizenship.

Naomi Shihab Nye is the author of many books, including *The Turtle of Oman, Transfer, Habibi, Sitti's Secrets, 19 Varieties of Gazelle*, and *Going Going*. A childhood resident of Ferguson, Mo., she has also lived in Palestine, and San Antonio, TX, and travels all over the world as a visiting writer.

Tom Sleigh's books include the poetry collections *Station Zed, Army Cats*, winner of the John Updike Award, and *Space Walk*, winner of the Kingsley Tufts Award, a book of essays, *Interview With a Ghost*, and a translation of Euripides' *Herakles*. His work appears in *The New Yorker, Virginia Quarterly Review, Poetry, Best American Poetry, Best American Travel Writing*, and *The Pushcart Anthology* and elsewhere. His honors include the PSA's Shelley Prize, awards from the American Academy in Berlin, the American Academy of Arts and Letters, the Lila Wallace Fund, the Guggenheim and NEA. He teaches in Hunter College's MFA program.

Ahdaf Soueif's work includes the Booker shortlisted *The Map of Love*, the nonfiction books, *Mezzaterra: Fragments from the Common Ground*, an account of events in Egypt, and *Cairo: a City Transformed*, and a translation of Mourid

Barghouti's *I Saw Ramallah*. She founded Engaged Events, a UK based charity, whose first project was the annual Palestine Festival of Literature held in occupied Palestine and Gaza. She was shortlisted for the Liberty Human Rights Award, and has won the Metropolis Bleu, the Constantin Cavafy Award, and the inaugural Mahmoud Darwish Award. She was named to the list of 100 people with most influence on the English reading public (*Guardian*) and 100 most powerful women in the Arab world (*Arabian Business*)

Adam Stumacher's fiction has appeared in *Granta, The Kenyon Review, The Sun, The Massachusetts Review, TriQuarterly, Best New American Voices*, and elsewhere, and won the Raymond Carver Short Story Award. He holds degrees from Cornell University and Saint Mary's College and was a fellow at the University of Wisconsin Institute for Creative Writing. He has lived in the Middle East, Latin America, and Asia, and he has many years experience as a teacher in inner city high schools, for which he was awarded the Sontag Prize in Urban Education. He is working on a short story collection and a novel.

William Sutcliffe is the author of six novels, including the international bestseller, *Are You Experienced?* and *The Wall*, which was shortlisted for the Carnegie Medal. His novels have been translataed into twenty-five languages. *Concentr8* will be published by Bloomsbury USA in 2016

Janne Teller is a New York based Danish novelist and essayist of Austrian-German origin. Her books include *Odin's Island*, and the bestseller *Nothing*. Her prize winning passport book about life as a refugee, *War—What If it Were Here*, she adapts to each country where it's published. Among her awards are the Michael L. Printz Honor Award for Literary excellency and the Drassow's Peace Prize. Her work is translated into more than 25 languages. She is an international speaker, who has worked for the UN and EU on conflict resolution worldwide, and today a member of the Jury of the German Peace Prize.

Philip Terman's is the author of five books of poetry, including *Our Portion: New and Selected Poems* (Autumn House Press, 2015). His poems have appeared in many journals and anthologies, including *Poetry, The Kenyon Review, The Sun Magazine, Tikkun, The Bloomsbury Anthology of Contemporary Jewish Poetry*, and *99 Poems for the 99 Percent*. He teaches at Clarion University, and is co-director of The Chautauqua Writers Festival.

Diego Vázquez Jr is a poet, novelist, storyteller. He comes from indigenous migrants who crossed invisible lines to become immigrants under a common sky. He has never met an illegal human. Vázquez is grateful for his ongoing participation in The Women's Writing Program at the Ramsey County Correctional Facility and the Sherburne County Jail in Elk River. This remarkable experience allows him new insights into the strength and joy of the human heart. Vázquez is the author of *Growing Through the Ugly*. He is completing work on a forthcoming novel, *Border Town Sky*.

Alice Walker is a writer, poet and activist whose books include seven novels, four collections of short stories, four children's books, and volumes of essays and poetry. She won the Pulitzer Prize in Fiction in 1983 and the National Book Award. Her works include *The Temple of My Familiar, By The Light of My Father's Smile,* and *Possessing the Secret of Joy* (1992), which was made into a documentary film, "Warrior Marks: Female Genital Mutilation and the Sexual Blinding of Women," a collaboration with British-Indian filmmaker Pratibha Parmar, and *We are the Ones We Have Been Waiting For: Inner Light in a Time of Darkness.*

Steve Willey lives in Whitechapel, London, and is the author of *Elegy* (Veer Press, 2013). His ongoing project. *Living In,* has been published as 'Slogans' in *Better Than Language* (Ganzfeld Press, 2011), as 'Signals: Letters to Palestine' in *Dear World and Everyone In It* (Bloodaxe Books, 2013), and as 'Mirror: Flag' in *Spiral Orb Nine* (2014). In 2013 Steve completed doctoral work on the subject of 'Bob Cobbing 1950–1978: Poetry Performance and the Institution' (awarded, 2013). He was the Summer Resident at the University of Arizona Poetry Center (August, 2014). He blogs at www.stevewilley.com and Tweets @swilley17.

Phillip B. Williams is a Chicago, Illinois native. He is the author of the forthcoming book of poems *Thief in the Interior* (Alice James Books, 2016). He is a Cave Canem graduate and received scholarships from Bread Loaf Writers Conference and a 2013 Ruth Lilly Fellowship. His work has appeared or is forthcoming in *Callaloo, Kenyon Review Online, Poetry, The Southern Review, West Branch* and others. Phillip received his MFA in Writing from the Washington University in St. Louis. He is the poetry editor of the online journal *Vinyl Poetry*.

Tiphanie Yanique is the author of the novel *Land of Love and Drowning,* which won the 2014 Flaherty-Dunnan First Novel Award from the Center for Fiction, and the American Academy of Arts and Letters Rosenthal Family Award, and collection of stories, *How to Escape from a Leper Colony,* which won the BOCAS Prize for Caribbean Fiction, and placed her on the National Book Foundation 5Under35 list. The *Boston Globe* chose her as one of sixteen cultural figures to watch out for. Tiphanie is from the Virgin Islands and is a professor in the MFA program at the New School.

Clarence Young (at times Zig Zag Claybourne) is the author of the novels *By All Our Violent Guides, Neon Lights,* and *Historical Inaccuracies.* His essays, poems and short stories have appeared in a variety of places but not, as yet, Oprah's desk. He is a lifetime resident of Detroit but enjoys the wandering soul given everyone at birth. As such, violence, no matter what form it takes, baffles him. He can be reached via his website www.writeonrighton.com or his woefully neglected blog thingsididatworktoday.blogspot.com.

Acknowledgments

I was raised in a culture underlined by Buddhism, a theology of many lives that makes us used to the long-term. As such, when I began this work, I expected both that I would continue knocking on doors and that most doors would remain closed to me. I was surprised therefore by the overwhelming support I received from friends and strangers. These are a few of them.

Alan Shapiro's and Tom Sleigh's enthusiastic embrace of this project gave me necessary courage and Jane Hirshfield, Marilyn Hacker, Nathalie Handal, and Tess Gallagher introduced me to poets and writers whom I would otherwise have never approached. This anthology would be much poorer if not for their ongoing support and mentorship.

Rick Simonson from Elliott Bay Books and Rob Spillman from Tin House lead me to Colin Robinson, who took on this publication. I am grateful to all three of them, and most specially to Colin who agreed to let a perfect stranger talk him into this project with nothing but the skills of persuasion and, possibly, determination, to recommend her.

Graywolf Press's poetry editor, Jeff Shotts, read through many of the submissions I was considering, and shared his "poetry mind" with me, an exercise I found educational and affirming. His willingness to undertake this work for an anthology which was not in his control, and whose entire shape he could not see, was beyond generous. If I chose, albeit infrequently, to disregard the wisdom of his advice, it was only because I felt the inclusion of a certain work provided a necessary link between other submissions. I will remain ever grateful for having had his careful company on this journey.

My youngest daughter, Kisara, did the work of converting print to text, and correcting the errors of technology with 'Pastoralia' and 'Cathal's Lake.' I believe it was good for her.

I am grateful, always, to my family which has had to share our good times and bad with better and worse times of my making and which harken to people and projects that may seem far from their lives. I can only hope that they will continue to keep a forgiving and joyful space in their hearts for me.

Permissions

Excerpts from "On Paradise" by Roger Reeves will appear in *Ploughshares* in 2015.

"Cathal's Lake" from *Fishing the Sloe-Black River: Stories* by Colum McCann. Copyright © 1993 by Colum McCann, used by permission of The Wylie Agency LLC.

Excerpt: "Cathal's Lake" from the book *Fishing the Sloe-Black River* by Colum McCann. Copyright © 1993 by Colum McCann. Used by permission of Henry Holt and Company, LLC. All rights reserved.

Sinan Antoon's translated excerpt comes from Ibtisam Azem, *Sifr al-Ikhtifa'* (*The Book of Disappearance*) (Beirut & Baghdad: Dar al-Jamal, 2014), pp. 21–25, and is reprinted with the permission of the publisher and author.

"Verbatim Palestine" by Ed Pavlic appeared in "Dispatches from PalFest," *Wasafiri* (Volume 80: Fall 2014), pp. 30–36. Print. It will also appear in *Let's Let That Are Not Yet : Inferno* (Fence Books 2015). Reprinted with the permission of Fence Books and the author. "The Goal is Clarity: War, Sports and the Dangerous, Delightful and Disgusting Elasticity of Experience" first appeared in *Africa is a Country*, July 18 2014.

"The Fruit of the Land", "A Mother Walks Around", "The Story of the Arab Who Died In A Fire" translated by Chana Bloch, Chana Kronfeld and Ido Kalir, from *Hovering at a Low Altitude: The Collected Poetry of Dahlia Ravikovitch* by Dahlia Ravikovitch, translated by Chana Bloch and Chana Kronfeld. Copyright © 2009 by Chana Bloch, Chana Kronfeld, and Ido Kalir. English translation copyright © 2009 by Chana Bloch and Chana Kronfeld. Use by permission of W. W. Norton & Company, Inc.

Alicia Ostriker. Nakedness of the Fathers: Biblical Visions and Revisions. Copyright © 1994 by Alicia Ostriker. Reprinted by permission of Rutgers University Press.

"East Jerusalem" by David Gorin previously appeared in the *Boston Review*.

Terman, Philip. "Our Jerusalem" from Our Portion: New And Selected Poems © Copyright 2015 by Philip Terman. Reprinted by permission of Autumn House Press.

Naomi Shihab Nye's preface is excerpted with the permission of the author from the Washington Post Online. "Before I was a Gazan" first appeared in *Red Wheelbarrow.* "Everything Changes the World" first appeared in *Sojourners,* November 1, 2014.

"Of the Leaves That Have Fallen (Stevens, Like Decorations in a Nigger Cemetery)" by Rickey Laurentiis first appeared in the *Boston Review* March 31, 2014. Reprinted with the permission of the author.

"The Sadness of Antonio" by Jason Schneiderman first appeared in the *American Poetry Review,* January/February 2014.

"News Back Even Further Than That" from *Into It* by Lawrence Joseph. Copyright © 2005 by Lawrence Joseph. Reprinted by permission of Farrar, Straus and Giroux, LLC.

"My Daughter Davis-Monthan Air Force Base, Tucson, Arizona," "My Daughter Not You," and "My Daughter Emily Dickinson" by Farid Matuk first appeared in *Mizna,* Volume 15, Issue 2.

"All Day the Light is Clear" and "Love Poem to be Read to an Illiterate Friend" by Tess Gallagher first appeared in *Midnight Lantern: New and Selected Poems* (Graywolf, 2011) and "I Have Never Wanted to March" first appeared in *Dear Ghosts* (Graywolf, 2008).

"La Frontera" by Leslie Jamison first appeared in *Empathy Exams* (Graywolf, 2014).

"We are all African" by Corban Addison first appeared on the Huffington Post. It is reprinted with the permission of the author.

"Shadowboxing: Eyeless in Gaza and Ukraine" by Askold Melnyczuk first appeared in *Agni.*

"Extraordinary Rendition" by Tomas Q. Morin first appeared on The Awl; "112th Congress Blues" first appeared in *American Poetry Review.* "At the Supermarket" first appeared in *Narrative.*

"The Diary of Teju Cole" by Teju Cole first appeared in the *Financial Times.* It is reprinted with the permission of the author.

"Pastoralia", from *Pastoralia: Stories* by George Saunders, copyright © 2000 by George Saunders. Use by permission of Riverhead, an imprint of Penguin Publishing Group, a division of Penguin Random House LLC.

'The Luncheon" from The Tree of the Doves: Ceremony, Expedition, War by Christopher Merrill (Minneapolis: Milkweed Editions, 2011). Copyright © 2011 by Christopher Merrill. Reprinted with permission from Milkweed Editions. www.milkweed.org

Excerpt from *The Wall* by William Sutcliffe (Bloomsbury, 2013) reprinted with permission by the author and publisher.

"Three Variations on Fado Themes" by Marilyn Hacker first appeared in *A Stranger's Mirror* (Norton, 2015).

Excerpt(s) from *The Routes of Man: How Roads Are Changing the World and the Way We Live Today* by Ted Conover, copyright © 2010 by Ted Conover. Used by permission of Alfred A. Knopf, an imprint of Knopf Doubleday Publishing Group, a division of Penguin Random House LLC. All rights reserved.

"The Trial: A Real Farce (1988)" by Ammiel Alcalay was first published in *Memories of Our Future* (San Francisco: City Lights, 1999). "Letter to the Americans (2014)" first appeared at *Warscapes Weekly*, August 15, 2014 (http://www.warscapes.com).

Excerpt from interview with Hayan Charara first appeared in *The Normal School: A Literary Magazine.*

"A Heart at Sea" by Nathalie Handal first appeared in *World Literature Today* on July 29, 2014. Reprinted wtih the permission of the author.

"Letter to Palestine (with Armenian Proverbs)" by Nancy Kricorian originally appeared in *Clockhouse Literary Review,* Volume 2 (2014), and is reprinted with the author's permission.

An amended version of "Last Stop Jerusalem" by Ahdaf Soueif first appeared in the *Guardian* on May 26, 2010, under the title "The Dig Dividing Jerusalem." It is reprinted with the permission of the author.

"The Concrete of Bint Jbeil", from *An Individual History* by Michael Collier. Copyright © 2012 by Michael Collier. Used by permission of W. W. Norton & Company, Inc.

"A Wedding at Cana, Lebanon, 2007" by Tom Sleigh first appeared in *Army Cats* (Graywolf, 2007).

"The Familiar Picture of Dis" and "Installation/Occupation" by Philip Metres first appeared in *To See the Earth* (2008). Excerpt from *A Concordance of Leaves* first published by Diode Editions, 2013.

Credit: Brenda Carpenter

Ru Freeman's creative and political writing has appeared internationally. She is the author of the novels *A Disobedient Girl* (Atria/Simon & Schuster, 2009) and *On Sal Mal Lane* (Graywolf, 2013), a *New York Times* Notable and Editor's Choice Book. She blogs for the Huffington Post on literature and politics, is a contributing editorial board member of the Asian American Literary Review, and has been a fellow of the Bread Loaf Writers' Conference, The Corporation of Yaddo, Hedgebrook, the Virginia Center for the Creative Arts, and the Lannan Foundation. She is the 2014 winner of the Sister Mariella Gable Award for Fiction, and the Janet Heidinger Kafka Prize for Fiction by an American Woman.